INDIAN THOUGHT

INDIAN THOUGHT

AN INTRODUCTION

Edited by
DONALD H. BISHOP
College of Sciences and Arts
Washington State University

A HALSTED PRESS BOOK

JOHN WILEY & SONS
New York Toronto

Published in the U.S.A., Canada, Latin America
and the Middle East by Halsted Press,
a Division of John Wiley & Sons, Inc., New York

ISBN 0-470-07580-5

Library of Congress Catalog Card Number: 73-13206

Printed in India at Prem Printing Press, Lucknow

FOREWORD

For more than a century Indian thinkers have been seeking to understand the mind of the West. They are naturally eager to master the science and technology it has developed, but they have also realized that its philosophies pose a distinctive challenge, especially in the area of social and political thought. When independence was won India chose to become a democracy, perceiving that its basic values are those she wished to realize in her new organization of society.

Western thinkers have been slow to recognize that they need to understand the mind of India, for the sake of an enriched perspective as well as for the peaceful collaboration between peoples that mutual understanding fosters. But during recent decades this recognition has become increasingly evident. Signs are multiplying that intercommunication in depth is going on and will continue—very likely at an accelerated pace.

One important way of contributing toward this inter-communication is exemplified in the volumes now appearing which aim to interpret India to the West. *Indian Thought, An Introduction* is a welcome addition to the list. It covers the whole field as an introduction should, and those who have cooperated in writing it are men respected both for reliable scholarship and for breadth of insight.

May it play a significant part in making Indian philosophy better known to Western students and others who seek larger understanding.

E. A. Burtt

Ithaca, New York

II

I met Dr Donald Bishop on the two successive visits he paid to India to plan this book. I had known him before through his articles in Indian journals on Indian thought. They were written with insight and perceptive understanding. His two chapters in this book, on the Gītā and Buddhism, show his scholarship and deep interest. His book is a symposium on Indian Philosophy and not merely a 'history' of the 'schools'.

Although ancient, the Indian cultural tradition is still alive, and is not irrelevant to the contemporary human situation. Indian culture began at the very beginning and struggled through inquiry and the pragmatic experiment of its own experience to the highest peaks. The Himalayas are also there in Indian philosophy and culture! Moreover the story of Indian Culture as its "experiment with Truth" is still going on and is unfinished.

Yajña (sacrifice), yoga (ways to reunion with the divine) and Sannyāsa (renunciation of possessions and the possessor) are the fundamental concepts of classical Indian thought. To this, modern India has added a fourth, Satyagraha (the power of truth in action). And Gandhi has made the same impact on the modern world that the Buddha made in ancient times. Moreover, in its conception of Man and the possibility of the integral evolution of his consciousness to higher and higher rational levels, traditional Vedānta is seen not to be incompatible with modern science. Vedānta does not contradict science and is not contradicted by it.

The United States is a meeting place of races and cultures. Its culture is like the sea into which many rivers flow. Therefore there is a visible "openness" in it. While other traditions may limit themselves to their own, the "open" American mind learns or must learn from all, assimilates from all, and in its creative adventure brings into synthetic focus Human Culture and the diversity of its unfinished manifestations. This book is a symbol of the openness and the adventure of American education and the American educator.

I welcome this book, therefore, and congratulate Dr Donald Bishop on his successful perseverence.

N. I. NIKAM

Bangalore

PREFACE

This book is a collection of original essays written especially for this volume by persons, the majority of whom the editor met while in India in 1967 and 1971.

It is intended for use as an introductory text in Indian and western universities and for the lay reader wishing to acquire some knowledge of traditional Indian thought. One characteristic of our times is the efforts of an increasing number of westerners to learn more of eastern ways of thinking and to discover truths and insights relevant and helpful today. Many are searching for a philosophy whose roots are world-wide.

The editor and contributors believe that India has much to offer such seekers. This book is presented in the hope that insight into Indian thought will be helpful to them and that, by bringing about such understanding, peace and good-will may result.

The length, breadth and depth of the Indian tradition makes a discussion of all of it impossible in a single volume. The editor hopes that as much as possible of the most important has been dealt with; and, if the volume stimulates the reader to continue further elsewhere, a major goal will have been accomplished. Toward that end numerous references have been included and a bibliography for each topic has been furnished. To aid the reader a glossary, with pronunciation, has also been added.

I would like to thank those who helped in the selection of contributors, Professors Ray and Chatterji for suggesting Debiprasad Chattopadhyaya, Professor Barlingay for suggesting S. R. Talghatti and G. N. Joshi, Professor Saran for suggesting G. S. Bhatt and T. K. Mahadevan for suggesting R. R. Diwakar. I am very grateful to Professors Burtt and Nikam for writing forewords and to the latter especially for his help and encouragement when I was in India.

Thanks goes also to those who have helped in the preparation of the manuscript, especially Mrs Laura Webb of Pullman, Washington.

DONALD H. BISHOP

Pullman, Washington

CONTENTS

PART FIVE : THE MODERN PERIOD

CONTRIBUTORS

S. S. BARLINGAY, Professor and Head, Department of Philosophy, University of Poona. Received M. A. and Ph. D. from Nagpur. Post-doctoral scholar at Oxford 1958-59. Taught Zagreb University, Yugoslavia 1962-64 and University of Western Australia 1968-70. Author of *A Modern Introduction to Indian Logic* in Hindi. Contributed numerous articles to Indian and international journals. Editor, *Indian Philosophical Quarterly.*

G. S. BHATT, Reader and Chairman, Department of Sociology, Dayananda Anglo-Vedic College, Dehradun. Has written two books in Hindi—*Sociology, Race and Culture in India* and *Indian Renaissance: Leaders and Movements.* Has contributed a number of articles to Indian journals. Currently engaged in the study of *panthas* (religious brotherhoods) among low castes of Dehradun.

DONALD H. BISHOP, Professor, Department of Philosophy, Washington State University. Degrees from Cornell University, Yale Divinity School and The University of Edinburgh. Member, American Philosophical Association. Received Fulbright Award 1964. Received Fellowship from Society for Religion in Higher Education, 1966-67. Travelled in the Far East 1964, 1967, 1971. Has written over sixty articles in American, British, Indian and Japanese journals.

PRITIBHUSHAN CHATTERJI, Head, Department of Philosophy, University of Calcutta. Writes on various aspects of Indian and Western thought. Author of two books in English, *Studies in Comparative Religion* and *The Philosophy of Josiah Royce.* Has written books in Bengali on general psychology, educational psychology and social psychology. Editor of two philosophy journals in Bengali. He is past president of The Indian Philosophical Congress. Fields of interest include comparative philosophy, comparative religion, social philosophy and philosophical psychology.

DEBIPRASAD CHATTOPADHYAYA, Professor of Philosophy, City College, Calcutta. Author of *Lokayata-darsana.* Leading authority on Indian Materialism.

R. R. DIWAKAR, Journalist, Administrator and Parliamentarian. Took active part in the freedom struggle. Elected to the Constituent Assembly of India in 1946. Minister of State for Information and Broadcasting 1949-52. Governor of Bihar, 1952-57. Chariman, Gandhi National Memorial Trust, 1957 Awards. Chairman, Gandhi Peace Foundation, 1959 Awards. Editor, *Samyukta Karnatak* and allied journals. General Editor, *Builders of Modern India* series. Joint editor, *Book University* series. Member, International press, President, Indian & Eastern Newspapers Society, 1962. Travelled abroad extensively; led delegations to Washington and London in 1962 to press for cessation of nuclear testing. Publications include *Glimpses of Gandhi, Mahayogi–Life and Teachings of Sri Aurobindo, Paramahamsa Ramakrishna, Satyagraha in Action, Satyagraha: the Pathway to Peace.*

G. N. Joshi, Professor and Head, Department of Philosophy, Fergusson College. Post-Graduate Teacher and Research Guide, University of Poona. Graduate of Bombay and Gujarat Universities. Member of Board of Studies in Philosophy at Bangalore University and the University of Poona, Member of the Board of Editors of the *Marathi Encyclopaedia of Philosophy;* read papers at a number of annual sessions of the Indian Philosophical Congress; Vice President of the Indian Philosophical Association; Author of *Ātman and Mokṣa* and of numerous articles in professional journals in English and Marathi.

T. K. Mahadevan, editor of *Gandhi Marg,* quarterly publication of the Gandhi Peace Foundation. Publications include *Freedom From Fear, Whither India, Civilian Defence, Gandhi: His Relevance for Our Times, Non-Violence After Gandhi, Truth and Non-Violence, Quest for Gandhi,* and *Gandhi My Refrain.*

T. M. P. Mahadevan, Professor and Head, Department of Philosophy, University of Madras. Director, Centre for Advanced Study in Philosophy, University of Madras. Known especially for his work on Śaṅkara and Advaita. Lectured at Cornell University, Columbia University, the University of Texas and University of Pennsylvania. Participated in second and third East-West Philosophers' Conference in Hawaii. Awarded Padma Bhushan in 1967 by the Indian government. Elected member of International Institute of Philosophy, Paris, 1971. Author of numerous publications including *The Philosophy of Advaita, Outlines of Hinduism, The Upanishads, Time and the Timeless, Invitation to Indian Philosophy.*

S. S. Raghavachar, Professor and Head, Department of Post-Graduate Studies in Philosophy, Manasa Gangotri, University of Mysore. Publications include *Vedartha Sangraha of Ramanuja, Vishnu Tattva Nirnaya of Madhav, Naiskarmya Siddhi of Sureswara, Ramanuja on the Upanishads* and *Introduction to Vedartha Sangraha* as well as numerous articles in Indian journals.

K. S. Ramakrishna Rao, Lecturer, Department of Philosophy and Logic, Maharani's College for Women, Bangalore. Graduate of Mysore University. Member, Board of Studies in Philosophy, Bangalore University. Has written book reviews for *Visveswan and Indological* and articles for *Vedanta Kesari, Ahimsa* and *Prabuddha Bharata.*

B. G. Ray, was Professor of Comparative Religion, Visva-Bharati. Studied at the Universities of Calcutta and Dacca. Principal of the College of Graduate Studies, Visva-Bharati, 1961-63. Active in Indian Philosophical Congresses. Books include *Contemporary Indian Philosophers, Gandhian Ethics, The Philosophy of Rabindranath Tagore, Religious Movements in Modern Bengal* and *God and Karma in Indian Religions.*

V. Madhusudan Reddy, Professor and Chairman, Department of Philosophy, Osmania University. Graduate of Madras and Osmania Universities. Director Sri Aurobindo Darshan, The University of Tomorrow. General Secretary, Institute of Human Study, International Centre. Secretary, Andhra Pradesh Philosophical Society, Editor of *New Race,* Osmania University *Journal of Philosophy.* UNESCO Fellowship 1961. Fulbright Visiting Professor in U. S., 1969. Books

rhood and

losophy,
f Indian
Hnman
Acharya
Sarvodaya
lism and

read
N. A. NIK——M

iversity.
Visiting
Professor in U. S., 1962-63. Visiting Professor of Philosophy, Christopher Newport College, Virginia, 1971-72. Member, Sardul Research Institute, Bikaner. Honorary Professor of Philosophy of Religion, Ahimsa Research Institute, New Delhi. Life member, Indian Philosophical Congress. Chairman, All-India Philosophical Congress, Poona, 1970. Books include *India's Democracy and The Communist Challenge, Ethical Philosophies of India.*

S. R. TALGHATTI, Lecturer, Department of Philosophy, University of Poona. Graduate of Fergusson College and University of Poona. Has contributed articles to the *Marathi Encyclopaedia of Philosophy* and to several Indian journals.

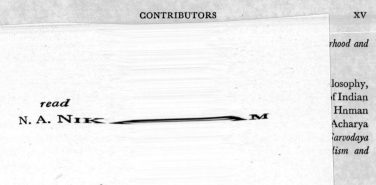

1

PROLOGUE

Donald H. Bishop

I

There are many terms Indian thinkers use as a matter of course which are unfamiliar to western students. An effort has been made in this text to keep their number at a reasonable level. Often terms are explained in parentheses. Also a glossary is found at the end of the book. The reader should expect to learn some terms, however. This is a part of the discipline of studying any body of knowledge, and an exception should not be expected or made for Indian philosophy.

II

From a historical standpoint Indian thought may be separated into three periods. D. S. Sarma, for example, uses the typical divisions of Ancient, Medieval, and Modern. Works of the first period best known to westerners are the Bhagavad Gītā and the Upaniṣads. The Medieval period consists of approximately five hundred years beginning around A.D. 1000. In it the Bhakti Schools arose as a response to the earlier Advaita Vedāntism of Śaṅkara. The Modern period is characterized by an increased Moslem influence, the penetration of the West and western thought, the revival of Hinduism and a renaissance of Indian philosophy.

Many Indians, however, prefer to view Indian thought in terms of schools (Darśanas) distinguishing two types, the orthodox who accept and the heterodox who reject the authority of the Vedas. Examples of the latter are the Cārvākas, Buddhists and Jains. The orthodox schools are divided into two groups, the Mīmāṃsā and the Vedānta whose teachings are based directly on the Vedas and Sāṃkhya, Yoga,

Nyāya and Vaiśeṣika whose views are indirectly related to the Vedas.

There are some who find the "Schools" approach too mechanical and tedious. To avoid this other alternatives have been devised, such as the topical and historical. Each method has its strengths and weaknesses. This book uses a combination of the historical, schools, and topical approaches, hoping to take advantage of the merits of each.

III

An understanding of Indian thought will be facilitated if one recognizes that there are, as Charles A. Moore points out, certain "principles, attitudes, and methods which are, by rather common agreement, considered characteristics of Indian philosophy as a whole."[1] One is its refusal to make a sharp distinction between philosophy and religion. The majority of Indian thinkers do not view them as separate fields of study or realms of life. M. Hiriyanna points out in his *Outlines of Indian Philosophy* that "religion and philosophy do not stand sundered in India," the reason being that "their purpose is in the last resort the same, a seeking for the central meaning of human existence."[2] Similarly Jadunath Sinha writes in his book, *Introduction to Philosophy*: "Philosophy and Religion have common objects. Both of them try to grasp the nature of the universe, and to understand man's place, function and destiny in it."[3]

This attitude is due in part to Indian philosophers' broad definition of philosophy as reflection or reflective thinking on all of reality. Philosophy is not restricted solely to empirical matters. In his book, *Indian Idealism*, S. Dasgupta writes that "philosophy may be defined as the theory of a subject matter taken as a whole."[4] Moore, editor of *The Indian Mind*, characterizes Indian philosophy by saying its goal is "the total truth about reality as a whole."[5] Moreover the relationship between philosophy and religion is believed to be a supplementary, not an antagonistic or conflicting one. In *Indian Culture through the Ages*, S. V. Venkateswara writes: "Indian philosophy is not the denial but the fulfilment of religion".[6] The two are not hostile but rather reinforce and support each other. Sinha declares philosophy to be a rational attempt to "integrate our knowledge and interpret and unify our experiences."[7] Those experiences include religious as well as aesthetic, social, moral and scientific. The Indian philosophers declare, for example, that the dichotomy between faith and reason is a false one. They cannot, therefore, conflict.

In the second place Indian philosophy does not make an absolute distinction between the material and the immaterial, the sentient and the insentient. One reason for this is the strong strain of monism in Indian thought. In his book, *Indian Philosophy*, S. Radhakrishnan writes, "If we can abstract from the variety of opinion and observe the general spirit of Indian thought, we shall find it has a disposition to interpret life and nature in the way of monistic idealism."[8]

The Indian tendency is to view reality as an integral whole. Reality may be characterized by a single category such as existence or being and made up of different types of beings or existences. That is, reality is seen in terms of gradations rather than dualities, levels or strata. Indian philosophers do not deny the existence of diversities and pluralities but deal with them in at least two ways. One is to set diversity in the context of unity and claim that reality is a matter of unity in diversity. The pluralities of reality are manifestations of a One which is the ground of all being. A second is to assert that diversity characterizes reality on the relative level while unity is its primary nature on the absolute level. In either case, as Hiriyanna says, "no part of this diversity can be ultimate."[9] If one adds to the view of the oneness of reality that it is spiritual in essence also, the implications are many. The Indian view that the cow is sacred would be quite understandable, for example.

A third characteristic of Indian thought is its willingness to accept a variety of data, grounds, evidence and experiences as a basis for philosophy or truth. It refuses to be exclusivistic. It will consider all possibilities and alternatives, ruling nothing out beforehand. Regarding India's contribution to world philosophy D. M. Datta in his book, *The Chief Currents of Contemporary Philosophy*, writes, "its attempt to base philosophy on all aspects of experience and not simply on sense experience" deserves special attention, as does "its conviction that the Ultimate Reality manifests itself, or can be conceived, in different ways."[10]

Moore recognized this aspect of Indian thought when he noted "the almost infinite variety of philosophical concepts, methods, and attitudes that make up the Indian philosophical tradition." He declared that "there are many differing approaches to reality, to life, to truth, and to philosophy itself in the Indian tradition."[11] One is reminded again of Radhakrishnan who wrote: "The criticism that

Western metaphysics is one-sided, since its attention is confined to the waking state alone, is not without its force. There are other states of consciousness as much entitled to consideration as the waking. The whole truth must take all the modes of consciousness into account."[12] S. K. Saksena in the book edited by Charles Moore contrasts the Indian view with the western rationalist's premise that anything not the product of or acceptable to reason is unphilosophical and contends that such an "atomistic view of the faculties of man" is itself most unphilosophical.[13]

The Indian's belief that Ultimate Reality manifests itself in many ways reflects the attitude of tolerance which has long characterized Indian thought. This openness of view is both a strength and a weakness. It infuses Indian philosophy with depth and at the same time makes it liable to attacks or misunderstanding. For an outsider may equate one emphasis with all of Indian thought. Note the typical western stereotype of Indian philosophy as "mystical", for example.

The attitude of tolerance is basic to a fourth attribute of Indian thought, its synthetic character and approach. Indian philosophy wants to include all within its scope. Every field is its domain. The Indian thinker is not content to restrict himself to but one area of thought or reality. He believes Philosophy should still be the queen of the sciences even as it once was in the West.

Philosophy's scope and task as a comprehensive one is well stated by Sinha when he writes that philosophy is "the art of thinking rationally and systematically of reality as a whole. It systematizes our scientific knowledge, and moral, aesthetic and religious experiences. It endeavours to reach a conception of the entire universe. It is not contented with a partial view of the world. It seeks to have a synoptic view of the whole reality; it tries to have a vision of the whole."[14] Indian philosophy insists on a synthetic, not separatist, methodology also. In their book, *An Introduction to Philosophy,* Chatterjee and Datta write: "Indian philosophy discusses the different problems of Metaphysics, Ethics, Logic, Psychology and Epistemology, but generally it does not discuss them separately. Every problem is discussed by the Indian philosopher from all possible approaches, metaphysical, ethical, logical, psychological and epistemological. This tendency has been called by some thinkers the synthetic outlook of Indian philosophy.[15]

This aspect of the Indian view is based on the premise that reality is not compartmentalized and therefore thought cannot be. To the Indian the philosophical mind must be a comprehensive mind. It must synthesize as well as analyse. It must integrate as well as dissect. The practical implications of this outlook are many and numerous. Datta denotes one of them when he writes that one of the "main trends of Indian thought which deserve special attention at this critical age of our planet" is "its recognition of the fundamental unity of all beings, particularly mankind, and the consequent consciousness that our moral or religious duties are towards all, and not simply to the members of our own group, country, or race."[16]

It ought to be noted that the Indian philosopher does not accept the charge that breadth leads to superficiality or lack of depth. Such an assertion is based on the false premise or assumption that the two are mutually exclusive. But this is not necessarily true. One can have depth as well as breadth of mind.

Another characteristic of Indian thought is its insistence that philosophy be meaningful or relevant to the everyday world. To the Indian "Philosophy becomes a way of life, not merely a way of thought," Hiriyanna asserts.[17] Datta states that "the Indian systems are more than theoretical discussions; they are ways of moulding life."[18] Similarly, Radhakrishnan writes that "Indian philosophy has its interests in the haunts of men, and not in supra-lunar solitudes. It takes its origin in life, and enters back into life after passing through the schools."[19] From the Indian standpoint then, if a belief is to be valid, it must stand trial in the court of experience.

Hiriyanna makes an interesting observation that "philosophy in India did not take its rise in wonder or curiosity as it seems to have done in the West; rather it originated under the pressure of a practical need arising from the presence of moral and physical evil in life."[20] It is not to be wondered then, that, as Datta points out "the express function of each system, except the materialist, is practical. It is to attain a state of perfection beyond suffering."[21] Buddhism is an outstanding example of this. It begins with suffering and ends with Nirvāṇa, the eight-fold path being the means from one to the other.

To the Indian the goal of philosophy is personal growth. In regard to the individual Hiriyanna states that "the value of philosophic training consists essentially in making him what he was not before."[22] But philosophy is relevant to society as a whole also. In describing ancient Indian culture Venkateswara declares that "The principles of philosophy were welded into the life of the people."[23] Philosophy, then, is not a mere spectator sport or intellectual pastime. To be philosophical is to be involved in and with life. The task of philosophy is twofold, to discover and root out personal bias and prejudice, and to understand and reconstruct society in terms of basic ideals and values.

Moreover, in the Indian tradition, philosophers themselves are expected to be models of what they teach. "Philosophy becomes a way of life, not merely a way of thought," Hiriyanna writes, and "the ancient Indian did not stop at the discovery of truth but strove to realize it in his own experience."[24] The term "realize" or "realization" is often used by Indian writers, and this is exactly what is meant. Truth and virtue are not just something we know. They become meaningful only when realized or practised.

Of course this is a hard task to accomplish for, as Radhakrishnan points out, "the highest triumphs of philosophy are possible only to those who have achieved in themselves a purity of soul."[25] Nevertheless those philosophers who do so earn the gratitude of many. In Radhakrishnan's words, "they comprehend experience on behalf of mankind, and so the latter are eternally grateful to them."[26] Gandhi is perhaps the best example in the twentieth century of the Indian emphasis on beliefs being put into practice. Gandhi not only advocated but lived the philosophy of satyāgraha and ahiṃsā; indeed he even died for it. That the emphasis is still much alive today is reflected in Datta's statement: "Philosophy, of even the most catholic kind, if confined to mere intellectual discussion, will remain a helpless spectator of war, intrigue, and devastation repeatedly carried on by persons with narrow outlooks and uncontrolled passions."[27]

A sixth attribute of Indian thought is its introspective character or its emphasis on introspection. From the Indian view philosophy begins with the self not the external world. "'See the Self' is the keynote of all schools of Indian Philosophy," Sharma writes.[28] And, as Radhakrishnan points out: "The philosophic attempt to determine the nature of reality may start either with the thinking self or the objects of thought. In India the interest of philosophy is in the self of man."[29] Two schools of thought in which this emphasis reached its climax are Yoga and Buddhism. "Creatures from mind their character derive; mind-marshalled are they, mind-made. Mind is the source either of bliss or of corruption," Buddha said.[30]

The emphasis upon the inner is seen in the fact that the study of psychology was cultivated early in India's history. Moore writes of the Indian's "deep concern with the inner man and with the introspective approach to truth" and says that one distinction of the Indian tradition is its "emphasis upon and great achievements in the area of psychology in its broadest and most comprehensive sense."[31] The goal, as H. Nakamura insightfully points out in his book, *Ways of Thinking of Eastern People*, and the reason "the ancient Indians set a high value on introspection" and "exercised the silent meditation of Yoga" was to "attain serenity of mind."[32] Its attainment, they believed, could be achieved independent of the external world.

Other reasons for the introspective character of Indian thought may be mentioned briefly. It was believed that to be was of greater significance than to do. A person is to be measured not by what he has or does but by what he has become. Furthermore, as Moore points out, for the Indian "the transformation of the inner self is primary, while concern with changing or controlling the outer world is distinctly secondary. . . ."[33] As the Buddhist would say, one must purify oneself before he attempts to purify the world. Moreover, outsiders have often mistaken or interpreted reflection as inactivity or passivity. But to the Indian reflecting or meditating is an activity, is a form of doing. It is, as a matter of fact, a rather important activity, even though it is not related to any immediate impact on the external world. To be is to do, form an Indian view. Perhaps what we have here is a fundamental difference between East and West. The West attributes greater credibility, merit, significance, truth, and reality to the external and the East to the internal.

Two more points may be added. The Indian philosopher views man as a microcosm of the universe. Thus to know man is to also know the universe. In addition the Indian believes that scientific investigation or experimentation is not necessary in order to know the material world. It can be known through reflection and meditation.

The emphasis on transcendence is dominant in Indian thought also. The Indian urges us not to stop with the *is* or the immediately experienced for they are of the category of the relative or conditional. Indian philosophers in general believe that true or final reality is not material reality; instead "An unconditioned reality where time and space along with all their objects vanish is felt to be real."[34] Radhakrishnan typifies the Indian view when he writes that "The principal categories of the world of experience, time, space and cause are self-contradictory. They are relative terms depending on their constituents. They have no real existence."[35]

One reason for emphasizing the transcending of the material is the basic belief that the material is an epiphenomenon of the spiritual. The inner and the spiritual are the real and the material and the external their manifestations. Thus the Indian, as Venkateswara points out, asserts a non-biological view of evolution. To him "the unfolding of Prakṛiti is not a mechanical evolution but one directed by the spirit (Puruṣa)."[36] Aurobindo is an outstanding twentieth-century exponent of epiphenomenalism as we see in his following statements regarding Indian thought:

> "Its idea of the world, of nature, of existence is not physical, but psychological and spiritual. Spirit, soul, consciousness are not only greater than inconscient matter and force, but they precede and originate, and force and matter cannot exist without them. The Force that creates the world is a conscious will or an executive power of the Spirit; the material universe is only a form and movement of the Spirit."[37]

Reason must be transcended also. The Indian does not deny its validity and appropriateness but only its ultimate insufficiency. "Our intellectual categories can give descriptions of the empirical universe under the forms of space, time and cause, but the real is beyond these," Radhakrishnan writes.[38] He states that "Our limited mind cannot go beyond the bounds of time, space and cause, nor can we explain these, since every attempt to explain them assumes them," and, "The absolute can never become an object of knowledge, for what is known is finite and relative."[39]

Indian philosophy advocates intuition as the means of transcending reason and knowing ultimate truth and absolute reality. Sinha typifies this position in his statements that "Logical reason is subordinate to intuition"; "Reason is subordinated to the authority of the Vedas, which is regarded as the authority of intuition"; "Intuition is immediate apprehension of reality which transcends discursive thought"; and "Reasoning should be carried on under the guidance of intuition."[40] Sharma points out that one meaning of the word "darśana" is "vision and also the instrument of vision. It stands for the direct, immediate and intuitive vision of Reality."[41] In regard to knowledge of God four steps are delineated—hearing (the scriptures), reflection, meditation and "intuitive apprehension of Brahman." Sinha writes that the Advaita Vedāntist Śaṅkara "... does not abjure reason, but he subordinates reason to the scripture. Hearing must be followed by reflection which includes reason. Reasoning in conformity with the scripture is conducive to the intuition of Brahman, and therefore should be employed."[42]

Hiriyanna's statement "...the goal of Indian philosophy lies as much beyond Ethics as it does beyond Logic,"[43] illustrates another commonly accepted thesis of Indian thought, that ethical legalism must be transcended also. The ideal state of "beyond both good and evil" is exulted in the Bhagavad Gītā and other Indian literature. This is the basis for the further statement by Hiriyanna that "... philosophy as understood in India is neither mere intellectualism nor mere moralism, but includes and transcends them both."[44] "Mere moralism" or "common morality" is not enough for it is based on the motive of rewards, doing the good because one will derive some benefit from it. This is not genuine morality. It is grounded in the motive of doing good for the sake of goodness itself. The reward motive must be transcended.

Actually this attitude toward ethical legalism is a part of a larger emphasis on the necessity of self transcendence. The self must be surpassed in the sense that egoism must be rooted out, for it is grounded in selfishness. Ethnocentrism, which is a combination of selfishness on the group level, the feeling of superiority and other factors, must be eradicated also. Hiriyanna writes that "In addition to personal egoism... the egoism of the species which leads inevitably to the belief that the sub-human world may be exploited for the benefit of man...also must be got rid of, if man is to become truly free."[45] Radhakrishnan notes that "The passionate physico-mental individual is not the real man."[46] The true self is more than or transcends the passions, body and mind.

The emphasis on transcendence found in Indian thought is based upon at least two premises. One is that the real is of the nature of the universal. Its basic attribute is universality. This is a correlate of the monistic thesis that reality is one. Thus that which divides, separates, is dualistic, is not the real. The real is that which unites. The second premise is that the ideal or the perfect, not the imperfect, is the real. That is to say, the more perfect an entity is, man for example, the more real it is. This is the reason the Indian thinker defines philosophy as a quest for the ideal and the attempt to realize it.

IV

An awareness of the distinctive features described above will facilitate an understanding of Indian thought presented in the following chapters. The reader will gain more also if he keeps in mind some basic questions as he reads on. A major query is how Indian thought compares with western. In answering this one needs to look for both similarities and differences. Are there common values upheld by Indian and western thinkers alike: What life-goals are there about which there is universal agreement? On the other hand are there some differences between East and West which simply cannot be reconciled? If so, what is the next step? Should the reader keep only this set of questions in mind, his study will be much more profitable.

PART ONE

Early Indian Literature and Thought

INTRODUCTION

I

India's philosophical and religious literature is one of the most ancient and extensive in the world. It has become known in the West only relatively recently. Occidental scholars were introduced to Indian writings in the nineteenth century by men such as Georg Bühler, T. W. Rhys Davids, E. B. Cowell, S. Beal, Paul Deussen and F. Max Müller whose extensive labour gave birth to the fifty volumes Sacred Books of the East series. In the twentieth century, especially since World War II, India's literature and traditions have become much more widely known in the West, in part because of the many paperback editions we have before us presently.

II

The sheer bulk of the literature of India, the multitude of ideas considered, and the length of time over which it was written makes variety inevitable. It also makes neat categorizing, classifying and dating of the literature difficult. Further obstacles arise because of the large number of authors involved and the early tendency not to claim or attribute authorship to a particular work.

Nevertheless there is agreement among Indian scholars on various items connected with the literature. For example, the basic distinction between Śruti and Smṛiti writings is generally accepted. Śruti is the original, primary scripture and authority, whose truths were directly revealed to or intuited by the early seers or ṛiṣis. They are accepted as sacred, infallible and God-made. Smṛiti literature is derivative or takes its authority from the first. They are of human, not divine origin, and were written to explain and elucidate the Śruti and make them understandable and meaningful to the masses. Prabhavananda writes that "They record civil laws, social obligations, and ceremonies performed at the birth of a child, during initiation into Vedic mantra, at marriage, and at the moment of death. They comprise, in short, the daily duties, usages, and customs to be observed by the several castes and by people in different stages of life. . . ."[1]

Indian literature may be divided into the Ancient, Medieval and Modern periods which roughly parallel their western counterparts chronologically. It was in the Ancient period that the works called the Śruti—the Vedas or Vedic Literature—came into existence. The terms Vedas and Vedic literature are sometimes used in a confusing manner. The Vedas proper are four in number, originating chronologically as follows—Ṛig, Yajur, Sāma and Atharva. Each Veda consists of four parts—Mantras, Brāhmaṇas, Āraṇyakas and Upaniṣads. Again, for convenience at least, each part of each Veda may be thought of as originating chronologically. The term Vedas is sometimes used to refer to only the mantras of each of the Vedas; at other times authors use it in reference to all four Vedas and the four parts of each. The term Vedic literature, however, usually denotes all the Vedas and all parts of each. Only by seeing it in context can one tell whether an author is using the term Vedas in a narrow or broad sense.

The main point to be remembered is, again, the distinction between Śruti and Smṛiti. The four Vedas in their totality make up the Śruti. Scholars such as D. S. Sarma divide Smṛiti literature into five groups—law codes, epics, Purāṇas, Āgamas and Darśanas. The Darśanas or schools of philosophy are separated into two types—the heterodox which reject the authority of the Vedic scriptures, namely the Buddhists, Jains and Cārvākas, and the orthodox which accept Vedic literature or the Vedas as authoritative. The orthodox schools are six in number and are divided into two groups. The Vedānta and Mīmāṃsā claim to be based directly on Vedic literature and the Nyāya, Vaiśeṣika, Sāṃkhya and Yoga see themselves as being based on grounds different from but not contrary to the Vedas. Each Darśana or school has a number of Sūtras or writings attributed to its founder, plus a number of commentaries on them written by followers later.

III

Let us now go on to describe briefly the various types of literature or scriptures indicated above. We should note that early Indians made no sharp distinction between sacred and secular literature. One reason is that in their daily lives they did not separate the sacred and the profane. Rather they attempted to live in terms of the ideal that all our thoughts and actions are sacred and should be directed toward Brahman.

The Ṛig is the oldest and most important of the four Vedas. The mantras (Saṃhitās) are hymns of incantation and supplication addressed to the deities at times of worship and sacrifice. In this early period represented by the mantras natural forces and phenomena were personified and deified. Whatever occurred was believed to be due to the deities. Man is subject to them and the natural forces. He should obey and propitiate them; hence the birth of religious sacrifices and ritualism. The Brāhmaṇas are written in prose and also "deal with the rules and regulations laid down for the performance of the rites and sacrifices."[2] Religion had become institutionalized by this time and the priests or Brahmins were an important group. They insisted on a strict and proper adherence to the rituals and ceremonies and the Brāhmaṇas were written to guide them in their sacred duties.

The Āraṇyakas or forest treatises were authored by hermits who had withdrawn into the quiet of the forests to meditate. They not only dealt with the proper performance of the sacrifices and rituals but also gave them a symbolic and spiritual interpretation. As a contemporary author points out, they mark the "transition from ritualistic to philosophic thought."[3] That change reaches its climax in the Upaniṣads.

The Upaniṣads are known as Vedānta, meaning "the end of the Vedas," because they come last and contain the essence or high points of Vedic thought. Their authors and exact dates are not known. Their content is more important. They are the works of saints and seers who had personally experienced highest reality. The Upaniṣads, as we have them, are not tightly constructed, logically argued, philosophical essays and treatises but are instead disclosures of the intuitive insights, visions, and trans-rational experiences of the seers. Their antagonism towards sacrifices and ritualism led to a lesser emphasis on them in the Upaniṣadic period.

Religion and worship may include but must go beyond ritual and sacrifice for true religion, according to the Upaniṣads, is knowing and experiencing Brahman directly.

IV

The law codes (Dharma-Śāstras) are the first of the Smṛiti literature. The best known of the codes is the Laws of Manu, Volume XXV, in the Sacred Books series. It consists of twelve parts and contains prescriptions and regulations governing individual and corporate life. In it is a detailed account of the creation of the universe and the social order. The main purpose of the Laws of Manu was to demarcate a type of society which would be just and enduring. Self-control, non-injury, generosity and non-attachment are some of the virtues extolled as a basis for such a society. Kauṭiliya's Arthaśāstra on state-craft, Vātsyāyana's Kāmaśāstra on love and pleasure, Yājñavalkya's and Paraśara's social and legal Śāstras, in addition to Manu's Laws have had a lasting effect on India. They have provided a model which her people have accepted and attempted to realize through the ages.

The Rāmāyaṇa (life of Rāma) and the Mahābhārata (great Bhārata) are two well-known Indian epics. Vālmīki is the author of the Rāmāyaṇa. It tells of the experiences of King Rāma and his consort Śiva. In the derivative epic, the Adhyātmya Rāmāyaṇa, the symbolic meaning of the lives and experiences of the principals is brought out. Rāma represents the impersonal Brahman and Śiva the personal. Rāma is also regarded as the embodiment of all virtues, especially truth. God is truth. Whoever loves God seeks and loves truth, and Rāma's finally being installed king is regarded as a symbol of the ultimate triumph of truth.

Vyāsa is the author of the Mahābhārata which is sometimes called the fifth Veda because of its wide influence on the masses. It is a story of the descendants of King Bharata and deals with a great dynastic war in the ancient kingdom of the Kurus. Again its central theme is that truth and righteousness eventually prevail. The object of the Rāmāyaṇa and Mahābhārata was to instill the truths and virtues enjoined in the Smṛiti in the minds and lives of the people through the use of stories involving real or legendary heroes. The people or characters in the Epics embodied the ideals which the masses accepted and strove to follow. The influence of the Epics is indicated by one author who writes: "In the quiet hours of the evening, when work is finished, men, women and children meet together in villages throughout the land, and listen eagerly to recitations from them by especially trained story-tellers. Thus are brought to the humblest cottage the essential moral lessons and the great spiritual truths of an immemorial tradition. The beneficient effect upon the vast masses of the Indian population can scarcely be exaggerated."[4]

The Bhagavad Gītā, the most popular scripture of India, is found in the Mahābhārata. It is so important that it is often called the Bible of India. Its message is timeless and universal. It gives spiritual guidance to all types of devotees—karma, bhakti, dhyāna and jñāna. It proclaims the ideal Yogin as a man of contemplation and action. The Bhagavad Gītā opposes excessive ceremonialism and ritualistic sacrificing. They are not necessary for the "realized" individual. The sacrifice of the inner self is what is really needed. One should perform one's duties unselfishly, for they are a means to one's purification.

The chief characters of the Bhagavad Gītā are Kṛiṣṇa and Arjuna. Kṛiṣṇa symbolizes the belief that all reality is a manifestation of God. Kṛiṣṇa represents God; Arjuna represents man and the dialogue between them symbolized the divine-human encounter found throughout history. The Gītā emphasizes the concept of avatāras or divine incarnations born into the world periodically to establish truth and righteousness. Brahman is viewed as having many manifestations and thus can be worshipped in a variety of ways. Man's goal is union with Brahman. Self-renunciation is a prerequisite to such union.

The Purāṇas are next to the Epics in importance as "instruments of popular education."[5] There are eighteen main ones, six devoted to Viṣṇu, six to Brahman, and six to Śiva. Their author is believed to be Vyāsa who wrote the Mahābhārata. The Purāṇas are accounts of either real or legendary kings. The concept of the avātara is fully developed in the Purāṇas, which describe a large number of them who either have or will come. Viṣṇu, who symbolizes the preserving principle in the universe, had ten incarnations, for example.

The Purāṇas also contain creation accounts. They project the accepted theory that the universe moves in terms of cycles. A major function of the Purāṇas is to personalize and thus make more meaningful the ethical and the abstract spiritual truths of the Vedas and Upaniṣads. They stress God's grace, power and mercy. The Bhāgavata Purāṇa is probably the most widely known Purāṇa. Its emphasis on love and devotion to God is especially attractive to the Vaiṣṇavas and the account of Kṛiṣṇa and the gopis dancing and playing, which is often misinterpreted by westerners, symbolizes man's unreserved, complete love of God.

Another body of Smṛiti literature or scriptures is the Āgamas or Tantras. They may be thought of as worship manuals. Their exact date and authorship is unknown. Buddha evidently was acquainted with them so they predate him. There are three groups of Āgamas associated with three deities, the Vaiṣṇava Āgamas with Viṣṇu, the Śaiva Āgamas with Śiva, and the Śākta Āgamas with Śakti. Śakti, Mother of the Universe, represents fertility or the creative principle or aspect of Brahman. The Śākta Āgamas are the most popular, and often most abused, of the Tantras.

The Tantras are divided into three parts—sādhanās or spiritual practices and disciplines ; siddhi, the results attained from such practices, especially Mokṣa ; and the philosophical-religious background for such practices based on the Upaniṣads. Sādhanās are to be undertaken under the direction of a guru. Their goal is to transcend worldly or sensual pleasures through exposure to them and thus attain union with Brahman. Four forms of worship are detailed in the Āgamas from the highest of pure meditation on the impersonal God to the worship of the personal God through symbols and images. Thus the Tantras stimulated both contemplation and meditation on the one hand and temple worship on the other, since they recognized that most men require visible objects and prescribed rituals as aids to spiritual realization although a few do not.

As mentioned earlier, the Darśanas or schools of philosophy are divided into the heterodox and orthodox. Buddhism, Jainism and Cārvāka will be dealt with subsequently. In each case, and especially the first two, an extensive literature grew up furnishing devotees with a knowledge and means of expressing their faiths. Buddhist and Jain literature was in Prākṛit, the spoken language of the period, and not the scholarly or priestly language, Sanskrit. Early Buddhist literature was divided into three piṭakas or baskets. The Vinaya Piṭaka or "Discipline Basket" was concerned with the Saṅgha, the monastic order founded by Buddha. The Sutta Piṭaka consists of the sermons and discourses of Buddha and his chief disciplines and so is called the "Sermon" or "Dhamma" basket. The Abhidhamma or "Exposition Basket" come later as it is made up of the teachings and commentaries of scholars in the Buddhist schools and monasteries of ensuing centuries. The canonical works of Jainism contain the teachings of its founder Mahāvīra (great hero). They consist of twelve Aṅga or "limbs" codified some two hundred years after Mahāvīra's death.

The literature of the six schools grew out of and is an extension and expansion of Vedic thought. Once the Aryan invasions ended and the inter-mixing of invader and native had been accomplished, life in India became more stable and orderly. Hinduism took a variety of forms and developed such basic concepts as Karma, Dharma, Ṛita and Mokṣa. These conditions made reflection and contemplation natural and the six schools of philosophy were the result.

The primary sources or literature of each school are called Sūtras (the term is often applied to early Buddhist and Jain literature also). Each of the schools except Sāṃkhya had its own—the Brahma sūtra of Bādarāyaṇa for Vedānta ; the sūtras of Jaimini for Mīmāṃsā ; the sūtras of Gotama for Nyāya ; those of Kanāda for Vaiśeṣika, and Patañjali's for Yoga. In time commentaries to expound and clarify each sūtra came into being. These in turn gave rise to further commentaries, treatises and independent works. The object of the sūtras and treatises was, as M. Hiriyanna points out, "to consolidate the teaching of the particular school to which they belong, and to criticize others when they diverge from it."[6] Vedānta sūtras emphasize and justify the speculative aspects and Mīmāṃsā sūtras the ritualistic aspects of the Vedas, for example. Since the literature of these schools was primarily philosophical in nature, the sūtras deal with basic ethical, metaphysical and epistemological questions. For instance, it was quite common for them to start with the question of pramāṇas or the means to valid knowledge. The sūtras develop and refine the concepts mentioned earlier, each school giving its own interpretation and refuting those of others.

VI

As indicated at the beginning of this discussion there are several factors which make the dating of Indian literature often uncertain. The division, found in the West also, between Ancient, Medieval and Modern has been noted. The literature described thus far belongs in the Ancient Period. One scholar divides it into five ages.

The Vedic Age from 2000 to 560 B.C. is the time during which all the Vedic literature came into being. It is divided into the three ages of the Mantras, Brāhmaṇas and Upaniṣads. The next division is the Age of the Kalpa-Sūtras from 560 B.C. to 200 B.C. A Kalpa Sūtra consists of three parts—a Śrauta sūtra which is a manual on the scriptures, a Gṛihya sūtra dealing with domestic religious ceremonies, and a Dharma sūtra concerned with rules of conduct. Many Kalpa Sūtras were written in this period. Portions of the Mahābhārata may have been written at this time and an important literature of this period is the early Buddhist and Jain scriptures.

The Epic Age comes next from 200 B.C. to A.D. 300. In it the Rāmāyaṇa and Mahābhārata receive their final form. The codes of Manu and Yājñavalkya appear here also, as well as the minor Upaniṣads and some of the Purāṇas. Mahāyāna Buddhism made its appearance at this time with its own writings and scriptures. The Epic is followed by the age of the Purāṇas and Darśanas from A.D. 300 to A.D. 650. In India's history this is the period of the Guptas, one of the times when Indian culture was at its peak. The extensiveness of the Purāṇas and Darśanas has been indicated already. Of this period D. S. Sarma writes, "Thus the brilliant age of the Guptas carried on the Hindu Renaissance of the preceding period by popularizing Hinduism on a vast scale through Purāṇas and Tantras on the one hand and by systematizing Hindu philosophy through the philosophical sūtras on the other."[7]

The last age of the Ancient Period is that of the Later Purāṇas and Darśanas from A.D. 650 to A.D. 1000. As mentioned before, commentator followed commentator and critic followed critic; thus it is no wonder that there are similarities and one period merges into another. Nevertheless in this period the Purāṇas and Darśanas took a more definite and comprehensive form. One sees this in the works of Śaṅkara, the first systematic exponent of Advaita Vedānta based on the Upaniṣads. He was born in A.D. 788. His philosophy was an outstanding intellectual achievement and was balanced by an earlier Bhakti movement carried on by Vaiṣṇava and Śaiva saints and mystics. The Vaiṣṇava mystics were known as Aḷvars, the two best known being Nammaḷvar and Tirumangai.

They travelled throughout south India expressing their devotion to God in songs and poetry eagerly acclaimed by the people. The hymns of the Aḷvars are known as the Nalayira Prabandham. In Śaivism the Nayanmars were the counterparts of the Aḷvars, performing identical roles and achieving similar results. The Bhāgavata Purāṇa is the best known of the Purāṇas of this period. Sarma calls it "one of the seminal books in the religious literature of India"[8] and it gave rise to five later Bhakti schools.

The writings of the Ancient Period outlined here came into being over a period of some two thousand years. They are varied in type and content, yet they have a common end. Prabhavananda points out that "...their avowed purpose is to aid all men to attain the highest spiritual development."[9] Their aim is to dispel man's ignorance and this can be done by "...direct knowledge of ultimate truth obtained through purification of the heart, and through a constant striving for detachment of the soul from worldly desires."[10] Another author writes that "...just as all our scriptures have a common source, they have a common aim. Their aim is to make man a perfect spirit like God and one with him."[11] And D. M. Datta in his book states that "...the original and express motive of each system...is to attain a state of perfection beyond suffering."[12]

VII

Some scholars include Śaṅkara in the Medieval Period. There is a rationale for this, since his views and those of the founders of important schools in the tenth through the twelfth centuries are counterposed. The literature of the Medieval Period includes the works of Rāmānuja, Madhva and Meykandar, the founders of Viśiṣṭādvaita, Dvaita and Śaiva-Siddhānta. The works of the Bhakti schools of Rāmānanda, Vallabha and Chaitanya are also important, as was the Rāmāyaṇa of Tulsīdās (1532-1623). Outside of Hinduism in the Medieval Period we have the writings of Nānak (1469-1538), the founder of Sikhism and the literature of the Moslem Sufi mystics and Kabīr who was neither Moslem nor Hindu.

VIII

We find two literary traditions, one native and one foreign, in India in the Modern Period. Regarding the latter, India was exposed to both the sacred and secular literature of the West beginning in the 1700's. The Christian Bible on the one hand and the works of the French Physiocrats and the English Utilitarians on the other found their way into India at this time.

One result of the introduction of western literature and views was social, political and religious reforms. Organizations such as the several Samājs arose, their leaders' writings reflecting two trends, a "back to the Vedas" movement such as Dayānanda and the Ārya Samāj, and an integration of East and West exemplified by Keshub C. Sen and the Brāhmo Samāj. The extensive writings of men such as Rammohun Roy, Ranade, Gokhale, Debendranath Tagore and Vivekananda in the many journals and newspapers they founded roused public support for the overthrowing of suttee (widow-burning), caste distinctions, degradation of women, restricted education, and religious bigotry and parochialism.

The writings of Rabindranath Tagore and Mahatma Gandhi have had wide public influence in the twentieth century. Tagore was the leader of the modern literary renaissance. Gandhi continued the reform zeal of the nineteenth century. In religious philosophy Aurobindo's works are monumental and in twentieth century philosophical circles we find men such as Radhakrishnan whose writings reflect the attempts by Indians to achieve a synthetic world view.

THE VEDAS

V. Madhusudan Reddy

I The Nature and Importance of the Vedas

The Vedas are a group of hymns, chants and treatises containing the thought and experiences of the Aryan people at a certain period in their collective advancement. Chronologically they are the earliest documents of the Aryans, and to many they are unparalleled for their intrinsic excellence and spiritual content. They contain the highly intuitive experiences of the Ṛiṣis, the ancient mystics of India, and are written in Sanskrit, a very old language, whose norms of expression are highly symbolic and therefore not easily translatable into simple terms. While the Vedas reveal the Truth to the initiate, to the pragmatist they appear to be myth and ritual. They received their name meaning knowledge because they embody the highest Truth. Moreover, as Aurobindo points out, "In the fixed tradition of thousands of years they have been revered as the origin and standard of all that can be held as authoritative and true in Brāhmaṇa and Upaniṣad, the Tantra and Purāṇa, in the doctrines of great philosophical schools and in the teachings of famous saints and sages."[1]

The Vedic Ṛiṣis were one of the first to discover the lofty truths of this life and the beyond. The Vedas are declared to be ageless in content and to constitute the earliest spiritual literature of mankind. B. G. Tilak and H. Jacobi date them from 4500 to 6000 B.C. In them more importance is given to the truths discovered than to the discoverers. Those truths were heard by the inner ear and seen by the inner eye of the Ṛiṣis ; hence the Vedas are called apauruṣeya, not written by men, or Śruti, that which is heard.

The four Vedas (Ṛig, Sāma, Yajur and Atharva) were compiled at a later date by Vyāsa. They are divided into four parts—

Mantras, Brāhmaṇas, Āraṇyakas and Upaniṣads. The Mantras are poetic compositions whereas the Brāhmaṇas dealing with the ritualistic aspect of the Vedic literature are written in prose. The Āraṇyakas (forest treatises) and the Upaniṣads are philosophical and mystical writings. The Mantras are classified in two ways. In one they are divided into eight parts (aṣṭakas) which are subdivided into eight chapters (adhyāyas). The adhyāyas fall into different groups (vargas) which on an average consist of five hymns (Ṛiks). The second classification divides the Saṃhitās (four Vedas) into ten Maṇḍalas. Each Maṇḍala is subdivided into anuvakas which are divided into Sūktas containing a number of Ṛiks. The latter classification is more popular and is in vogue. The Ṛig-veda, the epitome of the Vedas, contains 10,552 mantras or hymns, the Sāma-veda 1,875, the Yajur-veda 1,975 and the Atharava-veda 5,987 making a total of 20,389.

The Vedas are generally accepted as the true foundation and starting point of later spiritual movements and philosophies in India, including even the modern renaissance. They constitute the very fibre of Indian religion and culture. S. Radhakrishnan underlines their importance by declaring "A study of the hymns of the Ṛig-veda is indispensable for any adequate account of Indian thought" and in *The Cultural Heritage of India* we read :

> "The Hindus trace the original source of their cultural life to the Vedas which they hold to be divine truths revealed from time to time to the Ṛiṣis, seers in their supernormal consciousness. Their religion, philosophy, ritualistic practices, civic conduct, and even social relations are guided by certain codes which are known as Smṛitis, but all of them are based upon the sacred sanction of Vedic authority. Even the Itihāsas and Purāṇas are to be read as commentaries on the sacred Vedas. Manu, the greatest law-giver of India, has explicitly stated that these should be considered as an elaboration of the Vedas. It is a recognized rule of procedure that whenever there seems to be a difference between the Śruti (the Vedas) and the Smṛiti, the Śruti has to be upheld as the supreme authority and the Smṛiti has to be interpreted in consonance with it. No school of philosophy will be recognized as orthodox, if it is not supported by the authority of the Vedas. The whole life of a Hindu, from conception up to the last funeral rites, has to be sanctified

by the recitation of Vedic mantras (sacred text). From these facts, it may easily be conceived, how profound has been the influence of the Vedas upon this great and most ancient of the civilized nations of the world."[2]

The Vedas made the Upaniṣads possible as they are but a continuation and development of the Vedas, bringing out clearly what lies concealed in symbolic language in them. The Upaniṣadic authors recapture the Vedic vision of Truth within the framewok of pure intellect and, to establish their doctrines, often refer to the Vedas. This is seen in the following comparison:

"The face of the Truth is covered with a golden lid: O fostering Sun, that uncover for the law of the Truth, for Sight. O fosterer, O sole Ṛiṣi, O controlling Yama, O Sūrya...He am I."

Īśā Upaniṣad, 15-16

"Hidden by your truth is the Truth that is constant for ever where they unyoke the horses of the Sun. There the ten thousands stand together, That is the One: I have seen the supreme Godhead of the embodied God."

Ṛig-veda, V. 62-1

The sun in both the Vedas and Upaniṣads stands for Rit-chit (Truth consciousness) which is the same as the Vijñāna of the Upaniṣads. The various Upaniṣadic sādhanās or Vidyās (Madhu, Dhara, Satya, Puruṣa-vidyā, etc.) dealing with different aspects of the Supreme and the means of approaching it have been borrowed from the Vedas also.

The Gītā too takes freely from the Vedas and holds the Ṛiks in high reverence. Of post-Vedic literature the Gītā truly attempts to bring out the spiritual significance of Vedic symbolism. Like the Vedas the Gītā does not consider the world an illusion; and it accepts life in its totality. The Brahma Sūtras are in a way an aphoristic summary of the main teachings of the Vedas. In the post-Vedic period the Upaniṣads, Gītā and Brahma Sūtras are considered the authoritative scriptures. The Dharma Śāstras too are rooted in the Vedas, repeatedly invoking Vedic authority to establish their doctrines. Even the epics Mahābhārata and Rāmāyaṇa are founded on the Vedas. The former has been called the fifth Veda; and people generally give the Purāṇas the status of the Vedas. For they have brought the high philosophical truths and visions of the Vedas and the Upaniṣads to the common man.

The physical images in the Epics and Purāṇas have psychical and mystical significance and amplify the meaning of the Vedas. For example, when the Purāṇas speak of Viṣṇu reclining on the multi-hooded snake, Ananta, upon the ocean of milk, it means that the supreme Lord rests upon the Infinite coiled upon the waters of eternal Existence. Viṣṇu is the all-pervading Godhead; Ananta is the world of infinite possibilities, and the ocean of sweet milk is the unalloyed bliss of eternal existence. The Āgamas (manuals of worship) also speak of the Vedic origin of the Tantra (the literature of Śakti worshippers). Tāntric philosophy results from the esoteric doctrines of the Vedas. The gods of the Veda continue to adorn the Tāntric pantheon, and the spiritual positivism of the Vedas is upheld by the Tantras. The Tantras take up all aspects of Truth and work out their highest and fullest significance.

The spiritual experiences of the Vedas are subjected to logical criticism and systematic analysis in the six systems of Indian philosophy, and the critical aspect of philosophy becomes as important as the speculative. Considering Buddhism and Jainism to be against the Vedic vision of Reality is invalid. They revolted only against excessive Vedic ceremonialism and ritualism. Reality is One and Many, and different systems of philosophy, including Jainism and Buddhism, emphasize its particular aspects and regard them as the whole Truth. The modern Indian Renaissance represents the increasing fulfilment of the integral vision of the Vedic Ṛiṣis. It implies a rebirth of India's soul into a new body of energy, a return of spirituality to life. The same spirit that brought the light in ancient times renews and expresses itself through instruments more rich and suited to comprehend the complex and ever enlarging conditions of the times including the social, economic, political and cultural aspects of human life and existence.

II Vedic Commentaries

The Vedic hymns lend themselves to a ritualistic interpretation by those who are interested merely in the early secular history of India and not its spiritual attainments. Most European scholars have taken such an interpretation, contenting themselves with the etymological explanation of words. From Yājñavalkya (c. fourth century A.D.) to Aurobindo there have been a number of Vedic commentators in India who have interpreted the Vedas in various ways. Among them are Skanda Swami, Marayana and Udgitha (A.D. 630), Yāska, Lakṣmaṇa (A.D. 1100), Madhvachārya (A.D. 1198-1278), Sāyana (14th century A.D.), Chatruvedaswami (15th century A.D.), Swami Dayānanda (A.D. 1824-1883) and Sri Aurobindo (A.D. 1872-1950). More important commentaries on the Yajur-veda, Sāma-veda and Atharva-veda are those of Hari Swami (A.D. 638), Bharat Swami (A.D. 1303), Sāyana, Guṇa Viṣṇu (13th century A.D.), Mahidhara (A.D. 1600), Śobhākar Bhaṭṭa (15th century A.D.) and Swami Dayānanda.

Yājñavalkya is the first commentator to interpret the Vedas spiritually and the authors of the Brāhmaṇas the first ritualistically. Nonetheless, the Brāhmaṇas have passages emphasizing the spiritual import of the Vedas and explaining the rituals symbolically. Yāska, author of the Sanskrit etymology and lexicon, Nirukta and Nighantu, is a great Vedic commentator. His view is that etymology is a part of Vedic learning and a proper study of the Vedas is impossible without it. According to him the meaning of the Ṛiks is difficult to grasp, for they are formulations of the spiritual experiences of the Vedic Ṛiṣis. His is a naturalistic interpretation and is as symbolic as the Vedic hymns. By the time Yāska wrote his Nirukta, the spiritual interpretation of the Vedas was almost lost. Yāska insists on a right understanding of the hymns or Mantras, for he believed in their secret import and supreme authority and considered them more authoritative than the Brāhmaṇas.

Coming immediately after Yāska, Bṛihat Devatā also testifies to the existence of several schools of interpretation of the Vedas. He supports the psychological theory of the Vedas. His special insight is summed up in the words : "He knows the Gods who knows the Ṛiks." Madhvāchārya, the founder of the Dvaita school of Vedānta, also attempted a spiritualistic interpretation. He did not rule out the ritualistic interpretation but was not prepared to mistake the performance of the ritual for the essential message of the Vedas. While he admits the ritualistic use of the Mantra, he insists that the Mantras are addressed to gods who are the different powers of the supreme God, Viṣṇu, and who have a distinct consciousness of their own.

Sāyana, another great scholar and commentator, greatly

influenced succeeding scholars. His renowned commentary, the Bhāṣya, takes the Brāhmaṇas as a basis. According to him the Vedas speak of supernatural methods for the achievement of desired and avoidance of undesirable objects. He accepts mainly the ritualistic tradition, and was of great help to European scholars of the Vedas in their attempts to understand the Sanskrit of the Vedas. No doubt the Bhāṣya is indispensable for Vedic studies, for it gives all the relevant information regarding Vedic grammar, literature, tradition, myth and legend. Sāyana distorts the hymns to suit his own thinking, but nonetheless clearly admits the possibility of a spiritualistic interpretation. The Vedas have a terminology of their own, and words like ghṛitam, go, ashya, ṛitam, etc. will have to be understood in a particular sense. It is only then that the Vedas yield a consistent and coherent meaning.

Recent commentaries on the Vedas include the historical interpretation by Abinash Chandra Das, geographical by Umesh Chandra Vidyavrata, scientific by Paramasiva Iyer and astronomical by Balgangadhar Tilak. None of these consistently interpret the Vedas entirely. Tilak in his monumental works, *Orion* and *The Arctic Home in the Vedas*, generally accepts the findings of the European scholars and, taking an ingenious and fresh approach, concludes that the Aryans had their original home in the Polar regions, putting their date at 6000 B.C. But the Aryan invasion of India, some say, is only a myth, Aurobindo claiming, for example, "It is indeed coming to be doubted whether the whole story of an Aryan invasion . . . is not a myth of the philologists."[3] The Aryans were the original inhabitants of the country and were "autochethonous" to her. Iyer takes pains in his *The Ṛiks* to compare the Vedic Age and the Glacial Period and to prove that the whole of the Ṛig-veda is only "a figurative representation of the geological phenomena belonging to the new birth of our planet after its long-continued glacial death in the same period of terrestrial evolution."

V. G. Rele's interpretation is biological, seeing in the Ṛiks only an account of the physiology of the nervous system of the human body in figurative language. Besides these S. Radhakrishnan's and A. K. Coomaraswamy's views regarding the Vedas are noteworthy. The former, in spite of his erudition, hesitates to set aside the traditional interpretation of Sāyana or the views of European scholars on the subject. Nonetheless his later writings strengthen the view that the Vedas constitute the essential foundation of the entire Indian spiritual tradition for they are the products of spiritual intuition and vision. Coomaraswamy in his work, *A New Approach to the Vedas*, supports the psychological theory.

Max Müller, a great Vedic scholar, translated for the first time the whole of the Ṛig-veda along with Sāyana's Bhāṣya. In spite of his great love for India and her culture he could not discover the key to the understanding of Vedic symbolism, although he successfully awakened Europe as well as modern India to the glory of ancient Indian civilization. The Vedas speak of many gods—Indra, Agni, Varuṇa, Mitra, Vāyu, Aświns, Maruts.

This led Max Müller to believe that the Vedas teach polytheism. But Vedic polytheism is only a phase of its monotheism. All the gods are the several powers or personalities of the one supreme Godhead—"The One Existent is called variously by the wise."[4] Each god is raised in turn to a supreme status and is invoked as the one and the only God encompassing within Himself all the rest. Max Müller uses the word henotheism to describe this phenomenon; but Indian monotheism has always believed rather "in the unity of Gods in God, than the denial of gods for God."[5] Max Müller, however does not rule out the spiritual import of the Vedas, for he writes, "I know from my own experience how often what seemed to me for a long time unmeaning, nay, absurd, disclosed after a time a far deeper meaning than I should have ever expected."[6] Other European scholars are Brunnhofer, Wilson, Griffith and Bloomfield who have mostly contributed to a naturalistic and exoteric interpretation of the Vedas.

Dayānanda and Aurobindo are two of the more authoritative, recent Vedic commentators. Dayānanda's greatest contribution has been his herculean effort to make the Veda once again a living and inspiring scripture. "In the matter of Vedic interpretation," Aurobindo declares, "I am convinced that whatever may be the final complete interpretation, Dayānanda will be honoured as the first discoverer of the right clues. Amidst the chaos and obscurity of old ignorance and age-long misunderstanding his was the eye of direct vision that pierced to the truth and fastened on that which was essential. He has found the keys of the doors that time had closed and rent asunder the seals of the imprisoned fountains."[7] It was a formidable task for Dayānanda to make people forget the ritualistic interpretation of Sāyana's commentary on the Vedas. Having accepted the Veda as his firm foundation Dayānanda tries to build on it "a whole education of truth, a whole manhood and a whole nationhood...." He taught Vedic wisdom in its original purity and established the Veda once again as "the source of all sanctions and standards of all truth," and accordingly proceeded to reconstruct the entire fabric of Hindu society in the light of Vedic authority.

In interpreting the Vedas, Dayānanda pursues the Nirukta of Yāska, the Sanskrit Grammar Aṣṭādhyāyī of Pāṇiṇi, the Mahābhāṣya of Patañjali and the Brāhmaṇas, but not without reservations. In his introduction to the commentary on the Vedas (Ṛig-vedadi Bhāṣya Bhūmikā) he outlines broadly the principles of his interpretation. To him the Vedas are revealed, and contain germinally the truth of all science as well as of religion. The Vedic authors were only the hearers of truth, the real author being God himself. The Vedas themselves are a part of God's knowledge and are, therefore, infallible, self-existent, authoritative, and co-eternal with Him. He quotes several authorities to support this view.[8] According to Dayānanda the Brāhmaṇas are not revealed scriptures; they are the works of the Ṛiṣis and consequently products of the human intellect. The Vedas normally deal with four subjects, Vijñāna, Karma, Upāsanā and Jñāna—scientific knowledge, common human activity, behaviour turned towards liberation and spiritual knowledge. All the Vedas have God as their common subject. He is the creator of the universe, the source of all true knowledge, omnipresent and omniscient. He is Eternal, the Infinite, Just, Merciful and All-Beatitude. God is the subject matter of not only the Vedas but also the other śāstras. The Vedic Ṛiks are hymns written in praise of the One Supreme under many names, names designed to express His many powers, for example, "Even He is Agni, He is Āditya, He is Vāyu, He is Chandramās, He is Śukra, He is Brahmā, He is Āpa, He is Prajāpati."[9] Dayānanda believed the Ṛiks reveal this secret import only to those initiated in the spiritual life and those pure in mind and possessing the highest erudition. The uncultured and mundane, no matter how intelligent, cannot interpret them rightly.

In his estimation of the Vedas as records of intuitions and revelations Dayānanda is the forerunner of Aurobindo. According to Aurobindo the Vedas are "a great scripture of the mystics with a double significance," an exoteric for the many and esoteric for the few. The Ṛiks, being couched in a very ancient language, are capable of varied interpretations. To establish their esoteric significance he fixes the import of certain Vedic terms, deciphers a number of the Vedic symbols, elaborates the psychological functions of the many gods and explains inconsistencies in the Vedic texts. By doing so the Vedas become a consistent, coherent scripture. The symbolic and figurative language of the Vedas testifies to a psychological or esoteric interpretation. Its spiritual hypothesis is proved by this very internal evidence which is fixed and invariable. There is a uniformity in the meaning of the basic words used in the Vedas and a consistent diction which give a coherent account of them. Sometime the words used yield a double meaning resulting in both ritualistic and spiritualistic interpretations. This double meaning was deliberate; it was meant to save the common man from the danger of being exposed to the utterly spiritual. The spiritual import was meant for the inwardly evolved, the spiritually fit and the initiated.

Such use of language was natural with the Vedic Ṛiṣis, for in the Vedic period language was not conventional as it was later. Originally words were fluid in their meaning; they were not fixed and hence were capable of a number of applications. At first words were communal in their character; only later did they become rigid and subjected to the idea. Aurobindo writes "...in the first stage of language the word is as living or even a more living force than its idea; sound determines sense. In its last stage the positions have been reserved; the idea becomes all important and the sound secondary."[10] With the passage of time the progression in language has been from the concrete to the abstract, from a pluralistic to a particular, single meaning, thus greatly diminishing the bearing capacity of words. The Vedic Ṛiṣis used their words in their original sense and natural context, and not in their particular and restricted sense. The deciphering of the meaning of Vedic words is of great importance for a spiritualistic interpretation of the Vedas as the following illustrate: Aditi=Mother of gods, Indivisible Consciousness; Agni=Truth-Conscious, Seer-Will, Divine Energy; Bhūḥ=Earth, Physical Consciousness; Go=Light, Rays of illumination from Higher Consciousness; Soma=Divine Ānanda; Varuṇa=Pure Wide Being; Yajña=Action consecreted to gods. A right understanding of the meaning of the many Vedic words and their symbology reveals that the many gods mentioned in the Vedas are the several special powers of the Divine who increase the spiritual consciousness of the aspirant. On the external side they are the powers of creation. Indra is the god of rain; Maruts are storm-gods; Uṣas is the god of Dawn, etc. The gods thus have micro-cosmic as well as macrocosmic functions. Agni is the physical fire as well as the inner aspiration that makes man move God-ward. Similarly Vāyu, the wind-god embodies the life-principle in man's inner being. Each of the gods is thus an aspect, a power and a personality of the Divine.[11]

III Vedic Thought

Hindu culture, religion and thought have their origins in the Vedas. The Vedas take life in its fullness and endeavour to effect a harmony between man's spiritual and material quests. A contemporary author writes, "We do not find in the Vedas any evidence of the tragedy of the divided soul, and the anguish and misery that accompany it (as we find among the Greeks). Nor do we come across signs of repression or self-torture, accompanied by morbid sin-consciousness, sometimes found...among followers of the Hebraic religions. No negative attitude, induced by disillusion-ment..., no world-weariness is in evidence in the Vedas. Vedic sages are positive in their acceptance of life and death...of the ulti-mate values, of truth, goodness, beauty—and of the Eternal Law Ṛita...."[12]

The Ṛiṣis were intensely spiritual and felt the living presence of the Divine in the entire physical universe. They loved life as well as God, and, placing themselves under the discipline of Satya, Ṛita and Tapas (Truth, the Eternal Law and penance), they led a life of utter dedication and consecration to the Divine. The revelation in their souls of the Supreme Truth was creatively expressed in songs marked for their power, purity and austerity, their language being cryptic and symbolic, signifying a deep, mystical truth. As one author has written, "The visions of the beauty of life and nature in the Vedas are extremely rich in poetic value. Perhaps nowhere else in the world has the glory of dawn and sunrise and the silence and sweetness of nature, received such rich and at the same time such pure expression."[13]

Vedic religious thought has survived numerous social and political upheavals through the millenniums and in doing so adopted many of the more enduring features of those movements. Vedic culture was many-sided and synthetic as well as deeply philosophical and ethical in dealing with life-problems. The basis of its social and material existence and literary and artistic creations has been spiritual and intuitive. The Vedas claim there is one Supreme Reality and many ways to approach it. The Divine can be realized not only through an expansion of consciousness but can be met by each individual soul in itself, for the individual and the universal are essentially the same. The Vedic view of the Divine is much subtler and deeper in spiritual content than the words monotheism and polytheism convey. Max Müller calls the view henotheism; but it too does not convey the full significance of the spiritual idealism of the Vedas. They picture the Divine as the One in Many and the Many in One. Henotheism describes the Divinity as One, as well as conceiving of it as a God. It also contemplates many gods and extols each as the Supreme Being. Though henotheism is marked by a general devotional attitude, it does not bring out the truth of Vedic theism which contemplates the worship of the One in many names and forms, thus asserting the unity not only of God but of all orders of reality. The gods are many in form but in spirit they are all one, for they are the powers and personalities of the one Supreme Being. Vedic religion is an expression of this vision of the Truth.

The Vedic vision of Reality is also one of beauty and splendour. He is "the shining One" as well as Satya-dharman, "the one for whom truth is the law of being." According to the Vedas the Supreme reveals Himself as Ṛita, the Eternal Order. This oneness of the Divine is also presented by the Vedas as a spiritual essence as in the statement "the One Being the wise call by many names."[14] Sometimes the One Being is described as the All God.[15] The one Divine Being understood essentially and metaphysically is the One which pervades all; and the Vedic description of this in the neuter singular, in masculine and feminine, or in dual and plural do not contradict each other. Everything becomes unified in the all-pervading reality of the Supreme "In whom all find one nest." The idea is brought out clearly in the Atharva-veda: "He is the One, the One alone, In Him all Deities become One alone."[16] In the mystical experience of the Ṛiṣis the One is real, as are the Many. This is seen in the verse in the Ṛig-veda: "One is Agni kindled in many a place; One is Sūrya shining over all. One is Uṣas illumining all this. That which is One has become this All."[17] Vedic religion believes in Ṛita, the Eternal Law upholding the universe. Agni was invoked as adhyakṣam dharmanam, Lord of Eternal Laws."[18] According to the Atharva-veda Dharma is the fundamental principle of existence—"Truth, Eternal order that is great and stern, Consecration, austerity, prayer and ritual—these uphold the earth."[19]

No doubt in ancient India as in Greece and Rome people worshipped nature Gods. But the Vedic Ṛiṣis did not deify or personify the forces of Nature. They believed instead that the Gods presided over the elements of the physical universe—Sun, Moon, Heaven, etc. The many gods represent the spiritual functioning of the one Godhead under different names and personalities. T. V. Kapali says: "It is enough if we remember that the Gods whose identities with the objects and forces of Nature in the physical universe are quite assured are not really and deeply the external things meant as objects of ritual worship, but are much more and are intensely divine in their true form and nature, superb and intimate in their workings as powers of the Godhead in the hidden and occult layers of our being as well as in the Cosmic existence."[20]

The Gods of the Ṛig-veda are the different powers or personalities of the Supreme Truth, not entirely separate from It, yet Its definite manifestations. They are the limbs as it were of the Supreme Godhead functioning in the field of Cosmic action. The Devas (gods) are manifestations of the power and intelligence of the Supreme, acting in the various spheres of His Cosmic existence. The esoteric sense of the Vedas reveals that these gods who have their cosmic functions also work as psychological and spiritual powers within man. The benefit of the presence of these gods is always available to man when he outgrows his limited existence and enters into the domain of their help and influence. The Vedas emphasize that the means with which man enlarges his existence "is the same instrumentation by which the supreme One, the Creative Godhead produced, manifested, or created the Universe of Many, the world of creatures out of His own being."[21] It is by self-giving or sacrifice (Yajña) that the supreme Puruṣa made the creation of this world-existence with its beings and gods possible.

By self-giving man can also participate and earn the help of gods to re-create himself in the life of the Supreme Spirit. This is the true inner sacrifice of which the outer ritual is only a symbol. The self-offering of the aspirant makes it possible for the gods to be born in him and increase their own substance in him, thereby helping man to reach his own inner heights. This upward procession or spiritual evolution passes through several stages "the triple world of Earth (pṛithvī), the Middle-world (antarikṣa) and Heaven (dvauh)." Yajña, or the inner sacrifice, is thus the way to realize the supreme ideal of manifesting the Divine in man.

The Vedic Ṛiṣis' ideal was to realize the Sun of Truth, the world of Supernal Light. They sought to become a part of the immortal world of undying light where the Sun of Truth shines forever—"Settle me in that Immortal world that never decays nor dies, wherein the Light of Heaven, the Sun-world is set and the Lustre shines forever...."[22] The Sun World is symbolic of Truth-consciousness or the Supermind. The Ṛiṣis' realization of the cosmic Godhead qualified them for becoming a part of the immortal world of Solar Effulgence. They were also aware of and sensitive to the suffering of their fellow beings and prayed for a common ideal, feeling and well-being. The world for them was a virtuous place to lead a good life under the protection of gods.

The Ṛiṣis accepted and led a full and integral life. They were convinced that the Eternal and the Supreme is involved and immanent in the material universe, and that It increasingly and progressively manifests itself as higher and higher levels of reality—life, mind, vijñāna, Truth-consciousness and Ānanda (Bliss). India's religion, philosophy and social and political life have been built upon this high realization of the Ṛiṣis. Progress for her has been the progressive self-unfoldment of Spirit. It is the founding of life upon this exalted conception and the continued aspiration and effort to realize the Truth and manifest it in life that constitute Vedic civilization. Above all dogmas, beyond all theology, an endless quest for Spirit and the ultimate authority of spiritual experience in all matters of life and existence has been the ruling passion of its culture.

IV Conclusion

In concluding we might summarize the Vedas as follows. They have been accepted traditionally as an infallible source and standard of truth and virtue. Their truths are considered uncreated, eternal and trans-sensuous. The Ṛiṣis declared that on the highest level of religious experience one transcends the intellect, sees the truth directly, and experiences God immediately. Though the Ṛiṣis recognized the inadequacy of words to express ultimate truth, they used them any ways, as it was the only medium they had.

A variety or progression of religious beliefs and practices can be discerned in the Vedas. People in the Vedic Period lived close to nature. It was only natural for them to associate nature and the Divine. At times they personified and deified various aspects or forces of nature. At other times they looked beyond them to a supreme being of which nature in its manifold aspects was a manifestation. At still other times their religion was not rooted in nature but in what we might call "pure thought" alone. We find the Vedas stressing the need for worshipping God regularly and systematically, thus the development of ritualism in the Vedic period and the detailed rituals and sacerdotal practices enjoined. On the other hand some emphasized by-passing or minimizing ritualism and going to or communing directly with God.

It was generally recognized that God is a being with whom one seeks union. This union is man's goal, attainable in various ways, all requiring self sacrifice and discipline. Added to the ritualistic sacrifices must be a sacrifice of self. One must offer oneself to God inwardly as well as outwardly. Self discipline leads to self purification which is a prerequisite to a vision of and union with God. The Vedas picture God as the creator and source of goodness and truth. One's life should be dedicated wholly to God. However, this does not rule out the living of a full life here and now, for reality is good and is to be enjoyed. Spiritual pursuits do not exclude material ones when rightly carried on. The latter is always to be given a lower priority however.

Their experiences with the pattern of natural phenomena led Vedic people to the concept Ṛita, the belief that reality is orderly. Orderliness is one factor which makes for the goodness of reality. The ethical correlate of Ṛita or cosmic order is the principle of Dharma. As there is a certain order inherent in the natural world, so there is a moral order immanent in human life. This was combined with the concept Karma, the belief that deeds have consequences, and therefore everyone is responsible for his actions and their consequences. Thus ethics and self responsibility were considered the foundation for both society and individual life.

One of the Vedas' greatest gifts to India's spiritual heritage is the attitude of tolerance. There are many ways of conceiving of the Supreme and numerous means of approaching Him; and it is both invalid and harmful to insist that one's own is the only way. This tolerance is rooted in the kind of doubt reflected in the last verse of the Hymn of Creation,

> "None knoweth whence creation has arisen;
> And whether he has or has not produced it:
> He who surveys it in the highest heaven,
> He only knows, or haply he may know not."[23]

It is this hesitancy which has minimized religious dogmatism and arrogance in India's past and which will continue to in the future.

Perhaps the most profound and significant concept, germinal in the Vedas, is the belief in the oneness of reality. All is one. Brahman and Ātman are one. Man is one with God. Man is divine. All is divine. The unity of reality has two facets. One, indicated already, is that God and man are one. The second is the oneness of mankind. All men are brothers under Brahman. The Unity of man and God has as its correlate the oneness of man and man. The belief in the integral oneness of all reality has been both the stimulus and the ideal for India through the ages. Her future will be glorious only if she continues to accept and strive toward that ideal.

3

THE UPANIṢADS AND UPANIṢADIC THOUGHT

S. R. TALGHATTI

I THE IMPORTANCE AND MEANING OF THE UPANIṢADS

The Upaniṣads occupy a unique place in the history of Indian philosophy. They constitute the concluding portions of Vedic Literature and are, therefore, called Vedānta, the others being the Saṃhitā (Mantra), Brāhmaṇas and Āraṇyakas. It is to the credit of Upanṣadic thinkers that, for the first time in the history of Indian philosophy, philosophical thinking seems to have been consciously and purposely undertaken in the Upaniṣads. Though the Upaniṣads thus mark the beginning of philosophizing in India, the philosophy they have produced is not to be considered crude. "Beginnings are crude" is not a universal principle. At least it does not hold in this case. On the contrary, we find that the subtlety with which problems are raised and answered in the Upaniṣads is remarkable. These philosophical problems are, again, as fundamental as they are subtle, and their solutions reveal a profound understanding and deep insight into human nature and experience. That is why Upaniṣadic philosophy has remained ever-fresh, commanding the respect of its students from generation to generation.

Another consideration bearing on the importance of their study is that the seeds of many of the later schools of Indian philosophy, especially the Vedānta and Sāṃkhya are found in the Upaniṣads. This makes the study of Upaniṣadic thought indispensable for an understanding of the development of Indian philosophy. Thus the importance of the study of Upaniṣadic thought cannot be over-emphasized. In regard to its meaning and the sense in which it is applied to the philosophical works called by that name, the word Upaniṣad is derived from upa+ni+sad meaning 'to sit near' or 'to approach'. This evidently refers to approaching a teacher for instruction. The importance of a teacher is expressed in the Chāndogya Upaniṣad as follows: "Knowledge (Vidyā) learnt from a teacher alone helps one to attain the best."[1] The way to approach a teacher, who is, of course, the Knower of Brahman, is also described in the Upaniṣads. Instruction, however, was not imparted to any and every student who approached, but only to the qualified. The qualifications of a pupil are also mentioned in the Upaniṣads. Instruction was considered to be sacred, and therefore, secret. Thus it was that upaniṣad gradually came to mean the teaching or instruction itself which was imparted by the teacher. The language in which this instruction is given is usually indirect, being metaphorical and allegorical, having what may be called secret import. Therefore, the term Upaniṣad further meant esoteric (secret or mystic) doctrine (vidyā). Being vedānta, Upaniṣad also signifies the 'secret of the vedas'.

However, one must not think there is something mysterious or mystical about the doctrine or teaching itself. This will be evident from the account of Upaniṣadic thought presented here. What is perhaps meant is that the Upaniṣads expound a doctrine or view which reveals the secret of an eternally happy or blissful life. Upaniṣad is, thus, the 'doctrine revealing a secret'. A direct reference to this is found in the Muṇḍakopaniṣad where it is said that a student should humbly approach for instruction a spiritual teacher (guru) who is well versed in the scriptures (vedas) and is established in Brahman. Such a teacher should then teach or explain to him the principles of Brahma vidyā (knowledge of Brahman), whereby one knows the person, the truth, the imperishable.[2] The description of ātman as 'lodged in the cave' (of the heart) also lends support to this meaning. On the basis of the internal evidence itself, then, it can be shown that Upaniṣad finally came to mean the esoteric doctrine of Ātman or Brahman, i.e. Brahma-Vidyā.

There is a characteristic description of the process of attaining knowledge or realization of Brahman in the Chāndogya Upaniṣad which throws light on what sitting near means: "When he becomes strong, he becomes a rising man. Rising, he becomes an attendant. Attending, he becomes attached as a pupil. Attached as a pupil (sitting near), he becomes a seer, a hearer, a thinker, an understander, a doer and a knower (or realizer)."[3] The meaning of Upaniṣad covers all these stages, taken in a broader sense. But its essence is doctrine or knowledge of Brahman. And it is in this sense that the word Upaniṣadic is used to denote the various Upaniṣads.

II The Principal Upaniṣads and Problems Taken up

Though there may be many more, the number of Upaniṣads published so far is one hundred and eight.[4] Not all of them are taken to be standard or authentic. There is, however, as little difference of opinion about the principal older Upaniṣads as there is about the division of the Upaniṣads into two groups—old and new. The principal Upaniṣads are generally accepted to be thirteen in number, and they are Īśā, Kena, Kaṭha, Praśna, Muṇḍaka, Māṇḍūkya, Taittirīya, Aitareya, Chāndogya, Bṛihadāraṇyaka, Śvetāśvatara, Kauṣītaki and Maitreyī. Some accept only eleven Upaniṣads as principal and do not include the last two in the list. It is not necessary for our purposes here to enter into the discussion of the age and chronological order of the Upaniṣads. Suffice it is to say that the account of Upaniṣadic thought presented here is based only on these principal Upaniṣads and that the author's interpretation, wherever necessary, is based entirely on the original texts of the Upaniṣads. My aim throughout has been neither criticism nor comparison, nor again joining issues with other interpretations, but only a clear exposition, as far as possible, of the central features of the Upaniṣadic thought as I understand it.

Before stating the specific philosophical problems which occupied the Upaniṣadic thinkers, we need to know what they conceived the purpose of philosophical inquiry to be. Often it is believed that philosophy is an entirely intellectual affair arising out of a quest after reality and having no concern for practical life. This is expressed by saying that philosophy is the child of wonder. The problem of 'summum bonum' they reserve for ethics. But there also, the approach to it is primarily intellectual. In terms of this, the serious concern for practical life seen in the Upaniṣads is striking. This is not to say that Upaniṣadic thinkers were in quest of the Life-Ideal (Parama-Puruṣārtha) only. They did seek to know reality in itself, but at the same time they were also occupied with the attainment of the ultimate goal of life which they variously called śreyas, śānti, ānanda, amṛita, etc. More probably, the search for reality itself was undertaken by them only at the end of the realization of that ideal.

In any case the search for reality and for the summum bonum was combined in a single approach to reality which may be described as the value or ethical as distinct from the epistemic approach. What is meant by this will be clearer after we have considered the nature of reality. Here I want to underline the implication of this approach for philosophy itself, namely that philosophy, according to the Upaniṣadic thinkers, is not merely the 'child of wonder' but is something much more vitally connected with the basic human aspirations which make up what is called the supreme goal, the ultimate end, or the summum bonum of life. Thus the purpose of Upaniṣadic philosophical inquiry is twofold, ontological and ethical, together leading to a sound philosophy of life. In other words, philosophy is so intimately connected with life that any attempt to sever the two is bound to be discredited, as it will leave philosophy barren and practically worthless. This conception of philosophy may contribute something to the present-day discussion of the nature of philosophy.

What has been said above will be understood better if we look at the main philosophical problems raised and discussed by the Upaniṣads. In the Muṇḍakopaniṣad, it is asked, "Through understanding of what, pray, does all this world become understood, Sir ?"[5] This is clearly an inquiry into the nature of the ultimate reality of the world. Another question is found in the Kenopaniṣad where it is asked, "By whom impelled soars forth the mind impelled ? By whom enjoined goes forth the earliest breathing ? By whom impelled this speech do people utter ? The eye, the ear—what god, pray, them enjoineth ?"[6] In the Śvetaśvatara Upaniṣad, we find a more comprehensive inquiry, "What is Brahman, the cause ? Whence are we born ? Whereby do we live ? And on what are we established ? Overruled by whom, in pains and pleasures, do we live our various conditions, O ye Knowers of Brahma ?"[7] We must bear in mind that all these philosophical inquiries become meaningful and worthwhile only when we make them with the definite purpose expressed in Maitreyī's question in the Bṛihadāraṇyaka Upaniṣad, "What should I do with that through which I may not be immortal ?"[8] It is instructive to note in this connection the distinction made between the lower and higher kinds of knowledge (Aparā and Parā Vidyā) in the Muṇḍakopaniṣad. It is stated that even the Vedas belong to the realm of lower knowledge, while the higher is "that whereby that Immortal (or Imperishable) is apprehended."[9] This clearly indicates how, in the eyes of the Upaniṣads, parā vidyā, that is philosophy, is really the attainment of the immortal, which is not only reality, but the ultimate goal of life. In the Īśopaniṣad also, where the term vidyā is used for knowledge or philosophy, it is said that "with Knowledge wins the immortal."[10]

We need to clarify the Upaniṣadic use of vidyā and other terms. Generally vidyā stands for philosophic knowledge. The Muṇḍakopaniṣad has called it parā vidyā. Tattvajñāna or philosophy is knowledge of reality which is characterized by the Upaniṣads as the imperishable or the immortal (Akṣara). Since this reality is Ātman or Brahman according to the Upaniṣads, philosophy is nothing but Ātma Vidyā or Brahma Vidyā. Throughout this discussion, I have also used philosophy in the same sense. We have also to note that vidyā and jñāna are used almost synonymously, though a distinction is possible. Ātma-Jñāna (Knowledge of Ātman), however, is not knowledge in the epistemological sense of the term. But more about this when we discuss the nature of Ātma-Jñāna (or Brahma Jñāna). It is because reality and summum bonum merge in the single ideal of the immortal that philosophy, which is the attainment of this ideal, is considered of highest importance. For example, Brahma-Vidyā is described as "the foundation of all knowledge,"[11] and we are advised to arise, awake and get this knowledge from worthy teachers. We are warned further that only if we have this knowledge in this life and world can we be said to have attained our goal (or good); otherwise "great is the destruction."[12] It will be useful, in this connection to note the distinction made by the Kaṭhopaniṣad between the good and the pleasant (Śreyas and Preyas). It says that "the wise man chooses the 'good', indeed, rather than the 'pleasant'. "[13] The Śreyas (good) is of course the attainment of Brahman or Ātman.

The account above should give a fairly good idea of the nature of the basic philosophic problems taken up in the Upaniṣads as well as the purpose of their inquiry. The whole thing is summarized in the form of the famous Upaniṣadic prayer which beautifully expresses the characteristic yearning of the human soul everywhere:

"From the unreal lead me to the real!
From darkness lead me to light!
From death lead me to immortality!"[14]

III Views of Reality

The reality which the Upanṣadic sages sought is, to state in anticipation of the result of their inquiry, Ātman; and the goal of human life is its realization. The most explicit statement of this is from Yājñavalkya in the Bṛihadāraṇyaka where he tells Maitreyī:

> "Lo, verily, it is the Ātman that should be seen,
> that should be harkened to, that should be thought
> on, that should be pondered on, O Maitreyī, Lo,
> verily, in the Ātman's being seen, harkened to,
> thought on, understood, all this world is known."[15]

Here he has answered the question, mentioned earlier, "Through understanding of what, pray, does all this world become understood, Sir ?" In other words, it is Ātman that the Upaniṣads are in quest of both as the ultimate reality and end to be realized. Both ontology and ethics lead to Ātman.

While searching for reality or the immortal (akṣara), the Upaniṣadic thinkers followed two paths which may be described as individual and cosmic. The former consists of the search for reality through a thorough analysis of the psycho-physical functionings of human personality. The latter consists of the search for reality through a critical analysis of cosmic processes and functionings. Both these paths lead the seeker to one and the same reality called Ātman in the former case and Brahman in the latter. Ātman and Brahman are not two realities but one. That is why they are used synonymously in the Upaniṣads. The statements of their identity are well known and numerous—"This Ātman is Brahman;"[16] "Both he who is here in a person and he who is yonder in the Sun—he is one;"[17] "he who is yonder, yonder Person—I myself am he;"[18] "I am Brahman;"[19] and "That art thou."[20]

We may now see how the sages have followed the paths leading to this reality. Along the psycho-physical path they found that the Ātman is "the hearing of the ear, the thought of the mind, the voice of speech, as also the breathing of the breath, and the sight of the eye."[21] In more specific terms the same Upaniṣad further says, "That which is unexpressed with speech, that with which speech is expressed—That indeed known as Brahma, Nor this that people worship as this."[22] The same is the condition of thought, sight, hearing and breathing. This description is meant to emphasize that the sense-organs are not reality, but that which supports their functionings, i.e. Ātman, is alone reality. This is summarized by the Praśnopaniṣad—"truly, this seer, teacher, hearer, smeller, taster, thinker, conceiver, doer, conscious self, the person—his resort is in the supreme imperishable Ātman."[23]

In the Māṇḍūkya Upaniṣad the relation of Ātman to the various states of consciousness, viz. waking, dream, and deep sleep, is considered; and it is pointed out that none of them is Ātman, though Ātman is their ground in different forms. Ātman is beyond these three states and represents the fourth which is described as "...non-thinkable, that cannot be designated, the essence of the assurance of which is the state of oneness of the self, the cessation of development, tranquil, benign, without a second—(such) they think is the fourth. He is the Ātman. He should be discerned."[24] This fourth state is called Turīya in the Bṛihadāraṇyaka and Turya in the Maitreyī Upaniṣad. The name Turīya has now come to stay.

Just as we find in the Māṇḍūkya the discussion of Ātman with reference to the three states of consciousness, similarly, we find Ātman discussed with reference to what are called the five sheaths (pañca-koṣas) in the Taittirīya Upaniṣad. The so-called doctrine of five sheaths is very important as it throws light on the subtler understanding of human personality by the Upaniṣadic seers, who, unfolding it layer by layer, tried to arrive at the Ātman. Of course, the term koṣa (sheath) is not used by the Upaniṣads but is a later addition to our philosophical vocabulary. What we actually find in the Upaniṣad is the progressive realization of Brahman from gross layer to subtler layer till its true nature is reached. In the very beginning of the third chapter we find one of the most important declarations about Brahman which is the goal of philosophic knowledge. It says, "That, verily, whence beings here are born, that by which when born they live, that into which in deceasing they enter—that be desirous of understanding. That in Brahman."[25] Bearing in mind this general characterization of Brahman, the pupil Bhṛigu is asked to understand Brahman by austerity. The first knowledge to dawn on him was that 'Brahman is food' (anna). This being untrue, he was asked to probe further. Then he came in turn to understand Brahman to be Breath (Prāṇa), Mind, Understanding (Vijñāna) and lastly, Bliss (Ānanda). The search ended with Ānanda as Brahman.

We have here five graded conceptions of Brahman in terms of good, breath, mind, understanding and bliss. These are referred to as five sheaths. They are called sheaths because they are not Ātman, but the covers of Ātman. It is generally accepted that Ātman is beyond all these five sheaths of Ātman or layers of personality. A difference in one respect from this view may be noted. Brahman is certainly beyond the first four sheaths, viz. food, breath, mind and understanding, though it supports them; but there is nothing in the text of the Upaniṣads to show that Brahman is beyond Ānanda, also. What I am suggesting is that according to the Upaniṣads, Brahman is Ānanda which is beyond the other four sheaths. This is borne out by the fact that Bhṛigu is not asked to know Brahman further by austerity when he approached his teacher Varuṇa declaring that Brahman is Ānanda. In fact, this knowledge is said to be 'established in the highest heaven'; and it is assured that "He who knows this becomes established."[26] Without dwelling on this point further I may only suggest that the doctrine of the five sheaths and the view that Brahman is beyond all the five would need revision in the above light.

From the personality point of view it is obvious that food and breath represent the physiological aspects, while mind and understanding represent the psychological aspect of human personality. Ānanda is that which sustains the whole personality immanently, though itself beyond the psycho-physical aspects mentioned. It is that reality which, being also the supreme value, governs life and activity. Thus the individual psycho-physical path of investigation led Upaniṣadic thinkers to Ātman as the supreme reality.

That same reality throbs in the heart of the cosmos. On investigating cosmic phenomena, the sages came to know that they are all grounded in and moved by the omnipresent and omnipotent Brahman alone. In the Kenopaniṣad[27] we have a story or rather allegory of the gods, Yakṣa and Umā. They represent cosmic phenomena, Yakṣa representing Brahma and Umā Vidyā. The gods Indra, Agni (fire) and Vāyu (air) really derive their power from Brahman itself and have no power of their own. The story tells us, that, when the gods were ignorantly exulting in the victory of Brahman and boasting of their greatness, Yakṣa, (i.e. Brahman) asked them to exert their might on a straw. But no one could do any harm to it. Then it was revealed to them by Umā that their power is really the power of Yakṣa, i.e. Brahman, without whose support they cannot break even a straw.

In the Vedas we find that philosophical thought developed from polytheism through what is called henotheism to monotheism. There are, however, certain statements which show that in the Vedas themselves philosophical monism was clearly enunciated, especially the famous statement—"Reality is one, the wise call it by many names."[28] The same theme is developed to its utmost by the Upaniṣads, as is evident from the above study where the Vedic gods are said to derive all their power from Brahman, the ultimate reality.

Essentially the same view is expressed in many ways. Brahman is said to be the lord or governor (Īśā) of everything. As described by Kaṭha, he is the "Lord (Īśāna) of what has been and what is to be." Again "Whence the Sun rises, and where it goes to rest—on Him all the gods are founded; and no one ever goes beyond it."[29] Another way of saying this is that all the deities perform their tasks from fear of Brahman; e.g. "From fear of Him fire doth burn. From fear the Sun gives forth heat. From fear both Indra and Wind, and Death as fifth, do speed along."[30] In the Muṇḍaka it is said that "He on whom the sky, the earth, and the atmosphere, are woven, and the wind, together with all the life-breaths, Him alone know as the one Ātman...."[31] Many more quotations can be given; but those already given show sufficiently that it is the same reality called sometimes as Ātman, sometimes as Brahman, "From which everything comes, in which everything lives and to which everything returns," to use Upaniṣadic language.

The next question which would naturally arise is "what is the nature of this reality ?" The most forthright answer is that reality is beyond words or description. As is said, "Reality is that wherefrom words turn back together with the mind...."[32] Though words are incapable of expressing the nature of reality, they can at least serve as sign-posts pointing to it. It is in this capacity that the Upaniṣads use words to describe reality. I shall refer here to some important descriptions giving us a glimpse into the nature of Brahman, the Supreme Reality.

I have already referred to Brahman's omnipresence and omnipotence. The whole universe including man is pervaded in all directions and respects by Brahman alone. There is Brahman everywhere and Brahman alone. This is graphically expressed as "Brahma, indeed, is this immortal. Brahma before, Brahma behind, to right and to left. Stretched forth below and above,

Brahma, indeed, is this whole world, this widest extent."[33] Brahman is the inner soul of all things; Īśāvāsya says that "By the Lord enveloped must this all be whatever moving thing there is in the moving world..."[34] The culmination of this description we find in the most important mahā vākya (great statement)—"verily, all this is Brahma."[35] This gives us the unity of Being underlying the multiplicity of becoming, the one in many.

On the side of knowledge it is said that by knowing Ātman all this is known. This is expressed beautifully in another way, by more than one Upaniṣad as "This whole world is illumined with his light."[36] Here we have a unity of knowing, whic his precisely stated, again, in another great statement, "Brahman is knowledge."[37] Of course, here we do not have an epistemological but an ontological conception of Knowledge (Prajñāna). That is why it is said to be Brahman.

The most famous description of Brahman is—"Brahman is the real, the knowledge, the infinite."[38] It covers the two aspects mentioned above, the unity of being (sat or satya) and knowledge (cit or Jñāna). The concept of infinity here is to be taken to represent the all-pervading, all-inclusive nature of Brahman which is unlimited and which pervades all things both from within and from without. It is not merely the opposite of finite but suggests positively that Brahman itself is the limit, the end of the universe ; but again, Brahman is immanent as well as transcendent. This may be called, to coin a new word, its 'transimmanence'. Brahman is in everything; everything is in Brahman. This sounds like pan-Brahmanism.

The concept of perfection (pūrṇa) or fullness is also to be taken in a similar sense. In the famous declaration we are told:

"The yon is fullness, fullness this
From fullness, fullness doth proceed
Withdrawing fullness's fullness off,
E'en fullness then itself remains."[39]

Here, perfection means fullness and as applied to Brahman, it means that whatever is, is Brahman only. This is his fullness. It is because of this fullness that Brahman transcends the sphere of relativity. Yet, to call it absolute will be to give a one-sided picture. Therefore the Upaniṣadic seers describe it in seemingly paradoxical terms suggesting thereby that it is both, and yet beyond both. For example, the Īśāvāsyopaniṣad says, "It moves. It moves not. It is far, and it is near. It is within all this; and it is outside all of this."[40] Again, Śvetāśvatara describes it as "More minute than a minute, greater than the great."[41] Such paradoxical descriptions are possible only because Brahman is all, and is, therefore, beyond the dualities which are characteristic of the world of relativity. It is, similarly, beyond space and time, being their ground at the same time. In other words, its fullness is perfect or complete. That is why it cannot be described this way or that.

I now turn to the symbolic representation of Brahman in the form of Om[42] or Praṇava as it is called. The whole of the Māṇḍūkya Upaniṣad is devoted to the discussion of the nature of this Om. In the very beginning it is said that "Om !—This syllable (or, imperishable) is this whole world. The past, the present, the future—everything is just Oṃkāra."[43] It is further stated that all this, which is Om, is Brahman; this Ātman is Brahman. The Upaniṣad goes on to describe further how Brahman pervades the three states of waking, dreaming and deep sleep in the forms of Vaiśvānara, Taijasa and Prājña and remains in the fourth in its reality as Ātman. Corresponding to these three states, we have three essences or elements of Om, viz. 'A', 'U', and 'M'. The last abiding state is beyond the essences or pure existence, to use existentialist language. Thus, Om is Ātman indeed.

There are a number of places in the Upaniṣads where Om is identified with Brahman and is praised as such. For example, the Taittirīya states: "Om is Brahman. Om is the whole world."[44] It is needless to multiply quotations. What is important to know is why such a symbolic representation of Brahman (as Om) is offered by the Upaniṣads. It seems to me, theoretically, that it indicates that Brahman (AUM) is the source or ground of speech, and therefore, beyond words. Further, it, being an open-texture symbol, can be interpreted in various ways, and all these interpretations will hold good, since Brahman, which it represents, is everything. Practically, Om is prescribed as the object of meditation and also as the name of the Lord to be chanted for the attainment of union with Him. Thus, Om has both theoretical and practical applications.

I had deferred the consideration of Brahman as Ānanda (Bliss) until now in order to discuss it at some length, as I consider this conception to be of utmost importance. In connection with the so-called doctrine of the Pañcakoṣas I have pointed out that Brahman is Ānanda or Bliss. A fuller statement of this is found in the Taittirīya Upaniṣad—"He understood that Brahman is bliss. For, truly, indeed, beings here are born from bliss, when born they live by bliss, on deceasing they enter into bliss."[45] The concept of rasa (essence) is also basically that of Ānanda (or the subtle source of all the kinds of happiness). The Upaniṣad says, "Verily, what that Being (su-kṛita = Well done—Being), is, that, verily, is the essence (rasa). For truly, on getting the essence, one becomes blissful. For who indeed would breathe, who would live, if there were not this bliss in space! For truly, this (rasa) causes bliss." This declaration is followed by an elaborate discussion of bliss ending with—"He who knows the bliss of Brahman, fears not from anything at all."[46] In the Kaṭha we read "This is it! Thus they recognize the highest, indescribable happiness."[47]

An elaborate discussion of the blissful nature of Ātman or Brahman is found in both the Bṛihadāraṇyaka[48] and Chāndogya Upaniṣads.[49] It is described as the "doctrine of honey." Here, honey (Madhu) represents bliss; and it is repeatedly said that the ultimate source of all kinds of happiness found in the world of dualities, etc. is, in reality, the Ātman which is the Immortal, the Brahman, the All. As the Bṛihadāraṇyaka puts it, "This Ātman is honey for all things, and all things are honey for this Ātman. This shining, immortal person who is in this Ātman, and with reference to oneself, this shining, immortal person who exists as Ātman—he is just this Ātman, this Immortal, this Brahman, this All."[50] This is the same bliss (Ānanda) which is variously called fearlessness (Abhaya), Immortality (Amṛita), Peace or Tranquillity (Śānti), etc. This is obviously, what we are in quest of; that is to say, this is not only true Reality but also the Life-Ideal, Supreme Goal of Life, or Summum Bonum at the same time. And this view is extremely important as, in it, both the metaphysical and the ethical points of view meet. The Vedānta summarizes the description by saying that Brahman is reality, knowledge and bliss (sat cit ānanda).

While discussing the nature of reality, I have pointed out that according to the Upaniṣadic sages, all this, i.e. the world, is Brahman only. It arises from, lives in, and returns to Brahman. What is meant here is that the moving plurality, characteristic of the world, is but a multifarious manifestation of the one and same reality which is the imperishable (Akṣara), the immortal (Amṛita). Multiplicity is not denied altogether; it is said to consist only of forms and names, and is not different, in reality, from Ātman or Brahman. What is denied is the plurality of reality but not the expressions of the same reality. In other words, there is a unity of reality underlying the diversity of names and forms. When it is said that all this is Brahman, it is evident that Brahman can only be "one without a second."

The same idea is expressed in the Chāndogya as "In the beginning, my dear, this world was just Being (Sat), one only without a Second....It bethought itself: "Would that I were many! Let me procreate myself!"[51] Here, there is a reference to a creation of the world out of itself by Brahman. What kind of creation is it? In the Muṇḍaka Upaniṣad we have an analogical description of the process. "As the spider emits and draws in (its thread), As herbs arise on earth, As hairs of the head and body from a living person, So from the Imperishable arises everything here."[52] In another place it is said, "...as small sparks come forth from the fire, even so from this Ātman come forth all vital energies, all worlds, all gods, all beings. The mystic meaning (upaniṣad) thereof is "the Real of the real."[53] Because of this, Brahman is supposed to be both the material and the efficient cause of the world. But it is very difficult to apply the notion of causation here. It would be more proper to say that the world is the natural manifestation of Brahman (or its creative activity); that Brahman variously manifests itself in and through the manifold universe; it becomes the world without any loss to it.

Becoming is not opposed to Being but is the dynamic and multiple unfoldment of Being, i.e. Brahman. Since here multiplicity does not destroy unity but only displays it, it is not real multiplicity. In short, the same Ātman takes different names and forms. As put in the Kaṭha Upaniṣad, "As the one fire, entering the world, becomes corresponding in form to every form, so the one inner soul (Ātman) of all things corresponds in form to every form, and yet is outside."[54] This shows the transcendence as well as the immanence of Brahman; transcendent because it is not exhausted by the becoming and immanent because it is Ātman that becomes (the world). The world is full of Brahman, but at the same time, Brahman is full in itself. This is beautifully stated by the Bṛihadāraṇyaka, as quoted earlier, "The yon is fullness...fullness than itself remains."[55] At another place it is elaborately stated by Yājñavalkya, in answer to Gārgī's questions, that it is Akṣara (Brahman) "Across which the whole universe, including Ākāśa, is woven, warp and woof."[56]

That the world is the sport (creative activity) of Ātman is suggested in the Śvetāśvatara, "It is He who resides in the body, the city of nine gates. He is the Soul that sports in the outside world. He is the master of the whole world, animate and inanimate."[57] The concept of causation involves a reference to a time-series on the one hand and an event-series on the other. But since these series are themselves the expression of Brahman, they cannot be applied to their own creation. Only by analogy may we say that Brahman is the material, efficient and even final cause of the world. The metaphor of fire and sparks, which is significant in many ways, suggests a kind of emanation theory. The world with all its variety emanates from Brahman. But emanation only suggests a common source or origin, while Brahman is not only the source but also the sustainer and end of everything. I would prefer, therefore, to say that the world, according to the Upaniṣads, is Brahman's natural self-expression. This expression may be infinite and yet it might not have expressed Brahman entirely. On the contrary, there still remains infinite possibilities for its further expression. In other words, the expression is never complete. This is why Brahman is said to be Ananta—Infinite-limitless. It is exactly this that is conveyed by saying, as already quoted, that "even after taking out fullness from fullness, what remains is fullness again." This shows that the relation between Brahman and the world is very peculiar. In fact, it is not proper to speak about relation here, as Brahman and the world are not two in reality. The world is just the manifestation of reality, its self-expression.

It is true that the Upaniṣads deny multiplicity (Nānātva). But we must understand what exactly is meant thereby. The Bṛihadāraṇyaka says that "By the mind alone is it to be perceived (that) here there is no multiplicity whatsoever."[58] This statement is to be understood in the light of the explanation given by the Chāndogya that "Just as, my dear, by one piece of clay everything made of clay may be known—the modification is merely a verbal means (distinction), a name; the reality is just 'clay'."[59] The clay may express itself in different forms under different names; but the reality is clay only. Similarly, reality, i.e. Brahman, may express itself in infinitely various forms and names, yet that reality as such is one and the same. Obviously the Upaniṣads do not deny the multiplicity of the world altogether, but they point out that underlying this multiplicity of forms and names (i.e. individual expressions), there is only one reality, viz. Ātman or Brahman. This does not mean that the world is an illusion. It only means that the world is not something different from Brahman, but its expression. I may suggest the analogy of personality and say that, just as the personality, even of a finite individual, expresses itself in and through each and every mode of thought, word and deed, and yet remains open for further expression, similarly the personality of Brahman or reality expresses itself in and through each and every form and name, i.e. the world, and yet remains to be expressed in infinite ways. In fact, Brahman is conceived of as the Puruṣa or Person in the Vedas and the same idea is accepted by the Śvetāśvatara Upaniṣad. It is said of this Cosmic Person or as I have put it, the Personality of Reality, that "The Person has a thousand heads, a thousand eyes, a thousand feet. He surrounds the earth on all sides, and stands ten fingers breadth beyond...The Person, in truth, is this whole world, whatever has been and whatever will be...It stands encompassing all."[60]

It will be seen from the above account that the Upaniṣads have a positive and healthy attitude towards the world and all that it signifies. Now we understand why they say about reality that "by knowing it everything in the world becomes known." This does not prevent anybody from trying to know that the reality of which they are manifestations is Ātman only. One may know, create and enjoy various forms or modifications of clay with different names, but philosophically it is sufficient to know that the reality of them all is clay only. In fact, various scientific and other pursuits themselves add to the richness of the self-expression of Ātman. Thus there is no opposition between the world and Ātman or Brahman. The dynamism found in the universe is also meaningful as it brings out the dynamic nature of Ātman's expression. We must remember that no particular or finite expression of Brahman, nor all of them put together for that matter, can exhaust the infinite possibilities of its further expressions or manifestations owing to their finitude. If you go in the direction of manifestation, there is infinite multiplicity. But if you go in the direction of Ātman, the ultimate reality, there is infinity itself or imperishable unity, unexhausted and inexhaustible by its infinite expressions. It remains full (Pūrṇa) in spite of infinite self-expressions. Thus, in my opinion, the world, according to the Upaniṣads, is neither real by itself, nor unreal altogether, but the self-expression of reality, i.e. Ātman or Brahman. The concepts of causation, creation, emanation, etc. seem to be somewhat inadequate from this point of view.

IV Knowledge of Brahman

I have already pointed out the distinction made by the Upaniṣads between Parā and Aparā Vidyā (Higher and Lower Knowledge). Brahma-Vidyā is Parā Vidyā by which the Imperishable is known or comprehended. If we try to understand this distinction further, we see that the Upaniṣadic sages want to convey something very important by the concept of Parā Vidyā, since even the Vedas are said to belong to the category of Aparā Vidyā along with Grammar, Astrology, etc. Roughly, Parā Vidyā may be said to be philosophy or philosopical knowledge. But such knowledge does not give us an idea of the nature of Brahma-Jñāna. The clue lies in the description of the Vedas as Śabda or word. In other words, Aparā Vidyā consists of verbal knowledge. Parā Vidyā, therefore, has to be conceived to be non-verbal knowledge. What this means is made clear by a pointed statement which I consider to be the master-key that opens the gorgias vista of Brahma-Jñāna as conceived by the Upaniṣads. The statement is: "He, verily, who knows that supreme Brahman, becomes very Brahman."[61] There are parallel statements, e.g. "He, knowing all, becomes all."[62]

This shows that knowledge of Brahman, which is the purpose of philosophical inquiry, is different from ordinary knowledge, the subject matter of epistemology, wherein the subject-object polarity or the triputi (trinity) of knowledge-known-knowledge is involved and which is entirely conceived, based and expressed in language. In this sense all knowledge is verbal, excepting existential knowledge, if we may use that phrase, which is non-verbal, as Brahma-Jñāna is. It is, in fact, very difficult to call it knowledge—having epistemic status—at all. It is really 'being'—having ontic status. In other words, to *know* Brahman is *to be* Brahman. There is no scope for language or words and dualities of any kind.

This is the purport of the above and similar Upaniṣadic statements. The same is expressed in describing the fruit of Brahma-Jñāna as being (one with) Brahman. This is Parā Vidyā, (beyond knowledge or one may call it meta-knowledge) which is beyond words, description and epistemic duality or trinity. This is why even the Vedas are said to be only Aparā Vidyā. I think that the sages would say the Upaniṣads themselves, in so far as they give us ony epistemic, theoretical knowledge may be of Brahman itself, or constitute only Aparā Vidyā. Thus philosophical knowledge itself is to be conceived in two aspects—epistemic and theoretical, and non-epistemic and practical. The latter's nature is well brought out by substituting the term realization (Sākṣātkāra) for Knowledge. Thus Brahma-Vidyā, though the highest of all the vidyās, is only Aparā in its verbal, intellectual, epistemic, objective aspect; it becomes Parā when 'that imperishable is realized or attained.' And this realization can be only subjective or individual.

Concerning philosophical knowledge of Brahman, the Upaniṣads seem to have followed the method of analysis of experience emphasizing the Knower, especially from the point of view of the attainment of imperishable happiness—the Supreme Value in man's life. As for the realization of Brahman, it is subjective, being non-intellectual, and for this, naturally, the psycho-ethical method of attitude and conduct is prescribed. It is the description of this method which in fact constitutes Upaniṣadic ethics. Thus the Upaniṣads follow the philosophical method (or if you wish, metaphysical method) of constructive analysis, involving a critique of values also, in order to arrive at Brahma-Jñāna; they prescribe the psycho-ethical method for Brahma Sākṣātkāra. The former is the prerequisite of the latter which alone leads one to realize Ātman as Bliss. It is an integrated approach to life and reality.

The aids to the knowledge of Ātman according to the Bṛihadāraṇyaka are understanding Upaniṣadic teaching (Śravaṇā), pondering over it, (Manana) and constant thought of it (Nididhyāsana).[63] While describing the nature of Upaniṣad (secret doctrine) or Brahma-Vidyā, the Kenopaniṣad says, "Austerity, restraint and work or duty are its foundation. The vedas are all of its limbs. Truth is its abode."[64] Tapa (austerity) is also suggested by the Taittirīya, where it says that having performed austerity he understood that Brahman is bliss. At one place the inadequacy of merely intellectual means is pointed out. The text says, "This Ātman is not to be obtained by instruction, nor by intellect, nor by much learning. He is to be obtained only by the one whom He chooses; to such a one that Ātman reveals His own person."[65] This means only that Ātman is not just to be known theoretically but to be practically realized.

V Upaniṣadic Ethics

The discussion of the nature and means of Brahma-Jñāna (Knowledge of Brahman) leads us to a consideration of Upaniṣadic ethics which aims at guiding conduct on the path of Ātman-realization. We have already seen that the whole of Upaniṣadic thought is directed towards the attainment of the Imperishable or Immortal or Bliss. From the cosmic and metaphysical point of view, it is reality, while from the human and ethical point of view it is Supreme Value or the ultimate goal of life, the summum bonum. Here, metaphysics and ethics help each other to culminate in the realization of Brahman, which is reality cum bliss.

As such the Upaniṣads give us not only ethics but a comprehensive way of life manifesting Ātman (or Brahman) in the form of Ānanda. This makes Upaniṣadic ethics, technically, not only teleological but also hedonistic, although, of course, pleasure and bliss belong to different levels altogether. We may call it Hedonism par excellence, if we bear in mind this distinction. In fact, the Chāndogya Upaniṣad clearly states that all activity is directed ultimately towards the attainment of pleasure only. It says: "Verily, when one gets pleasure one is not active. Only by getting pleasure is one active. But one must desire to understand pleasure." And then the most important statement is made that "Verily that which is Bhūman (Great or Infinite) is pleasure. There is no pleasure in the finite."[66] This describes in a nutshell, the goal as well as the means of its attainment. The goal is pleasure or Ānanda, and the means is becoming Great (Bhūman) or infinite. Bhūman is said to be the same as the immortal and the small to be the same as the mortal.

It will be seen from the description of this Great or Bhūman, that it virtually stands for Brahman, the one all-inclusive, infinite reality without a second; and small, finite pleasures are only imperfect or partial manifestations of this great or infinite pleasure. We find a mathematical account of the hierarchy of pleasures given in the Upaniṣads aimed at giving an approximate idea of the Brahma-Ānanda, the infinite pleasure, about which it is said that "On a part of just this bliss other creatures have their living."[67] The clue to the path of its attainment is found in the very description of this

Great or Bhūman. One, who sees, hears, and understands nothing else as different from oneself, is great (Bhūman); one who so sees, hears, and understands is small. What is meant here is that bliss consists in seeing all this to be oneself, i.e. Ātman or Brahman. This vision of the essential unity of being in which multiplicity is dissolved is all that one has to attain. The Kaṭha puts it negatively: "He obtains death after death who views this world to be many." In reality—"here there is not many, whatever," meaning, that there is only one reality without a second, viz. Ātman. So far as its realization is concerned, the seers knew that it cannot be be physical. The Upaniṣad says, "By the mind, indeed, is this (realization) to be attained."[68] Or more elaborately, "He (Brahman) is to be conceived or comprehended by the heart, by the intellect, and by the mind."[69] This means you have to cultivate or develop this vision or attitude of non-duality, and it is done by what Kaṭha calls 'Adhyātma yoga'.[70] The purpose of Upaniṣadic ethics is to describe what it is.

A keen intellect is the first requirement for "seeing Ātman hidden in all things."[71] It gives us an intellectual grasp of reality. But it is insufficient, for the highest state is described as: "When the five (sense) knowledges cease together with the mind, and (even) the intellect does not stir, that is, they say, the Supreme State."[72] To attain this state of bliss, which is the same as Ātman, one has to follow what I have called the psychoethical method or path. Its necessity is emphatically expressed by the Upaniṣad as: "Not he, who has not ceased from bad conduct, who is not tranquil, who is not composed, who is not of peaceful mind, can obtain Him by intelligence."[73] Here, two more requirements are mentioned—a composed, tranquil mind and good conduct.

The mind is composed and tranquil or the heart pure only when it is free of desires. That is why the Upaniṣad says: "When are liberated all the desires that lodge in one's heart, then a mortal becomes immortal and therein reaches Brahman."[74] The practical instructions for achieving this state are also given. It is very important to know them; but they can be properly understood only through the guidance of great and learned seers because this path is as hard and difficult to traverse as the sharpened edge of a razor. The instructions are: "An intelligent man should merge (or control) his speech (i.e. all senses) in the mind, the mind he should merge in the intellect, the intellect in the great self (Ahaṃkāra) and he should merge it in the tranquil Ātman."[75] This summarizes the psychological aspect of the Adhyātma Yoga or the psychoethical path. It makes man, psychologically, not only in tune but one with the infinite. This is described as the attitude of 'being that'. It means viewing everything as nothing but the manifestation of Ātman, or as essentially non-different from oneself. This real Brahmacarya, as it is 'living in the Brahman'.

When this vision or attitude of non-duality is imbibed, it has a revolutionary impact on conduct. The senses are controlled; the mind is tranquil; the intellect is purified, and one experiences union with all beings. No opposition, no conflict can affect you from the outside or inside since you have mastered all desires, and therefore all attachments and infatuations. Such is the life of Ānanda, which the Upaniṣads ask and help one to live. This is the gist of the Upaniṣadic ethics; and, if we are asked to suggest any one Upaniṣad wherein its basic principles are laid down, we can without hesitation, point to the Īśāvasyopaniṣad. The principles are the same, of course, as outlined above. But they are presented in an ethical idiom and in a socially oriented way. I shall conclude this section with a brief account of them.

Its positive and healthy attitude to life is found in the very acceptance of Karma (activity) as unavoidable. As it says, "Doing deeds alone, here, may one wish to live a hundred years." The idea of living a hundred years is in itself attractive enough. But it tells us further, that so long as we live, we cannot but be active. Thus, there is no escapism entertained. The question is not whether to live but to live so that life becomes a glorious expression of Ānanda, the imperishable. The secret lies in the dictum: "It is not the Karma (activity) that binds a man."[76] It is attachment, owing to the false, dualistic attitude, which is really the cause of misery or suffering.

Then what should be the attitude governing life and activity? It is stated in the very first verse as: "By the Lord pervaded (enveloped) must this all be—whatever moving thing there is in the moving world." This is the foundation of Upaniṣadic ethics. Here Lord means Ātman or Brahman. As we have seen, everything in the world is only its self-expression. We are, therefore, enjoined to base our life and conduct on this basic truth. Such a life will be one of sacrifice or renunciation leading to the highest enjoyment of Ānanda in its infinite manifestations. In it, there is no room for greed, delusion or conflict. That is why the Upaniṣad says: "With that, renounced, thou mayest enjoy. Covet not the wealth of any one at all."[77] The reference to wealth here is significant, for man hankers after wealth without limitation as if it is the ultimate goal of life, forgetting the truth stated by the Kaṭhopaniṣad: "a man is never to be satisfied with wealth."[78] The Bṛihadāraṇyaka is even more emphatic on this point when it says: "Of immortality, however, there is no hope through wealth."[79]

What is the ultimate ethical principle of conduct based on this view of reality and the summum bonum? According to the Īśāvāsyopaniṣad, it is, "treat others as yourself." This embodies the vision of the ultimate unity of beings, discarding duality and therefore all conflict and strife. Only by reforming our personalities in this mould of Advaita or non-duality, can we hope to attain bliss or the immortal. The Upaniṣad states this principle beautifully: "Now he, who always looks on all beings as just in the Self (Ātman), and on the self as in all beings, thereafter, is never disgusted with anybody. In whom (or in whose view) all beings have become his very self (Ātman), for such a seer who perceives the unity, what delusion and sorrow can there be?"[80]

If we work out the implications of this principle of the vision or attitude of non-duality, then we find that, in fact, we are asked to lift ourselves above moral binding and accept the open morality of the saints and the heroes. Love, kindness, benevolence, sympathy, forgiveness, sacrifice, and other such saintly virtues belong to this morality. A little exhibiting these excellent human qualities is a truly religious or spiritual life. Thus from the non-dualistic Upaniṣadic point of view, morality culminates in spirituality. There is no binding here, as binding requires duality. One is naturally moral, i.e. one does not feel the binding. In fact one is more than strictly moral. That is why it is said that he who reaches the highest is above all laws. "Him does afflict the thought, 'why have I not done what is good? why have I committed evil?' "[81] He is beyond good and evil. "Verily, he overcomes them both. What he has done and what he has not done do not affect him." This is so because, "This eternal greatness of Brahman is neither increased nor diminished by action (deeds). One should know it. By knowing it one is not stained by evil action. Therefore, having this knowledge, having become calm, subdued, quiet, patiently enduring and collected, one sees the Ātman in oneself, and everything as

Ātman. Evil does not overcome him, he overcomes all evil. Evil does not burn him, he burns all evil. Free from evil, free from impurity, free from doubt, he becomes Brahman."[82]

Thus, in Upaniṣadic ethics, the psychological aspect of human personality plays a very important and twofold role. On the one hand, we must attain a tranquil mind and pure heart by conquering all passions; on the other hand, we have to imbibe and develop the attitude of unity or non-duality. With this psychological transformation, man's life is bound to radiate bliss, because it then becomes the easiest expression of the realization of Ātman or its worship. This is the state of being which everyone aspires for and which is the end of all moral endeavour.

Ātman, as Ānanda, being the ultimate goal of life, is the supreme value. The value of everything else speaking practically, depends on it. This is quite elaborately pointed out by Yājñavalkya to Maitreyī. The essence of his teaching is that "Lo, verily, not for the happiness (love) of all that all is dear, but for the happiness (love) of Ātman that all is dear." Here priya (dear) stands for value.[83] This is but natural because Ātman (or Brahman) is "the delight of life and mind, abounding in tranquillity, immortal."[84] It is for this reason that Ātman, which is reality, is also the supreme value, the ultimate ideal of life. It is this view of reality that is signified by what I have called the ethical or value-approach to reality.

VI The Distinctiveness of Upaniṣadic Thought

It will be seen from the above account that Upaniṣadic thought is of a distinctive nature. It cannot be described either as purely metaphysical or as purely ethical, or again as merely a combination of the two. It presents a unified view of reality and life, or to be precise, reality in life. Reality is to be found in all kinds of existence and knowledge or experience and what is important, it affects individual human beings, their attitudes and behaviour in what may be called a valuational way, involving an ultimate reference to their happiness. Thus a comprehensive and integrated view of reality takes in reality in its fullness, in all its aspects and expressions. So far as it is possible for man to understand it, reality is not something that is only outside man, given to him in a so-called objective way; it is also in man as well as the universe. In a sense it is manifested more in man, since the phenomena of knowledge and value or the experience of Ānanda (happiness) are found only in the man. If, then, we want to know reality in all its aspects that can be possibly known, it is to be looked for not only in the universe outside but in the personality and life of man also. This is exactly what the Upaniṣadic seers did; but while doing so, they constantly kept in view man's earnest quest of imperishable happiness or immortality, the profoundest expression of the reality of human life. That is why the purpose of their inquiry is not just theoretical, namely the satisfaction of intellectual curiousity by knowledge in the epistemological sense, but most practical in the sense of being concerned with the attainment or realization of imperishable happiness, the eternal ideal of human life. This led them from knowledge to realization, from mere knowing to being, i.e. beyond the boundaries of epistemology which presupposes language and dualities. This was the natural outcome of their conception of reality as not only sat (being), but also Prajñāna (pure knowledge of experience as such) and Ānanda or Śānta (peace, tranquillity). The term used by the Upaniṣads for reality is very significant from this point of view. They call it the imperishable, the immortal (Akṣara). Vedānta describes it as sat-cit-ānanda and not merely as sat.

This, I think, is the key to the understanding of Upaniṣadic thought. It explains the preoccupation of the Upaniṣadic seers with immortality, their acceptance of both Ātman and Brahman to be one and the same reality, their conception of reality as sat-cit-ānanda which covers all the expressions or manifestations of reality known to man, and their emphasis on the psychoethical path for the realization of the summum bonum.

As for the method of investigation to which the conclusions they have drawn are due, it seems that the Upaniṣadic thinkers have followed the method of an analysis of experience coupled with a critique of values based on a deeper understanding of human nature and life. The object of experience or knowledge which, in its totality, is the universe at large, yielded to their analysis reality as Brahman, while the subject or the knower himself proved to be reality as Ātman underlying all experience. The one is primarily of the nature of being (sat), while the other is of the nature of experience or knowledge (consciousness, prajñāna or cit) also. Add to this the ideal of human life found to underly all activities and to determine the value of everything, viz. Ānanda or Śānti (everlasting happiness or peace abiding), and you have the conception of reality in its fullness, as Sat-Chit-(Prajñāna)-Ānanda, called either Ātman or Brahman. Actually it is bṛihat-ātman (infinite or great ātman), i.e. Ātman in its all-inclusive, non-dual form and not in its usual individualistic, exclusive form. That is why, the attainment of Brahma-jñāna is not merely a matter of intellect, but involves the whole being of man, his awareness, attitude and acts. Hence the prescription of the psychoethical path, in addition to that of knowledge, for the realization of the Ātman that is Brahman.

This Brahma-Vidyā, we must remember, is not opposed to scientific or other noetic pursuits. It is concerned primarily with man's attitude toward life and the world outside, with a view to the attainment of bliss or a happy, peaceful and contented life. It is thus concerned more with being than with knowing. Hence it is called Parā Vidyā (higher knowledge) to distinguish it from all other knowledges grouped as Aparā Vidyā. The latter is termed Avidyā in the Īśopaniṣad, and is given due importance by saying that it helps us in 'crossing death,' meaning 'removing pain, misery or evil' which is relative in character. The Vidyā, i.e. Parā Vidyā, on the other hand, helps us in the attainment of immortality, i.e. happiness or peace which is everlasting and absolute. This is a clear indication of the healthy and positive view taken by the Upaniṣadic seers of man, his life, and the universe. Let the other vidyās (sciences or knowledges) prosper and help man to be happy and to remove evil, as far as they can. But whatever man would be able to attain with their help, would be only the perishable (Kṣara). It is the Upaniṣadic Brahma-Vidyā that would help man to attain the imperishable, the immortal. Hence it is called the ground (or crown) of all sciences or knowledge.

If I am asked to give out the Upaniṣad (secret) of the Upaniṣads, in one word, I would immediately say Śānti (peace, tranquillity or contentment). It is not without reason that both at the beginning and at the end of the recitation of every Upaniṣad, there is an invocation for peace, and even that always ends in the pronouncement of 'O M' followed thrice by 'Śānti', as:

Om! Śānti! Śānti!!
Śānti!!!

4

THE BHAGAVAD GĪTĀ

DONALD H. BISHOP

I INTRODUCTION

The Bhagavad Gītā can be read from two perspectives, as a piece of literature containing the basic tenets of Indian thought which serve to guide everyday living or as a treatise presenting a profound philosophy of cosmic consolidation of great import. Both aspects will be discussed in this chapter.

The Bhagavad Gītā forms a part of the great epic, the Mahābhārata. The contents of the text are brought out in the form of a dialogue between Kṛiṣṇa, whom the Indian tradition believes to be the Lord incarnate, and Arjuna, a warrior prince of the Kuru dynasty. The situation in which both the characters are placed is a battlefield wherein Arjuna has come to fight, by force of circumstances, his own cousins, nephews, elders of the family, teachers and friends. Metaphorically the battle and battlefield is life itself. For in life we are constantly engaged in a struggle both within and without between the forces of good and evil. The Gītā on the one hand gives us guidance or a set of beliefs to help us in that battle and on the other hand it provides a metaphysical or cosmological foundation for life, for reality and for these beliefs.

II THE GĪTĀ AND EVERYDAY LIFE

One such belief is that Brahman is in all things. This is found in a number of statements in the Bhagavad Gītā: "I am the Ātman that dwells in the heart of every mortal creature: I am the beginning, the life-span, and the end of all;" "Who sees his Lord within every creature, deathlessly dwelling amidst the mortal, that man sees truly;" "His heart is within Brahman, his eye in all things sees Brahman equally present, knows his own Ātman in every creature and all creation within the Ātman."[1]

The Bhagavad Gītā carries on an earlier tradition in this respect for in the Laws of Manu we read: "He who sacrifices to the Self, equally recognizing the Self in all created beings and all created beings in the Self becomes like an autocrat and self-luminous."[2] In the Īśā Upaniṣad we find an added note: "The wise man beholds all beings in the Self, and the Self in all beings; for that reason he does not hate anyone."[3]

Two practical implications of this belief might be noted here. The first is that it provides a basis for human brotherhood on a world level. All men are brothers because they are children of Brahman or are divine. Everyone shares in a mutual heritage, has a common origin and destiny. Such a theistic foundation is a much more solid one for world brotherhood because it does not set human relationships within the context of self-interest.

Non-self-interest is the second implication of the belief that the Divine is in all, for it stimulates a non-exploitative attitude toward life and all of reality. It leads us to see people, for example, not as objects to be used for our own benefit but as persons worthy of dignity and respect in their own right. It enables us to be compassionate toward them in their suffering and to be joyful with them in their happiness. The Bhagavad Gītā describes the highest type of person as: "Who burns with the bliss and suffers the sorrow of every creature within his own heart, making his own each bliss and each sorrow, him I hold the highest of all yogis."[4] In another section it declares: "A man should not hate any living creature. Let him be friendly and compassionate to all."[5] Such statements enjoining universal compassion remind us of Gandhi's statement about Ahiṃsā: "It is very necessary because God is in every one of us and, therefore, we have to identify ourselves with every human being without exception."[6]

A belief in the divinity of all results in our having a different attitude toward the material world also. We do not see nature or material things as existing for us to grab hold of and possess exclusively for ourselves. Instead an attitude of sharing is prompted. The good things of nature are not to be the monopoly of a few; nor should the few or the many exploit nature's bounties carelessly or wastefully and without thought for the future. We should see ourselves as stewards or trustees of nature. For it was given to us by a benevolent Deity and it is our duty to care for it carefully and tenderly.

The concept of trusteeship is related to a second tenet found in the Bhagavad Gītā, the desirability and value of the attitude of non-attachment. You have the duty or right to work, the Gītā states, but "You have no right to the fruits of work;" therefore "Renounce attachment to the fruits."[7] The Bhagavad Gītā is telling us that many undesirable results will accrue if working for self-gain or profit is the primary motive for work or action. For example, "Thinking about sense-objects will attach you to sense-objects. Grow attached and you become addicted. Thwart your addiction, it turns to anger. Be angry, and you confuse your mind. Confuse your mind, you forget the lesson of experience. Forget experience, you lose discrimination. Loose discrimination, and you miss life's only purpose."[8]

If a rewards motive for action yields such unfortunate consequences, what should be the motive for working? The Bhagavad Gītā's answer is God or Brahman: "Perform every action with your heart fixed on the Supreme Lord. Renounce attachment to the fruits...you must perform every action sacramentally, and be free from all attachment to results."[9] One's motive is to make Brahman manifest in all one says and does. This does not mean that one should be unconcerned about the immediate necessities of life and not work for them; rather it sets the immediate in the broader context of Brahman and declares that the latter supercedes without eliminating the former.

There are several results of working without attachment. One is that we are freed from "anxiety for the results." We can attain peace and serenity of mind. "Cut free from the act, a man finds peace in the work of the spirit," the Gītā states.[10] One is reminded of the Roman Stoic Epictetus' statement on the same theme: "The great blessings of mankind are within us, and within our reach, but we shut our eyes, and like people in the dark, we fall foul upon the very thing which we search for without finding it. Tranquillity is a certain equality of mind, which no condition of fortune can either exalt or depress."[11] A second result of non-attachment is that it liberates us from the bondage of the law of Karma. As the authors of one text point out: "All actions, of which the motives are desires for certain gains here or hereafter, are governed by this law. Disinterested or passionless actions do not produce any fettering effect or bondage . . . The performance of disinterested actions helpes us to exhaust and destroy the accumulated effects of our past deeds done under the influence of hatred and infatuation. . . ."[12] A third result is self-realization, perfection or union with Brahman. The Gītā states that "By working for my sake only, you will achieve perfection" and "In the calm of self-surrender, the seers renounce the fruit of their actions, and so reach enlightenment." In addition, "Whosoever works for me alone, makes me only his goal and is devoted to me, free from attachment, and without hatred toward any creature—that man shall enter into me."[13]

Finally, through non-attachment we are freed from delusions, the major one being the delusion of absolute selfhood. The Bhagavad Gītā asserts that a man ". . . must free himself from the delusion of 'I' and 'mine'."[14] The statement has several implications, two of which are that we should try to see things from the viewpoint of others and not just our own, and we should stop looking at the world from the standpoint of desiring to own or possess it. We need to get over our egotism, both in an ontological and economic sense. This view is found in both East and West. In regard to the economic, Seneca, the Roman Stoic declared: "property, the greatest cause of human trouble" and that, if we look at the causes of evils in the world, the evils caused by money "will far outweigh the others."[15]

From the Indian standpoint the concept of non-attachment found in the Gītā provides man with the right motives for working, namely, unselfishly and for Brahman. Its practice brings about good results on both the social and personal levels. Vinoba Bhave, Gandhi's successor, notes this in his statements that ". . . nonpossession is a force for social good", and "We have long known that nonpossession brings about individual purification."[16] The question of purity of motives is raised continuously throughout the Bhagavad Gītā. In ethics the question, "Why should one do the good?", is a universal one. Undoubtedly rewards is the motive impelling most people. A good deed is done because the doer's reputation is enhanced or he will receive some material benefit in return. Such action, however, is based on a "barter" type ethics which in the end is no ethics at all but simply an appeal to selfishness. For one will do the good only when he gets something from doing it.

A passage in the Gītā which notes the self-interest motive and offers a better one is "A gift may be regarded as proceeding from sattva when it is given to a deserving person, at a suitable time, and in a fit place; not because of past benefits, or in the hope of a future reward, but simply because the giver knows that it is right for him to give. Whatever is given in the hope of a like return, or with any selfish motive, may be known to proceed from rajas. From tamas comes the gift which is given to an unworthy person, at the wrong time in the wrong place, without regard for the feelings of him who receives it."[17] The better motive offered above is the doing of good for its own sake, "because the giver knows that it is right for him to give." As Immanuel Kant points out, when one acts in terms of that motive, he is much more apt to do the good at those times, which are many, when there is no reward in sight.

The emphasis upon duties is a fourth one found in the Bhagavad Gītā of immediate relevance to us. For instance, we have a duty to do the good or the right, if for no other reason than that we are rational, moral beings. We are reminded again of Immanuel Kant and his well-known statement regarding the universal "obligation to benevolence"—"Every one of us, in enjoying the good things of life must have regard to the happiness of others.... Since God's providence is universal, I may not be indifferent to the happiness of others. If, for instance, I were to find in the forest a table spread with all manner of dishes, I ought not to conclude that it is all for me; I may eat, but I should also remember to leave some for others to enjoy....Recognizing, therefore, that Providence is universal, I am placed under an obligation to restrict my own consumption, and to bear in mind that nature's preparations are made for all of us. This is the source of the obligation to benevolence."[18]

The contemporary western world, despite thinkers like Kant, stresses the concept of rights much more than duties, and we find this trend in India too, today. Traditional Indian thought is more "duties" oriented. In the Laws of Manu, after the duties of each social group are enumerated, a set of duties incumbent on all is listed: "Contentment, patience under injury, self-subjugation, honesty, restraint of all sensual organs, purity, devotion, knowledge of the Deity, veracity, and abstinence from anger, these form the tenfold summary of duty."[19] The Gītā suggests one's duties are determined by natural temperament: "Seer and leader, provider and server, each has the duty ordained by his nature, born of the gunas."[20] Elsewhere it states, "he who does the task dictated by duty, caring nothing for the fruits of the action, he is a yogi."[21] According to Indian political thought: "A king should attend to all urgent business; he should not put it off." He takes a vow to engage in "energetic activity" and "his sacrifice is constituted of the discharge of his own administrative duties." The king is under obligation to promote public well-being—"The welfare of the king does not lie in the fulfilment of what is dear to him; what is dear to the subjects constitutes his welfare." Vivekananda adds, "...the result of this teaching is that all the duties of the world are sanctified. There is not duty in this world which we have any right to call menial; each man's work is quite as good as that of the emperor on his throne."[22]

The question of whether duties or rights should have priority has been long debated. Some societies emphasize the former and others the latter. Two critiques to be used are individual happiness and social stability. Which is more conductive to them? The Bhagavad Gītā would assert duties: "A man's own natural duty, even if it seems imperfectly done, is better than work not naturally his own even if this is well performed."[23] A person motivated by the concept of duty is more apt to be contented and moral. Social harmony and peace are more likely when duties are given first place. If rights are to be asserted, it should be a consequence of duties having been fulfilled.

Regarding the concept of God in the Bhagavad Gītā at least two emphases stand out. One is that Brahman is a universal Being in that no single person or group can claim Him as exclusively their own. Nor, on the other hand, does Brahman chose any one or any group as exclusively his own. A major theme of the Gītā is that salvation is open to and that Brahman accepts all. Kṛiṣṇa tells Arjuna that "My face is equal to all creation, loving no one, nor hating any....Even those who belong to the lower castes—women, Vaiśyas, and Śūdras too—can reach the highest spiritual realization if they will take refuge in me...whatever path men travel is my path. No matter where they walk it leads to me."[24] Brahman is pictured as impartial and without bias. The practical implication of this is, of course, that man should be also.

Secondly, as universal Being, Brahman manifests himself many times and in many ways. Perhaps the best known passage in the Gītā is "In every age I come back to deliver the holy, to destroy the sin of the sinner, and to establish righteousness."[25] This view is in contrast to the emphasis on a single saviour or incarnation found in western religious thought. One of its correlates is the willingness to allow for at least four ways of salvation or paths to Brahman—jñāna, rāja, karma and bhakti. In addition a variety of objects may be used by different worshippers as aids to devotions. Each picks that which suits him best. A major result of such pluralism in religious belief and practice is the attitude of tolerance which Indian thought has long been noted for.

A final emphasis in the Bhagavad Gītā which is of everyday value to us is its picture of the "ideal man". Every society has a concept of what the ideal man is like. What is the Indian one, as far as the Bhagavad Gītā is concerned? Several aspects have been mentioned already. He does not hate, has compassion on all, is non-attached, does the good for its own sake and is free of delusion. Ramakrishna makes an interesting distinction between the attached and non-attached person: "There are two kinds of ego—one ripe, and the other unripe. The unripe ego thinks, 'This is my house, my son, my this, my that.' The ripe ego thinks 'I am the servant of the Lord, I am his child; I am the Ātman, immortal, free, I am Pure Consciousness'."[26]

The Gītā indicates additional traits of the ideal man as follows: "He must accept pleasure and pain with equal tranquillity.... His resolve must be unshakable. He must be dedicated to me in intellect and mind....He neither molests his fellowmen, nor allows himself to become disturbed by the world. He is no longer swayed by joy and envy, anxiety and fear. Therefore he is dear to me. He is pure and independent of the body's desire....He does not rejoice in what is pleasant. He does not dread what is unpleasant, or grieve over it. He remains unmoved by good or evil fortune....His attitude is the same toward friend and foe. He is indifferent to honour and insult, heat and cold, pleasure and pain. He is free from attachment. He can control his speech....He rests in the inner calm of the Ātman, regarding happiness and suffering as one. Gold, mud, and stone are of equal value to him."[27]

Forgiving further characterizes the ideal man. He does not harbour grudges or malice. He is patient and steadfast. He perseveres through misfortune and he does not let good fortune go to his head. He knows himself and thus praise and honour does not appeal to his vanity. At the same time he can accept blame without being overcome by it. He is self-controlled and does not lash back when insulted. He is impartial. He is not overly nationalistic or ethnocentric. He is contented even if he does not have a great deal. He has an inner calm, serenity and peace and so is not upset by external events. He is not filled with anxiety or fear. From the above, we see the ideal man pictured in the Gītā is the ethical man. He is the non-aggressive, independent, purified man. He is not a military hero or economic giant. Instead he is the spiritual hero Ramakrishna pictures thus: "The true hero is he who can discipline his mind by devotional exercises while living in the world. A strong man can look in any direction while carrying a heavy burden on his head. Similarly, the perfect man can keep his gaze constantly fixed on God while carrying the burden of worldly duties."[28]

III The Philosophy of the Gītā

We might note first that the Gītā gives us an estimate of Reality, not as viewed by man, one of its constituents, but by Reality itself. Kṛiṣṇa is the representative or manifestation of the Real and his is the voice of the Real speaking to us. If we place the Gītā in its historical context, this means that the Gītā is not an apology for any one of the religious sects or philosophies—Sāṃkhya, Vedāntism, Kṛiṣṇaism—existing in India at the time the Gītā was written somewhere between the first and second centuries B.C. Instead it transcends all of them giving us a synthesis of the great truths in each. Swami Prabhavananda says that the Bhagavad Gītā is not "...the fruit of the traditional religious thinking of any particular sect; rather, one should say, it contains metaphysical truths in their diverse aspects, and embodies every form of religious thought, practice and discipline."[29]

The Gītā declares reality to be a totality, a whole, a One. In this sense it supports a monistic metaphysics. Nevertheless it recognizes that man does make distinctions such as the finite and the infinite. Thus the Gītā deals with at least three major questions: "What is the nature of the infinite?"; "What is the nature of the finite?"; "What is the relation between the two?" Answers to these questions will give us an insight into the cosmology or philosophical aspects of the Gītā.

In regard to the first question, in some parts of the Gītā Brahman is pictured as having attributes and in other parts as not. Some of them are wisdom, compassion, concern, love, generosity, power, benevolence, harmony, equanimity and creativity. This viewing of the Brahman as having attributes may be an example of the tendency to conceive of God personally or as in some sense a person. This does not mean that the Bhagavad Gītā has not transcended the crude anthropomorphism or animism of an earlier time, for it has. It only implies, and this is a universal phenomenon, that for some, probably the majority of people, God is much more meaningful if conceived of in personal terms. The Gītā reminds us that Brahman is in himself perfect in all those attributes. His wisdom and goodness is perfect while ours is imperfect. Those who view God personally start with attributes they find incomplete in themselves and envision and experience them in Brahman in their fullness or perfection.

Brahman without attributes (Nirguṇa) is pictured as pure Being or the Absolute. He is other than the qualities or characteristics we experience in this world. "Who knows me birthless, never beginning, Lord of the Worlds, he alone among mortals is stainless of sin, unvexed by delusion," the Bhagavad Gītā states.[30] Brahman without attributes is the unqualified, the unconditional absolute Self. He is beyond all categories; any categories we can conjure up do not apply to him. Nirguṇa Brahman is undifferentiated or undivided. He is one without second. He is beyond name and form. He is beyond time and space.

One way of demonstrating this view of Brahman is to picture Brahman as having two opposite characteristics such as divisible yet indivisible, which in the end cancel each other out leaving nothing, or pointing to the idea that Brahman in its purity transcends opposites or characterizations. An example in the Gītā is the statement "You are what is not, what is, and what transcends them."[31] Brahman without attributes is absolute, not relative existence. Thus Brahman is not subject to such change as growth and decay. Nor is he subject to cause and effect since they operate only in the realm of becoming and not in the realm of pure or fully-realized Being.

Brahman without attributes is God without limitations—"Universal Form, I see you without limit, Infinite of arms, eyes, mouths and bellies. See, and find no end, midst, beginning." Nirguṇa Brahman is the impersonal God or Deity. In contrast

Brahman, when he becomes the personal God or God as person, is a being with self-imposed attributes and thus limitations. Brahman without attributes is Brahman on the Absolute level, the Trans-personal Deity. Brahman with attributes is the personal deity, Brahman self-projected on the relative level. One who asserts this view of Brahman recognizes the inadequacy of words and concepts to fully express their object. Thus the most we can say is that "Brahman is" and is to be experienced for, "You alone know what you are by the light of your innermost nature."[32]

A further question regarding the nature of the Absolute, the Infinite or Ultimate Reality may be raised in terms of the categories pluralism, dualism and monism. Which of the three characterizes it? In some places in the Gītā we find the Infinite described from a dualistic standpoint. It is a qualified dualism however, and not the strong dualism found in the traditional western religious thought which sharply differentiates the natural and the supernatural or man and God, making of them two different orders and being related only through divine initiative.

From the standpoint of the qualified dualism found in the Gītā, the Absolute in its māyā form is the world of sense and object or ordinary experience. It is the relative world of reality, the finite and the limited. It is Brahman in its conditional form or manifestation. From a qualified dualism standpoint the universe is an extention of Brahman but is not Brahman, for on the māyā level a distinction is made between Brahman and his actions or evolutes. Thus the modified dualist pictures Brahman as creator, preserver and destroyer. He is Brahman with attributes, characterized by action and will.

In its māyā form Brahman is characterized by such attributes as materiality, plurality and apparent dualisms. Brahman māyā is sentience in its corporal form. It is Brahman on the secondary, differentiated level. It is like the shadow of an object, the shadow being real but real only because of the presence of the object. In this state Brahman super-imposes names and forms on himself. He does not suffer any diminution thereby, however.

There are several religious implications of this metaphysical view. One is that God is personal and with attributes. The concept of a personal God, therefore is not an invalid one. A second, as noted already, is that Brahman is the author of creation. This is seen in such statements as "I am where all things began, the issuing forth of the creatures" and "I am the beginning, the middle and the end in creation."[33] The third is that Brahman is a being separate from us and thus an object of worship and devotion. Another implication is the concept of salvation as the union of man and God, a bringing together of the Ātman, the individual self, and the Paramātman, the Universal self.

Turning to monism, the main tenet in the monist's view is that there is no real division of Brahman and non-Brahman. Brahman cannot be separated even from its extensions or manifestations, for they are not two but one. What the dualist calls its manifestations is Brahman itself. There is no dichotomy in the being of the Real. God is not everywhere or in everything. God is everything. Brahman does not exist in time and space for Brahman is time and space. The dualist is caught in the spell of ignorance, illusion or māyā when he asserts a separation.

The monist views reality in terms of one category. It may be called Consciousness, Sentience, Being or Existence. Differences may be a matter of degree or gradation, not of kind however. There are different levels of consciousness in reality, but there is only one category. All of reality is illuminated in different degrees. The concept of potentiality is important in the monist's framework. Everything has within it a divine potential which is realized to a particular degree at a particular point or stage in its existence. And what Kṛiṣṇa says to Arjuna in the Gītā is that, if you want to realize your full, truly divine self, then metaphorically, engage in battle or, non-metaphorically, participate in reality.

The monist must use finite concepts and language to describe Brahman or the Absolute, although he insists on their inadequacy even while using such descriptive tools. Thus he says that God is in time and space; God is beyond time and space; God is beyond both being in and outside of time and space. As the Bhagavad Gītā says: "Brahman transcends the mortal and even the immortal." He is "Equally beyond what is and what is not."[34] While the language the monist uses to describe the Real may be dialectical in nature, the Real itself is non-dialectical because it has both incorporated and transcended all dualities. That is to say, from the point of view of the Infinite, nothing is finite, for the Infinite is all.

The monistic view of reality is present in the Gītā in such statements as "You are what is not, what is, and what transcends them," and "This very day you shall behold the universe with all things animate and inert made one within this body of mine."[35] They remind one of the medieval mystic Eckart's assertion that "God is nearer to me than I to myself"[36] and the contemporary poet Gibran's statement "Say not that God is in my heart, rather I am in the heart of God."[37]

An important religious implication of a monistic metaphysics is the defining of religion as realizing the divine within. If God is everything, then God is each individual; and religion, for the individual, becomes a matter of realizing his divine nature, his divine potentiality, of doing those things which leads to full spiritual realization. Another important implication is the oneness of all men in God or a divine basis for world brotherhood mentioned earlier. We are reminded of Josiah Royce, the nineteenth-century western religious philosopher, who conceived of God as "Universal Will" and the ground for "World Community".[38] Thirdly, a monistic metaphysics would lead to the conceiving of salvation as not a union of ātman and Ātman but as a loss of or merging of the self or ātman completely in the Ātman.

Pluralism as well as monism and dualism is found in the Gītā. It is not a positivist type, however, which divides reality up into a multitude of distinct, separated, unrelated empirical entities completely divorced from Brahman. It is instead what might be called a theistic pluralism in which pluralism and monism are combined. From the standpoint of theistic pluralism the Absolute is one in itself but a plurality in its manifestations. The world with its great diversity which we experience here and now is the manifestation of the Absolute but is not the Absolute. The Absolute is to be conceived of in terms of harmony and consolidation for the Absolute is a harmony which consolidates all elements in it without contradiction. There is a creative dialectic between the One and the many which in the end transcends all dualities or dialectics, for the Ultimate is beyond the dichotomies of one and many.

This monism and pluralism might also be described by saying that in its essence the Real is one but in accident, that is in terms of its temporal, material aspects, it is many. In its non-manifest state it is a unity; in its manifested state it is a plurality. From such a view everything which exists in our experienced world has a dual nature—materiality and immateriality, sentience and insentience, the latter being impermanent and the former permanent.

When we view reality from this standpoint we recognize that the Infinite has ways of preserving Itself beyond distinctions and that it suffers no loss of its indivisible wholeness when it becomes diversified. The Infinite in its māyā form puts forth from itself a great variety of forms and movements of which man as a species is one. There is no loss therein as each form and each individual is eventually taken back into the Infinite itself. Thus the oneness is preserved in the midst of plurality. The tendency toward consolidation fulfils itself. The One is realized as identity-in-difference, as unity-in-diversity. All the multitudinous types or varieties of existents we experience on the relative, conditioned level are but manifestations of the One, the Real on the absolute level or in the unconditional state.

Demonstrating the theistic pluralism view in the Gītā is the statement "Then the son of Pāṇḍu beheld the entire universe in all its multitudinous diversity, lodged as one being within the body of the God of gods."[39] It reminds us of Plotinus' statement in one of the Enneads: "...all the loveliness of this world comes by communion in the Ideal-Form...where the Ideal-Form has entered it has grouped and coordinated what from a diversity of parts was to become a unity; it has rallied confusion into cooperation; it has made the sum one harmonious coherence; for the Idea is a unity and what it moulds must come to unity as far as multiplicity can."[40] The same view is expressed by the Sufi mystic Jalal Rumi: "The lamps are different, but the Light is the same; it comes from beyond. If thou keep looking at the Lamp, thou art lost; for thence arises the appearance of number and plurality. Fix thy gaze upon the Light, and thou art delivered from the dualism inherent in the finite body."[41]

The religious implications of a theistic monism are noted in the Gītā. One is the idea mentioned earlier of many and not a single incarnation. A second is the four mārgas or paths to God. There are many equally valid ways of worshipping or becoming one with Brahman. Monism, dualism and pluralism are three views found in the Bhagavad Gītā. The Gītā does not claim only one of them is valid but that each is valid in its own way. It adds, however, if we could view reality as the Real itself views it, we would recognize that the three can be harmonized or synthesized into a single view. That is to say, the Real is a synthesis of all three.

The criticism often made of Hinduism that it asserts the

experienced world is an illusion is invalid. From the synthetic viewpoint of the Gītā that world is real but not ultimate reality. It is of a lesser degree of reality than Brahman. Critics of Hinduism criticize from a dualistic standpoint of either real or unreal and their criticism misses the point. It is a matter of one category, Being; and Being manifests itself in different degrees and ways, fully in Brahman, partially or incompletely in the māyā world of empirical and sense reality.

The questions of the nature of the finite and its relationship to the Infinite may be answered together. One point to be made is that the metaphysical foundation for the individual's life, which the Gītā presents us with, provides a ground for the assertion that to fulfil or reach his true self the individual must become a part of or one with that which is greater than himself. On the one hand this means going beyond himself or fulfilling himself through union with Brahman; on the other it means identifying or becoming one with others in the promoting of universal good. This is because reality is a whole. It is ultimately indivisible and the individual always lives in the context of the whole. He cannot separate himself from it or shirk his duties toward it.

This means that there are no separate, unrelated, self-contained selves. There are no finites which exist unto themselves. The Gītā states this in the following analogy: "For as the vast air, wandering creatures, are always within me." Whatever being finites have is granted to them by Brahman. The basic tenet of Indian religious thought which the Bhagavad Gītā reflects is that all existence is a manifestation of Brahman, that God exists in all beings and in all things and that a realization of this enables us to reach the final goal. In the words of the Gītā: "Who sees the separate lives of all creatures united in Brahman, brought forth from Brahman, himself finds Brahman." Finites, then, do not find fulfilment in themselves. In themselves they are incomplete. They become complete or fully realize themselves in God. "Take refuge in that Primal Being from whom all this seeming activity streams forth forever," the Bhagavad Gītā urges.[42]

The Gītā portrays the relationship of the finite to the Infinite as one of contingency. The finite is dependent on the Infinite because it is an extension or part of the latter. To use another set of terms, each particular is not a self-contained existent but is a manifestation of a universal. The universal is prior and takes the form of particulars. Thus particulars are not independent entities but have their being in their related universal. Likewise existing universals, taken as a whole, have their being in the Supreme Universal, the Real. The finite or the individual is under the spell of the illusion when he fails to recognize his contingency and instead asserts his independence and self-will.

The result of such self-assertion is that the individual becomes egoistical, selfish and greedy, a condition which can only end in grief and despair. His life becomes static and not dynamic, and the individual is no longer in tune with reality. For the Gītā pictures reality as being dynamic, always active, filled with vitality. It is Brahman which "...makes all our activities possible and, as it were, sanctions them, experiencing all our experiences." Further, "the creative energy of Brahman is that which causes all existences to come into being" and "My energy enters the earth, sustaining all that lives."[43] Brahman is the vital force, the dynamic element in reality.

This gives rise to the interesting view of the individual as a process not a thing. There are some who view the self as substantial, as a thing-in-itself. This leads to the notion of owning or absolute ownership which the Gītā rejects, as mentioned earlier. There are many places in the Gītā where the emphasis is on a process view of the self. The individual is, or should be, always in a state of constant growth, development, becoming. The growth is to be always from being to Being, finite to Infinite, the particular to the universal, self good to the good of all.

It might be noted that the Sāṃkhya view of man in terms of the three guṇas may be interpreted from the process view too. The usual interpretation is to say that the three guṇas as extensions of Prakṛiti are manifested in individuals in that, while all three are present in each individual, one predominates, thus determining the nature of that individual and his actions. Suppose however that we view the three guṇas as types of existence or levels of being. In that case it is a matter of growth through these different levels of being as a result of a purification process. The man of tamas or the man living on the tāmasik level evolves through a process of purification to the rājasik level. As he continues to be purified, he rises to the level of sāttvik existence.

Tāmasik, rājasik and sāttvik being or existence, however, is still Brahman in his māyā form. Thus the individual to become fully one with Brahman or the Real must transcend even sāttvik existence. When he does this, he has reached the final state, complete union with or absorption in Brahman. This is asserted in various places in the Gītā, one being, "He who has experienced Brahman directly and known it to be other than Prakṛiti and the guṇas, will not be reborn, no matter how he has lived his life."[44]

It would be interesting to see if the three yogas can be interpreted in the same manner. It is customary to think of them in terms of the path analogy. Each is a path or road one goes on to reach the same end, Brahman. Each person follows the way most suitable to him. One statement of the ways in the Gītā is: "Some, whose hearts are purified, realize the Ātman within themselves through contemplation. Some realize the Ātman philosophically, by meditating upon its independence of Prakṛiti. Others realize it by following the Yoga of right action. Others who do not know these paths, worship God as their teachers have taught them." In a general sense each way is a method by which the divine potential becomes actual in each of us. They are means of raising the individual beyond his finite, immediate, limited self to his full, true self. A basic idea is that people are different and so will use different means to achieve their ends. This holds for religion too. Thus "for the contemplative is the path of knowledge" and "for the active is the path of selfless action."

From a metaphysical standpoint this view is a natural corollary of a monistic combined with a pluralistic metaphysics. The One manifest himself in the many; there are various ways to the One. As stated in the Gītā: "Whatever path men travel is my path. No matter where they walk, it leads to me."[45] It is also compatible with the concept of many devas and each person worshipping the deva he finds to be the most meaningful expression of Brahman. Again, it does not matter what deity a devotee choses to worship—"If he has faith, I make his faith unwavering. Endowed with the faith I give him, he worships that deity and gets from it everything he prays for. In reality, I alone am the giver."[46]

At the same time the paths may be thought of not as methods or techniques but as states of being or kinds of activity in which union with Brahman can be accomplished. The devotee of karma yoga, for example, reaches the state of full karma being or consciousness when he works unselfishly rather than for himself, when he acts to enhance universal well-being and not just his own. He dedicates his effort to the glorifying of God, not self. When one works in such a state of being or with such attitudes, he has reached the highest state, or the Real has come down to him: "Quickly I come to those who offer me every action..."[47]

Jñāna yoga, the path of knowledge, can be viewed similarly. Brahman is truth. The jñāna devotee is one who seeks truth. He attempts to rid his mind or consciousness of all errors, delusions and falsehoods. When his mind is in such a liberated state, he becomes one with Brahman, for Brahman is truth or knowledge. The jñāna practitioner strives to purify the mind or rid it of prejudice, hatred and partiality. When he has accomplished that completely, he and his mind takes on the nature of God or becomes the same kind of existence, consciousness or being as Brahman. For Brahman is itself pure impartiality or entirely devoid of hatred or prejudice. Also the purified mind is one which is freed from all dualities or opposites. It is then able to lead the devotee to a state of oneness with all reality. Having reached that state, the devotee has become one with Brahman, for Brahman is itself oneness or unity. The Bhagavad Gītā describes the jñāna devotee as follows: "They keep all the sense in check. They are tranquil-minded and devoted to the welfare of humanity. They see the Ātman in every creature. They also will certainly come to me."[48]

The follower of Bhakti is one who lives in a state of complete faith and devotion to that Self which is greater than himself. His life is a state of self-surrender, of complete self-giving-up. His faith has been completely purged of doubt, his love of unselfishness. His devotion is to Brahman only. When one reaches such a state of being the Divine responds: "Because they love me these are my bondsmen; and I shall save them from mortal sorrow and all the waves of life's deathly ocean."[49] Bhakti, karma and jñāna may be thought of, then, in a metaphysical sense. Brahman manifests himself in different states or types of being which can be called Bhakti, karma and jñāna. The individual's task is to purify himself so that his being, no matter what its type, becomes that Pure Being which is Brahman.

The message of the Gītā is that the tendency of the universe is toward consolidation through purification. That consolidation consists of the harmony of man with man and with nature on the māyā level and the union of man with Brahman on the absolute level. That union is accomplished through participation on the part of both man and God, man becoming purified in the process. The Gītā, as a synthesis of Indian thought, describes different ways of joining with Brahman. It does not declare one to be better than the other, for each leads the sojourner to his true destination, God.

It was pointed out at the beginning of this chapter that the Bhagavad Gītā is a book which offers us direction in the battle of life and that it contains a basic metaphysics or cosmology. We might close by noting that it is a book of devotion especially appealing to the Bhakti devotee. This is because the Gītā is a part of that type of Indian literature known as the Purāṇas, described by one author thus: "A leaning toward Bhakti is, however, predominant in all the Purāṇas, and this is very appealing to popular minds and hearts. Their interest lies more in inspiring the lives of men than in establishing any particular metaphysical views."[50]

One reason the Gītā is a source of inspiration is because it presents to its readers the concept of God as personal (Īśvara), and this is the most meaningful concept of God as far as the majority are concerned. A personal God is a being who knows every sorrow and is a witness of all our grief: "I am time never ending. I am the creator who sees all." A personal God is a being who is our refuge in times of distress, our hope in days of despair, our light in nights of darkness. With his great power he lifts us from weakness to strength, from sorrow to joy, from smallness to greatness, from isolation to oneness.

To those whose lives are tainted—and whose is not—the Gītā offers new hope: "The devoted dwell with Him; they know Him always.... Made free by his knowledge from past uncleanness of deed or of thought, they find the place of freedom, the place of no return."[51] Īśvara, the personal God, accepts us as we are and purifies us: "Though a man be soiled with the sins of a lifetime, let him but love me, rightly resolved, in utter devotion. I see no sinner. That man is holy. He shall not perish."[52]

The man of faith and devotion finds assurance in the Gītā's declaration: "No one who seeks Brahman ever comes to an evil end." The true devotee finds himself in God and God in him: "I am victory and the struggle for victory. I am the goodness of those who are good." No one is excluded from Brahman's loving care. All stand as equals before Him. All are accepted alike by Him no matter what his duty or work: "I am the same to all beings, and my love is ever the same. Those who worship me with devotion, they are in

PART TWO

The Heterodox Schools

INTRODUCTION

The three heterodox schools of Indian thought are Cārvāka, Buddhism and Jainism. The time of origin of the first cannot be fixed exactly as no early Cārvāka works are extant. According to some authorities the Cārvāka school had developed before Buddha. Bṛihaspati is accepted by some as the founder and Cārvāka his chief disciple. Others say that Cārvāka is the name of the originator. Still a third claim is that Cārvāka is not the name of a person but a word signifying pleasure. As to why Cārvākism came into being Chandradhar Sharma writes that:

> "It must have arisen as a protest against the excessive monkdom of the Brahmana priests. The externals of ritualism which ignored the substance and emphasized the shadow, the idealism of the Upanishads unsuited to the commoners, the political and the social crises rampant in that age, the exploitation of the masses by the petty rulers, monks and the wealthy class, the lust and greed and petty dissensions in an unstable society paved the way for the rise of materialism in India in the post-Upanishadic and pre-Buddhistic age."

The basic characteristic or "the essence of Cārvāka's thought" is its materialism. Its metaphysical claim is that matter is the only reality. Matter consists of four elements—earth, water, fire and air —mixed in various ways and proportions and in terms of laws inherent in them to form objects. Since ether can only be inferred, not seen, its existence is rejected. The mind is simply a particular combination of the four elements. Consciousness is an outcome of matter, a result of a certain combination of the elements. It is an epiphenomenon or by-product of matter.

The Cārvākist believes that perception is the only means of tru knowledge. He rejects inference as invalid. Cārvāka epistemolog is very much like that of David Hume and contemporary positivism A further similarity is its atheism. God as an inference from th material world is not acceptable. Moreover God is not necessar to account for the world and its operations. An internal explanatio is sufficient. The early Cārvākists are said to have believed religio to be an "opiate of the people" given by the priesthood to retai their preeminent position in society.

Its denial of the soul and immortality leads the Cārvākist to plac a major emphasis on this world and life and thus to propose a hedo-nistic ethics. Like the British utilitarians, he asserts the good to b whatever is useful for maximizing pleasure and minimizing pain Sensual happiness is considered the supreme good and goal of life Values are man-created, and have no a priori existence or theisti grounding. Kāma (pleasure) is the end of life and Artha (wealth the means of realizing it.

As to the extensiveness of materialism, it is generally agreed tha it never became a dominant philosophy in India. C. Sharm declares: "...materialism in Indian Philosophy has never bee a force" and "Materialism as metaphysics has never found favou with the Indian philosophers." Its major contribution has bee that it "...saved Indian philosophy from dogmatism to a grea extent" by introducing an element of scepticism or agnosticism into the Indian philosophical stream. The major cause of it downfall in the seventh and sixth centuries B. C., Sharma declares was its "denial of all human values which make life worth living." Jainism and Buddhism, he asserts, "...arose immediately an supplied the ethical and spiritual background which ejecte Materialism."

Changes in contemporary India brought out a renewed interes in materialism. Indian society, as elsewhere, has become mor secular in the sense of a greater emphasis on and justification o material values. The rise of science and technology has stimulated thinking and investigation into ways in which science may or may not be reconciled with philosophy and religion. Are they in-evitably opposed to each other or can the presuppositions of each be harmonized? Hopefully, new insights will result from the raising of questions such as this.

5

JAINISM

K. S. Ramakrishna Rao

I History

Jainism is said by many to be as ancient as Vedic religion. References are found in the Ṛigvedic mantras to Ṛiṣabha and Arstānemi, the two Jain Tīrthaṅkaras (saints or ford-finders), the former being the founder of the Jain Dharma (the Eternal Law) of the present age. Jainism was taught by twenty-four Tīrthaṅkaras who attained liberation. Ṛiṣabha was the first and Vardhamāna Mahāvīra, a contemporary of Buddha, was the last. Vardhamāna was born in 599 B.C. and died in 527 B.C. He was called the Jina, meaning the spiritual conqueror, or Mahāvīra, the great hero, just as Siddhārtha was called Buddha, the Awakened, after his illumination.

Jainism was in part a protest movement against Hinduism, much like Protestanism in the sixteenth-century West. The early Jains repudiated Vedic rituals and practices, declaring that religion consisted of a way of life and thought and not the performance of prescribed exercises. In the Kritanga Sūtra we read, "By self-invented rites common people seek holiness; they are full of deceit and shrouded in delusion."[1] A. Chakravarty writes, "The Jainas insist that right faith can be attained only if . . . superstitious beliefs are discarded," such as, "that bathing in certain rivers, going round certain trees, etc. purify a man" and "the belief in gods and worshipping them for getting rid of diseases . . . ."[2]

It was the extensive rituals described by A. L. Basham as "involving much preparation, the slaughter of numerous animals, and the participation of several well-trained priests"[3] which the Jains objected to especially. The killing of innocent birds and animals as a sacrifice was directly contrary to their belief in Ahiṃsā. Furthermore, the Jains rejected the need and authority of the Brāhmin priests. They did not accept the supremacy and teachings of the Vedas. It is not to be wondered that Jainism has been classified as one of the heterodox schools of thought.

In the beginning the Jains consisted of a small group of monks and lay followers. Growth in numbers was slow. Then in the fourth century B.C. the famous king Chandragupta, who defeated the Greek invader Alexander, became a Jain after abdicating his throne. This led to a notable increase in the number of Jains and eventually Jainism spread throughout all of India. A split occurred in the first century B. C. between the Śvetāmbaras (the white-clad) and the Digambaras (the sky-clad). Monks of the former were willing to wear a minimum of clothes of a white colour while those of the Digambaras insisted on following Mahāvīra's example of total nudity. To them the discarding of clothes symbolized the absolving or cutting away of all bondages to the world. The two sects disagreed over the Jainist canon also. In the fifth century the Jain teachings, which had been transmitted orally previously, were written down. The Śvetāmbaras accepted the written canon but the Digambaras did not and eventually produced their own writings.[4]

A common core of beliefs were accepted by both groups, however, and through the centuries Jainism flourished and its adherents increased in number. A minor schism occurred in 1473 within the Śvetāmbaras when a group at Ahmadabad broke away in protest against the worship of images of the Tīrthaṅkaras. Today Jainism has from one and one half to two million followers found almost exclusively in India. Their influence is far out of proportion to their numbers, as they are engaged mainly in commercial and professional occupations, and have greatly influenced Indian literature, architecture, ethics and philosophy.

II Ahiṃsā

Jainism is said to be noted for its three major concepts or practices—Ahiṃsā, asceticism and anekāntavāda. The doctrine of Ahiṃsā is central to Jain ethical thought. According to S. Radhakrishnan, "The Jainas were the first to make ahiṃsā, non-violence, into a rule of life."[5] Chakravarty suggests that, being preached by Riṣabha, it is ". . . possibly prior in time to the advent of the Aryans in India and the prevalent culture of the period."[6] Regardless of its origins, the practice of Ahiṃsā has been staunchly upheld by Jains through the centuries, and it influenced Mahātmā Gandhi, one of the great leaders of our time.

Ahiṃsā is the doctrine of non-violence, non-injury or non-killing. It is enjoined repeatedly in Jain literature. The Ākārāṅga Sūtra states that "Knowing the course of the world, one should cease from violent acts," and that the Brahman, following the Jain's example, ". . . should not kill, nor cause other to kill, nor consent to the killing of others." A person must not do violence to oneself or others: "One should do no injury to one's self, nor to anybody else . . ."[7] Furthermore Ahiṃsā is to be applied even to one's enemies. Thus, "When men rise up in enmity and wish to fight, it is not cowardice, say the wise, to refuse the challenge. Even when your enemies do the utmost evil, it is right to do no evil in return."[8]

But the uniqueness of Jainism lies in the urgency with which it extended the practice of Ahiṃsā to all forms of life. "The Arhats and Bhagavats of the past, present and future, all say thus, speak thus, declare thus, explain thus: all breathing, existing, living, sentient creatures should not be slain, nor treated with violence, nor abused, nor tormented, nor driven away," one verse asserts.[9] In a later verse this is declared to be "the doctrine of the worthy" while the "doctrine of the unworthy" is that "All sorts of living beings may be slain, or treated with violence, or abused, or tormented, or driven away." One verse pictures the "great sage" as one who "neither injuring or injured, becomes a shelter for all sorts of afflicted creatures, even as an island, which is never covered with water."[10]

The importance of Ahiṃsā is reflected in its being the initial one of the five great vows taught by Mahāvīra—"The first great vow runs thus : I renounce all killing of living beings, whether subtile or gross, whether movable or immovable. Neither shall I myself kill living beings, nor cause others to do it, nor consent to it."[11] To aid the devotee to fulfil such a vow he should meditate on five things—"carefulness of speech, carefulness of mind, care in walking, care in lifting and laying down things, and thoroughly seeing to one's food and drink."[12] By meditating on them the Nirgrantha (freed from bonds) is "careful in his walk, not careless" and ". . . searches into his mind" for harmful thoughts. He "searches into his speech" before speaking. He is "careful in laying down his utensils of begging . . ." and ". . . he does not eat and drink without inspecting his food and drink."[13] From such teaching comes the phenomenon seen today in India of the white-clad Jain monk straining the water before he drinks it and sweeping the walk in front of him as he goes along.

As to the basis of Ahiṃsā, A. Chakravarty writes, "Ahiṃsā does not mean merely a negative virtue of non-violence. It is based upon the positive quality of universal love which is the result of a recognition of kinship among all living beings. One who is actuated by this ideal cannot be indifferent to the suffering of others."[14] Statements from the Jain sūtras reflect this view: "For all sorts of living beings pain is unpleasant, disagreeable, and greatly feared;" "All beings with two, three, four, or five senses . . . in fact all creation knows pleasure and displeasure, pain, terror and sorrow." The similarity continues with the statement: "Not I alone am the sufferer—all things in the universe suffer."[15] Recognizing the universality of suffering, one should have compassion. One verse insists that "...one must meditate upon compassion for all living beings, delight at the sight of beings more advanced than ourselves, pity for the afflicted, and indifference toward those who mistreat you."[16] And in one Jain story of a king converted to Jainism, he says to his unregenerate brother, "If you are unable to abandon pleasure, then do noble actions, O King; following the Law, have compassion on all creatures...."[17] Seeing pain in the world, the true Jain will not do things to increase it: "Observing the pain of mundane existence, one should not act with violence."[18] A recognition, then, that all men share a common heritage of suffering and pain leads one to empathy and compassion, from which Ahiṃsā or non-violence grows.

Jainism accepts the principle of Karma in the sense of cause and effect. An act will give rise to effects which are of the same nature as the act and for which the doer is responsible: "Every good deed will bear its fruits to men; there is no escape from the effects of ones' actions."[19] An everyday example is found in the verses: "If you send a calf into a herd of cows, it will find its mother with unfailing skill. So past deeds search out the man who did them, and who must surely reap their fruit."[20] It is because of the principle of Karma that Ahiṃsā produces positive results. It alleviates quarrels and wars. Furthermore, it enables the individual to free his soul from the bond of Karmic matter. This view is found in the two verses: "Examining Karman and the root of Karman, viz. killing, examining it and its contrary, he is not seen by both ends (he is not touched by love and hate, which cause death)" and "Reflect and observe that whether you go to this world or to that beyond, in the whole world those who are discerning beings, who abstain from cruelty, relinquish karman."[21]

Hiṃsā (violence) and lack of compassion are not the only causes of the bondage of souls and evils in the world. Four passions producing the same effect are anger (krodha), pride (mana), infatuation (māyā) and greed (lobha). They give rise to bhāva bandha (bondage caused by passions) in contrast to dravya bandha (bondage resulting from the permeating of the soul by matter particles).

In a more general sense desires and pleasures are the primary causes of both rebirth and the world's ills. "From desire of pleasure arises the misery of the whole world, the gods included . . .", one sūtra states. Elsewhere we read, "Those who are led by their desires . . . are born again and again . . . the miserable, afflicted fool who delights in pleasures . . . is turned round in the whirl of pains . . . . Those who acquiesce and indulge in worldly pleasures are born again and again . . . . Desirous of pleasures they heap up karman."[22] In another part of the sūtras the term "colour" is used to denote the objects of the senses and desires—"Colour attracts the eye; it is the pleasant cause of Love, but the unpleasant cause of Hatred . . . . He who is passionately fond of colour will come to untimely ruin . . . . He who is very fond of a lovely colour hates all others. . . . He who has a passion for colours will kill many movable and immovable beings; a passionate fool, intent on his personal interests, pains and torments those beings in many ways . . . . When he is not satisfied with those colours and his craving for them grows stronger and stronger, he will become discontented, and unhappy by dint of his discontent, misled by greed he will take another's property."[23] Desires and the drive for pleasure become the primary sources of evil. Out of them grow the passions which bind the soul and cause so much trouble in the world.

The cure or means of overcoming ills, avoiding rebirth and getting rid of the Karmic element is self effort and discipline. Jainism holds to this solution in common with Buddhism, especially Therāvāda. In the Dhammapada of Buddhism we read: "By oneself evil is done; by oneself one suffers; by oneself evil is left undone; by oneself one is purified. Purity and impurity belong to oneself, no one can purify another." Jainism emphasizes perhaps even more strongly that each one reaches Kevala, the state of blessedness, through his own efforts. There is no divine redeemer or saviour who will do it for him. Through self-conquest the true Jain rids himself of passions and desire: "Though a man conquer a thousand brave foes in battle, if he conquers only himself, this is his greatest conquest . . . the wise man avoids wrath, pride, deceit, greed . . . when he ceases to desire the objects of the senses, his desire for pleasure will become extinct."[24] Even the gods praise the self-disciplined person. When King Nami gave up his throne and life of pleasure, the God Indra praised him—"Well done, you have conquered anger . . . pride . . . delusion . . . craving."[25]

We find in the Jain sūtras an emphasis similar to that in the Bhagavad Gītā on the giving up of attachment. Both emphasize that becoming attached to the things of the world leads to greed, jealousy, suffering and injustice. The best course is to sever such attachment; thus the injunction in one sūtra: "You who hoard up wealth, give it away. Tomorrow the funeral drum will beat." One verse warns that "He who grasps at even a little . . . will never be freed from sorrow."[26] The ideal of non-attachment is presented in the following terms: "I shall become a Śramana who owns no house, no property, no sons, no cattle . . ." and "That sage has seen the path to final liberation for whom there exists no property."[27] The hardest attachment of all to overcome, according to one verse, is to women, for "To those who have overcome the attachment to women, all others will offer no difficulties; even as to those who have crossed the ocean, no river, though big like the Ganges, will offer any difficulty."[28] He who has through self-conquest crossed the ocean, conquered desires and passions and given up attachment will be a source of peace and joy to the world. He will reach the state of Kevala or rise to Aloka-ākāśa. He will be an example for others to follow.

The cure for worldly wrongs and individual rebirth has been formalized by Jainism in the teaching of the "Five Vows" and the "Three Jewels".[29] The first vow of Ahiṃsā has been discussed already. The others, as found in the Jain sūtras are: "I renounce all vices of lying speech arising from anger or greed or fear or mirth. I shall neither myself speak lies, nor cause others to speak lies, nor consent to the speaking of lies by others. . . . I renounce the taking of anything not given, either in a village or a town or a wood, either of little or much, of small or great, of living or lifeless things. I shall neither take myself what is not given, nor cause others to take it, nor consent to their taking . . . I renounce all sexual pleasures. I shall not give way to sensuality . . . I renounce all attachments, whether little or much, small or great, living or lifeless; neither shall I myself form such attachments, nor cause others to do so, nor consent to their doing so . . . ."[30]

Vows two through five are characterized as satya (truthfulness or not uttering falsehoods), asteya (non-stealing), brahmacharya (chastity or abstention from sensuality) and Aparigraha (non-greed, non-attachment, renunciation of worldly things). The five vows or principles of conduct are standards for the Jain monk to uphold. Laymen are expected to follow them also, although, as Chakravarty points out: " . . . in the case of the householder the five principles are enjoined with limitation."[31] While householders are expected to conscientiously practise the first three vows, the fourth implies for the layman a "strictly monogamous life" and "sexual relations only with his wife." As for the fifth, Charkravarty notes that Jain leaders insisted "on the principle of limited possession as an essential principle to be observed by all householders."

The "Three Jewels" of Jainism are Samyak Darśana (right faith), Samyak Jñāna (right knowledge) and Samyak Cāritra (right conduct). Right conduct has been discussed above. Right faith is an acceptance of belief in the Jain scriptures and the teachings of the Tīrthaṅkaras. Right knowledge is an understanding of Jain philosophy, its epistemological and metaphysical views for example, which will be discussed subsequently. Jainism differs from other traditions in its insistence that all three must be practised simultaneously if the individual is to be liberated. Bhakti alone is not enough, nor is Jñāna. The mōksa-mārga or path to salvation is a threefold one.

III Asceticism

That asceticism is a major emphasis of Jainism is apparent from the discussion of Jain ethics above. Jainism advocates the practice of asceticism or "austerities" throughout all of one's life and not in just the fourth stage. One must not conclude that asceticism yields a life of joylessness. Instead it leads to a state of inner serenity and calm which no external events can disturb. Further, it is not a state of joylessness because asceticism is voluntarily, freely or gladly practised because one is aware of the good results it produces and the evil results indulgence leads to.

An ascetic is not to be confused with a fatalistic view of life. Jainism recognizes the uncertainty, brevity and vanity of life. Jain works remind us of the Book of Ecclesiastes in the Old Testament portion of the Christian Bible for in the sūtras we read: "No one on earth has escaped death, and fled, and gone free"; "Life in this world is transient; though your life lasts a hundred years, you die as a short-lived man . . . . When calamity befalls him or the end of his life draws near, he must come and go alone"; "The body is of a fragile, decaying nature . . ."; "All singing is but prattle, all dancing is but mocking, all ornaments are but a burden, all pleasures produce but pains;" "Life drags on towards death continuously . . . When they have burned with fire on the funeral pile his forlorn, helpless corpse, his wife and sons and kinsfolk will choose another man to provide for them."[31] Yet, because it offers a way out, Jainism is not fatalistic. It would be better characterized as realistic for it sees life as it is and at the same time as it might be, and it provides a way from one to the other. The first step toward raising life is to recognize how low it is.

Asceticism in Jainism has as its goal the purification of the individual so that two results may follow. One is the reaching of the state of kevala. The other is to enable the individual to see his world more clearly, understand it more profoundly and emphasize with it more deeply so as to make it a better world. The basic thesis in regard to the latter is that man's inner life must be cleansed, purified or set right before he can set his external world a-right.

Asceticism, then, does not mean a running away from the world. It does not imply passivity. Jain scriptures, like the Bhagavad Gītā, state that work is necessary. The question is: "From what motive should one work?" Enough has been said about Jain ethics already to enable us to infer that the Jain answer is that one is to work for unselfish not selfish ends or purposes. How else would one account for the emphasis on "limited possessions" for example? When one recognizes the transient nature of oneself and whatever one possesses, one realizes the foolishness of making them the chief purpose or end. From the Jain standpoint asceticism enables a person to have right views because he is not attached to things and thus is not bent on defending and preserving them. Asceticism is the basis of a non-legalistic ethic as one voluntarily does the good rather than being forced to by rules or laws. Asceticism leads to an unclutterred life. Through austerities the vestiges of Karma are dissolved and destroyed. Karma's hold on the soul is loosened and the Jīva is restored to its original purity and splendour.

The Jain's emphasis on austerities or asceticism is seen most forcefully in the life of the monk who serves as an example for the householder. The monk is to practise austerity daily. A monk "on a begging-tour should not resolve to go to a festival, preceded or followed by an entertainment . . . ." Elsewhere the monk is warned not to accept perfumed cloth from a householder: ". . . do not wipe or rub it with perfume. If you want to give it to me, give it such as it is." Moreover he is not to dye the clothes he wears: 'A monk or a nun should beg for acceptable clothes, and wear them in that state in which they get them; they should not wash or dye them . . . . A monk should not . . . colour colourless clothes."[32] They should not colour or accept coloured clothes for it will stimulate the pride of the giver and lead to competition to see who can give the brightest clothes. Similarly a monk is to reject costly clothes: "A monk . . . should not accept very expensive clothes . . . made of fur . . . goat's hair . . . of muslin, or silk." In addition, "A monk or a nun wanting to get a bowl, may beg for one made of wood or clay" only; they shall not accept ". . . any very expensive bowls . . . made of iron, tin, lead, gold, brass . . ." or ones "which contain a band of precious materials . . ."[33]

Even the few things he uses daily the monk is not to consider as exclusively his own. If the concept of "limited possessions" is to guide the householder, the ideal of the monk is that of complete detachment or non-attachment. The sūtras state that the monk ". . . should be free from attachment, wise, controlling himself, seeking the Law, earnest in the performance of austerities . . . knowing the highest Law, he should perform his religious duties, and regard nothing as his own."[34] He is not to "long for gold and silver" and "should not eat for the sake of the pleasant taste of the food but for the sustenance of life." He does "not act on the motives of the world." He is the sage who "has seen the path to final liberation for whom there exists no property" or possessions.[35]

The practice of austerities leads to both bodily and mental discipline. Of the Mahāvīra himself the sūtras state: "Always well-guarded, he bore the pains caused by grass, cold, fire, flies, and gnats." In his travels when "the dogs bit him" or when "he was struck with a stick" or when "they cut his flesh," he endured it all: "Bearing all hardships, the Venerable One, undisturbed, proceeded on the road to Nirvāṇa."[36] Likewise the monk is one who "bears the three kinds of calamities arising from beasts, men, and gods." He "patiently forebears all unpleasant feelings"[37] and "In whatever house, village, city or region he may be, if a monk be attached by men of violence, or suffers any other hardships, he should bear it all like a hero." Moreover, as a result of his disciplined mind, "If another insult him, a monk should not lose his temper, for that is mere childishness— a monk should never be angry. If he hears words harsh and cruel, vulgar and painful, he should silently disregard them, and not take them to heart. Even if beaten he should not be angry, or even think sinfully, but should know that patience is best, and follow the Law."[38]

In one sūtra a contrast is drawn between the "ill-behaved" and "well-behaved" monk. The former "is liable to the following fourteen charges . . . and does not reach Nirvāṇa : if he is frequently angry; if he perseveres in his wrath; if he spurns friendly advice; if he is proud of his learning; if he finds fault with others; if he is angry even with his friends; if he speaks evil even of a good friend behind his back; if he is positive in his assertions; if he is malicious, egotistical, greedy, without self-discipline; if he does not share with others; if he is always unkind; then he is called ill-behaved."[39] The well-behaved monk is the opposite or does not commit the fourteen charges. Instead he is free from "deceit, greed, pride and wrath."[40] Through such freedom, which results from practising austerities or living an ascetic life, the monk wears away the Karma which encases his soul. In doing so he decreases the evil and increases the good in the world and acts as an example for the house-holder to follow.

IV ANEKĀNTAVĀDA

Anekāntavāda is the basic metaphysical and epistemological view of Jainism.[41] It is what might be called a view of reality as being pluralistic, many-sided or expressing itself in multiple forms. The result is that no absolute predication of reality is valid. Whatever we assert about reality must be probable or relative. We can at the most say a thing "may be" but we cannot validly claim that "it is absolutely this or that." There are, then, different points of view (nayavāda) and each is conditional (syādvāda). Together this is the doctrine of anekāntavāda or many-sidedness.

In contrast to western dualistic thinking which insists on two predications, "either X is or X is not" Jain epistemology emphasizes seven. Called the Sapta-bhaṅgī, they are : A thing may be (Syāt asti); A thing may not be (Syāt nāsti); A thing may or may not be (Syāt asti nāsti); Maybe is inexpressible or indescribable (Syāt avaktavyah); Maybe is not and is inexpressible (Syāt asti ca avaktavyah); Maybe is not and is inexpressible (Syāt nāsti ca avaktavyah); Maybe is, is not and is inexpressible (Syāt asti ca nāsti ca avaktavyah).

The Jain view is different not only from western dualism but from other Indian systems which are called ekāntavāda or the view that reality has but one true nature, which, were it so, would make absolute predication possible. From the Jain standpoint ekāntavāda is wrong because it commits the fallacy of attributing to all of reality what is true of only one part. Examples of such an error are found in both West and East. The Greek philosopher Heraclitus maintained that ultimate reality is in a state of constant change or flux while his counterpart Parmenides asserted the opposite. In India the Advaita-Vedānta school of thought insists on the ultimate unity and identity of reality while Buddhism attributes perpetual change or becoming to reality. In each case the adherents do what Mallisena in his thirteenth-century commentary cautions should not be done: ". . . each naya in its own sphere is right, but if all of them arrogate to themselves the whole truth and disregard the views of rival nayas then they do not attain the status of a right view."[42]

The Jain doctrine of many-sidedness is found in the well-known story of the blind men and the elephant. A king called all the blind men of Savatthi together and presenting an elephant to them, asked them to touch the elephant and then describe it to him. Having done so the blind man who touched the elephant's head declared the elephant was like a pot. The man who touched its trunk said the elephant was like a plough. The one who touched its leg said it was like a pillar, and so on. Then they started shouting and quarrelling with each other. That is the trouble with ekāntavāda, the Jain says. It leads each one to think that his is the only right view and all others are wrong and are not to be countenanced.

The Jain feels that his view is an antidote to such intellectua arrogance. Holding that the finiteness of man and the complexit of reality together makes man's knowledge partial and limited Jainism has contributed greatly to the tradition of tolerance whicl we find in India.

According to Jainism there are five kinds or sources of knowledge.[4] They are mati, ordinary cognition or perception; śruti, knowledg gained through scriptures or authority; avadhi, direct knowledge c things at a distance in time or space, that is, clairvoyance; manaḥ paryāya, direct knowledge of the thoughts of others or telepathy and kevala, perfect knowledge or knowledge par excellence. Th first two belong to the class of mediate or indirect knowledge sinc they depend on the senses as a medium. The other three ar immediate or direct. It is interesting to note that the last two kind of knowledge have purity of the knower as their prerequisite. On cannot know others or enter into the minds of others until he ha purged his own mind of hatred, jealously and prejudice. And on cannot attain kevala-jñāna until one has ridden the soul of it Karmic bondage. When all the Karmas which obstruct knowledg are removed from the soul, the mind can have absolute knowledg or omniscience. Thus in Jainism, as in other Indian traditions, w find a common insistence on the necessary relationship betwee ethics and epistemology. The knower must be purified before hi knowledge can be complete.

V Metaphysical Views

According to Jainism reality is of two types, Jīva and Ajīva.[4] Jīva is that part of reality characterized by consciousness, animatio or life. Jainism extends the range of the living farther than othe Indian systems do from one sense to beings with six senses. Thos of a single sense are plants, trees and microscopic organisms. Worm have two senses, touch and taste. Ants have smell in additior Four-sensed life forms like bees possess touch, taste, smell and sight Higher animals have a fifth sense, hearing. Six-sensed organism such as man have the attribute of mind or reason as do the deva (gods) and narakas (inhabitants of hell).

The Jīva is made up of body and soul in its unliberated state When liberated the Jīva is pure spiritual being freed from all Karmi substance. The inborn and original nature of every jīva is perfec knowledge and peace, perfect potentiality and power. It is the condition to which the bound jīva seeks to return. Owing to the association of the Karmic forces the original glory of the jīva becomes tainted. It is like gold covered with rust. Just as the coating of rust is an obstacle to the glittering of the gold, so the Karmic forces, made up of subtle particles of matter which permeate the soul, are obstacles in the way to the perfection of the soul, just as the bright light of a lamp is diminished and blurred by the formation of soot around it. Just as, when the soot is removed, the brightness of the light is revealed, so also, if a person attains Jñāna, the Jīva shines in its original glory. The purpose of practising the Jain ethical teachings is to remove this bad association of Karma and made the jīva pure. It is like giving a bath to the jīva and restoring it to its original purity.

The other part of reality, Ajīva, is that which is inanimate, without consciousness or life. Ajīva consists of five entities. The first is pudgala or matter. The smallest unit of matter is the atom. Atoms combine to form human bodies and material objects. Ajīva also consists of space (Ākāśa). Since bodies are extended, space must exist. Two kinds of space are presupposed. One is loka-ākāśa or finite space, the space in which material objects or bodies are in motion or at rest. The other is aloka-ākāśa, empty or infinite space beyond the realm of finite space and in which the pure Jīvas and Tīrthaṅkara abide.

Ajīva consists, further, of Dharma and Adharma. The term dharma does not have ethical implications to the Jain. Rather it is the principle of motion, while adharma is the principle of rest. In a more refined sense dharma is the necessary condition or context in which movement takes place, just as water is the necessary medium for the fish to swim in. Adharma on the other hand is what stabilizes things or gives rise to immobility.

Pudgala, Ākāśa, Dharma and Adharma have the attribute of extension. Time does not. It is a-astikya. We know that time is real or exists because we observe modification or change. As Chatterjee and Datta point out: "A mango can be green and ripe only successively, i.e. at different moments of time; and without the supposition of time-distinctions we cannot understand how a thing can possess such incompatible characteristics."[45] For the Jain time is infinite just as the universe is eternal. The universe goes through an infinite number of cycles and each cycle is characterized by a period of improvement or ascendence (Utsarpiṇī) followed by one of decline or descent (Avasarpiṇī).

From the Jain standpoint reality is characterized by origin, decay and permanence. As mentioned before Jainism opposes the Vedāntist view that reality is unchanging and the Buddhist view of reality as constantly changing as both being one-sided. Reality is characterized by change, that is, birth, growth and decay, on the phenomenal or accidental level; but permanence characterizes it in its essence. The body, for instance, is made up of matter, comes into being, exists for a while and then goes out of existence; but the soul is eternal and unchanging. What happens to it is, as mentioned before, that it becomes encrusted with Karmic matter when in its bound state.

The Jain doctrine of the threefold nature of reality is analogous to the Hegelian view of nature as dialectical—thesis and antithesis reconciled and held together by synthesis. Or it is like the biological principle or process of metabolism which is a reconciliation and synthesis of the two opposite processes of katabolism and anabolism. Reality then, according to Jainism, maintains its identity and permanency through the continuous process of changes consisting of origin and decay, identity in the midst of variety, and permanency through change. Neither the permanency or the process of change can be separated from each other. Each is indispensable to the other and hence cannot be separated in reality, though one may be differentiated from the other in thought and speech.

Jainism asserts that reality is dynamic, vitalistic, filled with life. It is illuminated with consciousness. This view has several implications. One is the doctrine of Ahiṃsā, namely, do not seek to exploit or harm reality; instead, try to harmonize with it. A second is the concept of self-illumination or the doctrine, again, that each jīva or soul has to save itself. A third implication is an epistemological one, namely, that there is a correlation or direct relation between the illumined mind and the illumined object. Thus physical processes in the object become psychical facts in the mind and immediate knowledge is possible.

Jainism takes a realistic and pluralistic view of reality. Its pluralism is reflected in the view already discussed that reality is manifold and complex, made up of innumerable souls and objects consisting of unlimited combinations of atoms. Its realism is reflected in the Jain's assertion of universal ethical principles such as

Ahiṃsā and the metaphysical principle of cause and effect—"All iving beings owe their present form of existence to their own Karman," and "All men must suffer in due time the fruits of their work."[46]

VI Non-Theism

Associated with this realism and pluralism is a naturalism which denies theistic type explanations of the universe. It is neither created nor sustained by a supernatural being, a God. Instead it has existed eternally, and operates in terms of natural law. One sūtra urges the mendicant to "not trust in the delusive power of the gods."[47] The ninth-century Jain teacher Jinasena wrote n his Mahāpūraṇa: "Some foolish men declare that Creator made he world. The doctrine that the world was created is ill-advised, and should be rejected. If God created the world, where was he before creation? . . . No single being had the skill to make his world. For how can an immaterial god create that which is material? . . . If out of love for living things and need of them he made the world, why did he not make creation wholly blissful, free from misfortune?"[48]

The attributing of natural causes rather than God to events is seen in a paragraph in the Akārāṅga Sūtra: "A monk or nun should not say: The god of the sky! the god of the thunderstorm! the god of lightning! the god who begins to rain! the god who ceases to rain! may rain fall or may it not fall! may the crops grow or may they not grow! may the night wane or may it not wane! may the sun rise or may it not rise! may the king conquer or may he not conquer! They should not use such speech. But knowing the nature of things he should say: The air, the follower of Guhya, a cloud has gathered or come down; the cloud has rained."[49]

The passages above demonstrate the Jain's refusal to associate reality with any supernatural being. In this sense Jainism is not a religion in the ordinary usage of the term. The early Jains did not personalize and deify natural forces as did other early people. They had no conception of an anthropomorphic-like Deity who came to man's aid. Instead everything operates in terms of natural laws. This has at least three results. It disallows a fatalistic attitude: "may the king conquer or may he not conquer." It prevents men from rationalizing their misdeeds in terms of God or the carrying out of God's will and it necessitates man's being responsible for and saving himself.

Jainism may be called irreligious in its not presupposing a Supreme Being, although even in that respect, one should note statements such as those of Basham: "Jainism, like Buddhism, is fundamentally atheistic, in that, while not denying the existence of the gods, it refuses them any important part in the universal scheme. The world, for the Jaina, is not created, maintained or destroyed by a personal deity, but functions only according to universal law."[50] Jainism does have much in common with the great world religions, however, in its emphasis on the ethical and on the sacrifice of the self, in its concept of liberation and man's need to transcend his lower and false self, its belief in the soul and kevala, its stress on the search for truth and its attitude of tolerance.

Jainism has much in common with Buddhism, apart from its rejection of the latter's metaphysics of impermanence. On the other hand Jainism is quite unlike the Cārvāka school of thought with its emphasis on materialism and hedonism. Basham writes that "The general attitude of the materialist schools, according to their adversaries, was that all religious observance and morality were futile."[51] The Jains also disagreed with a third unorthodox sect of the period, the Ājīvikas. They were ascetics like the Jains but upheld a much more strict determinism. They denied the commonly accepted doctrine of Karma that ". . . though a man's present condition was determined by his past actions he could influence his destiny, in this life and in the future, by choosing the right course of conduct."[52] The Ājīvikas believed the universe was determined in every detail by the impersonal cosmic principle, Niyati, or destiny.

The seventh and sixth centuries B. C. were a period of discontent, suffering and stress in India. Men sought new answers or solutions to the age-old questions and problems which baffled them. Earlier explanations did not suffice and schools of thought like the Cārvākas, Ājīvikas, Buddhism and Jainism arose to fill the vacuum such a dissatisfaction created.

6

LOKĀYATA MATERIALISM

DEBIPRASAD CHATTOPADHYAYA

I BACKGROUND

It is generally assumed that Indian materialism can be discussed today only on the basis of what the others had to say about it. Not that nothing is accepted as authentic statements of the materialists. A few scraps are indeed admitted to be so. Peculiarly, however, even these are recovered from the writings of their opponents. Such, then, is supposed to be the characteristic limitation of our knowledge of Indian materialism. This, though not wholly true, contains an important element of truth, about which it is necessary for us to be clear first. This is perhaps best done by way of recapitulating the main historical data that we have.

The Indian proto-philosophical literature of c. the 7th century B. C., called the Upaniṣads, contains a number of references to distinctly materialist views. In default of any ground to think that these are all references to a unified world-view deserving to be called the materialism of ancient India, we are left to presume that during this period there are many thinkers with a positively materialist proclivity. The Upaniṣads themselves do not tell us who they are, their views being generally branded as characteristic of the devils (asuras). Or, the story is told that when the great battle between the gods and devils is going on, Bṛihaspati, the preceptor of the former, goes in disguise among the latter and preaches this degenerating philosophy to bring disaster to them.

Not many centuries after the Upaniṣads, in the Pāli canons of early Buddhism, we frequently come across the name Lokāyata, meaning either "that which is essentially this worldly" or "that which is prevalent among the common people." But these works are peculiarly vague about the nature of the view referred to by this name. This is all the more peculiar because the works are fully aware of the materialistic or proto-materialistic tendencies of the age, which are sometimes associated with individual thinkers like Ajita Keśakambali and Pāyāsi but never identified with the Lokāyata. This leads some modern scholars to think that in the Pali Buddhist works the name Lokāyata does not stand for any philosophy at all; it means instead something like "nature-lore".

However, it is different in the Arthaśāstra, the famous work on Indian polity which could have been as old as the 3rd century B. C. According to it, Lokāyata is definitely the name of a philosophy, and, as a matter of fact, one of the three logic-oriented philosophies it recognizes. The name also occurs in the epics Mahābhārata and Rāmāyaṇa as an undesirable heretical view. These epics moreover speak of a certain demon called Cārvāka, who, because of his arrogant impiety, had to be burnt alive by the pious Brahmins.

The grammarian Patañjali of c. 150 B.C. refers to a commentary on some original Lokāyata work. The Buddhist work Divyāvadāna —which probably assumes its present form in the 4th century A. D. but which undoubtedly records a much older tradition—also speaks of an original work on the Lokāyata and of some commentary on it. But such Lokāyata works, evidently once in circulation, are irrevocably lost. The recent furore created by the discovery of an allegedly Lokāyata text—the Tattvopaplavasiṃha by Jayarāśi Bhaṭṭa of c. 8th century A.D.—is dying out. With the actual study of this book it is being increasingly realized that the evidence connecting it with the Lokāyata is really worse than flimsy and the text has nothing to do with materialism excepting an outright rejection of it.

After the early mention of the Lokāyata, Indian literature—both philosophical and non-philosophical—is peculiarly silent about it for several centuries. Roughly from the middle of the 8th century, however, the more sophisticated Indian philosophers begin to show a great deal of renewed interest not only in the old name Lokāyata—now somehow identified with the Cārvāka—but also in the basic tenets which it is supposed to stand for. This interest, though primarily negative or polemical, is nevertheless keen. Here are just a few examples of it.

The earliest available compendium of Indian philosophy—the ṣaḍ-darśana-samuccaya by the Jaina philosopher Haribhadra of c. 8th century—takes note of only six systems of Indian philosophy, one of which is Lokāyata, also called Cārvāka. Its renowned commentator, Guṇaratna, shows the most hair-splitting scholasticism for elaborately refuting one of the basic Lokāyata tenets. The same is shown by the famous Buddhist idealists, Śāntarakṣita and Kamalaśīla of the 8th century. Śaṅkara (A.D. 788-820), the Advaita Vedāntist, proposes to refute the Lokāyata view in more than one place in his magnum opus. Jayanta Bhaṭṭa of the 9th century A.D., one of the maturest exponents of Indian logic and atomism, takes a great deal of care to refute the Lokāyata views. Indeed, it may not be an exaggeration to think that from the 8th century onwards practically all the outstanding Indian philosophers follow this procedure. It is no wonder, therefore, that the most important compendium of Indian philosophy, the Sarva-darśana-saṃgraha by the Vedāntist Mādhava of the 14th century, opens with a rather detailed description of the Lokāyata or Cārvāka philosophy; for, from Mādhava's own point of view, this is the philosophy that must be rejected first.

At the present stage of historical research, it may be premature to conjecture on the real cause of this renewed interest in the Lokāyata philosophy roughly from the 8th century. What particularly concerns us, however, is its effect on the making of the contemporary image of materialism in ancient and medieval India. While enriching this image, it damages it also.

For understanding Indian materialism, what contemporary scholarship gains from the polemics against the Lokāyata is of course obvious. Since a considerable number of advanced Indian philosophers persistently try to refute a number of definitely materialist tenets as tenets characteristic of the Lokāyatas or Cārvākas and since it is being irresponsible to imagine that they are all fighting a fiction, modern scholars are obviously justified in trying to reconstruct the otherwise lost account of Lokāyata materialism from the polemics against it. At the same time, the general tendency of modern scholars to understand Indian materialism as such exclusively on the basis of these polemics, imposes certain limitations on their understanding of it. Two of these limitations are particularly prominent. First, it easily misleads them to identify Lokāyata materialism with Indian materialism as a whole, i.e. it prevents them from seeing the materialism and materialist proclivities of many other Indian philosophers, inclusive of some who want anxiously to be dissociated from the Lokāyata. It is like imagining that since the opponents of materialism in European philosophy persistently oppose Democritus, the materialist tradition of Europe is to be equated with the philosophy of Democritus. Or, it is like imagining that Marx and Engels are not materialists because they dissociate themselves from the French materialists of the 18th century.

Secondly, even the nature of Lokāyata materialism is sometimes seriously misunderstood, the characteristic limitation of the source of our knowledge of it being taken as the characteristic peculiarity of the Lokāyata itself. Thus, the opponents of the Lokāyata find it necessary to refute it only on the context of defending certain positive tenets of their own. They are therefore more anxious to say what the Lokāyata does not admit than what it does. This is construed to mean that the Lokāyata is interested only in demolishing certain philosophical positions and not in positively building up of any. The decisive thing about Indian materialism, as an eminent modern scholar comments, "is its purely negative interest" (Frauwallner). This is an error, not only because it is based on a rather superficial understanding of the available data about the Lokāyata but even more because it shows no understanding of the dialectics underlying Indian philosophical methodology.

From the Indian point of view, the essential precondition of philosophical activity is "doubt" (saṃśaya or vimarṣa) and the precondition of "doubt" itself is the open confrontation of the "thesis" (pakṣa) with the "antithesis" (pratipakṣa). As a result, it is not at all permissible for a serious Indian philosopher to state his own "thesis" without first negating its "antithesis," called the pūrvapakṣa. Naturally, therefore, in Indian philosophical writings, this "antithesis" looks largely negative from the standpoint of the "thesis," just as this "thesis" itself looks negative from the standpoint of its own "antithesis". But this does not mean that neither the "thesis" nor the "antithesis" is barely negative in content. The fact that we have the account of the Lokāyata only in the form of the "antithesis" may give it a deceptive appearance of negativism. But this is not to be taken as the decisive thing about the Lokāyata, far less of Indian materialism as such.

Of these two limitations of the current understanding of Indian materialism, in the present essay, there will be little scope to remove the first. A survey of materialism and the materialist trends outside the Lokāyata means the survey of an extensive field of Indian philosophy—particularly of atomism (paramāṇu-vāda) and of the philosophy of primeval matter (pradhāna-vāda)—which, again, is difficult without being often controversial. The present essay will, therefore, primarily be a positive account of Lokāyata materialism and it will barely hint why our idea of Indian materialism as such needs to be much broader.

II Lokāyata Epistemology

The assorted polemics against the Lokāyata, along with the philosophical compendiums by Haribhadra and Mādhava, give us the unmistakable impression that the opponents of the Lokāyata are bothered by it, particularly because of the positions it takes in epistemology, ontology and social ethics.

In epistemology, the position seems to be that of the primacy of empirical knowledge. The Indian way of putting this is that sense-experience (pratyakṣa) is supremely important as a source or instrument of right knowledge (pramāṇa). But this is readily misinterpreted as a purely negative attitude to the rational faculty, or, in Indian terminology, as the condemnation of inference (anumāna). That this is a wrong understanding of the actual Lokāyata position can be judged from two important evidences. Purandara of c. 7th century A.D., whom others refer to as "an author representing the Cārvāka standpoint," is quoted by a Jaina philosopher as clarifying the Cārvāka position as follows. Cārvāka "admits the usefulness of inference as determining the nature of all worldly things where perceptual experience is available; but inference cannot be employed for establishing any dogma regarding the transcendental world, or life after death or the law of Karma. The main reason for upholding such a distinction between the validity of reference in our practical life of ordinary experience, and in ascertaining transcending truths beyond experience, lies in this that an inductive generalization is made by observing a large number of cases of agreement in presence together with agreement in absence, and no cases of agreement in presence can be observed in the transcendental sphere; for even if such cases existed, they could not be perceived by the senses." (S. N. Dasgupta)

This is corroborated by Jayanta Bhaṭṭa who says that, from the Cārvāka standpoint, ordinary everyday inferences—like that of fire from smoke—is not questioned at all, because inferences like these have for their basis previous perceptual knowledge, i.e. the experience of the invariable co-presence of fire with smoke. What the Cārvāka actually rejects, says Jayanta, is the inference of God soul and the other world, i.e. inference supposed to have no relation at all to previous empirical evidence.

Incidentally, such a position in epistemology is not fundamentally different from the classical one of Indian logic as represented by the Nyāya-sūtra, which also mentions previous perceptual evidence as an essential precondition of legitimate inference. Hence, from the Nyāya standpoint, sense-experience is the most basic of all the sources of knowledge—pramāṇa-jyeṣṭha, literally "the eldest of the sources of knowledge"—and any inference going against the evidence of sense-experience is to be summarily rejected as a pseudo-inference.

However, where the Lokāyata seems to differ from the Nyāya is in the motivation for the somewhat similar understanding of legitimate inference. While for the Nyāya, the main interest for assigning primacy to sense-experience is mainly its science-orientation, that of the Lokāyata is frankly practical, or, more specifically, socio-ethical. Thus, we are persistently told that, according to these materialists, a great deal of cheating is going on in society with the talk of God, the soul and the other world. They are, therefore, anxious to show that such talk is a mere hoax, because these are never directly experienced and hence cannot be proved by inference either. This hoax, they further argue, is not really purposeless. It is deliberately designed to serve as a source of livelihood for the social parasites, i.e. in Lokāyata terminology, of those that share in neither intellectual nor manual labour (buddhi-pauruṣa-hīnāḥ).

III Social Ethics

This leads us to a discussion of the social ethics of the Lokāyatas. Certain "authentic popular verses" (prāmāṇika-lokagāthā) are persistently attributed to them by their opponents mainly to show how very impious these materialists are. However, in the general atmosphere of casteism, scripture-mongering, obscurantism and the economic drainage of futile rituals, the debunking of all these by the Lokāyatas in defence of the normal pleasures of this worldly existence still retains a great deal of scientific and social interest for us. It is impossible to retain in English translation the biting satire of their simple verses. But here is a rough translation of some of these as compiled in Mādhava's Sarva-daraśna-saṃgraha:

"Heaven and liberation are mere empty talks. There is no soul that is imagined to go to the other world. The actions prescribed for the caste-society (varṇāśrama) do not really yield their alleged results."

"The Agnihotra sacrifice, the three Vedas, the holding of the three staves and (the practice of the religious professionals of) smearing the body with ashes—all these are nothing but the sources of livelihood for persons that share neither in intellectual nor in manual labour."

"If, (as claimed by the priests), the animal killed in the Jyotiṣṭoma sacrifice attains heaven straightway, why does not the sacrificer kill his own father (and thus ensure heaven for him)?"

"If the performance of the śrāddha (i.e. the rite performed for the dead—a main source of the priest's income—in which food is offered to the dead) causes satisfaction to those that are already dead, oil put into the lamp even after it is blown off should as well make its flame ablaze."

"Besides, the same assumption (namely that food offered in śrāddha actually feeds the departed) should make it superfluous for the traveller to carry provisions with himself, because he should as well be satisfied while travelling afar by the food offered to him at home in the form of śrāddha."

"If, what is offered in śrāddha can satisfy beings supposed to be in heaven, why not offer food down below for one actually on top of a tower?"

"As long as you live, live happily. Feed yourself with butter, even though on loan. Once the body is reduced to ashes, how can it ever return again?"

"If after quitting the body one goes to the other world, how is it that one does not return again drawn by the love for friends and others?"

"Hence, it is only as a source of livelihood that the Brahmins here have introduced the rites for the dead. There is nothing more in all these."

"The authors of the three Vedas are just cheats and cunning thieves. All the pendantic formulas, the meaningless spells—jarpharī-turpharī—like the wife taking the horse's phallus (i.e. a part of the Aśvamedha sacrifice), are nothing but the inventions of cheats for the purpose of obtaining their sacrificial fees."

It is not difficult to see that the main theoretical basis of this social ethics is the denial of the soul over and above the body and hence also the denial of the other world where this soul is supposed to migrate after death. Put in Indian terminology, the point is para-lokino'bhāvāt-paralokābhāva: the fiction of the other world because of the fictitious nature of that which is imagined to go to the other world. This is of course a negative way of putting the point. for all that we know of the Lokāyātas, however, it is obvious that they are also anxious to put their point positively. Thus, it is repeatedly said, in the Lokāyata view only four material elements—earth, water, fire and air—are real. Human beings, like everything else in the world, are made of only these. So it is useless to assume any spiritual substance—the soul—to explain human nature. Or, what the others imagine to be the soul is nothing but the physical frame with its physiological functions.

IV Consciousness

The most formidable problem in taking such a position is evidently that of the fact of consciousness. If nothing but crass matter goes into the formation of the entire psycho-physical organization, how can the presence of consciousness in human—or, more broadly, animal—bodies be explained? After all, the gross physical elements like earth, water, etc., are by themselves admittedly unconscious. How, then, do the Lokāyatas propose to explain the indisputable evidence of consciousness in human beings consistently with their assumption that nothing but intrinsically unconscious material elements go into the making of everything about it?

When we look back at these materialists, their understanding of the nature of matter cannot but appear to us to be rudimentary and naive. Nor do we expect of them any knowledge of the central nervous system, particularly of the brain. In other words, the scientific data actually at their disposal is, in modern standards, miserable indeed. It is therefore extremely remarkable that, in spite of the severe limitations under which they are historically obliged to work, they do make a bold attempt at an explanation of the origin of consciousness from matter. And their main lines of argument, as far as we can judge them from the account given by their opponents, still have distinct theoretical interest for us. Three of their lines of argument deserve special mention.

First, the origin of consciousness from the material elements, each of which is itself unconscious, appears impossible to others because of one assumption. It is the assumption that an altogether new quality cannot emerge from some peculiar combination and transformation (viśeṣa-pariṇāma) of certain things that are by themselves distinctly devoid of this quality. But this assumption itself is an undue one. The fact, on the contrary, is that there are definitely observed cases of such new emergence. As the most typical case of such observation, the Lokāyatas are said to mention the following. None of the ingredients used to prepare spirituous liquor or alcohol possesses the quality called "intoxicating power" (mada-śakti). Yet the fact is that when these ingredients are combined and transformed in a special form we get spirituous liquor with its intoxicating power. Evidently, the Lokāyatas are yet to know the full explanation of such a fact. Nevertheless, the fact is there, and it proves that the emergence of a new quality altogether is not really as absurd as others may view it. And, if it is really not absurd, the view of the emergence of the new quality called consciousness from the peculiar transformation of the material elements in the form of the body cannot be ruled out as prima facie absurd.

Secondly, there are sound positive grounds to think that consciousness cannot but be the product of matter, i.e. of the material elements when transformed into the body. That this body is made of matter alone is admitted by all. Therefore, the question is: Is there any ground to view consciousness as a quality of the body, or as an effect of the body? There are, assert the Lokāyatas. In Indian terminology, the causal connection between two phenomena can be established on the basis of anvaya confirmed by vyatireka, which we may roughly translate as "uniform co-presence" confirmed by "uniform co-absence". Thus, fire-cum-wet-fuel is proved as the cause of smoke because the observation of the uniform co-presence of fire-cum-wet-fuel is confirmed by the observation that the absence of fire-cum-wet-fuel is always connected with the absence of smoke. So, argue the Lokāyatas, is the case of body and consciousness. Wherever there is the presence of body there is also the presence of consciousness. Further, wherever there is the absence of body there is also the absence of consciousness. Hence consciousness is the effect of the body.

According to the norm of Indian logic, there are only two ways of refuting such an argument. First, by pointing to the evidence of the presence of the body along with the absence of consciousness. Secondly, by pointing to the evidence of the absence of the body along with the presence of consciousness. There is no doubt that the opponents of Lokāyata explore both possibilities. Thus it is argued that in the case of the corpse there is a presence of the body along with the absence of consciousness. Besides, disembodied consciousness is possible in the case of the transmigrating soul that has left one body without yet acquiring another. From the Lokāyata point of view, there is no reason to take such arguments seriously. A corpse is not a body—i.e. a functioning physiological unit the materialists are talking of—no more than a pile of junk is an automobile or an airplane. As for the disembodied consciousness of the transmigrating soul the less said the better, for one cannot just assume the soul for the purpose of proving its existence.

From the writings of Jayanta Bhaṭṭa, we have a glimpse of another line of the Lokāyata argument proving consciousness as the product of matter. As Jayanta puts it, "It is commonly observed that a body well-nourished with food and drinks has improved consciousness. The reverse happens in the reverse case (i.e. in the absence of nourishment of the body, there is a deterioration of consciousness). Besides, the body of a young man who takes the Brāhmī-ghṛita (i.e. 'brain tonic' of traditional Indian medicine) shows a remarkable improvement of consciousness . . . . Thus the improvement and deterioration of consciousness is directly explicable by the presence or absence of the excess of material elements."

The argument is elemental in simplicity; palpably material things in the form of food, drink, 'brain tonic', etc., absorbed in the human body, go into the making of consciousness. How far, in Indian philosophy, the opponents of materialism successfully refute this rgument is of course a different question. For the present we have nother question of greater historical interest. From where does ayanta Bhaṭṭa collect this argument which he attributes to the okāyatas?

In view of the fact that the Lokāyata texts are lost presumably be- ore the time of Jayanta Bhaṭṭa himself, it would be impermissible to onjecture that he collects it from some extinct Lokāyata work. But t will be also impermissible to think that he collects it from nowhere, e. manufactures it himself. There exists a text in which the same rgument—or at least its unmistakable prototype does occur; and ayanta's personal lack of acquaintance with it can be thought of nly at the cost of sanity. This text is the Chāndogya Upaniṣad nd the argument under consideration is attributed in it to one of he first philosophers of India, called Uddālaka Āruṇi. Belonging s he does to earlier than the 7th-8th century B.C., we do not expect f him the later sophisticated form of putting a philosophical argu- nent. It is extremely remarkable, nevertheless, that he not only rgues on this line but also insists on an experimental verification of t. As a document of ancient Indian scientific thought, the passage f the Chāndogya Upaniṣad where this occurs needs to be read in ull, though we have room here to quote only a part of it.

Uddālaka Āruṇi was instructing his son Śvetaketu. The original ource of everything in the universe, he said, was primeval un- lifferentiated "being". From this successively evolved fire, water nd food. Everything in the universe—inclusive of the body and nind of man—eventually evolved from these three. In the imme- liate context of our discussion what interests us most is Uddālaka's iew of the origin of mind from the food assimilated into the body. Ve quote here only that part of his discourse which contains this iew.

Uddālaka Āruṇi said to his son Śvetaketu: "Food, when eaten, ndergoes a threefold division. Its coarsest constituent is trans- ormed into faeces; its medium (constituent is transformed) into the lesh and its subtlest (constituent is transformed) into the mind. Water, when drunk, undergoes a threefold division. Its coarsest onstituent is transformed into urine; its medium (constituent is ransformed) into blood; its subtlest (constituent is transformed) nto breath (prāṇa, life). Heat (i.e. in the form of oil, butter, etc.), vhen consumed, undergoes a threefold division. Its coarsest consti- uent is transformed into bone; its medium (constituent is transformed) into marrow; its subtlest (constituent is transformed) int speech."

The son Śvetaketu wanted to understand the view more fully So the father continued: "Of curd, my dear, when churned, tha which is subtle moves upward. It becomes butter. In the sam way, my dear, of the food that is eaten, that which is subtle move upward. It becomes the mind. Of water, my dear, when drunk that which is subtle moves upward. It becomes breath (life). C heat (oil, butter, etc.), when consumed, that which is subtle move upward. It becomes the speech. Thus, my dear, the mind consis of food, the breath (life) consists of water, the speech consists of heat.' The son wanted to understand the view even more deeply and s the father continued: "A person, my dear, consists of sixteen parts For fifteen days do not eat (any food, but) drink water as you please Breath (life), which consists of water, will not be cut off from on who drinks water."

So for fifteen days the son did not eat any food and then went t the father. The father wanted him to recite the Vedas. Śvetaket said: "These do not occur to me, Sir." To him Uddālaka said "Just as, my dear, of a great mass of fire only a single piece of coa of the size of a firefly may be left with which the fire would not there after burn much longer,—similarly, my dear, only one part of you sixteen parts is left and with it you fail to apprehend the Vedas Eat. Then you will understand me." Then the son ate and ap proached the father. This time whatever Uddālaka asked hin Śvetaketu answered everything. Then to him, Uddālaka said "Just as, my dear, of a great mass of fire only a single piece c (burning) coal of the size of a firefly is left, and covered with straw it is made to blaze up and this fire would burn much thereafter,— so, my dear, of your sixteen parts only the sixteenth was left over being covered with food, that is made to blaze up. With this yo can now understand the Vedas. For, my dear, the mind consists c food, the breath (life) consists of water, the speech consists of heat.' Then Śvetaketu understood what he said. Well, he understood

There is of course no ground to think that Uddālaka is a followe of the Lokāyata. In Indian literature, the name Lokāyata come in circulation after the Upaniṣads. However, if an advanced philo sopher like Jayanta Bhaṭṭa wants to look back at the basic suggestio of Uddālaka to illustrate how the Lokāyata wants to substantiat their view of the origin of consciousness from matter, it follows no only that the materialist tradition in Indian philosophy is older than the Lokāyata but moreover—and this is much more important—that our understanding of Indian materialism runs the risk of being too narrow in so far as it is identified only with the Lokāyata, as is usually done in textbooks on Indian philosophy.

V Lokāyata and Indian Materialism

The identification of Indian materialism with Lokāyata materialism, though mistaken, is not without a cause. We have already referred to it. Roughly from the 8th century A. D., the Indian philosophers themselves persistently refer to certain overtly materialistic tenets as tenets characteristic of the Lokāyatas. This, rightly understood, should have only meant that Lokāyata is a form of materialism—perhaps the most out-spoken and plain-speaking form of it. But this cannot and does not mean that in Indian philosophy there is no materialism outside the Lokāyatas. Even those that sharply differ from the Lokāyata, differ from it not necessarily for the purpose of differing from materialism as such. Some of them—particularly the Indian idealists—reject the Lokāyata materialism for this purpose no doubt. However, among those that represent the antithesis of idealism, there are at least some who dissociate themselves from Lokāyata materialism mainly because they want to defend a more advanced understanding of the nature of matter on the basis of which they hope to work out a better explanation of the universe. There are, moreover, obvious socio-ethical consideration on which these philosophers do not like to take the radical position of the Lokāyatas. Philosophically speaking however, their socio-ethical position is not even half as significant as their comparatively advanced understanding of the nature of matter.

Of such philosophies that differ from the Lokāyata materialism mainly on the question of matter, two are specially prominent. These are paramāṇu-vāda or atomism, defended particularly by the Nyāya-Vaiśeṣikas, and pradhāna-vāda or the theory of primeval matter defended by the Sāṃkhya philosophers.

I am fully aware that what I am trying to drive at is highly unconventional. To include paramāṇu-vāda and pradhāna-vāda in the materialist tradition of Indian philosophy is to most of its modern interpreters an atrocious distortion of fact. But the real reason for such an attitude is not the nature of these philosophies but a huge heap of intellectual debris that has somehow accumulated in the name of Indian philosophy. The resulting situation is so ridiculous that even the question whether an atomist is basically a materialist or not becomes highly controversial in the context of traditional Indian philosophy. Not that such debris cannot be cleared away. What is needed for the purpose, however, is the scope of a full-length study. This I have attempted elsewhere, which has led me to view the Indian materialist tradition as being represented mainly by three philosophies, the Lokāyata, Sāṃkhya and Nyāya-Vaiśeṣika.

7

BUDDHISM

DONALD H. BISHOP

I INTRODUCTION

It is impossible to deal fully with Buddhism in a single essay. I shall discuss, therefore, only some of its major doctrines, emphasizing the views attributed to Buddha especially, and later developments in Buddhist thought. Buddha was born in 563 B.C. near Kapilāvatthu, one hundred miles north of Banaras. Unusual events supposedly occurred at his birth. The blind received their sight. The deaf and dumb spoke. The lame walked. Angles rejoiced. Malevolent beings became kind. Peace reigned. Only Māra "was grieved and rejoiced not."[1]

Buddha's father, a rajah of the Śākya tribe, named his son Siddhārtha, Gautama being the family name. Siddhārtha means "wish-fulfilling", as Gautama fulfilled his father's wish for a son. Gautama is sometimes referred to as Śākyamuni, the "Sage of the Śākyas." Buddha, the "Enlightened One", is called also the Tathāgata, "one who has trodden" the path to Truth and can report to others what he has found.[2]

Warned by a sage that his son would become a ruler or mendicant, Buddha's father surrounded Gautama with princely luxury. Given a beautiful maiden, a son was born to them; all to no avail, however, for nothing could satisfy Buddha's inner restlessness. One day, journeying through the city, Buddha first saw a man crippled by old age. Subsequently he observed a man emaciated from fever, a corpse being carried to the cremation grounds, and finally a wandering mendicant of calm and serene composure. Determined to forsake all he had, Buddha returned to the palace and undertook the "Great Renunciation" that very night. After a last look at his sleeping wife and son, Buddha left with Channa his charioteer. The Yakkhas (heavenly helpers) raised the feet of his horse so they made no sound.

The palace gates opened and Buddha passed through unnoticed. At the edge of the city, Buddha bade Channa farewell and entered the forest.

Hoping to gain enlightenment, Buddha spent the next six years in self-mortification. Near Bodh-Gayā he met five ascetics. Fasting until near death, Buddha saw that it was to no avail. Leaving the ascetics he determined to gain enlightenment through meditation. For seven weeks he sat under a sacred pipal tree at Gayā while, according to legend, Māra attacked and tempted him. His army cast their weapons at Buddha. Māra's daughters danced and tempted him. He was promised all heavenly and earthly kingdoms. But Gautama was unhurt and unmoved. At the end of the seventh week, he arrived at the four noble truths and gained enlightenment. Overcoming all desires, he attained Nirvāṇa. He became the Buddha, the Tathāgata, the Exalted One.

Buddha's enlightenment presumably occurred in 528 B.C. His first converts were the five ascetics. Thus began the Saṅgha, the Buddhist monastic order. For forty years Buddha travelled and preached, gathering many followers. In his eightieth year, journeying to Kuśinagara with his cousin and close disciple Ānanda, he felt the end near. As he rested on the banks of the Hiraṇyavatī, word spread that his death was imminent and many followers gathered. After reminding them of the truths he had preached, Buddha drew Ānanda to him, saying, "Do not weep, do not despair, O Ānanda. From all that he loves man must part. All things are perishable; work out your deliverance with earnestness."[3] Thus ended the Buddha's earthly existence.

II The Four Noble Truths

Buddha's central teaching is the four noble truths. They are that there is suffering (dukkha), suffering has a cause, suffering can be overcome, the eightfold path is the means of doing so.

That suffering is universal is a fact of experience. Birth is painful and death is commonly looked upon with dread. Few are exempt from sorrow and disappointment. The four horsemen of the Apocalypse (war, conquest, famine, death) forever ride the earth. In Buddhist literature the parable of the Mustard Seed illustrate the universality of suffering. Kisā Gotamī, grief-stricken at the death of her son soon after birth, carried her child to her neighbours, seeking help. None could aid her and finally she was sent to Buddha. Asking for medicine, Buddha requested her to bring a handful of mustard seed from a house, however, in which the death of a child, parent or friend had never occurred. Hurrying from one to another Kisā found a ready supply of mustard seed but none from a house in which death had been absent.

As darkness fell, she sat down weary and helpless. Looking at the flickering lights of the city, the thought came to her, "How selfish am I in my grief. Death is common to all, yet in this valley of desolation there is a path that leads him to immortality who has surrendered all selfishness."[4] As dawn approached, her son's body was buried in the forest and Kisā returned to Buddha in whom she found refuge and comfort.

The second noble truth is that suffering is a result not of chance but specifiable causes. It comes, Buddha declared, from man's cravings, desires, thirst, attachment and ignorance. Men crave power, wealth and fame. They hanker after material things, vainly believing they will bring happiness. Cravings stimulate greed, jealousy and anger which breeds deceit and violence. Men thirst for sensual pleasures. Once attached to such delights, their lives become indulgent and mis-spent. Suffering results also from ignorance of the true nature of reality, the self and the effects of one's actions. Man's condition and Buddha's response is movingly described in the Upāsaka Sīla sūtra.

> "The Enlightened One, because he saw mankind drowning in the great sea of birth, death and sorrow, and longed to save them, for this he was moved to pity.... Because he saw them doing evil with hand, heart and tongue, and many times receiving the bitter fruits of sin, yet ever yielding to their desires.... Because he saw them afraid of birth, old-age and death, yet still pursuing the works that lead to birth, old-age and death. Because he saw them living in a time of wars, killing and wounding one another, and how that for the riotous hatred that had flourished in their hearts they were doomed to pay an endless retribution, for this he was moved to pity."[5]

The third truth, based on the principle of cause and effect or dependent origination is that suffering can be caused to cease. It has a determinable solution as well as cause. Buddha believed strongly that reality is inter-related and interdependent. Event *B* occurs as a result of the prior event *A*. Just as an act of suffering is due to a previous cause, so it can be overcome by a subsequent act or chain of events.

The fourth noble truth declares the way of overcoming suffering to be the eightfold path (mārga). The first step on the way is right views. Men must separate truth from falsehood when dealing with such questions as the nature of man, reality, right and wrong, death and immortality. The most important view or truth to be grasped, the Buddhist declares, is the rightness of the four noble truths.

The second step is right resolve. Once knowing the truth, one must resolve to practise it. The devotee should begin with himself and steadfastly shape his life in light of the truths discovered. He will renounce attachment, not have ill feelings and refrain from harming anyone. Right speech is the third step, for "wrong speaking" brings great harm to all concerned. The Dhammapada states: "If a man speaks or acts with an evil thought, pain follows him as the wheel follows the foot of the ox that draws the carriage."[6] Right speech means not slandering or vilifying another as Buddha pointed out in the well-known "Sermon on Abuse".[7]

The fourth step is right conduct. Thinking and talking are incomplete without action. "Like a beautiful flower, full of colour, but without scent, are the fine but fruitless words of him who does not act accordingly," the Dhammapada states.[8] Right resolution must evolve into right speech and conduct. What is right conduct? The Buddhist's answer is the five vows to abstain from destroying life, from theft, fornication, lying and drunkenness.

Right livelihood as the fifth step involves earning one's living by honest means. Further, a Buddhist should not engage in work which leads to harming or taking life. Buddha's exhortation to king Pasenadi offers a general rule of right livelihood: "Exalt not thyself by tramping down others...."[9] Similarly the Udanavarga states: "Hurt not others with that which pains yourself."[10] Any livelihood which debases and cheapens life or which leads to using others for one's own ends is to be rejected.

Right efforts is the sixth step. One meaning of right is constant—"...constant endeavour to maintain moral progress by banishing evil thoughts and entertaining good ones."[11] Continuous effort is needed to reach one's goal. The worthwhile requires effort to be realized. One must not be diverted by trivialities or fall back for lack of effort. Right mindfulness, the seventh step, means constantly keeping in mind what one should do and the goals set for oneself. Buddha aptly pointed out: "As rain breaks through an ill-thatched house, passion will break through an unreflecting mind. As rain does not break through a well-thatched house, passion will not break through a well-reflecting mind."[12] Buddha declared the seventh step important because "Creatures from mind their character derive, mind marshalled are they, mind-made. Mind is the source either of bliss or corruption."[13] The kind of thought determines the kind of character and the quality of a person's life.

Right concentration, the eighth step, is a more intense form of right mindfulness. It involves fixed concentration on the five meditations on love, pity, joy, impurity and serenity pointed out by Buddha. Right concentration is a sorting out process in which the insignificant is discarded and good and evil and truth and falsehood are seen for what they are. Concentration perfects one's wisdom and virtue. It is likened to the fourth Jñāna (state of mind) Buddha discussed with a disciple wherein purity and peace is attained.[14]

The four noble truths provide both a goal and means of reaching it. Buddha often referred to the eightfold path as the "Middle Way" between the excesses of self-indulgence and mortification. He declared the truths were neither divinely revealed nor the voice of priestly authority, but the product of reason and experience. Their verification lay in their being practised. The goal and means are available to all: "My doctrine is like unto the heavens, for there is room in it for the reception of all, for men and women, boys and girls, the powerful and the lowly."[15]

To Buddha the four noble truths are the way to break fetters and overcome saṃsāra (rebirth). Their practice would purify the individual and purge the world of evil. They emphasize self-responsibility. They are concerned with Dharma (righteousness). They accept the Anātman view of the self, view reality in terms of Karma and are grounded in the doctrine of Anicca (impermanence), topics which we shall turn to now.

III Ethics

The term Dharma is used by Buddhists in several senses—religious, metaphysical, ethical and legal. Its ethical import will be dealt with here. Buddha's ethical teachings may be analysed in terms of five questions: What is the good? Why do the good? What are the grounds of the good? How is the good achieved? How is evil to be dealt with?

As to the first, one answer is that Buddha associated the good with a set of attitudes—love (mettā), compassion (karuṇā), sympathy and joy (muditā), impartiality (upekkhā) and forgiveness (khanti).[16] The goal is to make them so much a part of one's self that one acts unconsciously in terms of them when making moral choices. Another answer is that Buddha associated evil with desires, pleasures and passions as seen in his statement: "not nakedness, no platted hair, nor dirt, nor fasting...nor sitting motionless can purify a mortal who has not overcome desires."[17] How does one deal with them? One answer is found in Buddha's exhortation to "cut down the whole forest of desires, not a tree only."[18] Desires are to be eradicated completely. A modification is presented in another passage: "The love of pleasure begets grief and the dread of pain causes fear."[19] One is reminded of the biblical injunction that "The love of money is the root of all evil...",[20] the answer being in both cases that desires or wealth are not bad in themselves.

In the second alternative Buddha is enjoining the principle of selectivity. Certain pleasure can be legitimately enjoyed up to a certain degree. Being joyful at the good fortune of another is surely admissable; delighting in another's misfortune is not. Eating to meet bodily needs is permissible; indulging to the state of gluttony is not. As Buddha said: "To satisfy the necessities of life is not evil. To keep the body in good health is a duty, for otherwise we shall not be able to trim the lamp of wisdom, and keep our mind strong and clear."[21]

The English philosopher, John Stuart Mill, also advocated a qualified hedonism. He distinguished between physical and mental pleasures, advocating the latter for their greater permanency. Buddha used the same criterion: "There is no satisfying lusts, even by a shower of gold pieces; he who knows that lusts have a short taste and cause pain, he is wise."[22] The Roman Stoic Epictitus advised selectivity also: "It is a mark of a mean capacity to spend much time on the things common to the body, such as much exercise, much eating, much drinking, much easing of the body, much copulation. These things should be done as subordinate things; let all your care be directed to the mind."[23]

Buddha associated the good with avoiding the extremes of self-indulgence and mortification. From his own experience he said: "What is that middle path, O bhikkhus, avoiding these two extremes, discovered by the Tathāgata—that path which opens the eyes, and bestows understanding, which leads to peace of mind, to the higher wisdom, to full enlightenment, to Nirvāṇa?...Let me teach you, O bhikkhus, the middle path....By suffering the emaciated devotee produces sickly thoughts in his mind. Mortification is not conducive even to worldly knowledge; how much less to a triumph over the senses."[24]

While Nirvāṇa is the end of moderation, freedom is the result noted in another statement: "He who lives for pleasures only, his senses uncontrolled, immoderate in his food, idle and weak, him Māra will certainly overthrow, as the wind throws down a weak tree. He who lives without looking for pleasures, his sense well-controlled, moderate in his food, faithful and strong, him Māra will certainly not overthrow...."[25] Moderation and control makes one free through avoiding the tyranny of extremes.

Aristotle's comparable statement on moderation is interesting: "By goodness I mean goodness of moral character, since it is moral goodness that deals with feelings and actions, and it is in them that we find excess, deficiency and a mean. It is possible, for example, to experience fear, boldness, desire, anger, pity and pleasures and pains generally, too much or too little or to the right amount. If we feel them too much or too little, we are wrong. But to have these feelings at the right times on the right occasions towards the right people for the right motive and in the right way is to have them in the right measure, that is somewhere between the extremes; and this is what characterizes goodness."[26]

Among other items regarding the nature of the good is Buddha's linking of virtue with self-denial and evil with self-assertion: "...there is no wrong in this world, no vice, no evil, except what flows from the assertion of self" and "...there is no evil but what flows from self. There is no wrong but what is done by the assertion of self."[27] Buddha correlated self-denial with sharing and self-giving, while self-assertion stems from selfishness and gives rise to anxiety and an exploitative attitude towards reality. Self-denial enables a person to centre his life around that which is other and greater than himself. In the Mahāyāna tradition the Bodhisattva personifies the ideal of self-renunciation, for he refrains from entering Nirvāṇa in order to aid others to reach it.

Buddha also associated the good with the universal. He replied to two young Brāhmaṇas: "The Tathāgata lets his mind pervade the four quarters of the world with thoughts of love. And thus the whole wide world, above, below, around and everywhere will continue to be filled with love, far-reaching, grown great, and beyond measure."[28] A Buddhist wrote in the Discourse on Loving-kindness: "Even as a mother would cherish her only child with her life, even thus towards all beings let him cultivate a boundless heart. Let him cultivate above, below and all around boundless love towards all the world, unhindered, without anger, without enmity."[29] A contemporary Buddhist also associates the good with the universal in his characterization of mettā and karuṇā: "They banish selfishness and disharmony and promote altruism, unity and brotherhood. They are thoughts to be cultivated towards all beings irrespective of race, caste, colour, community, creed, East or West, and therefore they are known as boundless states, for they are not limited, are not confined to watertight compartments. They unfold all beings without any partiality or grading according to rank, quality, position, power, learning, value and so on which keep men apart."[30]

In regard to love, for example, the Buddhist teaching is, then, that real love must be all inclusive. That person does not truly love whose love is limited to his own group, nation or race. Such love the Buddhist would call pema in contrast to mettā. It is partial and selfish rather than universal and unselfish.

Buddha's statements "Neither for one's own nor for others' sake should one do any evil; one should not covet a son, wealth, or a kingdom, nor wish to succeed by unjust means; such a man is indeed virtuous, wise and righteous" show his concern for the problem of means and ends. It is a continuing one, as the eighth-century poet Śāntideva wrote: "It is not desirable for me to obtain something, if the necessary action involves a moral obstacle to acquiring it; my acquiring will vanish here, but my evil will remain steadfast."[31]

Using evil means and seeking evil ends is contrary to common morality. Many, however, are tempted to believe that evil means can be justified by good ends. This Buddha disavowed. Only good means may be used to reach good ends. The reasons? A major one no doubt is that means and ends are inextricable and mutually influence each other.

In response to the question "Why do the good?" the Buddhist

oes not deny the Hindu's motive enjoined in the Gītā of doing the ood for its own sake. In a Buddhist sūtra of the New Wisdom chool we read: "Friendliness means to have hopes for the welfare of thers, to long for it, to crave for it, to delight in it. It is affection nsullied by the motives of sense-desire, passion or hope of a eturn."[32] The Buddhist would reinforce such idealism with ragmatism. Buddha said that one should see "evil as evil and e disgusted with it." When we see evil for what it really is, we oath it because we realize the untold human suffering evil brings bout. Evil is rejected because of its results, just as the good is ccepted for the same reason.

Buddha did not accept punishment and rewards as sufficient notives either, for he believed the stimulus for virtue must come from vithin. Rewards are impermanent. The recipient is happy when ewarded and miserable when not. Thus his state of being is dependent on what is external to him and he is not free. Once a person ealizes this, he will give up a rewards motivation.

Doing good "spontaneously" would surely be acceptable to Buddha, spontaneously not meaning thoughtlessly but rather because, as mentioned earlier, of the right attitudes being deeply ingrained in one. We are reminded of Epictitus' statement: "As he sun does not wait for prayers and incantations to be induced to ise, but immediately shines and is saluted by all, so do you also ot wait for the clapping of hands, and shouts and praise to be nduced to do good, but be a doer of good voluntarily, and you will e loved as much as the sun."[33] A spontaneous ethics takes into ccount effects but not rewards. It enables one to transcend thical dualism, the giving up of the thought of "both victory and lefeat", the going beyond both good and evil.

Buddha was concerned especially about rooting out all selfish notives. Even a good deed done from a selfish intent cannot be leemed truly good. The Bodhisattva, as an example, is to perform he ten Dharmas: "...with a heart disinterested and free from any hought of gain" and "may, as a result of this meritorious action, all eings be born unstained by the impurities of the womb."[34] Such omplete self-giving is possible only when selfish motives are absent ntirely.

One answer to "What is the grounds of the good?" is found in Buddha's statement to Anthapindika: "Let us abandon the heresy f worshipping Īśvara, let us no longer lose ourselves in vain speculations...; let us surrender self and all selfishness, and as all thing are fixed by causation, let us practise good so that good may resu from our actions."[35]

By causation Buddha meant the principle of Karma. Every dee has an effect; moreover the effect is like the deed. Good deeds hav good effects, evil deeds evil effects. Acknowledging Karma unde cuts any rewards motive. One does the good realizing it is inevitab that good acrue both for oneself and others but not because such goo results. Karma and rewards are easily confused. For exampl Christ's statements, "Blessed are the meek, for they shall inherit th earth" and "Blessed are the merciful for they shall obtain mercy", a rewards-oriented person might interpret, "My reward for bein merciful will be to gain mercy for myself and so I shall be merciful etc." However, from a Karma interpretation, all Jesus is pointin out is the irrefractable truth that mercy gives rise to mercy.

As to the fourth question of how the good is achieved, the Hīnayān tradition especially emphasizes "achieved". The good is the resul of long, unceasing effort and not the gift of a gracious Deity. "H who does not rouse himself when it is time to rise; who, though youn and strong, is full of sloth...that lazy and idle man will never fin the way to Enlightenment," the Dhammapada states.[37]

Moreover Buddha emphasized starting with oneself: "The fault o others is easily noticed but that of oneself is difficult to perceive A man winnows his neighbour's faults like chaff, but his own h hides, as a cheat hides the false die from the gambler."[38] W are reminded of the Hindu Purāṇas' statement: "The vile are eve prone to detect the faults of others, though they be as small a mustard seeds, and persistently shut their eyes against their own though they be as large as Vilva fruits."[39]

According to Buddha self-control is the means of achieving th good: "Let a wise man blow off the impurities of his self, as a smit blows off the impurities of silver, one by one, little by little, and fron time to time;"[40] "Restraint in the eye is good, good is restraint i the ear...good is restraint in the tongue...;"[41] "If some conquer i battle a thousand times a thousand men, and if another conque himself, he is the greatest of conquerors."[42] Self-control is no eas task: "Bad deeds, and deeds hurtful to ourselves, are easy to do what is beneficial and good, that is very difficult."[43] The results ar far-reaching however: "He who overcomes the fierce thirst, difficul to be conquered in this world, sufferings fall off from him, like wate rops from a lotus leaf."[44]

Buddha believed that "Self is the lord of self, who else could be ne Lord?"[45] Each is both his own master and responsible for imself: "By oneself evil is done; by oneself one suffers; by oneself vil is left undone; by oneself one is purified. Purity and impurity elong to oneself; no one can purify another."[46] Through his eeds one builds up good or bad Karma. Original Buddhism was nodified as it came into contact with non-Indian cultures. Pure and Buddhism in China was less individualistic, emphasizing he infinite love and compassion of Amitābha Buddha who saves hose who call on him in faith. Work and self-effort is supplemented y Amitābha's grace, whether for achieving the good or Nirvāṇa.

As to how to deal with evil, Buddhism and Hinduism reinforce ach other. Buddha and his followers emphasized the returning of ood for evil. It is the theme of the popular story by Buddha of Prince Dīrghāyu.[47] The Dhammapada states: "He who carries ut his purpose by violence is not therein righteous,"[48] and, "Let a nan overcome anger by love, let him overcome evil by good."[49] n his sermon at Rājagṛiha Buddha said: "Yea, cherish good-will ight and left, all round, early and late, and without hindrance, without stint... the rule of life that's always best is to be loving kind."[50]

Loving-kindness is to be expressed in thought, word and deed. Buddha's insistence that one love enemy as well as friend as the real est of Mettā and Karuṇā is reflected in the ninth of his ten precepts: "Cleanse your heart of malice and cherish no hatred, not even gainst your enemies;...embrace all living beings with kindness."[51] Śāntideva wrote similarly: "It is undesirable that there be sorrow, humiliation, reproach or disgrace for one's loved ones or oneself or, even contrawise for one's enemy."[52]

The universal love Buddha urged has patience, forbearance, endurance and forgiveness as a prerequisite. One should have the patience of the elephant, the Awakened One, and the Brahmin, and one should forgive as the Bodhisattva does.[53] Buddhists offer several vindications for love of enemy as well as friend. Buddha himself exemplified such. Secondly, it is practical for, as Buddha said: "Hatred does not cease by hatred at any time; hatred ceases by not-hatred...," and, "Conquer your foe by force, you increase his enmity. Conquer by love, and you will reap no after-sorrow."[54] Force begets force and love begets love. Thus the law of Karma justifies universal love.

Furthermore, returning evil for evil only increases rather tha diminishes the total amount of evil in the world: "Do ye think tha ye can destroy wrong by retaliating evil for evil and thus increasin wrong?"[55] Buddha also declared a person should not let his action be determined by others. If he does, he is no longer free and maste of himself: "Let us live happily then, not hating those who hate us... Among men who are greedy let us dwell free from greed."[56] Lov frees while hatred binds. A contemporary Buddhist writes: "Hat restricts; love releases. Hatred strangles; love enfranchises ...Hatred agitates; love quietens, stills, calms. Hatred divides love unites."[57] Love of enemy is a means of self-purification an freedom. Aśvaghoṣa, the Buddhist poet, wrote in the first centur A. D.: "If ill-will or the desire to hurt others should stir in you mind, purify it again with its opposite, which will act on it like wishing jewel in muddied water. Friendliness and compassio are their antidotes."[58]

The concept of suffering love, found in Mahāyāna Buddhisn especially, is a further justification for loving universally. Th Bodhisattva as the prototype of such love takes upon himself th wrongs of mankind. Out of love for man he pays the penalty fo such wrongs, so that he to whom the wrong is done need not requit the wrong-doing. Thus we read in the sūtras: "A Bodhisattv resolves: I will take upon myself the burden of all suffering....I hav made the vow to save all beings....The whole world of living being I must rescue from the terrors of birth, old age, sickness, death an rebirth, of all kinds of moral offence....I must give myself away a a pawn through which the whole world is redeemed."[59] Th similarity to the Suffering-Servant and the Messiah in the Judai and Christian traditions in the West is obvious.

In ethics a necessary distinction is between the real and th ideal. This analysis has dealt mainly with the ideal Buddha se forth. Buddhists have found it difficult to live up to, just as Chris tians have the Christian or Confucianists the Confucian ideal The failure to do so in each instance does not invalidate the ideal however.

Buddha was both an ethical realist and optimist. He admitte the world is full of hatred and injustice. He believed also that i need not be so necessarily. Buddha's was a humanist's ethics o self-realization as was Aristotle's who wrote: "We ought not to liste to those who counsel us 'O man, think as man should and O mortal remember your mortality'. Rather ought we, so far as in us lies, to put on immortality and to leave nothing unattempted in the effort to live in conformity with the highest thing within us."[60]

Buddha believed that to act compassionately is to act most highly. He believed man's natural response to suffering is compassion; an unnatural selfishness leads him often to react otherwise. Rousseau's concept of the "Noble Savage" is a western parallel. Man in his natural state is good but civilization corrupts him by stirring up egoistic and selfish tendencies. The twentieth-century emphasis on "objectivity" brings the same result. Compassion as the highest virtue leads to inner and thus true freedom. Though unrestrained externally, a person is not free if he is a slave of his passions. Buddha associated the good with the universal and unconditional. To practise love to all was Buddha's "categorical imperative", to use a Kantian term. Hate is like all limited and conditional things which the author of the Multitude of Graceful Actions describes as "...empty and powerless...conditioned by ignorance, and on final analysis does not exist...."[61]

Buddha's is an "attitudinal" ethics in that he emphasizes right attitudes. Thus it is also an inner-oriented ethics in that virtue must come from within and not be prompted from without. His is a non-legalistic ethics also, for Buddha did not emphasize extensive moral rules, laws or regulations. If right attitudes are truly a part of one, they will tell a person what to do. An attitudinal ethics enable Buddha to escape ethical relativism. For he would claim that such positive attitudes as love, compassion and forgiveness are universally applicable. They will work everywhere whether practised by an Indian, German, American, Russian or Chinese.

Finally, ethics was important to Buddha because he believed a person's worth depends on his character, not wealth, intelligence or place in society. So we find Buddha saying: "A man does not become a Brāhmaṇa by his platted hair, by his family, or by birth; in whom there is truth and righteousness, he is blessed, he is a Brāhmaṇa."[62] Similarly, a contemporary Buddhist asserts: "Rank, caste, colour and even wealth and power cannot necessarily make a man a person of value to the world. Only his character makes a man great and worthy of honour."[63]

IV The Self

Buddha once said to a group of disciples: "Cleanse yourselves of evil and sanctify your lives. Learn to distinguish between self and truth."[64] What is the "Truth" Buddha referred to? It is the Anātman doctrine that there is no absolute self or entity such as a soul which continues from one existence to another.

The Anātman view is well known and there is no need to discuss it at length here. Suffice it to say that Buddha believed the self is a temporary collection of five entities, an impermanent aggregate of form, feelings, perceptions, dispositions and consciousness. The self, Buddha told the Brahmin Kutadanta, is like all compound things which "...are transitory; they grow and decay." Does nothing continue on? Yes, Karma, the effects, good or bad, of our deeds, Buddha replied. Buddha's view is found in one of his sermons:

> "Paradoxical though it may sound: There is a path to walk on, there is walking being done, but there is no traveller. There are deeds being done, but there is no doer. There is a blowing of the air, but there is no wind that does the blowing. The thought of self is an error and all existences are as hollow as the plantain tree and as empty as twirling water bubbles. Therefore, O bhikkhus, as there is no self, there is not transmigration of a self; but there are deeds and the continued effect of deeds. There is a rebirth of Karma; there is reincarnation. This rebirth, this reincarnation, this reappearance of the conformations is continuous and depends on the law of cause and effect. Just as a seal is impressed upon the wax reproducing the configurations of its device, so the thoughts of men, their characters, their aspirations are impressed upon others in continuous transference and continue their Karma, and good deeds will continue in blessings while bad deeds will continue in curses.
>
> There is no entity here that migrates, no self is transferred from one place to another; but there is a voice uttered here and the echo of it comes back."[65]

Buddha justified his Anātman view primarily on pragmatic grounds. Its acceptance would lead to true religious practice. On observing worship in a temple Buddha declared: "Rituals have no efficacy; prayers are vain repetitions; and incantations have no saving ɔwer. But to abandon covetousness and lust, to become free from ·il passions and to give up hatred and ill-will, that is the right .crifice and the true worship."[66] It would facilitate rooting out :lfishness for "Self is the cause of selfishness and the source of evil."[67] : would lead to an attitude of non-attachment. The Charmasangiti ūtra states: "He who maintains the doctrine of Emptiness is not llured by the things of the world...." The same sūtra points out quanimity of mind as another result: "He is not excited by gain r dejected by loss." Purity of motive is stimulated also as there is o self to be rewarded: "Fame does not dazzle him...praise does ot attract him. Pleasure does not please him, pain does not trouble im."[68] A contemporary western Buddhist sums up the three results ·hen he writes that Buddhism teaches "life is not a situation from ·hich there is anything to be grasped or gained."[69]

Furthermore, if there is no absolute self, there is no ego to be efended when attacked or honour to be upheld when insulted. 'hus non-violence is more apt to be chosen. Unity with one's fellow-ıen is more likely, as self-pride does not get in the way. Openness nd communication are present when pride is absent. Finally, ıe attaining of Nirvāṇa is a major result of accepting the Anātman octrine. Salvation is gained when the I is lost.

A further aspect of Buddha's view of man is his belief in the neness of mankind, reflected in his statement to Kutananda: True wisdom can be acquired by practice only. Practise the ·uth that thy brother is the same as thou."[70] Others are subject › transitoriness like ourselves: "Thy self to which thou cleavest a constant change. Years ago thou wast a small babe; then, ıou wast a boy; then a youth, and now thou art a man."[71] Ioreover all experience similar joys and sorrow: "All men tremble t punishment, all fear death; remember that you are like unto them, nd do not kill, nor cause slaughter."[72] In addition all have the ame end; the Buddhist calls it Nirvāṇa, the Christian Heaven.

Mahāyāna Buddhism's emphasis on the metaphysical grounds of ıan's oneness is reflected in the Neo-Confucianist Chang Tsai's tatement: "Heaven is my father and earth is my mother, and even uch a small creature as I finds an intimate place in their midst. 'herefore that which extends throughout the universe I regard as ıy body and that which directs the universe I consider my nature. ll people are my brothers and sisters, and all things are my ompanions."[73] The contemporary D. T. Suzuki states similarly:

"When the clouds of ignorance are dispersing...we perceive tha our individual existences are like bubbles and lightnings, but tha they obtain reality in their oneness with the Body of Dharma."[74]

Philosophers of other traditions support Buddha's view of man' oneness. Mencius wrote that "The sense of mercy is found in a. men; the sense of shame is found in all men; the sense of respect.. the sense of right and wrong is found in all men."[75] Cicero state that "No single thing is so like another, so exactly its counterpar as all of us are to one another....The similarity of the human rac is clearly marked in its evil tendencies as well as in its goodness... Troubles, joys, desires and fears haunt the minds of all men withou distinction...."[76] The English clergyman John Donne wrote "No man is an island unto himself; every man is a piece of th continent, a part of the main,"[77] and Montesquieu asserted: " I knew something useful to my nation which would be ruinous t another, I would not propose it to my prince, because I am a ma before I am a Frenchman, or because I am necessarily a man, an only by chance a Frenchman."[78]

Buddhism also conceives of the individual as an end in himsel not a means. Hajime Nakamura notes that "Early Buddhis writings and other doctrines urge everyone to pay respect to other at all times."[79] To treat others merely as means is to deny thei inherent dignity and worth. By treating persons as ends i themselves Buddha placed human over material values. Person are not things or objects to be owned or manipulated as one pleases Using people as means leads to suffering and is the result of not havin given up cravings. We desire possessions, power and fame an willingly use people to attain them.

Buddha's belief in the essential goodness of man is one reason fo his refusal to treat others as means. Man is not mired in sin, unabl to save himself, a view of nineteenth-century orthodox Christia missionaries eastern people found revolting. Buddha is said to hav had "...the same sentiments for the high as well as the low, for th wise as well as the ignorant, for the noble-minded as for th immoral."[80] The Japanese Buddhist, Gitsuza Ashitsu stated a the 1893 Parliament of Religions "We ordinary beings are also calle Risoku Buddha, or beings with the nature of Buddha" and Banrie Yatsubuchi declared "...all beings have the nature of Buddhahoo ...the only difference between Buddha and all other beings is i point of supreme enlightenment."[81]

V Metaphysics

To the Buddhist the individual is a microcosm of the universe for it, like the self, constantly changes. According to the doctrine of Anicca, experienced reality is in constant transformation: "There is no inner and immutable core in things, everything is in flux. Existence for the Buddhist is momentary, unique and unitary."[82] Professor Burtt states of Buddha: "What is basic in this area of his thought is that all forms of phenomenal existence, including living creatures, are in constant change and must in time perish."[83] Buddha declared that "All created things perish. . . . All forms are unreal—he who knows and sees this is at peace though in a world of pain; this is the way that leads to purity."[84]

Buddha's might be called a "process" rather than "substance" view of reality. From the latter standpoint reality is characterized by concreteness, definiteness, continuity of structure and identity, or an unchanging substratum enduring forever. To the Buddhist, however, just as the self is "a stream of cognitions . . . a series of successive mental and bodily processes which are impermanent,"[85] so the world "is a number of accidents ever changing and being renewed at every breath and each moment disappearing, only to be replaced by a similar set."[86]

What, then, is permanent, if anything? Buddha answers the law of Karma. Metaphysically Karma refers to Cause and Effect or Dependent Origination found in Buddha's statement: "I will teach you the dharma that being present, this becomes; from the arising of that, this arises. That being absent, this does not become; from the cessation of that, this ceases;"[87] or "Every existence is organic, and the substance of its existence is a continuity of changes, each of which is absolutely determined by pre-existing conditions."[88] Both metaphysical and moral continuity was explained by Buddha using several analogies—the seal and the wax, the lute and its sounds, candles and their flames, the chariot and its parts. The figure of the wheel and its twelve Nidānas is used especially often in Buddhist teaching to illustrate the concepts of causation, change and rebirth.

Buddha rejected two traditional explanations of reality emphasizing permanence and impermanence and proposed instead the Anātman and Anicca doctrines, described by a contemporary as having "both a metaphysical and moral advantage, because they avoid the tyranny of eternalism and the hopelessness of nihilism."[8] Buddha believed his middle way would lighten the dead hand of the past and avoid the emptiness of nothingness. At the same time moral endeavour in this existence would bear fruit in the next.

To avoid the extremes of being and non-being Buddha emphasized the concept of becoming: "There is neither being nor non-being but becoming." The change experienced reality is undergoing constantly is not random or directionless but purposive. Everything has in it the possibility of becoming what it has not yet been but nonetheless can be. What others called the soul in man was for Buddha this capacity for becoming or for transformation on successively higher levels. That the concept of becoming was both infinitely relevant and liberating to the people of Buddha's day is averred by a contemporary: "It would be impossible to recapture or state the deep reaction of gratitude and hope with which people in India must have first received the message of Buddha. To learn that the miseries of life need not be; that one's history or past could not doom one to eternal suffering; that regardless of one's place or condition one could, by one's own efforts and intelligence, achieve freedom: what a sense of liberation and hope this must have generated among vast numbers of people!"[90]

A significant statement of Buddha's is: "All things are made of one essence, yet things are different according to the forms which they assume under different impressions.... Nirvāṇa comes to thee, Kassapa, when thou understandest thoroughly, and when thou livest according to thy understanding that all things are of one essence and that there is but one law."[91] Undoubtedly, Buddha is referring to the law of Karma, whose universality he is asserting. Nothing or no one is exempt from it. As to the "one essence", is Buddha advocating a metaphysical monism in keeping with the trend toward such at his time? Ch'en writes "Finally, the idea arose that the various gods were but different aspects and different names of the same supreme being. This monotheistic trend was to culminate in the Upanishads, which expounded the view that behind the diversities of the phenomenal world...there stands one absolute unity, the supreme Brahma."[92]

A metaphysical monism enables the Buddhist to not dichotomize cause and effect but view them as two aspects of the same reality. Cause becomes effect; that effect in turn becomes cause, etc. Means and ends cannot be separated sharply either; they are two parts of a whole. Buddha was reluctant to discuss metaphysical questions at length, believing them to be unanswerable ultimately, although pragmatic reasons could be given for choosing one alternative over another. In terms of the above quotes Buddha evidently rejected metaphysical dualism and taught a combined monism and pluralism. There is one universal from which all particulars spring. He did not set monism and pluralism in a theistic context however.

The implications for human reality of another statement of Buddha's from the same source is interesting: "As all things originate from one essence, so they are developing according to one law and they are destined to one aim which is Nirvāṇa."[93] A major one would be a monistic view of mankind as a brotherhood of innumerable individuals acting under the law of cause and effect, going on to an identical goal, Nirvāṇa. Here is the metaphysical basis for the oneness of man discussed earlier. Buddha recognized the practical need for such a brotherhood as the period in which Buddha lived "... was one of radical social readjustment and deepening religious need. Wars were frequent between the petty princes and rival clans in Northern India, and the organization of society was moving more and more in the direction of a rigid caste system."[94]

One pragmatic justification Buddha offered for his metaphysical views was that acknowledging the inevitable cause-effect relationship would make us more sensitive to our actions setting up a long chain of undesirable results. This is especially appropriate in our increasingly inter-dependent world today for whenever "... the egoistic values of one man or a few men are imposed on a multitude ... tenacious attachment to the ego can lead to disaster on a wide scale."[95] Accepting the principle of Karma would make us more conscious of self-responsibility in the moral realm also, as already indicated. Accepting the Anicca doctrine would have beneficial inner and external results: "All created things perish—he who knows and sees this is at peace though in a world of pain; this is the way to purity.... The world does not know that we must all come to an end here; those who know it, their quarrels cease at once."[96]

The acceptance of change would make one less apt to stubbornly uphold the social, political and economic status quo, especially if he is benefitting from it at others' expense. Detachment, would be easier, since there is nothing permanent one can own or be attached to. A good summary of the pragmatic results of the Buddhist metaphysical view is:

"The doctine of universal change, whether or not it is the whole truth about the world, is humanistically useful in opening up the possibility for men to change themselves. Similarly, the doctrine that the soul does not exist, while in dispute among philosophers, has functioned to facilitate non-egoistic thought, feeling and action; if you really believe that the soul is illusory, or, as in later Buddhism, that your soul is at one with the divine and universal Mind, then you are not apt to lust, drink, lie, cheat, steal, fight, and kill in its behalf. Again, if you believe that the only karma which you carry is the causal law of Dhamma, whereby your present state arises from the conditioning of some past state, then you are simultaneously freed of the yoke of Determinism and the gambling of Chance; you can undertake to change your state with resolution, confidence, and hope. Moreover, the Buddhist doctrine of rebirth, while difficult to understand as the mental or dispositional inheritance that passes from one body to another—save as we inherit our constitutions and hence our temperaments from our parents—has undoubtedly generated in men a deep sense of kinship and communion with all creatures. It has given men a 'world loyalty' and has helped them to feel as 'a humble instrument of the universal power'."[97]

VI Nirvāṇa

Buddha's statement, "...all things are destined to one aim which is Nirvāṇa," has been referred to already. What is Nirvāṇa and how can it be reached? Before replying we should note, as Suzuki points out, that "Nirvāṇa has become a very comprehensive term,"[98] and even Buddha supposedly replied to a questioner, "The term, Nirvāṇa, is used with many different meanings by different people."[99]

Buddhists generally agree that Nirvāṇa is man's ultimate goal. Buddha cautioned his followers: "Your talents may reach to the skies, your wealth may be untold; but all is in vain unless you attain the peace of Nirvāṇa."[100] However, Buddhism and Hinduism differed as to the nature of the goal. As Burtt points out "...the goal of spiritual attainment for Buddhism is not the realization of oneness with Brahman, but entrance into Nirvāṇa."[101] Self-effort is the means of reaching Nirvāṇa. It, like virtue, is a result of one's own actions. The Hīnayāna tradition places greater emphasis on elf-effort while the Mahāyāna offers Amitābha as an aid. Both emphasize mental and physical or sensual purification as prerequisites.

Through the centuries Buddhists have disagreed as to whether Nirvāṇa can be attained here and now. There is general agreement that Buddha did, for he said: "I have recognized the deepest truth.... I myself having reached the other shore, help others to cross the stream...."[102] Thus Buddha became the first of the three places of refuge, the others being the Dharma and Sangha. Contemporary Buddhists reiterate that Nirvāṇa can be attained in this life, Coomaraswamy claiming: "...Nibbana is a state to be realized here and now, and is recorded to have been attained by the Buddha at the beginning of his ministry...."[103] Dharmapala asserted at the 1893 Parliament: "Nirvāṇa is a state to be realized here on this earth. He who has reached the fourth state of holiness consciously enjoys the bliss of Nirvāṇa,"[104] and Suzuki writes that the last of the four forms of Nirvāṇa distinguished by Mahāyānists, "The Nirvāṇa that has no abode,"[105] is the one which can be lived now.

It seems, then, that Nirvāṇa may be reached either in the present or a future existence. Some have in this life for brief periods. Buddha evidently was in such a state constantly after his enlightenment. However, for the great majority, as one author points out, "...a continuous realization of salvation is only thinkable after death."[106] It might be said that, because only a few have but briefly realized Nirvāṇa here and now, does not mean that more could for longer periods. Perhaps what is lacking is sufficient will and effort.

Is Nirvāṇa an actual place or locale? One tendency has been to say no; for, if a Buddhist were to assert there is such, he would have to accept the corollary that there is an absolute self, since such a concept of Nirvāṇa is grounded in the view of reality as substantive. Buddha, however, denied the concept of a substantive self. His reply to a disciple about Nirvāṇa as a place is interesting: "In truth there is such a happy paradise. But the country is spiritual and it is accessible only to those that are spiritual."[107]

A variation developed in the Pure Land School in China with the doctrine of Amitābha and the Western Paradise. Nirvāṇa was associated with the Western Paradise "...created by Amitābha out of his boundless love for all sentient beings."[108] Ch'en pictures the Pure Land concept thus: "Amitābha, or Infinite Light, is the name of the presiding Buddha of the Western Paradise, whic is described as being rich, fertile, comfortable, filled with deitie and men but not with evil modes of existences. It is adorned wit fragrant trees...decorated with the most beautiful jewels and gem Rivers with scented waters give forth musical sounds....Heavenl beings sporting in the water can cause it to become hot or cold... Everywhere one can hear the words of the Buddha, teaching love compassion, sympathetic joy, patience, tolerance....Nowhere doe one meet with anything unpleasant or painful."[109] This concept c Nirvāṇa may exemplify how Buddhism acclimatized itself to natura human longings and to such aspects of Chinese thinking and cultur as its pragmatism and ancestor worship. For the empiricall oriented who tend to associate reality with substantiality, Nirvāṇ would more likely be thought of as an actual place or location others would turn to a different view.

As to whether or not there is complete extinction of the self i Nirvāṇa, it is often pointed out that the term Nirvāṇa means literally, a "blowing out", just as a candle-light is blown out Therāvada Buddhists tend toward such an interpretation an distinguish between Nirvāṇa and Parinirvāṇa. Buddha entered th former at the time of his enlightenment and at death passed int Parinirvana "which means utter extinction—no longer participatin in any desirable form of existence nor, indeed, of non-existence."[11

There are difficulties with the Theravāda view, however, such as the question of moral responsibility. Those who hold th opposite viewpoint to statements of Buddha's like: "Nirvāṇa doe not consist in simple annihilation and vacuity",[111] and Suzuk asserts: "Buddha's characteristic admonition to his disciples not t waste time but to work out their salvation with diligence an vigour" is contrary to the "...gospel of annihilation, the supposedly fundamental teaching of Buddhism."[112] There must be a continua tion of some form; otherwise, why work so diligently?

If the self continues, does it as a specific, separate, identifiabl entity? Pure Land Buddhists would answer yes, for the Pure Lan is itself a place one goes to on attaining Nirvāṇa. Another alter native, however, is to consider Nirvāṇa as a state where one ha become a part of a whole. Regarding this one authority writes "Whereas the Hinayāna thinks of nirvāṇa as the opposite of pheno menal existence, the Mahāyāna considers nirvāṇa to be the cessatior of all discriminations and dualisms and the realization that undifferentiated emptiness is the sole absolute truth. . . . He cannot distinguish himself from any other thing or even from the absoulte, for he has merged into the absolute."[113] Psychologically, Nirvāṇa might be a state of "...absolute surrender of the self to the will of the Dharmakaya,"[114] to use Suzuki's words.

The latter of the two views above minimizes individualism and is compatible with Buddha's views to the extent, at least, that he warned constantly against the evils coming from asserting absolute and separate self-hood. Practically, then, Nirvāṇa is better conceived as a state of "...deliverance from the sense of individuality"[115] in which "one realizes the oneness of all beings", a state of "absolute unity,"[116] the second of the "Eight Stations of Deliverance" where "unaware of one's own external form, one sees forms external to oneself."[117] The extinction of extreme and invidious self-consciousness is a minimum condition of Nirvāṇa. It, like the good, is a result of the giving up rather than asserting of the self.

Buddhists agree that Nirvāṇa is the extinction of the misery and suffering experienced in this life. Further, it is the cessation of becoming or rebirth because the conditions causing rebirth have been destroyed or bad Karma worked off. The problem whether or not there is an extinction of the self in Nirvāṇa is a difficult one for western people especially, as their tradition generally emphasizes reality as substantive and dualistic. Persons of such a background have difficulty visualizing there may be other possibilities than either there is or is not a substantive self. One is that "The ego is not the only content of the self though it is the only content that can be known objectively" or "...it does not follow that there is no self at all..." from the assertion "The self is not body, feeling, consciousness, etc."[118]

Undoubtedly the concept of Nirvāṇa has ethical connotations for Buddhists. It is "...a lasting state of happiness and peace, to be reached here on earth by the extinction of the fires of passions,"[119] not all, only the base ones, however. Selfishness and egoism are alien to Nirvāṇa. Dharmapāla claimed Nirvāṇa is "...beyond the reach of him who is selfish, skeptical, sensual, full of hatred, proud, self-righteous, and ignorant."[120] Buddha's teaching and example are cited when discussing the ethical aspects of Nirvāṇa. He lived a life of moral purity. He taught constantly that "Perfect peace can dwell only where all vanity has disappeared. . . . Blessed is he who overcomes wrong and is free from passion. To the highest bliss has he attained who has conquered all selfishness and vanity."[121] Buddha's thesis is that a person cannot validly claim to be truly religious or to have attained spiritual fulfilment if he is immoral.

Buddhist writers point out that Nirvāṇa is not a state of complete passivity or inaction. Suzuki declares: "In his last sermon Buddha did not teach his disciples to concentrate all their moral efforts on the attainment of Nirvāṇic quietitude disregarding all forms of activity that exhibit themselves in life.... The Buddha taught that Nirvāṇa does not consist in the complete stoppage of existence, but in the practice of the Eightfold path."[122] Nirvāṇa is not inaction but the absence of actions "...done under the influence of attachment, hatred, infatuation."[123] Moreover Nirvāṇa is a state of bliss or beatitude. Bliss is not to be equated with pleasure for "Pleasure is an empirical feeling which is transitory and therefore painful."[124] Bliss is permanent and not tinged with pain.

Buddhists often associate Nirvāṇa with perfection. Buddha declared that "Nirvāṇa is where the manifestation of Noble Wisdom expresses itself in Perfect Love for all; it is where the manifestations of Perfect Love expresses itself in Noble Wisdom for the enlightenment of all."[125] We have intimations of such perfection in occasional moments of complete joy and satisfaction in ordinary experience. Buddhists also assert that Nirvāṇa is a state transcending all conditional or experienced forms of reality. Buddha said to a group of monks: "There is, O Monks, a state where there is neither earth, nor water, nor heat, nor air; neither infinity of space nor infinity of consciousness, nor nothingness, nor perception nor non-perception; neither this world nor that, neither sun nor moon...neither coming nor going...neither death nor birth...it is the uncreate."[126] Contemporary authors hold that Nirvāṇa "...transcends all the forms of determination," that it is "...the realm of nothingness where complete absence of the subjective and the objective reference holds."[127]

In summary it may be noted again that Buddhists conceive of Nirvāṇa in a variety of respects. Such differences need not alarm us, as each tends to see in terms of his own experiences and temperament. Differences arise partly because Buddha was not explicit about Nirvāṇa himself, purposely so, some say. Furthermore, it may be true that the state of Nirvāṇa cannot be described by reference to ordinary experience and language. Indeed, it may be a state which cannot be described but only experienced.

VII EPISTEMOLOGY

Buddha emphatically upheld truth as a highly desired goal. In his last address to his disciples he said: "Hold fast to the truth as a lamp. Seek salvation alone in the truth."[128] A popular Buddhist story is of the marriage-feast in Jambūnada to which Buddha was invited. When asked to speak, he said that the "embrace of truth" gives greater happiness than the marriage embrace for "death will separate husband and wife but will never affect him who has espoused the truth."[129]

Commonly accepted sources of truth rejected by Buddha are seen in the statement to Kesaputta: "Do not believe anything on mere hearsay. Do not believe traditions because they are old. . . . Do not believe anything because people talk a great deal about it. Do not believe simply because of the written testimony of some ancient sage. Never believe anything . . . because the custom of many years inclines thee to take it as true. Do not believe anything on the mere authority of thy teachers or priests." Sources or criteria Buddha did accept are: "Whatever, according to thine own experience, and after thorough investigation, agrees with thy reason . . . that accept as true."[130]

In regard to how truth is attained Buddha answers mind-control. "Let us guard our thoughts that we do no evil, for as we sow so shall we reap;" "Unless you can so control your minds that even the thought of brutal unkindness and killing is abhorrent, you will never escape from the bondage of the world's life."[131] Both statements show that epistemology and ethics are closely associated in the Buddhist as in the Indian tradition in general, for "a mind swayed by passions and attached to the world cannot know truth;"[132] and the goal of truth or knowledge was seen by Indian thinkers as not the conquest of nature but self-purification and virtuous living.

Several general answers may be given to the question what is truth. It is that which unites. Between persons falsehood leads to separation and antagonism, truth to amity and unity. Metaphysically, the true is that which transcends dualities or distinctions. The Chinese Buddhist poet Sing Ts'an wrote: "Linger over either extreme, and Oneness is forever lost. . . . In the 'Not-Two' are no separate things, yet all things are included."[133] Buddhists also associate truth with the perfect and the ideal. Imperfection implies lack or blemish. The real in contrast to the ideal is always limited, finite, conditional.

Thus it would be invalid to associate truth with such states. That man seldom reaches the truth or the ideal in no way abrogates either

Further, truth, like the good, has the nature of the universal In this respect Buddhism in China was congenial with the Taoism reflected in Chuang-Tze's statement: "Great knowledge embraces the whole; small knowledge a part only. Great speech is universal; small speech is particular."[134] To Buddha the good is what "...is conducive to thine own weal and welfare, as well as the weal and welfare of other living beings."[135] Similarly the true is what is true for both oneself and others. The idea might be put differently by saying that Buddha urged seeing as a whole and not just from one's own view, as was the case with the man in The Blind Man and the Elephant story.[136]

To Buddhists truth is associated with love. Gandhi stated that "Ahiṃsā and Truth are so intertwined that it is practically impossible to disentangle and separate them."[137] Gandhi equated Ahiṃsā and Karuṇā. Buddha urged his followers to speak the truth in love (Karuṇā). He believed only a loving mind could know the truth. Love opens the mind; prejudice and hatred close it. A contemporary Buddhist writes: "Compassion cannot be cultivated by one obsessed with thoughts of selfishness."[138] The same is true for truth. Selfishness leads to partiality, our seeing only what is good or true for us and not others. Others having been left out, we have not entered the realm of universal truth or goodness.

Buddha was also concerned about how the truth is known. One way is through the senses. However, can the senses give us accurate and complete knowledge? The answer is no. The senses are limited and defective. Some animals can hear sounds, humans cannot. The senses are subject to illusions such as mirages. And sense knowledge is limited to material reality only. Also, as both perceived reality and the perceiver are constantly changing, how can genuine knowledge be gained in such a situation?

Does reason, as a second way of knowing, give us the highest truth? Buddha made a number of statements indicating no, such as, "And so, also, when he thinks or reasons, let him so regard his thought that being strenuous, thoughtful and mindful, he may, whilst in the world, overcome the grief which arises from the craving due to ideas, or to reasoning...."[139] In many situations reason is used to find means of satisfying rather than purifying desires. Or reason often sustains rather than eradicates prejudice. There is nothing in reason per se to guarantee its being used for good ends only.

Reason is also limited because it must be reinforced by the will. The distinction between knowing and doing the good is a universal one. The ancients pointed out that knowing does not lead axiomatically to doing the right, for the knower may lack the will or will-power to do what he knows is good or right. A good-will, then, becomes the final good, as Kant pointed out. Buddha was keenly aware of this.

A very trenchant commentary on reason and the senses is found in The Purpose of Being: "In the due course of evolution...sense-perception arose. There was a new realm of being....And the world split in twain: there were pleasures and pains, self and notself, friends and foes, hatred and love. The truth vibrated through the world of sentiency, but in all its infinite potentialities no place could be found where the truth could abide in all its glory. And reason came forth in the struggle for life. Reason began to guide the instinct of self...Yet reason seemed to add new fuel to the flame of hatred, increasing the turmoil of conflicting passions; and brothers slew their brothers....truth repaired to the domains of reason, but in all its recesses no place was found where the truth could abide in all its glory. Men broke down under the burdens of life, until the saviour appeared, the Great Buddha, the Holy Teacher of men and gods. Buddha taught men the right use of sentiency, and the right application of reason....He taught righteousness and thus changed rational creatures into humane beings, just, kind-hearted and faithful. And now at last a place was found where the truth might abide in all its glory, and this place is the heart of mankind! There is not room for truth in sentiency....Neither is there any room for truth in rationality. Rationality is a two-edged sword and serves the purpose of love equally as well as the purpose of hatred....The throne of truth is righteousness; and love and justice and good-will are its ornaments....This is the Gospel of the Blessed One."[140] In the Purpose of Being we see that grief arises from cravings due to ideas and from desires stirred by the senses. Reason is like a tool and is used for good or evil. We see the importance of a "good-will", the association of truth and virtues, and the heart as the seat of both.

Buddha's reluctance regarding metaphysical questions carried over into epistemology also. He criticized those who "...advance complex speculations and imagine that good results are attainable only by the acceptance of their theories."[141] On the other hand he talked about and claimed to have himself reached a state of trans-empirical, trans-rational consciousness, indescribable but nevertheless real. This aspect of Buddha's experience was emphasized by Mahāyāna Buddhists in their stress on transcendental wisdom and insight as seen in the statement: "The intellect alone can by no means unravel the mystery of our whole being into a region where absolute darkness defying the light of intellect is supposed to prevail. . . the only way that leads us to the final pacification of the heart-yearnings is to go beyond the horizons of limiting reason and to resort to the faith that has been planted in the heart as the sine quo non of its own existence and vitality."[142]

The transcendental state of being cannot be described by words and is not reached or known via the senses, reason, scriptures or ritual. A contemporary Buddhist points out that words build up a false world in which other people are reduced to sterotypes; even if description is accurate, it is not adequate because words dilute the intensity of immediate experience even when they do not distort it, and the highest mode of experience transcends the reach of words entirely. In regard to scriptures Ashitsu commented at the 1893 Parliament of Religions: "The sage regards the scriptures as guide-posts toward the Path of Mind; when he has found and entered that Path, he needs them no longer. It was said of old. All the Sūtras are nothing but fingers that point out the shining moon. When once we see the moon, pointers are no longer necessary."[143]

We must, then, go beyond words or language and the illusions they create. The unconditional cannot be characterized by anything which may be appropriate to characterize the conditioned. In the end the Buddhist might claim that transcendental reality is to be experienced, not known. Or he might define knowing non-cognitively as insight or wisdom (Prajñā), gained intuitively. While perhaps strange to a western mind, it only demonstrates that there are different ways of conceiving truth. Nakamura points out, for example, that "The dominant philosophical schools of Ancient India did not find truth in the agreement of subjective knowledge with the objective order, nor in inter-subjectively valid knowledge, but rather, they sought truth in the practice of ethics. . . Truth in the ancient Indian concept is no other than 'to be that' or 'to be such'."[144] Buddhism reflects this early Indian ontological view of truth. Truth is associated with the inner, with being or a state of being characterized by unity and purity.

PART THREE

Areas of Thought

INTRODUCTION

Indian philosophers have been long concerned with the areas of thought taken up in this section. They have asked themselves about the means, nature and grounds of truth. What ways of knowing are there? What is knowledge or what is the knowing process? An important concern has been whether we can have immediate knowledge of the world. Can we know reality directly? Furthermore, can we have knowledge of the whole or is our knowledge limited to parts only? In addition there is always the problem of how to avoid projecting our mind-made categories on reality rather than seeing it as it is, in its "suchness," as the Zen Buddhist would say. This leads to another epistemological question, namely, to what extent and in what ways is man's mind or intellectual faculties limited.

Indians have been concerned too, about the basic metaphysical question of the nature of that reality to be known. What is true reality characterized by, and how can we distinguish it? Is permanence or change the basic features of the universe? Is reality material or spiritual? What is the nature of matter? What do we mean by spiritual? Indian thinkers have asked themselves if the world of phenomena is all there is. Also, is reality made up of particulars only or are there universals which are as real and existent as particulars? A further question is whether the universe is orderly or is chance its dominant feature? What is the nature of relations? Is reality loosely or tightly connected? Another concern is that of similarities and differences. Which are more extensive and significant?

As persons, we are both individuals and members of a society. This situation gives rise to the question of which should be given greater preeminence, the individual or society. How can conflicts between the two be resolved? The social philosopher is concerned, too, with such questions as what the best kind of society is. In whom is authority to rest? Who is to rule and on what basis? What institutions are necessary for the proper functioning of society? A central social question is what enables a society to endure. Here Indian thinkers can surely offer valuable suggestions, as theirs is a society with a continuous existence of hundreds of years.

It would seem that for a society to endure there must be some fundamental principles in which it is grounded. What are they, as far as India is concerned? What common ideals and goal can a society be centred around? What about the problem of diversity? To what extent can it be allowed without disrupting social unity and cohesion? Perhaps here we are dealing with the problem of individual freedom. How much is desirable or possible? What is freedom, the right to simply do as one pleases? What is the relationship between freedom and duties or responsibilities? How significant is the concept of equality in Indian social thought? An important question any society must deal with is the relationship of the strong and the weak, the more gifted and the less gifted, the rich and the poor. What is India's answer to this question? We are interested not only in social questions of a theoretical nature, but we would like to know what Indian society actually is and has been like. What is the situation regarding caste? What changes in Indian society and social philosophy are occurring today? Where will they lead?

Indian thinkers have reflected on such questions in ethics as the nature, knowledge and grounds of the good. They have been concerned with the problem of relativism and absolutism. Are there universal rights and wrongs, or is the good and the right relative to individuals, time and place? A further question is whether morality is a matter of rules or something else such as attitudes. In addition, where do our ideas of the good come from? How do we resolve the dilemma of knowing and doing the good? Will doing the right automatically follow from knowing it? What about the question Kant raised regarding motives? Is a virtuous act performed from selfish motives really a virtuous act? Also what is the relationship of means and ends? Is it ethical to use evil means to attain good ends? This leads us to the question of whether the good is to be justified pragmatically or idealistically.

Finally, philosophers are driven inevitably to the question of man. What is his basic nature? Does he have such? Is man an animal or a being? Is he a solely sensual, appetitive entity or is he capable of projecting and realizing goals and ideals? If the latter, what is man's chief end and how is it attained? What is the purpose of life? What gives it meaning and value? Is man good or evil? Is he incurably selfish or is he sufficiently altruistic to make harmonious societies possible? Can he be as concerned for others' as his own good?

Indian philosophers are concerned with another aspect of the nature of the self, namely the relationship of particularity and universality. Is man a member of the category of the universal first and the particular second? Or we might raise the question by asking again whether the similarities between men outweigh differences. What we want to know is what is the true self. How can we distinguish the true from the false self? Two more questions regarding man may be posed. Is man a microcosm of the universe? Through self knowledge, or knowing himself, can he know the universe? Finally, is man free, and in what sense? Can he rise above the limitations of environment, heredity, his own nature and conditioning? What does it mean, to "realize" oneself?

We see, then, that Indian thinkers have been and are concerned with a number of significant questions. Their answers to them will be found in the selections which follow. Again, an item to keep in mind is how their answers compare with those given by philosophers in the West.

8

INDIAN EPISTEMOLOGY AND LOGIC

S. S. Barlingay

I Epistemology

Traditionally Indian philosophy is classified into six orthodox systems, Nyāya-Vaiśeṣika, Sāṃkhya-Yoga, Pūrva-Mīmāṃsā and Uttara Mīmāṃsā, and some unorthodox systems, namely Buddhism, Jainism, and Cārvāka. This kind of classification is inadequate, for, in the first place in addition to the systems mentioned above there are some other systems, e.g. the school of philosophy of Grammar. Secondly when philosophical writers said that they belonged to a particular system, it was not the case that they did not criticize the earlier writers or deviate from the views of their predecessors. However, in this chapter I am restricting myself only to the problems of knowledge and logic and here it does not appear to me that there was a separate theory of knowledge for each system although the writers of each system made some significant contributions to certain problems in the general area of logic and knowledge.

In the context of Indian philosophy although we talk of the problem of knowledge, there are, in fact, varieties of problems and not one. The problems are related, but one blanket theory of knowledge may not answer all the problems. When I say "I have knowledge of the table," or that "there is a flower-pot on the table," the problem concerning this kind of knowledge is different from when I say that, "I have knowledge of Brahman." The problem connected with the knowledge of Brahman is entirely different from the problem connected with the thing like a table or a flower-pot on a table. Again, when I say I have knowledge of a class of objects or a concept of knowledge of the absence of something, the problems connected with this kind of knowledge are again different from knowledge of concrete objects. When we have knowledge of concrete objects, this knowledge itself can be divided into definite and indefinite knowledge, or determinate and indeterminate knowledge. And the theories concerning them may not be of one kind. Then again, two different problems may face us. The first, how do you get knowledge? The second, what is the justification of knowledge?

At the outset it should be made clear that when the different systems of Indian philosophy talk of knowledge, they are not primarily concerned with every problem about knowledge. Pūrva-Mīmāṃsā which is concerned with what should be done and what should not be done, was not interested in the problem of knowledge as such, in the sense that the problem of knowledge is for example, concerned with knowledge of a table. But in later Pūrva-Mīmāṃsā, the problem of knowledge assumed importance and theories of knowledge were hotly discussed. In Sāṃkhya or Yoga, the problem of knowledge is not primarily important. But when we begin to ask questions about the self, we somehow or the other get involved in the problem of knowledge. This problem assumes importance in Śaṅkarācārya also. In a knowledge situation there is a subject and an object. The characteristics of the two are opposed to each other. But one may suppress the one with the characteristics of the other. This is what we do, to a certain extent, when we are supposed to know. But we go further and attribute the characteristics of the subject to the object and vice versa. This, of course, would be a fallacy. But the philosophic problems of knowledge, according to Śaṅkarācārya, arise on account of 'identifying' the subject with the object or vice versa.

Let us try to formulate the questions one by one. How do we explain the knowledge that there is a table or a flower-pot on the table? The first thing that Indian philosophy generally assumes is that knowledge is a kind of relation and it is an irreducible relation. It cannot be reduced to, or analysed into anything else: this is what the philosophers of Nyāya school would term the Viṣaya-Viṣayī-Bhāva or the epistemic relation between the subject and the object. Unless you accept a Viṣaya and Viṣayin[1] or the subject and the object and a certain peculiar relation between them, you cannot explain knowledge. This peculiar relation cannot be classed under any other kind of relations. One relatum of this relation is viṣayī or the knower and the other relatum is the object of knowledge. The relation, knowledge, is related to the knower by an inseparable relation termed "Samavāya". For, a knowee can always possess knowledge as his property. This is how the Nyāya philosophers regard knowledge as the quality of the soul and the quality is uniquely and inseparably related to the subject. But unlike other qualities this quality, namely knowledge, does not entirely belong to the knower, but is also related to the thing, or the object of knowledge. It is this relation which distinguishes knowledge from desiring, expecting, feeling and so on. Knowing is a transitive verb and for its existence it as much depends on the object of knowledge as on the knower. This peculiar complex in the theory of knowledge is known as the knowledge triad consisting of the knower, the known and the knowledge. And I believe that it is universally accepted by all schools of Indian philosophy.

It will be interesting to point out that, according to Śaṅkarācārya, knowledge is not a mental process or act like feeling or desiring. It is not something that a knower does. Finally, it is the thing that shows itself. This attitude is more or less accepted by philosophers of different schools. It is only because of this that finally a thing is known as a thing. If we do not regard knowledge as relation and merely regard knowledge as a quality only because *A*'s knowledge is *A*'s knowledge and is not shared by *B*, and *B*'s knowledge is *B*'s knowledge and is not shared by *A*, then we will have no other alternative except accepting the representative theory of perception. It is the acceptance of the relational theory of perception and the recognition that the subject-object relation is peculiar and unique that makes the Indian theory of knowledge of almost all varieties, a non-representative theory.

Indian theory recognizes that there is a knower and the object of knowledge but the psychological act of perceiving gives us only qualities of the object. Psychologically speaking, we cannot assert the existence of the thing once we proceed from our sensations. And it is a known fact that illusions do occur. But in order to distinguish illusions from veridical knowledge we are actually going beyond sensations. It means that we are inferring the objects of knowledge from our sensing them. Otherwise we would not have noticed silver at the place of a shell, water at the place of hot sand, and two moons in the place of one. Here perhaps one of the points which Indian philosophers would make is that psychological illusions presuppose some direct perception. We would not be able to have an illusion of two moons, unless we have the real, veridical perception of the moon.

Indian philosophers would not be satisfied with the kind of explanation the British Empiricists or the philosophers of the Sensum School would give of perception. When I say I perceive a certain object, is it merely a theoretical relationship between me and the object or is some practical relationship also involved? Is it not the case that the object is 'known' by me as the object in practical activity, in my using or handling the object? Starting from mere sensations we would never be able to distinguish a thing from the qualities of that thing. Perhaps it would be correct to say that a physical object is given to us not in the theoretical knowing of that object but in the practical relation which that object holds with the knower. This practical relationship goes beyond the relationship of knowing which is only secondary to the practical relationship. We realise that here is an object, although we may not know it through knowing. When I hold a flower-pot in my hand, it is not merely the sense of a flower-pot, nor a construct out of sense; we hold a thing in our hand and, whatever explanation we may give, for our practical purposes it is a thing that we are holding. Thus, when I have knowledge or when I assert that there is something, it is a kind of motor activity on my part, and not merely a sensory activity which gives me knowledge of a thing.

If knowledge of an object is distinguished into knowledge of a thing and the knowledge of the qualities of thing, the knowledge of the thing is not given to us by the senses, though it is given in the presence of sense-knowledge. The knowledge of qualities and relations on the other hand is given to us by the senses. This presupposition of a thing and its justification is called by Buddhists Arthakriyākāritva, and by Nyāya philosophers Saphalapravṛittitva. Artha is an object and the existence of an object is proved by the behaviour of the object itself. I do not perceive or describe the object; the object shows itself. The object shows itself in my doing, in my activities. In order to explain this action or "do-ness" Indian philosophers, particularly of the Nyāya School, think that, even in the act of our perceiving, the object of our perception and the one that perceives 'touch' one another.

Superficially this looks absurd; but, since the object of perception or the thing is not given to us in our senses, we must be discovering it, as a blind man does, by touch. A perception is supposed to be a conjunction, a touch of two substances. Without a touch perhaps it would not be possible for us to know a thing. So even when we perceive by our eyes a thing at a distance, the philosophers of Nyāya (and following them all Indian philosophers) say that our eye goes and touches the object. What perhaps they want to say is that some peculiar kind of action is involved in the act of perceiving. This action either accompanies perceiving or it is a part of it. Now, to say that my eye goes and touches the thing is absurd unless it is figuratively used. Modern optics tells us that through light it is the image which falls on the retina. But two important points arise here. (1) When the image falls on the retina the perceiver must be catching it. The 'doing' activity cannot be totally ignored. And (2) even though in perceiving a thing we act at a distance, the contact between the thing and the eye cannot be disregarded, e.g. if we put an opaque curtain between the eye and the object perception is prevented. It means that though there is a condition for light falling on the retina, it is prevented on account of the curtain. It means that there is no contact. The 'doing' part and the 'touching' part in the Indian theory of perception are intimately related. They convey something quite important. The only thing that is necessary to remember is that words like touch or doing are used figuratively, only to explain something on the basis of analogy.

Thus when a perceiver perceives, he perceives a thing or a substance and through the sense-organs he senses the qualities, etc. of the thing or substance. How a perceiver perceives a thing—a bare thing—is not explained but is taken for granted as a datum. But this is always done in the presence of sensing or experiencing. The first requisite of a perceptual experience is that it must be a kind of contact, and the metaphysical presupposition of this epistemological process is that there cannot be a kind of contact except between two things. Thus both the object of contact and the subject are taken for granted as things. This interesting theory is developed by the Nyāya philosophers in its full aspects. But though it has not been clearly worked out by philosophers of other schools, it appears to me that this was in the background of their philosophic or epistemological thinking too.

Let us work out the details of the Nyāya theory of perceptive knowledge. They say that we have perception through six different ways. They would say that there are six different kinds of Sannikarṣa. The first and the basic Sannikarṣa is, of course, that of 'touch' or contact. If *X* perceives *Y* then *X* is a substance and *Y* is also a substance, and both *X* and *Y* touch each other (either through the touch or through the eyes). It is because the two substances *X* and *Y* touch each other that a perception arises. Of course I have already explained above that this touch is to be understood not always as a physical touch but rather as the absence of non-contact; for if there is an absence of contact then no perceptive knowledge would be possible. But when we say we have knowledge it is never knowledge of the bare thing or substance. It is always a determinate specific knowledge. That is, it gives a particularity to that piece of knowledge, and it is always distinguished from other things. It is printed on the background of other unspecific things. Suppose I am seeing a radio set before me. Then it will not be correct to say that I am seeing a bare indeterminate thing. My object of perception is characterized by radioness and certain physical qualities of that thing like size, shape, cover, etc. A Nyāya philosopher would say that one 'guesses' the knowledge of the qualities through the senses, because the qualities belong to the thing and always belong to the thing. If I say I have knowledge of the qualities, I am a step removed from the knowledge of the thing. It is not the case that I have knowledge of the qualities and then I construct those qualities into some kind of a hypothesis about a physical thing. The qualities are permanently related to the thing. (I am doubtful whether this last part will be finally acceptable to other schools of Indian philosophers.) Thus when I have knowledge of the qualities I have first the knowledge of the thing and then the knowledge of the qualities; because the qualities belong to the thing. I have thus knowledge not of qualities but as qualities belonging to the thing. The qualities belong to things by a permanent relation; that is the qualities inhere in the things. The knowledge of the qualities is therefore through the contact of the thing and through the permanent relation between a thing and the qualities. This is termed as knowing through Saṃyukta Samavāya.

On the basis of the knowledge of the thing, however, we will not be able to discriminate one particular thing from other particular things. A thing is discriminated from other things on account of its being of a particular class. When I say I see a cow, I have already circumscribed, limited my knowledge by drawing a line of demarcation between a cow and other things. In western philosophy and logic a class is supposed to be a special kind of thing and the members of the class belong to the thing. The class is as if made of these members, although at some stage the concept of a class is regarded as different from the sum-total of all its members. In Indian logic and philosophy perhaps a similar concept of class might have existed in the very beginning. But very soon and in the quite early development of Indian Philosophy the concept of class underwent a change. Class was regarded not as a collection of things but as a common characteristic which is shared by all particulars to which we apply the term class. Thus the class "cow" does not mean a group of all individual cows. But it means the characteristic "cowness". Thus we will have to change the usual usage of saying that this particular cow belongs to the class cow. We will rather have to say that the class characteristic cowness exists in an individual cow. Thus to refer to the earlier example of a radio set, there will not be a class of radio sets, rather we will have to say that the radioness exists or belongs to a particular thing. It should, however, be noted that the extensional concept of class continued to exist in the inferential theory (see inference).

When we talk of a perceptive situation we not only talk of the class characteristic but also of the particular characteristics or qualities. When I see a flower, I do not merely see the thing with the class characteristic for flowerness. I also notice the colour; we may characterize that flower as having a particular colour; say, for example, red or rose or the like. This particular characteristic which belongs to the colour is explained by the Nyāya philosophers by what they term as Saṃyukta Samavāya. The qualities too have a class characteristic and the explanation of this knowledge will be a step removed and the model suggests that a quality inheres in a thing and the class characteristic of a quality inheres in a thing and the class characteristic of a quality inheres in the quality. In Nyāya language this is known as Saṃyukta-Samaveta-Samavāya.

The above theory, however, will not explain the perception that is concerned with hearing. The Nyāya philosophers think that hearing is of the kind of a sound and this sound is a quality of ether. Since ether is all pervasive, when a certain sound is produced it belongs to the whole ether. The auditory organ, so it is thought, is also ether and so the sound becomes a quality of this particular ether, the ear. This is how the sound produces similar sound waves in the ether and man is able to hear.

When one perceives an object, one is, so to speak, drawing a line f demarcation between that object and the other objects which he loes not perceive at that time. Similarly when someone does not erceive a particular thing at that time, someone perceives that some-ne does not perceive an object at that time. According to Nyāya hilosophers, this means that, just as we have knowledge of positive hings, similarly we have knowledge of the non-existence or absence f things. The Nyāya philosophers think that the non-existence is lso known through perception. Philosophers belonging to other ndian schools do not accept this contention of the Nyāya philos-phers. They say we have knowledge of the absence of a certain hing by a special faculty of knowing, viz. the faculty of knowing he absence.

It is difficult for anybody to say that all we perceive is actually the ase; illusions cannot be ruled out. How then do we distinguish llusions from veridical perception? If some times we can have illu-ions, how can we be sure that we do not have an illusion at any articular or all the time? The Nyāya philosophers start with n empirical outlook. There cannot be an illusion according to hem unless that of which it is an illusion already exists or existed nd was perceived. Thus if we have an illusion of water in a place of hot sand, the water must exist and be perceived somewhere and ometime. Similarly, if we have an illusion of a snake, then the snake nust exist somewhere. Some times we do have illusions like the illu-ion of a hare with horns or pink rats; but the illusions of the hare vith horns or pink rat is possible because the pink rat, for example, s a composite object consisting of two simples, the pink and the rat nd therefore we can, by joining these two simples, get an illusion of a pink rat. We can also talk of a barren woman's son because it s possible for us to conjoin the words like barren, woman and son. But in the strict sense of the term we can never have an illusion of a barren woman's son.

The Nyāya philosophers take it for granted that an illusion always presupposes a real veridical perception. To take the stock example, they would say that we do see some times that there is silver where there is only a shell. But when we ascribe silverness to the shell this is so because we know that there is silver; we have a memory of silver; we must have seen the silver in the goldsmith's shop and we must be aware of the usual qualities of silver. Thus when we see a shell, on account of the similarity of the usual sense of the shell and the silver, we can mistake the shell for the silver. The mistake is only with regard to the qualities and the class characteristics c those qualities. But there is never a mistake about the substance t which the qualities belong.

To a great extent this empirical point of view is accepted b philosophers of the Vedānta and Mīmāṃsā schools. One schoc of Mīmāṃsā accepts the contention of Nyāya. The other slightl differs from it. But even if it differs this school of Mīmāṃsā say that there is in fact no illusion; there is only the knowing c the elements in an illusion, because the wholes that we construc out of the composite parts are not the usual wholes. T consider the shell-silver illusion, a philosopher belonging to thi school of Mīmāṃsā will say that the shell is real and the silver is als real. But the whole of the shell and the silver is not real becaus the object that is shell belongs to one whole; the object that is silve belongs to another. In an illusory perception we are bringin together the parts of different wholes and combining them in one

The Philosophers of Advaita Vedānta raise very interesting issue in regard to the ordinarily accepted illusory phenomenon. If w consider the case of an illusion like perceiving a snake in place of a rope, they will say that it is difficult to verify whether something i actually a rope or a snake. For the only criterion, according to them is whether you actually perceive something. When you perceiv a snake at that moment, say at time T-1 you are actually perceiving a snake. Suppose at time T-2 you have perceived a rope instead o a snake; we have a tendency to believe that the snake was unrea and the rope was real. This is what is termed in Indian philosophy as Bādha. And all our common sense behaviour is based on this But let us analyse the situation further. At time T-2 we have seer a rope and, therefore, we infer that what we have perceived at tim T-1 was illusion. Now, there are several possibilities here. On possibility is that there was actually a snake and it disappeared another possibility is that there was a snake and it turns itself into a rope at time T-2; a third possibility is that there was indeed a snak and it does exist even at time T-2 but it went somewhere out of ou sight and when we were perceiving a snake at time T-1 the rope alsc existed there, but was unnoticed. All these theoretical possibilitie cannot be entirely denied. It may be argued that it is against com- mon sense to think that the snake turns itself into rope the next moment or the snake disappears the next moment and a new thing called rope comes into existence. In the common sense world w o believe in the permanence of things. But as a matter of fact it is his permanence which is challenged by the Advaita (Vedānta) philosophers. What we call permanent is not permanent according to hem. In this world we assume that a thing continues to be the same: table continues to be a table at time *T*-1, *T*-2, *T*-3, *T*-4, etc. But is difficult to conclude that it will continue to be a table all the me. Sometimes the table may break; it may be burnt and so on. Ordinarily we believe that if a thing has existed for sometime then would continue to exist. If the sun rises for all these days, then it vill tomorrow. If I deliver a lecture on every Wednesday, then I vould continue to deliver a lecture on Wednesday. The logicians ase their arguments on the belief that what continues to exist will ontinue to exist. But this is indeed fallacious. If I lecture on every Vednesday, then the correct conclusion would be that there will t least be some Wednesday when I would not lecture; for I may be o more. The Advaita philosophers make use of this. They say here is no reason to suppose that there is a distinction between the llusory' snake which exists for one moment and a thing belonging to ommon sense world which exists for a much longer time. Whether t is an illusory snake or a permanent thing in the common sense vorld, it has both a beginning and an end. And, therefore, there s some time when something did not exist and there is a time when omething would no more be. Thus one cannot say that if a thing xists for four moments, it is more real than a thing which exists for ne moment. Nothing can, therefore, be verified on the basis of reater length of time.

Although perception may be regarded as simple and something on-composite, we can distinguish in it several elements. For xample, when we say we perceive something determinate, our nowledge of the thing is always determined by a certain characeristic which, so to say, limits this knowledge. According to Nyāya philosophy this characteristic is related to the thing of which t is a characteristic by a certain relation. This concept of Nyāya has come to be accepted by almost all schools of Indian philosophy. The concept of characteristic, however, is only relative. For example, if we are perceiving a blue pot then the pot will be reported as a thing and blueness its characteristic. But if we are talking of pot alone, then potness itself is the characteristic which limits the otherwise non-determinate knowledge of the same *X*. Indian philosophers therefore distinguish two kinds of perceptive know-

ledge—one that is determinate and the other that is indeterminate
No one really has this indeterminate knowledge any time. Bu
because we distinguish between things and qualities or characteristic
and also between the knowledge of things and the knowledge of th
characteristics of things, the ancient Indian philosophers someho
jump to the conclusion that knowledge of things qua things, is no
only distinguishable from what we call knowledge—the composit
knowledge, but also that the bare things are separately and in
dependently known or perceived. From this they further conclud
that the bare things must be 'perceived' a moment earlier than th
composite or determinate object. They thus distinguish betwee
the knowledge of the bare things and the knowledge of the qualitie
This last part, I think, is a muddle; for here Indian philosophe
confuse between (1) the logically distinguishable and the physicall
separable and (2) also confuse that which is logically prior as tem
porarily prior. This knowledge of bare things is named by India
philosophers of almost all schools as nirvikalpa knowledge—o
knowledge without any construct.

There are, however, differences amongst Indian philosophers abou
the status and relations between the two kinds of knowledges
Nirvikalpa and Savikalpa or determinate knowledge. The Buddhis
(excepting perhaps those belonging to Yogācāra) think that in th
first moment of our perception (and by this they in fact mean visua
perception) we have knowledge of bare things. These bare thing
they term as Svalakṣaṇā—that which defines itself or that whicl
exists in its own right. Here of course comes the Buddhist meta
physics that what exists in its own right is just discrete unconnecte
moments, although the moments together would form a series o
continuum. The Nyāya philosophers on the other hand would tak
a realistic position. Just as from a long distance a thing is onl
vaguely perceived and the parts or qualities of the things are no
clearly distinguished and they become clearer and clearer onl
gradually as we approach the thing, similarly they also think tha
in the first moment we have knowledge of things qua things an
in the subsequent moment only we come to have determinate know
ledge. This is some kind of a compromise between Locke's positio
about qualities and the position of the naive realists. But in th
case of Nyāya there is no mental construction or projection whe
there is determinate knowledge. The knowledge of a thing an
determinate knowledge are only two stages of the act of perceiving

the stage of determinate knowledge being only later, deeper or clearer. This analysis is again based on Nyāya metaphysics, for they believe in the objectivity of the substance-quality model. The qualities according to Nyāya are not mind-dependent although they are substance-dependent; they exist objectively, although on account of the muddle between logical and temporal priority, philosophers belonging to the Nyāya school think that in the first moment of its existence a thing is a bare thing and the qualities which are otherwise inseparable from the things are born only the next moment of the existence of things.

The position of the Sāṃkhya school of thought is rather interesting in this respect. I shall indicate two important features of its theory. What we call knowledge arises only when Prakṛiti—matter (the nature or the natura naturata) and consciousness fall in each others' shadow, due to the criss-crossing of cosmocentric and anthropocentric points of view. Things (including the self) are distinguished on account of the ego or egoness or Ahaṃkāra. When a table is distinguished from a chair, it is due to nothing else except my intellect and my ego. From the cosmocentric point of view there is no distinction between a table and a chair. Both of them are only Prakṛiti or matter. Thus the distinction between a table and a chair is as much due to me or my ego (Ahaṃkāra) as my distinguishing myself from other men.

Another feature which one can bring out in the Sāṃkhya theory of knowledge, although perhaps by speculation, is the distinction between Tanmātra and Mahābhūta. Tanmātra is what exists in its own right and Mahābhūta means its magnification (I believe in knowledge). Corresponding to our five organs of sense there are, so it is speculated, five pure objects of sense (or sense data); they are pure data or objects of sound, touch, vision, taste and odour. Whether these are to be called objects of sense I am not sure. And why these should be an independent object of each sense is also a matter of metaphysics. However, the Sāṃkhya position can be interpreted in two different ways. (1) One can take Tanmātra as the object of one sense and then distinguish it from perception which, though it may primarily be due to one sense, is more complex in the sense that it includes the data from other senses. According to the Sāṃkhya theory of Pañchīkaraṇa in each of the objects of perception the object of one sense is dominant although the objects of other senses also form part of the thing perceived. (2) On the other interpretation it would mean that Tanmātra is something which exists in its own right; but, when it is subjected to perception it is perceived as a Mahābhūta—Mahābhūta signifying some kind of phenomenal reality.

The position of Advaita in this respect would be very similar to that of Buddhism. The philosophers of Advaita would distinguish between knowledge of bare things and determinate knowledge. Like the Buddhists they too would hold that it is the first kind of knowledge which gives knowledge of reality; the other kind of knowledge would merely give knowledge of phenomenal reality. However, since their presupposition is that Reality is one without the other, this would include knowledge of "reality along with the person who knows." This will have the form—'I along with the rest of the reality.' Such knowledge can never be had by perception. For in perception reality is always broken into the knower and the known. Advaita, therefore, holds that this knowledge is attained through some kind of intuition which is to be distinguished from perception. Advaita philosophers hold that at some stage this knowledge is obtained through Vedic sentences.

It will now be clear why a Vedāntin of Advaita thought thinks that knowledge of Brahman is of a different kind from knowledge of empirical things, although it is similar to it and so known as knowledge. First empirical knowledge presupposes the duality of the knower and the known. Unless the knower separates himself from knowable objects (the rest of the world) no knowledge of the empirical type is possible. Such knowledge is always characterized by some limitation; for by assumption it is not knowledge of the whole. The whole will include the knower also, whatever be his status. This cannot be the case when we are thinking of perception; and, if inference is also based on perception, it will not be possible even by inference. Knowledge of the logical form 'I am Brahman', then, cannot be had through perception through which we have knowledge of ordinary things. One would 'know' it intuitively when the duality between the knower and the known is eliminated and when he no more knows it but becomes it.

Perhaps the scriptures may give rise to it and intuition may be hastened on account of Upamāna where what happens in perception is reverted. When we know that something is Yak (if it is based on Upamāna), it is first given by description and then confirmed by comparing this description with the object of perception. Knowedge of Brahman also follows the same model. But there would be difficulty in the last part of the process. Brahman cannot be inally perceived as the object *of* Upamāna, as for example the Yak, an be perceived. For, as pointed out earlier, knowledge of Brahman, being knowledge of the whole will require the elimination of the subject-object relationship. How can such knowedge be possible? The Advaita Vedānta says that this relation is roken in the practical relationship, when the logical form is no more I know Brahman' but when it is 'I am Brahman'. It is not knowing, s knowing requires quality; it is being itself and so the duality is ndone. In fact this is in keeping with the pragmatic attitude of ndian philosophers towards knowledge. How does one know hat a thing is a table? From a distance it merely appears like a able. It is only in the practical use that it is confirmed as a table. The confirming of knowledge is living with it. And this is also true f knowledge of the whole or Brahman. Knowledge of Brahman s not something that is theoretical. It is not knowledge at all. t is only Brahman, and categorizing it as theoretical, etc. does not rise.

The philosophers of the Nyāya school seem to have a similar oncept of intuition. They are pluralists and atomists. But one annot have knowledge of the atoms in perception. They therefore hink that there is another kind of perception or rather intuition. They give it the name Alaukika Pratyakṣa (an extraordinary erception) and think that it is by this that one acquires knowledge f atoms. Knowledge of classes or generalities is also had through xtraordinary perception only. When one sees a table, for example, ne does not see merely a particular table but sees the whole class f tables. This is due to extraordinary perception. The later Nyāya philosophers have elaborated this concept of extraordinary erception still further. They think it is of three kinds. (1) Not nly knowledge of concepts or classes but also the relations between lasses or concepts is had by this kind of extraordinary perception. They give it a name, Sāmānya lakṣaṇā pratyāsatti (an extraordinary erception through which general concepts are given). (2) The ther kind of extraordinary perception is called Jñāna Lakṣaṇā. t is the same as what modern psychology terms as pre-perception r complication. Logically its form is that of analogy. One erceives one thing, but it immediately gives rise to another perception. One perceives a thing of sandal wood (at a distance). But (on account of memory) he connects (without specifically being conscious) it with fragrance. This connection is immediatel perceived, although it is not an ordinary type of perception (3) The third type of extraordinary perception is known as Yogaja-lakṣaṇā pratyāsatti. There has been a good deal of confusior about this concept amongst Indian philosophers. Often it i confused with the super human powers by which the Yogis ar supposed to know all the particulars in the past, present and future But the definition of Yogaja-lakṣaṇā pratyāsatti merely tells us tha through this perception one is able to perceive empirical generalizations and a connection between particular and empirically genera notions.

There is one small point which deserves our attention. Whil discussing the problems of perception, perception is described a knowledge arising out of contact of the object with some sense These senses are classified as external and internal. The fiv organs of sense are regarded as external senses. But there is a internal sense (Manas) too. Pleasure, pain, etc. are directly know through Manas; but Manas is also employed to know externa objects. Although Manas has been usually translated as mind understood in the technical sense, Manas does not mean mind It is more akin to the nervous system. Ultimately the object c knowledge is related to Ātman or the self (psyche) through the sens organs, external and internal. Therefore it is the Ātman alone whic is the knower in the ultimate sense of the term.

There is yet another important point connected with the genera discussion of perception. In perception, as we have seen there i a contact between the sense organ and the object of knowledg Knowledge is supposed to be possible because it is thought that bot the object of knowledge and the sense organ are made of the sam material. Thus the eye is supposed to be made out of light, the ea out of ether and the organ of cutaneous sensation out of air primaril The metaphysical presupposition is that knowledge becomes possib on account of the similarity between that which is known and that b which it is known. All that is known by our vision is thus made u of light and all that is known by hearing is made up of ether. Th so-called mystical perception of the Yoga system makes use of th concept. It is alleged that ether is all pervading; so, if the pow of the ear could be increased through concentration, then one's ea could be used to hear any sound anywhere. Our ear will act lik a wireless receiving station and one could adjust it according to a wavelength. Similarly if the power of the eye is increased one could see any object which has the capacity to be visual. Perhaps this would go against the modern theory of light and I need not try to defend it here although people may try to defend it using the notions of reflection and refraction.

When an Indian philosopher talks of the problem of knowledge he also talks of the sources of knowledge and gives it the name Pramāṇa. The followers of different systems give different sources of knowledge and grade them on a scale of merit. On this scale perception is usually accepted as of prime importance. All other sources of knowledge generally presuppose knowledge by perception or perception at least plays a significant role in the process. The Cārvāka school, representing an extreme type of empiricism, even goes further and rejects all sources of knowledge except perception. This helps them to reject causation, the unity of self, etc. The importance of perception is recognized even by the adherents of Advaita Vedānta like Śaṅkarācārya in respect to empirical knowledge. He said in his commentary on the Bhagavadgītā that even if one thousand Śrutis tell us that fire is cold it cannot be accepted, for it is contrary to experience.

II Logic

Until now we have generally discussed problems connected with perception. The other important sources of knowledge are Anumāna or Inference, Śabda or Authority (also language), Upamāna or knowledge by comparative description, Arthāpatti or semantical implication, and Anupalabdhi or knowledge by non-existence. All these, in one sense or the other, fall within the scope of logic and I shall now proceed to deal with them.

The word Anumāna (inference) literally means that which follows already existing knowledge. The word knowledge also needs to be properly understood. For ancient Indian thinkers a form of knowledge is not knowledge. Thus "two and two make four" or "All *M*'s and *P*'s, All *S*'s and *M*'s, ∴ All *S*'s and *P*'s" which gives the form of the first figure syllogism is not knowledge; knowledge must give information and that information is knowledge only when it is true. It must never be ignored that inference is a means of knowledge. The conclusion in the inferential machine gives this knowledge part and is jointly implied by the premises. It already exists in the premises and is carried through the premises to the conclusion.

The knowledge part in inference is called Anumiti in Sanskrit logic. Although Anumiti differs from knowledge obtained through other sources of knowledge, inasmuch as it is obtained through a different source, as knowledge it has the same knowledge content or characteristic as knowledge obtained through other sources. However, we will have to distinguish between Anumāna or the inferential structure that leads to knowledge and Anumiti or inferential knowledge. The inferential structure is empty. Only if it is filled in with information is it able to pass that information to the conclusion. The inferential structure, however, is regarded by logicians of all schools as infalliable. Validity is a necessary characteristic of this machine, although truth may not be. This structure is known as Anumāna only when truth is a characteristic of the premises so that it becomes a characteristic of the conclusion also. The empty machine, which has the ability to be a carrier of knowledge, is only a construct—vikalpa—according to the Buddhists (and other logicians) and is, therefore, neither concerned with truth nor with falsity (but is simply concerned with formal validity).

This peculiar view of (inferential) knowledge is largely responsible for the peculiar development of Indian logic. First, nothing is knowledge unless it is particular (or singular). A sentence of the form 'anything is *x*' is not knowledge. It should not be 'anything' but 'this definite thing'. Secondly it should not be '*x*' but some definite thing or a characteristic. Whereas 'anything is *x*' is not knowledge 'this is a blue pot' is knowledge. Even in perception it is only when the perception is definite that it is regarded as knowledge. A cognition of the form 'this is either a pillar or a man' is not knowledge. And this concept of knowledge is carried even in the region of inference. Thus the conclusion of the inference must necessarily be singular (particular). It can be easily seen that in order for the conclusion to be singular-particular, the premises also must have the core of singularity-particularity although it may not be visible always.

One cannot have knowledge that is characterized by particularity-singularity unless it is based on experience. The premises of inference then must be (1) either particular empirical propositions or universal propositions based on empirical observation. It is neces sary to ascertain further that they are actually based on empirical observation. That is, it must be asserted that there is at least one instance of the universal premise or Vyāpti Vākya as it is called in Sanskrit. Unless this is done one will not know whether the general premise has an empirical basis or whether it is empty.

It is stated above that the conclusion and premise of the inference-machine must be empirical propositions, but the inferential machine is not basically of the linguistic form or nature. It is only when it is for communication that it takes the linguistic form. So the inferential model that is linguistic (Parārtha—for others) is to be distinguished from the basic inferential machine that is non-linguistic and which exists for oneself (Svārtha). Some people tend to call it a psychological process of inference. But it is necessary to remember that it is not psychological in the sense that trains of ideas are psychological.

These presuppositions have had very important repercussions on the development of the Indian theory of inference. First, inferential knowledge is bound to be probably only and would never have absolute deductive certainty. Secondly, a universal general premise will be only probably and will not carry with it absolute certainty. In fact the history of Indian logic tells us that earlier there was no general premise in the inferential model at all. The inference model was only analogical. *A* has *P*, *S* also is like *A*, ∴ *S* also has *P*. It is only gradually that the premise '*A* has *P*' grew into 'All (or every) *A* has *P*', and *S* was brought under *A* as a member of the class of *S*. (It appears to me that when Indian philosophers talk of the general premise they use a concept of a class suggested by Vyāpti exactly the way it is used in western logic.)

It should, however, be noted that the general premise in Indian logic is never a proposition with a bare universal form. It is always accompanied by an instance. This would make sure (1) the possibility of predication and (2) ensure a (probably) particular conclusion, which would be impossible if the universal proposition had been empty. Again the kind of subsumptive relation which holds between a class and a sub-class is not accepted by Indians as inference. It does not fit in the accepted norm that knowledge must be particular-singular; a relation between a class and a sub-class is only general. (A Class or a sub-class cannot be an instance of a class in the sense that a particular is an instance of class.) Thus Indian logic will not have all those moods and figures which arise in classical

Aristotelian logic. It will also not give merely the relations of implication. Indian logic of inference is rather, to use W. E. Johnson's terminology, applicative. Not that subsumptive relations are not dealt with in Indian logic. But they are not called inference. They are regarded as simply rules indicating the relations between a class and a sub-class or Vyāpya-Vyāpakabhāva. Thus one could easily say that wherever there is potness there is earthness, and wherever there is earthness there is the characteristic of having odour; therefore wherever there is potness there is the characteristic of having odour. But this is not regarded as inference.

Indian inference is sometimes called Indian syllogism. I think this is a mistake. It does not have the syllogistic form although, if one means to bring it about, one could. It will be worthwhile to note that the form of inference in Indian logic is that of controversy and therefore it should be better called dialecticism and not syllogism. The form of inference that has come down to us as a form of inference for others (Parārthānumāna) is not that of three propositions, the major premise, the minor premise, and the conclusion—but that of five sentences required in the dialectics for convincing others.

The first is the enunciation of the position or the proposition to be proved. The second is the statement of the reason which would imply the enunciation. The third is a statement of an instance which is similar to the proposition of enunciation. In the course of history, the concept of concomitance between the middle term and the major term developed out of this instance by subjecting it to generalization and came to be known as universal relation or vyāpti. The fourth states that the enunciated proposition is similar to the instance with which the claim is supported. In the course of time, however, the relation of similarity was replaced by that of application of the universal proposition to the case under consideration. And in the final stage this concept was identified with *Parāmarśa* or comprehension. A discussion about this concept will follow. The fifth is the conclusion. This is the same as the proposition which was enunciated.

It will be proper to recall that in the earlier days of logic there were not only these five parts of arguments, which are mentioned above, but there were in addition five parts, making the total of the parts of argument ten. Thus it will be clear that the form of argument of inference is not that of a syllogism, but that of controversy or debate. That the five-part argument was not in the strictly logical form was clearly brought out by the Buddhist logicians Dignāga, Dharmakīrti and Dharmottara who said that only two parts representing premises and a conclusion were enough for the argument.

Before we proceed further it will be necessary to point out that although I said that according to Indian logicians inference proceeded from the general to the particular, Indian logicians would not allow any syllogism of the form 'All men are mortal', 'Some Greeks are men', ∴ 'Some Greeks are mortals' as inference. For inference must always be characterized by definiteness. When Indians talk of particularity they only mean singularity.

It is important to point out here that there is yet another difference between the Indian and Greek syllogism. From negative premises no affirmative conclusion can be drawn according to the Greek technique. But in Indian logic there can be a negative premise and an affirmative conclusion, and a conclusion can also be drawn from two negative propositions. This is so because (1) Negation has a very different significance in Indian logic. Being primarily empirical, Indian logic does not allow any negative entities. And in the final stage even non-existence was loosely understood as some form of conceptional existence. If we say that wherever there is smoke there is fire, then we say this because we have actually seen smoke somewhere and so there will be fire. Modus ponens is thus allowed. But modus tollens will have no place in Indian inference except for confirming the universal premise, by adhering to contra-positive or Tarka. And here too, the objective is not to prove something negative. The sole aim of Indian logic is to prove the positive concomitance between the middle term or the reason and the major term. In a sense it will not be very correct to say that the Greeks did not draw positive conclusions from negative premises. In a weak disjunctive syllogism form $p \vee q$, the conclusion p is drawn only by denying p, and p is drawn by denying q.

In the logical literature of India there is an allusion to three kinds of inference. In one book (Aphorism or Vaiśeṣikās) there is a reference to the fourth one too. But the theory of inference that is actually developed is of only one type. It is only the deductive one and is usually termed Sāmanyatodṛista or seen from the class or general characteristics.

Starting from these basic concepts, Indian logical theory developed in different ways. Since the inference proceeds from the class characteristics, the concept of class was profusely discussed. The earlier logicians did not accept anything except the natural class. The same object could not be classed under class *A* and class *B*. So also they did not accept the unit class. The later logicians, however, took the connotative view of the class, thought that classes need not have physical existence and depended on how we understand them. In fact they thought that classes were concepts, and we can think of them conceptually, even if there was not a member of the class. A half-man-half-lion, or Narasiṃha as it is called, they said, is either a case of unit-class or a case of null-class.

The basic pattern in which a thing was conceived was that of substance quality. Indian logicians conceived the structure of inference and of propositions too in the same way. The subject of a proposition was supposed to be the substratum, and the predicate superstratum. Similarly the form of the inference was that if on one substratum there were two characteristics always present then we could say that there was a concomitance between them. Thus, by bringing the substratum under a bigger class in which the substratum under consideration is a member, one could say that the member substratum would have a concomitance of those qualities. When we say, wherever there is smoke there is fire, we only mean that on all substrata smoke and fire go together. Now if this is so, then this will also be true in the case of the mountain, as mountain is only one of the members of the substrata which has smoke and fire.

The substance-quality, or the substratum-super-substratum relation, however, takes us to the logic of relations, the application of which, in a sense, is a speciality of Indian logic. When we say that the table is brown, the table is a substance, and brown is its characteristic; table is the substratum, brown is its super-stratum. They are inseparable and Indian logicians state this by saying that brownness "inheres in" the table. "Inhering in" is a kind of inseparable relation. When we say that a "table is on the ground", there is no doubt that the ground is the substratum and the table is the super-stratum. But the relation that is denoted by "on" is not an inseparable relation and is quite different from the relation "inhering in".

Indian logicians think that for a complete understanding of the substratum and the super-stratum the kind of relation which holds between them must also be added. We have seen earlier that in inference we infer from the class of substratum to a member substratum. Whether it is a class substratum or a member substraum the super-strata are related to the substratum, by a certain specific relation. The rule of the inference is that one can infer the super-strata and the relation between the super-strata and the member substratum, if and only if, the relation which holds between the member substratum and its super-strata is the same as the relation which holds between the class substratum and its super-strata. Only in such a case can the conclusion be validly held.

One of the important problems is how does one actually infer, i.e. proceed from premises to the conclusion. Suppose p is a premise and q is the conclusion, then can one simply say $p \therefore q$ if p and q are unrelated, if p and q do not overlap or are un-correlated in one's conceptual framework. Perhaps it is necessary to state that $p \supset q$, in order to draw the conclusion q from the given premise. That is, mere p as a premise is not enough to draw the conclusion q. One also needs another premise $p \supset q$. The same thing is true in the Logic of Terms. One cannot really conclude that Socrates is mortal from the premises 'All men are mortal' and 'Socrates is a man' unless the two premises are held together, unless the relationship is established between men, mortal and Socrates. In Indian logic this was pointed out by the concept of Parāmarśa. It acted like modus ponens and made room for the detachment of the conclusion. It also acted like the rule of transitivity. A parrot who says that there is smoke on the mountain and that wherever there is smoke there is also fire will not be able to draw the conclusion that there is fire on the mountain. The parrot only mentions concepts but does not use them. In using the concepts one is going beyond the coexistence of words. They become parts of one's experience and it is such experience which leads to inference. Parāmarśa of Indian logic tells us that two premises get fused in one experience and thus are able to imply the conclusion.

Although it was not there in the beginning, at a later stage the instance or example was developed into the universal concomitance. Earlier too, the reason (the middle term) was supposed to be identical in two instances, although the instances were different and particular. Indian logic was essentially empirical and, therefore, strictly speaking, there should not have been any place for implication. But the concept of implication did creep in. Whenever we say that wherever there is smoke there is fire, whether this statement is true or not we have already resorted to implication. And there is evidence that in Indian logic the concept of implication was made use of. According to the Buddhist logician, Dharmakīrti, the implication is (1) either based on the cause-effect relation or (2) is based on the relation between a class and its sub-class. Thus there is smoke implies that there is fire; because fire and smoke are related as cause and effect. So, since the effect cannot be produced without a cause, if there was the effect then it follows that there was the cause also.

However, since Indian logic is essentially empirical, how to get a universal proposition becomes a major problem. Observation is the main method for such inductive generalization. Usually counting many instances, or many types of instances (Bhuyo Darśana) is recommended. But it is also pointed out that whereas many instances may not prove, one instance may disprove, and sometimes even one instance may be enough to establish a necessary concomitance. If two things are found going together (Sahacāragraha), there is a tendency to think that they always go together. If one thing is present but another is absent, then they are not related by necessary relation. On the basis of these primary processes one may get (1) whenever there is A, there is B—a positive argument and (2) whenever there is $\sim A$, there is $\sim B$—a negative argument. On this basis a hypothesis that A and B are necessarily related is formulated and it is confirmed or proved false by means of Tarka. Tarka is sometimes called a proof by reductio ad absurdum or a case of counter-factual. But in form it is very different from both these, and I should like to call it the conditional transposition. The proposition wherever there is smoke there is fire, is tested on the ground that fire and smoke are cause and effect. So if there was no fire then there would be no smoke. But there is smoke. So there must be fire. Formally the argument would take the following form:

$((\sim q \supset \sim p) \cdot p) \supset q)$. This is of course equivalent to $(\sim q \supset \sim p) \supset (p \supset q)$ by exportation. And since $(\sim q \supset \sim p)$ is given $(p \supset q)$ will be proved by modus ponens.

While dealing with the theory of inference Indian logicians have also discussed fallacies. Fallacies are ultimately due to a fallacious reason; whether it is a wrong reason connected with the other terms it really comes to be a wrong reason. Hence, Indian logicians attribute all fallacies to fallacious reason. They give five requisites of good reason.

(1) The presence of a reason in the member substratum.
(2) The presence of the reason is co-substratum.
(3) Absence of the reason from that which is the substratum of the opposite characteristics.
(4) Non-contradiction of stronger proof.
(5) Absence of counter-balancing of reason.

Absence of these conditions leads to the fallacies. If the reason (middle term) is present in the substratum where the contrary of that which is to be proved (major term) exists, then the fallacy is called non-invariable relations (Savyabhicāra). (2) If the middle term and the major term do not exist on the same substratum but if they are asserted together, then there is a fallacy called *contradiction*. (3) If reason is assigned for a thing which is really not concerned with the case under consideration, then it is called unproved or Asiddha. (4) If by the middle term the opposite conclusion can also be proved, then the fallacy is called the real opposite or Satpratipakṣa. (5) When the conclusion is cancelled or refuted later on by some stronger reason, then it is called Cancellation or Bādhita.

It will be interesting to point out that in India an elementary system of modal logic was also constructed by the Jain logicians. They thought that in the world of matter of fact every attribute is compatible with every other attribute of a thing. So in this limited sphere the law of contradiction would not apply and to use modern language the only logical operator that is necessary is 'or' (V). On the basis of this they developed their logic of seven possibilities known as Syādvāda.

Some schools of Indian philosophy recognise Arthāpatti or semantical implication as an independent source of knowledge. It is independent inasmuch as the knowledge which arises is dependent on the meaning of the earlier sentences and not merely on the form of sentences as is the case in material implication, formal implication or inference. The argument from Arthāpatti, however, has the form, $p \supset (q \vee r)$ and by modus ponens, by asserting p we get $(q \vee r)$ and then by denying q we get r (disjunctive syllogism). However, the consistency of the argument depends on the meaning of p and the meaning of $(q \vee r)$. Further $(q \vee r)$ must be the only alternatives which are implied by p. The usual instance that is given is the following:

Devadatta who is fat does not eat during the day. The conclusion is drawn that he eats in the night. The implied propositions are

(1) One cannot be fat if one starves.
(2) One eats either during the day or during the night.

The detachment of $q \vee r$ from the original wff is due to the meaning of p and similarly the assertion of r after the denial of q which although it depends on the form $(q \vee r)$, is obtained through the meaning of the original argument. The logicians of the Nyāya school regard it as a case of inference. But if inference is defined as an argument from universal major premises to a particular singular conclusion, then it is plain that a universal major premise is not required for proving the case. Even when one tries to supply the universal premise, it is only forced. I call it 'semantic implication' because the suppressed premises can be supplied only if we take into consideration the meaning of the argument; and it is only on the basis of the meaning that the conclusion is drawn giving rise to new knowledge.

Upmāna or knowledge by comparative description is also regarded as a source of knowledge by the adherent of most schools of Indian philosophy barring of course Cārvākas, Vaiśeṣikās, Baudhhas and Sāṃkhyas. Some people call this an argument from comparison. In ordinary perception the existence of the object of knowledge is not only presupposed, but is actually felt. The object is presented to you and the description of the object arises from the object itself. However, if you perceive the object a second time, traces of the previous perception modify your second perception and you are able to recognise the object of perception. In psychology it is called apperception. If you see a table, for example, on two consecutive occasions, on the first occasion you may not know that it is a table; but once it is ostensively taught you that it is a table, on the second occasion when the table is presented to you, you would recognise it. However, even if the same table is not presented, but another table is presented, you would know that it is a table. That is, you are able to recognize different particulars under the same class.

In knowledge by comparative description or upamāna you are able to transcend this limit of one class. You are able to recognize the object belonging to a different class, although you have not seen it earlier. This is of course due to the similarity between objects of different classes and also due to the fact that the similarity has been earlier described to you. Knowledge by comparative description is like apperception except that the span of apperception is extended from the particulars within the class to the particulars outside the class. I perceive a cow. I am later told that a yak is similar to a cow and exists in the Himalayas. Although I have not seen a yak, when I see a strange animal which is similar to a cow and yet different from it, I recognize it as a yak even though I have not seen it earlier. It will be important to note that concept-formation also takes place in the same way. If I see a cow and know that it is an animal, even when I see a horse, I know it as an animal although it is not a cow.

Indian philosophers also recognize Śabda as an independent source of knowledge. The word Śabda is variously used to convey (1) ordinary language, (2) revealed language and (3) an authority. The word pramāṇa is also vaguely used to convey (1) the source of knowledge and (2) the authority of action. It is plain that when we are talking of prescriptions or actions we are not conveying any information or knowledge in the straightforward sense. The sentences (1) Open the door, (2) Do not do this or (3) Read a certain book, etc. do not convey information primarily. They are imperatives, although for the execution of these imperatives some elementary information is presupposed. Here the meaning of Śabda is 'authority for action', although this authority for action does not convey information exclusively. In Pūrva Mīmāṃsā, the word Śabda is used to convey such authority of action. But when Śabda is used as a source of knowledge, it conveys knowledge because the language or Śabda conveys information. The information can be clothed in language because someone has used this language to communicate this information. The information is regarded as reliable on the authority of 'that' someone, who is sometimes regarded as Āpta or the competent person. He is supposed to be not interested in deluding us. I read in the newspaper that the astronauts have landed on the moon. I believed it and regard it as information because I took it that the news agency which gave this news was interested in giving correct and not false news. Similarly I also believe that the newspapers which printed the news were interested in giving me correct information. Of course the authority of anybody and everybody is not accepted. The authority of a man is decided by some criteria. In one sense of the term then, when we talk of Śabda as a source of knowledge, we mean the authority of a competent person.

However, the competent person conveys this information through language. Some religious men hold that God and Messiah sometimes reveal sacred information which also is in language. The Vedas, the Bible and the Quoran are regarded as sacred books, and the language in those books is regarded as sacred and revealed. The truth of such revealed language is usually not challenged and is called in Sanskrit Alaukika Śabda.

But sometimes the information is conveyed in ordinary language and then the syntax and the symantics of the language become important. Indian philosophers have given various theories about language and its syntax. According to one, the Sphota theory, it is the sentence which is the primary unit of language. It is not the words which combine themselves in a sentence but it is the sentence which we break into 'parts of speech'. According to the second theory a sentence is made up of words; each word expects some other word till the sentence is complete. A word in itself could have many meanings, but in a particular context it is only the specific meaning of the word which is relevant. This is called competency. Again in order to yield the meaning, the different words must be proximate. If one word is uttered today and another is uttered tomorrow, it will not convey any meaning. However, the kind of syntax which Indians talk of is not a pure syntax; it is a composite syntax where the semantical part has also to be accounted for. Unless the intention of the speaker is taken into account the sentence will not yield any meaning and so will not be useful as a source of knowledge. In accepting language as a source of knowledge Indian philosophers give an elaborate analysis of language.

According to some systems of Indian philosophy a special source of knowledge is recognized for negative knowledge or the knowledge of non-existent phenomena. If a chair is not in this room I know it by perception according to the Nyāya philosophers. According to them the absence or non-existence (of a chair) is also known to me by the same sense organs by which I know positive objects. However, philosophers of some schools argue that, there is a difference in knowing that a thing exists from knowing that it does not exist or is not present. If there is no horse in this room, I cannot know it by perception. Therefore, non-availability (Anupalabdhi) is regarded as an independent source of knowledge, particularly by the followers of Pūrva-Mīmāṃsā and Vedānta schools.

How do we know that the knowledge which is conveyed through

ıese different sources is valid when we know that erroneous know-dge is made up of parts which are in themselves real. Thus, though ıe composite knowledge may be invalid, still, the units of knowledge annot be invalid. This is the view which is advocated by the Iimāṃsā schools and is known as the self-validity theory of know-edge. The Nyāya school believes in the self-validity of the ıference-machine and tests the validity of other knowledge by this ıachine. Therefore the Nyāya view is that no knowledge is valid y itself. The Buddhists think that things in themselves are only ıferred by us. Although they are presented to us directly and are nown to us at the first moment, due to our own projection and onstruction, our actual perception, consists of (1) actual reality, 2) our construction. Our macro-cognition then is not as a whole .nd so the validity of knowledge will have to be established and ustified by something else. The Buddhist theory is sometimes nown as the extrinsic validity theory of knowledge. That our nowledge is valid is a belief. Either we take it as valid in its own ight or test its validity. Then that by which we test it as valid in ts own right (or the validity of previous knowledge) is to be tested y further knowledge and this in its turn is again to be tested by urther knowledge. This is what happens in Buddhism.

9

METAPHYSICS

G. N. Joshi

I Introduction

Indian philosophy is so vast and varied that it is impossible to discuss it fully in a single, brief essay. The lack of a definite written record of the periods and dates of the many schools and writings, the authors' habit of not identifying themselves, the lack of materials such as paper and ink, the necessity of oral transmission and the resulting distortions and the very nature of Sanskrit makes the task even harder.

Some claim that philosophy, as in Greece, originated in a sense of wonder and curiousity about the world; however, it is doubtful whether that alone can stimulate philosophical thinking. Indian philosophy did not originate thus, as life was hard and burdensome for the early Indians. P. T. Raju asserts that "neither with the Upaniṣadic thinkers nor with Confucius, nor, again with Socrates and Plato did philosophy start in wonder. With Buddha it started with the idea of suffering. . . . It was a desire for some existence higher than the present, whether in the cosmos, society, or the state, that offered the motive force for every philosophy of life."[1] Indian philosophy, then, was not a mere intellectual pastime but was born out of a deeply felt need to be free from the sufferings of the world and to reach eternal peace and freedom from the cycle of birth and death. Indian people deeply sensed the misery of worldly life and were stimulated thereby to think profoundly on the root of all suffering and the causes of the world's ills. Indian metaphysics is motivated therefore by the desire to be free from all kinds of bondage and suffering and to realise Mokṣa (liberation), the supreme ideal of life.

By Indian philosophy we mean here all philosophy born in India, orthodox and heterodox, excluding Muslim philosophy. Indian metaphysics should be understood against the peculiar background, attitudes, approaches and perspectives of Indian thinkers. Among them are, according to Raju, the greater emphasis on Inwardness, which maintains the highest principle man has to realize is the Ātman (Self) within himself; the compatibility of Reason and Faith, God not being a conceptual abstraction but the experiencing of the identity of oneself with Him; the Ātman as the immortal principle and the highest in man and not his reason, that Self being known in a strictly personal and intuitive experience of identity with all reality; and the Ātman being the same as Brahman, the all-pervading, immutable, eternal Reality in which perfection is realized.

Indian and western philosophy is often contrasted, the former being supposedly spiritualistic, contemplative and mystical, the latter materialistic, empirical and activist. Several points may be made. The first is that we should be cautious about such generalizations as the above, for we find empirical philosophies in India and spiritualistic philosophies in the West also. Secondly, philosophers in the East and West are concerned with many of the same problems and we find both identical and different answers given by them. Differences between them may be one of degree of emphasis; on the other hand differences in the kinds of answers should not be glossed over. We should recognize that philosophy as meaning fundamental thinking is universal or knows no bounds. Therefore diverse need not be interpreted necessarily as conflicting answers. Indian philosophy emphasizes this point especially. It is based on a universalistic, synoptic, synthetic and unified vision of seeing one in many and the many as expressions of one single Reality. It believes in the central unity of life and existence, passes from oneness and unity to manyness and diversity and holds that the many reveal the richness and glory of the One which is the essential nature of every particular aspect of reality. Furthermore, it reminds natural scientists of the difficulties they face in their explaining of such phenomena as regularity, new creation and the adjustment of means to ends without taking into account the possibility of an intelligent and conative Cosmic power like God. Indian philosophy does not conceive it possible, desirable or logically feasible to explain natural phenomena and reality in an absolutely mechanical, objective and value-neutral way.

II The Vedas

India's earliest philosophical reflections are found in the Vedas. Being close to the earth Vedic people composed special prayers or hymns (Vedas) addressed to the earth and heaven. Their philosophers looked upon natural agencies as mystical divine power and so they chanted hymns in praise of the sun, fire, dawn, rain and wind to appease and seek their favour. The goddess Aditi, meaning "unlimited and unbound" is the name for the all-pervading, the infinite and invisible. It is the vast substratum of all that is here and beyond, having infinite potentialities. Every God or Goddess was considered to be supreme and so there was an "overlapping of divinities," a situation Max Müller calls "Henotheism". But Vedic philosophy upheld polytheism according to which the several powerful natural agencies were looked upon as Gods and Goddesses.

The Vedic view of the universe was quite crude containing elements of poetic fancy, awe for natural powers, and both an adoration and fear of natural agencies. Vedic thinkers were animistic also in their reading spirit in all moving, active objects and events. For example, in explaining natural phenomena they presupposed a principle of order in the midst of and behind the confusing changes, a uniformity in the midst of diversity, something unchanging and permanent in the midst of change, which they called Ṛita. Ṛita means "the course of things" and stands for orderly behaviour, regularity, law and justice. It was at the root of and responsible for the entire cosmic order and for the basic principle of morality and righteousness. It was binding on all natural phenomena and could not be violated even by the gods.

The concept Ṛita introduced elements of intelligence and will along with morality in the governance of the universe. It assured men that nature was not chaotic but systematic, orderly, harmonious and purposeful. It created a faith in men that life is not vicarious and fortuitous but that at its source is morality and righteousness. The principle of Ṛita gave solace to the hearts of men, tormented by uncertainty, insecurity and fear, that there is a superior power in the universe which recognizes the merit of individuals and rewards persons who sincerely follow the path of truth and justice.

Vedic philosophers believed that subtle and invisible realities can be perceived by wise men with keen insight and intuition. They tended to seek the unity of Godhead not in the form of one od above others, but as the common divine power that works ehind all the gods. Thus there was a kind of "philosophic ıonism". The many gods of Vedic times were personifications f particular natural functions and agencies. However, polyıeistic thinking in the Vedas gradually evolved through henotheism) monotheism and culminated in the monism of the Upaniṣads. 'edic hymns often lack clearcut, logical thought. Many Vedic ıonotheistic expressions also suggest a "Pantheism" which denies ny difference between the world and God and sees the whole world s divine. God is immanent in the world and the two become lentified. In the Vedic period an elaborate set of rituals and acrifices aimed at pleasing powerful, natural agencies developed; .owever, the sacrificialism and ritualism should be understood ymbolically, as Vedic thought was fast developing toward the ıonism of the Upaniṣads.

III The Upaniṣads

The main teaching of the Upaniṣads is that ultimate reality s an everlasting, infinite, immeasurable and all-pervading unity. t has two aspects, the external and internal. The external as the bjective side is called Brahman and can be known by man as his nnerself (Ātman). It is described like Spinoza describes substance. 3rahman as "that from which these beings are born, that in which, when born they live, and that into which they enter at death" is he source, support and end of all that exists.

The Upaniṣads do not deny the Buddhist view that everything s momentary but maintain that behind the changing world subject to origin, modification and destruction must be something unchaning. The gross material world is not totally unreal but enjoys only a limited reality. There are levels of reality, the senseworld being a lower one. As man rises in levels of experience and consciousness, he becomes aware of the higher reality, Brahman, which cannot be perceived by the senses because it does not possess perceptible properties. Because the categories of understanding do not apply to it, Brahamn cannot be known by concepts, described in language and therefore communicated to others in the usual way. Being vast and infinite it cannot be pictured positively but only negatively by such words as imperceptible, illimitable, indescribable and ineffable.

The Upaniṣads assert that Brahman is supersensible and thu cannot be known in the usual epistemological ways. Moreove the mind is limited and Brahman therefore is to be known only b direct, immediate, personal experience, by becoming one with it The subject-object duality does not enable us to know it. Ther can be no predicative knowledge of Brahman because the predicat states some attribute or class of the subject which is Brahman Being all-embracing and all-persuasive Brahman cannot limi itself to any particular attribute, though all attributes emanat from it. Thus it is said to be devoid of attributes (Nirguṇa) in no possessing any particular attribute or attributes and in transcendin all attributes because it is the highest and ultimate reality.[2]

Any attempt to restrict Brahman to any particular attribute quality or predicate will not only inevitably fail to give us the rea Brahman but will also falsify and negate it. Spinoza's famou formulation in regard to knowing Substance that "All determinatio is negation" is applicable to Brahman also.[3] Brahman is beyon names and forms. They are limited, to use Kant's terms, t "phenomenal reality", which is perceived by the mind and sense and limited in several ways. Brahman as unique is analogou to "noumenal reality", being the "thing-in-itself" to be known b reference. Having no connotation which can be stated, it can b only denoted or hinted at. Brahman cannot be known objectivel as an object of knowledge because it is the same as the knowin self. Its objectification and categorization is thus impossible Brahman can only be felt in an intuitive, personal, living experienc of identity with it.

Brahman is of two kinds, Nirguṇa and Saguṇa (with attributes) Saguṇa Brahman as God is not a different existence but is Nirguṇa Brahman on a lower plane. Saguṇa Brahman is the cause and governor of the world and becomes accessible to men as the object of worship because Nirguṇa Brahman, being beyond all attributes, cannot respond to the needs and prayers of men.

Māyā as cosmic illusion is another significant concept in the Upaniṣads.[4] The Māyā doctrine does not declare the world is absolutely illusory or unreal but only that it is not the ultimately Real or is not real as Ultimate Reality. It is real from an empirical standpoint or for those who rely on sense-experience. It is not for those who have experiences on higher planes of consciousness. The world appears illusory to those who have realized Brahman in personal xperience but not to others living on the phenomenal (worldly) lane. Another important contribution of the Upaniṣads is the Concept of Sheaths (Kośa). Though all is Brahman, there are ifferent levels and a hierarchy of existence. Ultimate Reality Nirguṇa Brahman) exists on the material plane in the form of food Anna Kośa), superseded by successively higher planes of existence—ital energy (Prāṇa Kośa), mind and will (Mānasa Kośa), intellect Vijñāna Kośa) and blissfulness (Ānanda Kośa). The five planes re arranged in an unbroken, continuous series, being manifestations f the same reality, Nirguṇa Brahman making qualitative appear-nces at the various planes of existence. The planes are recognized s an axiological hierarchy of the functions of life manifesting tself at the various levels of manifestations of the same single eality.

The concept of Sheaths illustrates how one single Reality is present n all aspects and levels of existence and even in one person. It hows also the stages from lower to higher in the evolution of life, n evolution in which there is not only lower-higher continuity ut the higher does not mitigate the lower. They exist together nd side by side. Each of the sheaths has its function and they omplement each other, the lower serving the higher ultimately to acilitate the realization of the highest principle, which is an expe-ience of perfect bliss. Reality as whole and continous is described s "Sat-Cit-Ānanda," Sat meaning that existence which is common o all things, Cit having consciousness or awareness of existence nd Ānanda pure joy or a sense of complete satisfaction or fulfilment. Existence cannot be only by itself. Unless there is an awareness f existence it is absured to assert that Ultimate Reality (Brahman) xists. The very assertion of the existence of reality implies aware-ess of it. Ānanda does not mean momentary pleasure but the onsciousness of nothing lacking or wanting. Ānanda as bliss neans an awareness of the perfection of Ultimate Reality. That Reality is not inert, dead and corporeal matter but is perfection itself, nd it has self-awareness of its own perfection or fulfilment. It nust be, therefore, a spiritual being.

Brahman is an immanent and inherent principle in conscious nd non-conscious realities. Smaller than the smallest and larger than the largest, the Chāndogya Upaniṣad describes it thus: "This myself within the heart, smaller than rice, or barley corn . . . ; this nyself within the heart is greater than the earth . . . the mid-region . . .

greater than all these worlds." Brahman is devoid of materialit dimensions and any quality. Yājñavalkya describes it negativel as "not gross, nor subtle, not short, not long. . . without air, withou space...without taste, without smell...without ears, without speech. without form and without either inside or outside." Thus the sam Ultimate Reality is everywhere, being all-embracing and all-pe vading. The Ātman which is the same as Brahman is the Univers Self immanent in all persons and things. It is the supreme obje of all knowledge. It is not a thought, but all thoughts are for i It is not a thing seen but is the principle of all seeing.

The Universal Self is the condition and presupposition of a empirical knowledge and is, therefore, the Transcendental Subjec It is ever the subject and not object of any knowledge. It is ofte expressed in the identity proposition "Tat-Tvam-Asi", "That ar thou", that the knower is Brahman itself.[6] In the final state th subject and object of knowledge lose their duality and become one Thus, according to the Upaniṣads, there is a correspondence be tween the states of consciousness of the Self and the different order of Brahman or the cosmic level.

IV Cārvāka

Cārvākism is a materialistic philosophy taking th metaphysical view that the universe consists of four eternal elements– earth, water, fire and air.[7] They consititute the body or the universe Consciousness is a function of their united action, and it is ar adventitious property of the living body. There is no soul as ar independent substantial entity; it is an epiphenomenon of th combination of the four elements. The soul disappears completel with the destruction of the body and nothing survives to be reborn Cārvāka does not accept the existence of life after death, Karma rebirth or heaven and hell. The empirical life of a person on eart alone is real and so, prudence lies in making the best of life on eart by enjoying the physical pleasures as fully as one can. Th Cārvākas advocated a hedonistic way of life without any considera tion for the life beyond.

Cārvāka metaphysics is the logical outcome of its epistemologica position which rejects all other sources of knowledge except per ception. It is more empirical and positivitic in its approach and sc it denies the existence of supernatural, trans-mundane and abstrac ntities. Cārvākism takes the position of even denying inference s a valid source of knowledge.[8] It delimits the scope of knowledge reatly by restricting all knowledge to direct perception and thus akes an extreme position which is philosophically and practically ntenable. The result of its narrow scope of knowledge is its denial f morality, social responsibility and commitment and supernatural agencies which affect and shape the lives of men. By reating death as the final end of life Cārvākism indirectly encourages n over-egoistic and selfish attitude in individuals. In its vehemence o oppose and criticize Vedic over-indulgence in sacrificialism and itualism it has denounced even obviously reasonable things and dvocated a crude and narrow eithics. The Cārvāka view exhibits n ignoble, sensualistic materialism. It is severely criticized by all ther systems of Indian philosophy.

V Jainism

Jainism is considered a heterodox system because it rejects the authority of the Vedas and atheistic since it denies the existence of God. It divides reality into two fundamental, independent and exclusive categories of Soul (Jīva) and Matter (Ajīva), the Soul being the conscious principle and experiencer of pleasure, pain and knowledge. Matter is devoid of consciousness and is the object of enjoyment. All animate beings have a body and soul. Ajīva is divided into classes, those with form (Rūpa) such as Pudgala (matter) and those without (Arūpa) like Dharma, Adharma, space and time. Substance is subject to changes and modifications, possesses qualities and performs functions. Things are permanent as substance and change in regard to their accidental features.

Jainism holds that reality changes, gains new qualities and loses old ones. Substance is inseparable from its qualities and persists in and through its qualities and modifications. It is unity in differences. It is dynamic and maintains identity in the midst of changes. Qualities (Guṇas) inhere in the substances. Jainism is pluralistic and relativistic as it recognizes an infinite number of Jīvas as well as material elements. Pudgala has two kinds of motion, Simple (Parispanda) and Evolution (Pariṇāma), and the qualities of colour, smell, taste, sound and touch are associated with it. Physical objects consist of atoms which are formless, infinitesimal, ultimate and eternal, having no beginning, middle or end.

Atoms possess weight, the heavy going downwards, the light upward. Gross things are produced by their various kinds of combinations and are subject to attraction and repulsion. The aggregates produced by combinations are called Skandhas. The qualities of atoms change in accordance with their combinations. Jains, unlike the Vaiśeṣikas, do not hold that atoms are qualitatively different from each other. All atoms are homogeneous, qualitative differences being due to the different kinds of arrangements and combinations of atoms, Souls are qualitatively similar; their differences are due to their empirical distinctions and different kinds of physical adjuncts. Unusual is the Jain's belief that the soul has variable sizes in its empirical life, becoming larger or smaller because of expansion or contraction according to the dimensions of the physical bodies the Jīvas occupy.

Souls are classified on the basis of the number of sense-organs they possess. The Jīva has the quality of experience and action. Inherently the Jīva is perfect, possessing infinite intelligence, faith, power and peace; but due to its association with the body its adherent qualities are obscured. Every person possesses both spiritual and material aspects. The soul's bondage is due to the predominant influence of the body. To attain liberation the soul continuously shakes off the influence of materiality so it can reveal its inherent excellences such as infinite knowledge and power in their fullness. Consciousness constitutes the essence of the soul and so it can know everything unaided and directly, provided there are no physical impediments obstructing its apprehension. The Jīva suffers from imperfect knowledge due to its association with the Karma obstructing the power of clear perception. The Jīva becomes omniscient and gains absolute knowledge directly when it is completely free from every Karma.

Karma is a kind of matter filling cosmic space and capable of developing the effect of merit or demerit. Karma penetrates the soul or sticks to it. Every action of the soul produces an effect on the Jīva through Karma and leaves its mark. The inflow of Karmic matter into the Jiva, which causes and strengthens bondage, is called Āsrava. Saṃvara is the stopping or blocking of the channels through which Karma flows into the soul.[9] Nijarā is that which wears away entirely all the sins committed by the soul. The Jīva falls into bondage due to wrong belief, non-renunciation, carelessness, and passions. In liberation, achieved by right knowledge and onduct, the Jīva experiences its native attributes of infinite knowedge, perception, power and bliss.

VI Buddhism

Buddhism like Jainism is atheistic, unorthodox and a reaction gainst excessive Vedic ritualism and sacrificialism. Buddha howed little interest in any other worldly life but sought to discover he means of improving man's moral life and releasing people rom their present sorrows and suffering.[10] Thus he did not ndulge in abstract metaphysical speculation; his approach was nore practical than theoretical.

Buddha propounded a theory of universal change, impermanence nd momentariness.[11] Everything in the universe is changing; nothing lasts for more than a moment. Reality is a continuous lux. There is nothing stable and permanent beneath and behind he changing scenes. Change is the stuff of reality. There is neither permanence nor identity. What we call identity is an ppearance, a deception caused by a rapid succession of similarities. Everything passes into non-being and the experience of permanence s an illusion. Only becoming is real.

Buddha declared that nothing exists in and of itself. He advocated he doctrine of soullessness. He also asserted the theory of Dependent Origination (Pratītyasamutpāda) which states that complex nd composite things developed out of the combination of several actors. For example, a flame is not a separate unit but is a visible esultant of several items such as wick, oil and fire working in a set pattern. A tree is not a whole tree as such but is a unity of several parts—roots, stem, branches, leaves, buds, flowers, fruits and seeds ll working in cooperation.

Thus everything depends on every other thing. Nothing has an xistence in itself; nothing has its being contained in itself. Nothing s self-created and sustaining. A thing is what it is because of its elations to other things. All is Svabhāvaśūnya (devoid of one's own nature). Causality is nothing but the coexistence and co-rdination of innumerable, momentary existences. Everything has relative stability and permanence. A thing comes into existence, becomes what it is, grows, changes its properties and disappears, but all this happens only in a single moment. What is supposed to be identity is nothing but an unbroken continuity of similar events.

Thus, according to Buddhism, every event happens in a realm o relations; everything is conditioned by and dependent on every othe thing and so there is only the reign of relativity. Buddha declarec reality to be a continuity of Becoming and an ordered succession There is no inner teleology in causation. There is necessity in th causal series only in that, once a series begins, it will not cease a long as the conditions under which it began continue. Thus with out positing any enduring substratum, Buddha advocated a theor of ceaseless change and infinite momentary existences.

VII Nyāya-Vaiśeṣika

The Nyāya-Vaiśeṣika systems founded by Gotama an Kanāda represent a kind of pluralistic realism which affirms the worl is real. It is different from the knowing mind, and all objects can b divided into seven categories—Dravya (Substance), Guṇa (Quality) Karma (Action), Sāmānya (Generality—Universal), Viśeṣa (Parti cularity), Samavāya (Inherence) and Abhāva (non-existence) Dravya is self-existent and self-subsistent, and qualities and actio inhere in it. There are nine ultimate substances possessing differen properties and relations—Earth, Water, Fire, Air, Ether, Time Space, Self and Mind. The first four exist in the form of extremel subtle supra-sensible atoms which are indivisible and eternal. Eacl is recognized by a unique, particular (viśeṣa) property, and thi unique particularity is fundamental. Therefore the system is know as Vaiśeṣika from the word Viśeṣa meaning unique particularity.

The atoms of earth are characterized by odour, water by taste fire by colour and air by touch.[12] Ākāśa is partless and infinit and therefore does not produce anything. The world is producec by the combination of those atoms in various proportions. Th atoms are uncreated, indestructible and eternal, but their compound are destructible. Atoms are supra-sensible and cannot be dis tinguished on the basis of their shape, size, weight, density, etc They have only qualitative distinctions and are known by inference The world comes into existence by their conjunction and its end i due to their disjunction. The world is non-eternal and therefor subject to destruction when the atoms separate from each othe The qualities of the atoms produce their corresponding qualities i the objects they constitute. Though each atom by itself is imper ceptible, their compounds which form gross objects become percep ible. At the time of the world's dissolution, the atoms segregate and emain in isolation. Their integration and disintegration are caused y the Unseen Principle (Adṛiṣṭa).

The world's creation happens according to the merit and demerit f souls. The Nyāya-Vaiśeṣika systems admit God as a Supreme Being and Governor of the world, but He does not create substances nd Karma. He administers the world on the principle of deserving r the merit and demerit of souls. God is guided by the principle f Adṛiṣṭa, thus being able to maintain justice and equity in the vorld. The Vaiśeṣika view atoms differently from the Greek philosophers Leucippus and Democritus who believed atoms differ in hape and size. Vaiśeṣika holds atoms to be extremely minute and imperceptible, having fundamental qualitative peculiarities of their own. The Vaiśeṣika distinguish seventeen qualities and five kinds of movement or action and pays more attention to the structure of the the universe and to its ontological aspect.

The Nyāya system is devoted more to the study of logic, epistemology and the means of knowledge. Sāmānya is recognized as a category along with Viśeṣa and their nature and interrelation are very meticulously studied. The concept of Samavāya is very peculiar.[13] It is a relation obtained between cause and effect, substance and qualities, whole and its parts, motion and object in motion, individual and the universal and is a relation of inseparability but not identity. It is different from a temporary conjunction (Saṃyoga) which is terminated by disjunction. It is an internal relation which cannot be terminated without the destruction of one of the objects. The relation between the cloth and its threads or that between the cloth and its colour is one of inherence. It is a peculiar type of relation not recognized in western epistemology.

The Nyāya-Vaiśeṣika systems recognize as real the causal law according to which cause and effect have an invariable relation. The cause precedes the effect and their association can be tested by the methods of Agreement and Difference. If the relation between the two is invariable, it rules out the possibility of a "Plurality of Causes". Nyāya recognizes three kinds of causes—material (Upādāna), efficient (Minitta) and accessory (Sahakārī).

According to the Nyāya, the soul is a substance possessing mental attributes such as desire, aversion, pleasure, pain and intelligence. It exists by itself and supports mental qualities. Consciousness is an adventitious not essential quality of the soul. Knowledge and other psychical qualities arise in the soul when it comes int contact with the world through the mind. The soul is also the sub stratum of merit and demerit in virtue of which it undergoes trans migration by assuming different births for which it is suited. Th Nyāya, like other systems, upholds liberation as the highest goal c life. The liberated soul becomes completely free of all its menta states, pleasurable and painful. It loses its contact with the worl and becomes free from the nine qualities of the self. It is free from sentience, its state being likened to a stone. It retains it potentiality for consciousness, however. Liberation can be attaine by a right knowledge of the world and the soul.

Both systems admit the existence of God as the Supreme Soul omnipotent, omniscient, guiding and regulating the working of th universe. The Jīvas (human souls) are infinite in number, suffe from the limitations of worldly life and are governed by the law o Karma. God's existence is justified on various grounds including the usual arguments from Design, Causality, Teleological Adjustmen and Perfection.

VIII Sāṃkhya-Yoga

The Sāṃkhya system takes a developmental or evolutionary view of the universe, emphasizing the continuity of life from the lowest to the highest level of existence. It advocates dualism and rejects pluralistic atomism. It distinguishes two independent, mutually exclusive, irreducible yet supplementary principles of Puruṣa and Prakṛiti. All Reality can be divided into these two fundamental principles. Puruṣa is characterized by pure consciousness, Prakṛiti by materiality and change. All aspects of physical existence except consciousness belong to Prakṛiti. It is the first cause and all-pervading principle of the entire physical universe in all its concrete and abstract forms.

The Sāṃkhya adopts the Satkārya theory of causation that the effect already exists in an unmanifest and latent form in the cause. The effect is not different from the cause, and in the process of development the latent effect becomes manifest. According to the Satkāryavāda theory nothing can evolve which is not already in the cause. Prakṛiti is the primal cause of the universe and is uncreated and imperishable. Though imperceptible, it can be known by inference. It is a metaphysical principle, is the basis of all objective xistence and the material counterpart of Puruṣa, the spiritual rinciple.

Prakṛiti is made up of three qualities (Guṇas) which are inferred, ot perceived—Sattva, Rajas, and Tamas. They are intertwined ke strands of a rope. Sattva represents the fine, light, consciousess, goodness and happiness; Rajas activity, movement, striving and hange; Tamas coarseness, obstruction and apathy leading to norance and sloth. Three functions are determined by the uṇas. Sattva manifests, Rajas activates and Tamas restrains. 'he guṇas are not physical entities. Though distinguishable they re not separable. In no object is only one of them present. They ix in varying proportions and a thing's quality is determined by he predominance of one guṇa over the other two. Tamas pre-ominate in all heavy things, Rajas in all active and moving and attva in fine, shining and transparent things.

When the three guṇas are in perfect equilibrium, Prakṛiti is at est. When their equilibrium is disturbed, an imbalance starts mong them. The guṇas try to supersede each other and activity ontinues in several ways. It is said that the first shock is received y Prakṛiti from Puruṣa by its simple presence or proximity. When uch a contact occurs, it excites activity in Prakṛiti.[14] It is difficult understand how Puruṣa, which is completely inactive, can start ctivity in Prakṛiti. Perhaps its influence can be compared with the ffect of a magnet over a piece of iron or the effect of an idea in starting physical activity. The relation between Prakṛiti and Puruṣa difficult to comprehend. Puruṣa is consciousness but totally nactive, and Prakṛiti is non-conscious but full of energy. Though pposed in nature there is full cooperation between the two. Their nion is somewhat like the union of a lame person (Puruṣa with good ision) mounted on the shoulders of a strong and powerful person Prakṛiti).

Like Aristotle's God, the Sāṃkhya Puruṣa is the unmoved mover, purely contemplative being.[15] Puruṣa is eternally free, but due a false identification with Prakṛiti feels itself in bondage. Its eeling of involvement and entanglement is due to non-discrimination om Prakṛiti. Puruṣa requires something different from it in order experience its immutability, aloofness and isolation. Prakṛiti is nly the accessory cause to the experience of liberation for Puruṣa. uruṣa can feel its freedom from Prakṛiti by isolating and detaching self from Prakṛiti by seeing its aloofness, and by becoming only a passive spectator of the activity of Prakṛiti.

Puruṣa is supposedly constituted of consciousness, incapable o activity and eternal, immutable, never the doer but only the ex periencer or enjoyer. It is beyond the three guṇas, and all know ledge and consciousness in the universe are due to it. There ar many souls (Puruṣas) in the world. This is due to their associatio with separate bodies which have separate sense organs and birth an death. If there were only one soul for all, all would have had th same experience at one time; but there are differences in the indiv dual experiences of persons. Similarly the law of Karma woul have no meaning if there were one soul for all persons. In everyday life the soul suffers pain because of its entanglement in the activitie of Prakṛiti due to non-discrimination (aviveka).

Prakṛiti is the first cause of the universe. After the origina equilibrium of the three guṇas is disturbed, a great commotion star in its bosom and creative activity begins. Prakṛiti is said to produc the entire universe out of itself in an orderly process. Maha produced first, is the basis of intelligence in the individual an is Buddhi in the cosmos. It is the subtle substance of all menta processes. Mahat is the will; its special function is ascertainmen and decision. In its pure condition it has attributes like virtu knowledge, detachment and excellence. When vitiated by th Tamas, it has the opposite qualities. Though Buddhi is neare to the self it is not identical with it.

The second product of Prakṛiti is the Ahaṃkāra, the basis of th feeling of "I and mine". Because of Ahaṃkāra the self wrongl considers itself to be an agent or cause of action. Ahaṃkāra of three kinds, according to the predominance of one or the othe of the guṇas. When Sattva predominates it is called Sāttvika when Rajas it is Rājasika and when Tamas predominates it Tāmasika. From the Sāttvika ahaṃkāra the eleven organs, i.e. fiv sense-organs, five motor-organs and the mind, are produced. Th five subtle elements are produced from the Tāmasika Ahaṃkār The Rājasika Ahaṃkāra provides energy to both.

The evolution of Prakṛiti is a gradual and progressive differentia tion into many qualities and objects. It is completely determine and, according to the Satkārya theory of causation, developmen is nothing more than an unfoldment of what already exists in a unmanifest and potential form. It is only the implicit becomin explicit, and there is no room for the emergence of what is absolutel

w. There is no room for uncertainty and novelty. In the
olution espoused by Darwin, Bergson, Lloyd and Morgan there
room for indefiniteness and the emergence of new qualities and
rms, but not in the evolution advocated by Sāṃkhya. In the
tter there is an inherent teleology implied, since the whole process
evolution serves a purpose, though it is not consciously willed
d pursued. Perhaps there is an unconscious teleology involved
the Sāṃkhya system because the Prakṛiti that evolves is not cons-
ous of the functions it performs; yet it acts indirectly to serve a
irpose and attain certain ends. The adjustment of Prakṛiti with
ıruṣa is said to be unconscious, like the secreting of milk by the
w nursing its calf. Similarly the activity of Prakṛiti serves some
ırpose of the Puruṣa without consciously willing it.

Adherents of Yoga philosophy accept the metaphysical views of
e Sāṃkhya. Yoga is not a philosophical discipline but aims at
ying down a method of psychological and moral preparation for
e individual's attaining of the experience of isolation delineated by
e Sāṃkhya system. Patañjali evolved a discipline for those desir-
g to attain the highest state of liberation, according to which such
person has to observe rigorous self-control by restraining his sense
ıd motor-organs and by observing a certain mental discipline.[16]
hat discipline consists of Yama and Niyama and enables a person
withdraw gradually from the external world, concentrate on his
lf, contemplate its real nature and ultimately experience the final
ate of Samādhi in which the self forgets its narrow, egoistic existence
ıd experiences the infinite, unbounded self detached completely
om Prakṛiti.

Yoga also accepts the existence of God and God not only becomes
n object of concentration of the mind but even the attainment of
amādhi requires God's grace. Patañjali accepts the entire
āṃkhya metaphysics and its theory of evolution. The steps for
amādhi follow a reverse order, however. The Sādhaka must begin
is concentration of mind on the gross elements, then on the subtle
lements, then progressively on the senses, manas, ahaṃkāra and
ıahat. When concentration is purified and perfected at the highest
vel, the Puruṣa realizes there is only a reflection of it in Prakṛiti
nd that it falsely identifies itself with Prakṛiti and its evolutes.
'he moment one realizes this, Prakṛiti ceases to be active for him;
ıe guṇas regain their equilibrium; the reflection disappears and
ıe apparent bondage of Puruṣa vanishes.

Yoga is not simply a correlate of Sāṃkhya but enjoys a uniq position in Indian philosophy. It is accepted as a very importa science and technique of self-discipline by such systems as Vedānt Śāktism and Śaivism. Its essential teachings even Jains an Buddhists have found useful, though indirectly. In fact Yoga h provided to all Indian philosophy unfailing guidance in cultivatir self-control, moral purification and psychical methods of conce trating and meditation, enabling seekers of Mokṣa to attain t ultimate experience of Samādhi. Yoga is the most proud an unique possession of Indian philosophy. In the twentieth centu Gandhi was in many ways both an outstanding exponent and e ample of it. To him the union of the individual and Brahman i Samādhi had as its correlate in the conscious state the union man and man. He taught self-renunciation as the means of i dividual purification and Ahiṃsā and Satyāgraha as the means purifying inter-personal relations. Meditation and contemplatic lead to Truth and Gandhi equated Truth with God.

IX Vedānta

Vedānta seeks to explain the essence of Upaniṣadic teaching Bādarāyana (c. 500-250 B.C.) tried to systematize the different philo ophical tendencies in the Upaniṣads and later scholars like Sāṅkar Rāmānuja and Madhva wrote commentaries on Bādarāyana Sūtras giving different interpretations—Advaita (Monism Viśiṣṭādvaita (Qualified Monism) and Dvaita (Dualism). Th central issue dealt with is the relationship between Brahman, th individual soul and the world.

Śaṅkara maintains that Brahman alone is real and to the man wh knows Brahman correctly the world appears illusory and unrea although not in an absolute sense. The world is quite real for thos who accept as valid sense-experience, sense-perception, qualities an their relations. The world of relations is one of dependence an interdependence and so is founded on relativity. All that is base on relations, dependence and relativity has only phenomen existence, however; and from the highest point of view in whic all distinctions, qualities and relations disappear, and in which the is undivided continuity, phenomenal existence is bound to appea false and unreal. Therefore, according to Śaṅkara, the empiric world is Māyā but in a definite sense; and it is unreal only for on vho has realized Brahman in his own experience, risen above all listinctions and felt the unity of life in spite of and in the midst of ıll objects of the sense-world and lives on the transcendental plane. Thus Śaṅkara believes in a hierarchy of levels of reality-empirical, phenomenal and transcendental to which corresponds hierarchical tates of experience—dream, waking and the experience of distinc-ionless unity.

As to Brahman's relation to the world, He is not deceived by mpirical reality. Śaṅkara declares God is like a magician who reates magic (the World) but knows that it is not real, and so is ıot deceived by the appearance of the world. In fact Māyā is the Śakti-power producing the plurality of souls (ātmans) and the insenti-nt material world. Brahman alone is real and the Śakti producing he world (Māyā) is unreal. Śaṅkara's interpretation of the relations between Brahman and the world is based on the concept of Adhyāsa vhich means superimposition. The world is superimposed upon Brahman and is seen by the perceiver where it does not actually xist. Experiencing the world instead of Brahman is due to gnorance; and, when real knowledge dawns upon a person, he eases to perceive the world as a real thing. He then begins to perceive Brahman everywhere and not the world.

Śaṅkara holds that Brahman and God are one and the same. Brahman is ultimate Reality, devoid of and beyond attributes—the Nirguṇa Brahman or the Absolute in western philosophy.[17] God s less than Nirguṇa Brahman; He is penultimate reality character-zed as creator, sustainer, and governor of the universe, real only in relation to the world and individual souls. God is Saguṇa Brah-nan possessing knowledge, power, goodness and such qualities in uperlative degree. From the highest transcendental position, how-ever, even God is not real or is an appearance or an existence of a lower order because, whatever has qualities has limitations and exists, therefore, on the plane of relativity and belongs to the level of phenomenal reality. For Śaṅkara only the highest Brahman devoid of attributes or qualities is real and only knowledge of Nirguṇa Brahman is the highest and liberating kind of knowledge.

According to Śaṅkara the individual soul is real only on the ultimate, not phenomenal, level. The individual soul (Jīvātmā) is not different from Bahman but is limited by and its individuality is due to its perishable adjuncts such as body, senses, buddhi, manas and antaḥkaraṇa. The Jīvātmā experiences the good and bad fruits of worldly life, suffers pain, enjoys pleasures, acquires Karm. and revolves on the wheel of birth and death. Its bondage is due t its false identification with the adjuncts. In reality the soul i Brahman itself; but it forgets this and through ignorance imagine itself separate from Brahman. It can regain its original infinite perfect and blissful nature by casting away its limitations due t ignorance. Thus for the soul mokṣa means a kind of self-recovery When it removes the crust of ignorance, the soul begins to shine The individual understands that the soul is Brahman itself, and i experiences a oneness with the whole of reality.

The liberated soul becomes univerzalized and feels no distinctions It attains perfect peace and joy and is freed from Karma and the cycl of birth and death. It accumulates no new Karma and that alread accumulated is burnt. The person who is completely detached maintains a perfect equilibrium of mind, is not affected by anythin around him, rises above all dualities, distinctions and desires bu continues to live and work in this world is called "Jīvamukta" When he casts away his gross body and has no more possibility o rebirth due to exhausting all Karma, he attains "Videhamukti" the final or bodiless liberation. He departs from the earth, never t return. This is the highest ideal of Advaita Vedānta.

Rāmānuja differs with Śaṅkara by identifying God with Brahman.[18] Brahman is God with whom souls can enter into a personal relationship by love and devotion (Bhakti). Further fo Rāmānuja the world and the Śakti which produces it are both real Also individual souls and the world are real as parts and manifesta- tions of the same Brahman. They are real as modifications or transformations of God or Brahman. Rāmānuja believes in the causal theory of Parināmavāda according to which the effect is an actual transformation of the cause, just as curds are nothing but tranformed milk. He advocates a Qualified Monism which holds individual souls and the world are adjectival to Brahman. They are Brahman but in a qualified sense. Brahman is like a substantive which can exist without the world and souls, which are its adjectives; but the adjectives cannot exist without the Substantive. Therefore the world and souls, being dependent on Brahman, cannot exist without and apart from it.

Śaṅkara believes that real knowledge of the Self (Brahman) can lead to the experience of liberation. This knowledge is not just a conceptual understanding of the Self. Conceptual understanding based on distinctions and differences and can give us only appearances, never reality. Brahman is beyond all conceptual understanding. Thus by knowledge Śaṅkara means an intuitive experience of identity of the soul with all existence requiring rigorous self-control, the observance of Yama and Niyama prescribed by Yoga and a mental detachment from all objects of experience. Rāmānuja believes such knowledge is insufficient for attaining Mokṣa. What else is needed is complete surrender (prapatti) and pure, unqualified devotion to God. Constantly repeating God's name, remembering Him always, singing songs of devotion and praise and receiving God's favour and grace are also necessary. The path of devotion emphasized by Rāmānuja was taken up by later Vaiṣṇava Saints and has become widespread and popular up to this day.

Madhva, while an Advaita Vedāntin, presents a Dvaiti interpretation. According to him ultimate Reality is Brahman, whom he calls Viṣṇu or Hari, who is self-existent, subsistent and dependent, every other thing being dependent on it. Brahman is the same as God who is omnipresent, all-pervading and possessing infinite qualities since He is the innermost reality and cause of everything. He is devoid of qualities (Nirguṇa) but becomes many yet still remains one without any defect or contamination.

Madhva is a dualist because he believes differences and distinctions in the world are real. In fact, he is not a dualist but a Bhedavādin who asserts there are the five real distinctions between God and souls, one soul and another, God and matter, soul and matter and one object and another.[19] Though Madhva accepts the reality of differences, he is a monist in that he believes ultimate Reality is only One, and that is God, who is omnipotent and impeller of all actions. Madhva believes these five kinds of differences are eternal. They do not disappear even in the deluge (Pralaya) of the universe.

Individual souls and matter are dependent, as they cannot exist apart from Brahman. God is the efficient but not material cause of the world and individual souls which are atomic in size and infinite in number. Souls possess limited power, knowledge and bliss as they are obscured by Karma caused by ignorance. Their actions, knowledge, ignorance, bondage and deliverance are caused by God in accordance with their Karmas. The soul possesses two aspects, the essential and unchanging, and the external and changing. The latter consists of the physical body, senses, mind, the subtle body and

10

SOCIAL PHILOSOPHY

G. S. Bhatt

I The Setting

In the social-philosophical thought of the Indian, particularly the Hindu, the secular and sacred, physical and metaphysical, the world in which man lives now and hereafter all merge into one. Man transcends into the Supernatural and the Supernatural manifests itself in human forms. Man and the Supernatural constitute a unity of the spiritual continuum, the realization of which man is to strive tirelessly for throughout his life and through the process of births and rebirths. Both man and the Supernatural are bound by the laws of the Cosmos. Within these laws man is the maker of his destiny which is spiritual, not mundane.

The term Darśana, translated as Philosophy in English, implies not only knowing but also seeing and realizing the soul and the material world as being part and parcel of the Supreme Soul pervading the universe.[1] The highest knowledge is that which enables one to realize spiritual oneness with all things and unity in diversity.[2] The social existence of man is only a means to attaining that unity which is, in turn, a further means to the highest end, mokṣa, or freedom from transmigration of the soul. To attain mokṣa is the natural trait of man. But man has to cultivate it through the process of socialization. Man cannot attain mokṣa without meeting the obligations of body and mind and without fulfilling the social obligations as entailed in the philosophy of the four principal ends of life.

In scientific thought man and other animals are products of the all-pervading process of organic evolution. In the evolutionary process man acquired a highly developed brain capable of conceiving ideas and norms and endowed with the capacities of self-reflection and symbolic communication in which language plays an important part. These capacities of the mind along with those of the body unique to man enabled him to become a culture-building anima As such, man is both a consequence and a cause of his existence.

In Indian thought man shares the traits of eating, sleeping, fearin and copulating with other animals. It is in having Dharm (righteousness) that man differs. Man is not a cause but a cor sequence of Dharma. Dharma circumscribes the individual an social life of man. It conditions his past, present and future in term of the way he orients himself to it. Man's birth, his future course c birth or freedom from it, his socialization, his role and status in th family, caste and society, the meaning and aims of his life and hi relation with the Supernatural are defined by and dependent o Dharma. Individuals come and go but the Dharma of man (mānava dharma) goes on. Dharma, therefore, transcends man and accom panies him in the world hereafter. It accumulates through th process of rebirth. It is a force, a power but not a supernatura power in the religious sense of the term.

Dharma binds even the Supernatural, as indicated in the Gita. Being ruler of rulers Dharma protects and preserves man in both hi physical and metaphysical existence, provided man does not dis regard and destroy Dharma. In Manu we read: "Therefore without causing pain to anybody, one should gradually accumulat Dharma for the sake of acquiring aid in the next world. For in th next world, neither father, nor mother, nor sons, nor wife, nor rela tions stay to help him through. Dharma alone stays to help him." As ordained by Dharma the end of man's life is to rise higher than th animal level of existence and to attain mokṣa by becoming th highest in man (narottama) which is the stage of mokṣa. Man ha to rise from the state of nāra (man) and become nārāyaṇa (man, th divine) on the way to becoming finally narottama (the highest in man)

II Dharma

Dharma and religion need to be distinguished, especiall as the latter term is used in the West. There religion is definec as a recognition of a supernatural power and a body of rites anc obligations, ranging from prayer to propitiation, directed toward it. While in western revealed religions man reaches his ultimate end by God's grace and aid, in Indian thought man can himsel through Dharma. Dharma is to be cultivated through practice in the private and public life of individuals, as both aspects of life are nterdependent. Dharma not only relates to the relationship etween man and the Supernatural but also to all relationships etween the individual and society.

In the Indian tradition Dharma is not limited to just one manifestaon. Individual and social expressions of religious experience re subject to the diversity of matt (religious belief), mārga (a way), anth (religious brotherhood), samāja and sampradāya. Sampraāya means "tradition, traditional doctrine or knowledge, a peculiar stem of religious teaching, a religious doctrine inculcating the orship of one particular deity."[5] The sampradāya is the religious roup organized around the dogma of religious experience. The piritual-social doctrine and associated symbols of a religious receptor and initiator constitute his matt. The body of ritual, eremonies, and other observances of a preceptor prescribed to realize ne Godhood according to his matt is his mārga. A panth is a rotherhood of those who follow a matt and its corresponding mārga nd are socially bound by a body of rituals and ceremonies and religious symbols with primary emphasis on initiation and the religious uthority of the hereditary Guru. The members of the panth owe llegiance to the original Guru who is held in a hallow of divinity nd miracles. When a panth's matt and mārga become dogmatic, laiming superiority over other panths, it becomes a sampradāya. n the nineteenth century, under the impact of Christianity and ne West, matts and mārgas of different preceptors grew into amājas like the Ārya Samāj, Brāhmo Samāj and Prārthanā Samāj. Vhile functioning like religious associations, they did not have the haracteristics of a sampradāya.[6]

An individual's experience of God becomes limited by the guṇa quality), Śrama (effort), deśa (place) and kāla (time) of that ndividual. Individuals vary in these four aspects. Hence their eligious experiences vary as well. The Truth or Brahman is one and ne same but men conceive and realize it differently. It is these issimilarities which lead to a plurality of sampradāyas. These aried ways of religious expression, or what might be called religions n the West, are not Dharma because they sectarianize Truth. Dharma stands for the realization of that Truth or Reality which is he highest and the One and which as such does not cause conflict or ifferences of any sort. Such a world view found in the Indian radition has been the primal source of pluralism and coexistence n religion and even in politics along with active neutrality. It is the origin of the philosophy of a synthetic socio-cultural existenc along with the steadfast belief in the rightness of one's own wa Herein lies the catholicity of the Indian way.

III The Four Ends

Indian social philosophy posits four principal goals (pur ṣārthas) man seeks to realize—Dharma, Artha, Kāma and Mokṣ Mokṣa is the stage of man's social evolution in which he mingles lives in the Super Soul. It is the highest end of life, attainable on by the individual himself, with the help and guidance of Dharm Artha and Kāma relate the individual to society, family, soci stratification (caste and varṇa) and the production of wealth. the basis of this as well as the other-worldly life, Dharma com first, then Artha and Kāma. Mokṣa as the last end signifies that i attainment is impossible without first fulfilling the obligations of tl other three. Dharma is, therefore, both individual as well as socia this-worldly as well as other-worldly. At the same time it is supr individual, supra-social and even supra-supernatural.

Socially Dharma is that which helps man to fulfil the obligatio of Artha and Kāma directed to the ultimate end of mokṣa. Dharn is, therefore, order, social duties, customs, morals, law and cultur all combined in one, yet, at the same time, different in differe contexts. The concept of Dharma may have been derived from ar superimposed on the early Vedic concept of Ṛita, the laws dete mining the order of the Cosmos. In Vedism Ṛita is a mystic force binding the universe to a natural order and man's soci existence to a moral order. In Vedic usage Dharma stands f custom, moral law, general law, duty and what is right. later literature the concept Dharma replaced Ṛita.[7] Grammatical Dharma means what holds together a phenomenon—material immaterial, organic or non-organic. This notion is extende further in the Mahābhārata: "People call Dharma that whic possesses, sustains, preserves, protects and holds together. Dharn holds, preserves and protects prajā (mankind)."[8]

Dharma, thus, is that which holds mankind together individuall socially, culturally and spiritually. It maintains social stability an unites the individual and society, enabling him to fulfil his psych moral needs and obligations within society.[9] Man's life, its happ ness and sorrows, is transitory; his soul is eternal. The etern happiness of the eternal soul can come only from that eternal Dharma which is true in all times and places and for all men. This is called the Dharma of Man, mānavadharma or sādhāran-dharma. Such Dharma consists of "contentment, forgiveness, self-control, abstention from wrongly appropriating anything, purification, discipline of the organs, knowledge, truthfulness and abstention from anger."[10] Viewed thus Dharma is the instruction, discipline, duty and law of the right path for man. It is the resource by which man can sublimate himself to rise to the level of the human-divine. It not only protects and preserves but also refines and polishes the individual and society. It, thus, also becomes saṃskāra, i.e. a body of rituals which refine and polish as well as socialize. Discipline and Saṃskāra lead to social-spiritual evolution and welfare. The collective result of this refinement is culture and Itihāsas (stories instructing in the ideal of puruṣārthas). So Dharma is the very temporal existence of man in which man and Dharma interact in the dynamics of time-place configuration, with Dharma ever unfolding and reaffirming itself under the protective role of incarnations and the halo of the divinity of the king, bound to the Dharma of the king and the state.

Mānavadharma and svadharma (one's own Dharma) are to be rationally blended. The latter grows out of one's obligations toward one's guṇa (quality), śrama (efforts), varṇa (social category), saṃskāra (rituals and ceremonies of one's social category), āśrama (stage in life), deśa (place) and kāla (time). During unusual times like war and famine one may deviate from svadharma and follow apadharma, the Dharma of calamity. In deciding what is Dharma learned ones must depend not only on the Vedas and other scriptures but also on their own wisdom and the time-place configuration. Along with what is prescribed in the Vedas, Manu recommends the path traversed by the learned and the great. Dharma is not dogma. Its ultimate test is an other, not self-regarding one.[11]

Dharma moralizes Artha and Kāma and through them the social conduct of man. Dharma also moralizes mokṣa, and mokṣa, in turn, spiritualizes Dharma. Through dharma, mokṣa spiritualizes Artha and Kāma as well. Artha stands for the "whole range of tangible objects that can be possessed, enjoyed and lost"[12] and which man requires in daily life for the upkeep of the household, raising a family, and the virtuous fulfilment of life. Artha also means the attainment of riches and worldly prosperity, advantage, profit and wealth. Poverty is the root of all ills. It and hunger drive man to commit any sin. Without wealth all the virtues of man vanish into nothingness and even a good lineage does not bring status. Without wealth even Dharma cannot be a source of happiness as wealth itself is a potent source for fulfilling the obligations of Dharma such as liberality (dāna). If one, according to the Mahābhārata, robs someone of his wealth, one robs him of his Dharma as well.[13] To Kauṭilya "wealth and wealth alone is important in as much as charity and desire depend on wealth for their realization."[14] He is against widespread renunciation as it interferes with production. He recommended that the state punish those who renounced the world without first having satisfied the claims of family and society. The production and acquisition of wealth is for liberality, for a proper blending of one's own welfare with that of society. Man's existence becomes meaningful only when he acquires both wealth and liberality. Kāma, as interpreted by Prabhu, refers to all the desires in man for the enjoyment and satisfaction of the life of the senses. The term refers to the native impulses, instincts and desires of man and his natural mental tendencies and finds its equivalent, we may say, in the use of the English terms desires, needs, basic motives, urges or drives, and the collective use of the term Kāma would refer to the totality of the innate desires and drives of man.[15] Ordinarily Kāma is taken to be the sex drive and its satisfaction and, as that, it is the lowest of all the puruṣārthas. As pure sex drive it is lust, sensuous enjoyment and an obstruction in the way of man's spiritual progress. As such it is an enemy of man, others being anger, greed, temptation, conceit and jealousy. At the same time, it is the basis of socially regulated mating, marriage, the propagation of the species and of the gṛihastha āśrama (householder stage) on which depend all other āśramas. Manu, therefore, ordains that the good of man consists in the harmonious coordination of the three puruṣārthas, i.e. dharma, artha and kāma—that coordination in which mokṣa alone would prove the best guide.

Mental and bodily happiness is the immediate object of Kāma. Its long-range end is Dharma leading to mokṣa. It is a source for disciplining the organs and freeing them ultimately from sensual lust. Detached indulgence is the way to mokṣa and that is possible only when man gradually regulates Kāma so as to be free from it and ultimately without the least trace of any longing for it. Besides Dharma and artha, good food and drink, pleasant and charming company, fine clothes, perfumes, ornaments and garlands are preeminent sources of Kāma.[16] But woman, the mystery of her beauty and attraction, is the major source of Kāma. In Indian thought many ideal-types of the male-female relationship can be identified. Men and women are manifestations of the Eternal Male and Female, the two all-pervasive cosmic forces, which complement each other and constitute the transcendental mystical entity of creation. They operate as the Eternal Companions, as couples which are humanly divine, like Rādhā-Kṛiṣṇa, Sītā-Rāma and Śiva-Śakti. In pre-medieval India, during the later phase of Buddhism, this speculation about the Male and Female degenerated into rituals and ceremonies of vāma-mārga (the left-hand ritual of the Tantras) in which women and copulation came to be viewed as ritualistic resources for attaining supernatural powers.[17] It finds expression in such ritual-oriented concepts as a woman as the Bhairavī (a young girl representing the goddess) and the Tripurasundarī (the beauty of the three worlds).

In the householder stage of life the ideal is the wife being a most desirable source of pleasure. The choice of a wife is regulated through the institutional sources of the family and its extensions—varṇa, caste and tribe. As in the case of such legends as Śakuntalā-Duṣyanta, Mālati-Mādhava and Śiva-Pārvatī, there could be marriage growing out of romance as well, but only as a forerunner of a socially recognized marriage. The eight types of marriage (Brahma, Daiva, Arṣ, Prajāpatya, Gāndharva, Asura, Rākṣaṣa, Paiśāca) are intended to legitimize all conceivable forms of acquiring a mate in order to ward off the social curse of illegitimacy.[18]

The Karud Purāṇa describes the ideal wife thus: "She who speaks sweetly to her husband and is a clever manager of household affairs, is a true wife. She who is one in spirit with her lord, and devotes her whole self to his happiness, is a true wife. . . ."[19] Not even dreaming of a person other than her husband is the ideal of pativrata (the Dharma of the wife's devotion to her husband) and satī (immolation on the husband's funeral pyre). Figuratively, the wife is half of her husband's body. She is a preserver of the family and the ritually ordained companion in the performance of household rituals. Matrimonial companionship is locked in the marital knot which is tied at the time of marriage and on the occasion of every ritual in which the wife is a ritual necessity. The marital knot goes beyond this life. It signifies the eternal matrimonial companionship which continues through rebirths.

On the other hand we find in the Indian tradition another view that the wife is not the source of pleasure arising from emotional and intellectual stimulation. The wife and the "beloved" are two incongruent views of women as two different sources of Kāma. Kṛiṣṇa, as portrayed in devotional poetry, loved Rādhā but took Rukminī as his wife. In the popular philosophical image, however Kṛiṣṇa's consort is Rādhā. The spiritualized myth of Rādhā as popularized through the Bhagvat Purāṇa and the poetry and painting of medieval India, may be taken as a culturally idealized projection of a society which denied its women a role combining the function of the wife and the beloved.

The pleasure of Kāma arising out of intellectual and emotional stimulation may be looked for also outside the wedlock. One of its socially projected expressions is the spiritual myth of the divine consort. Another is in the idealization found in the monistic philosophy of Bhakti of the soul's longing for Brahman and the conceptualization of God as the male or female beloved. On the earthly sensuous plane it finds expression in erotic poetry (both in Hindi and Sanskrit), particularly in the poetic delineation of the types of female beloved, in describing their bodily forms and decorations and their coquettishness and vivacity. Yet another form of its expression is the recognition of the social, cultural ritualistic and even political importance of the courtesan. In the forms of the gaṇikā (courtesan), nagaravadhu (bride of the tower) and veśyā (prostitute) the courtesan has a long social history dating back to Vedic times. Kauṭilya regards the ganika as an inevitable part of society and accepts her importance in diplomacy and espionage. The "man about town" in Vātsyāyana's Kāmasūtra is sophisticated enough to accept the pleasure of her company as legitimate happiness.[20]

In medieval India, under the interaction between Hinduism and Islam, the courtesan emerges as the socio-cultural focus of the cultured society—that cultural focus of intellectual and emotional stimulation in which the wife plays no part. The wife and the courtesan belong to two different social-cultural worlds. In the world of the wife society idealizes devotion and chastity in matrimony, but in the world of the courtesan society encourages its individuals to seek intellectual and emotional stimulation in culturally idealized permissiveness which was religiously and legally sanctioned and socially tolerated.

t also expresses itself in the institution of polygymy and "the keep" vhich until recently carried legal sanction. This leads to a sort of nconscious yearning and tolerance of the cultural ideal of per-nissiveness found philosophized in the case of Gods in religious nyths such as that of Kṛiṣṇa and the milk-maids of Bṛindāvana. The idol of Śiva and its pedestal which is an object of common wor-hip, symbolize the union of the genitals of the male and female. Along with all this also runs a quite powerful stream of puritan and nti-orgiastic thought in which man is instructed to shun the ompany of courtesan and musicians, to refrain from intoxicants nd the use of such things as stimulate sexually. Thus Kāma is ndesirable but a social and individual duty at the same time. It is mystery as well as both an art and science.

Being the ultimate value of man's social existence, the puruṣārtha of mokṣa is an end in itself. Beyond that, man has nothing to ttain. It is the stage where man's cravings cease and along with hat ceases the need for attainment and fulfilment. As the highest nd of life, the concept of mokṣa answers man's quest for the ultimate nd man's relation with the Supernatural. It is based on the ssumption that man and the supernatural are one in soul or spirit. They stand separated because of the role of māyā (illusion) and the īva's course in the process of transmigration as determined by the umulative consequence of the jīva's actions, past and present. Birth in human form is an opportunity for mokṣa because human ife itself is the result of good deeds. Man's ignorance (avidyā) nay arrest his spiritual evolution. It is up to man to liberate himself rom ignorance through righteous and just conduct for which the irst three puruṣārthas are his guide as well as resources.

There are two views of mokṣa. In the philosophy of monism he jīva (individual soul) attains mokṣa when it mingles in Brahman (the Super or Universal Soul) finally and eternally. In qualified nonism the individual soul is as eternal as are God and Nature and God is not the cause of this world but one of its factors, others being he jīva and prakṛiti (Nature). Consequently the world is real and eternal, from which there is no escape. Here mokṣa is not final ningling in God but it is living in God as long as one's Karmas warrant it. Whereas the former is other-worldly, the latter is this-worldly in the sense that it is not based on the concepts of the world being an illusion and man being unable to finally escape this vorld. In the attainment of mokṣa only Dharma can help, provided it has been cultivated through Artha and Kāma. He wh neglects them does not attain mokṣa. Preparation for mokṣ is done throughout one's life, first by cultivating Dharma and the discharging one's social obligations as entailed in Dharma-base Artha and Kāma, for that is the way to be freed of lust and longin Mokṣa comes out of self-knowledge, knowledge of the soul and th Supreme Spirit, the conscious realization of unity in diversity, th sources of which are self-control through the control of passions an worldly longings, a study of the Vedas, penance and right knowledg and learning.

Such knowledge is not within the reach of all. Therefore in th Bhakti panth, which became popular with the lower rungs c society, submission to God came to be emphasized as the way t mokṣa. But, as propounded in the Gītā, bhakti without jñān (knowledge) and jñāna without bhakti (submission) are not possibl and neither are possible without desire-free action (niṣkāmā karma) They are the three points of the equilateral triangle of man' individual-social existence in which one leads to and is dependent o the other two. They make the individual free from desire, contente and endowed with that attitude and world view in which pleasur and pain, youth and old age, dirt and gold, profit and loss and birt and death are viewed alike with an attitude of detachment. Suc an ego-free state of mind, flowing from desire-free action based o jñāna and bhakti, brings mokṣa.

IV The Four Āśramas

An āśrama, literally, is a halting or resting place. Th word, therefore, signifies a stoppage or stage in the journey of lif wherein one rests, in a sense, in order to prepare for the furthe journey to attain final liberation.[21] From birth to death the indivi dual's social and spiritual development passes through the fou stages of Brahmacharya, Gṛihastha, Vānaprastha and Sannyāsa The first is the student stage, the period of education in the theor of Dharma. The Gṛihastha āśrama (householder stage) is a tim for the practical application of Dharma in the pursuit of Arth and Kāma and the remaining two (forest hermit and homeles wanderer stages) for the application of Dharma to the pursuit c mokṣa. Each stage goes with a dominant theme of social an individual duties, with scripturally ordained "do's" and "don'ts or the individual. The four stages of life, Vyāsa says in the Mahā-hārata, form a ladder or flight of four steps which attaches to Brahman.[22]

In the present context saṃskāra stands for what polishes, refines, purifies and which, like a mould, casts its impression on the individual's body and mind. A saṃskāra is also a purificatory rite, a sacred rite or ceremony, or both. Thus, for the training and cultivation of the mind of the individual in society, to purify his body in the process of transition from one stage to another, to endow each transition with its required social, ritual and ceremonial significance and to polish and refine the individual culturally, the scriptures prescribe a number of saṃskāras from conception to death. They are based on notions of ritual pollution and purity and hence, they are symptomatic of the magico-religious world view which dominates Indian social life in interpersonal relations inside the family and in and between the caste and castes. In actual practice scripturally ordained rituals are coupled with the rituals of family, caste and region and are officiated over by the Brahmin priest, while the rituals of family and caste may or may not be. The higher the caste in ritual-social status, the greater is the participation of the Brahmin in the performance of rituals.

Ordinarily it is accepted that there are sixteen saṃskāras, socially functioning as rite de passage. Out of them garbhādhāna (the foetus-laying ceremony) and puṃsavana (the male-making ceremony) are pre-natal and jātkarma (ceremony at birth) nāmadheya (name-giving ceremony), annaprāśana (ceremonial feeding of infant with rice cooked in milk) and muṇḍana, i.e. chūḍā-karma (the first tonsure of the hair) are post-natal. Generally, with the muṇḍan infancy is supposed to end. With the performance of the sacred thread (upanayana) ceremony, the individual enters the first āśrama, the studentship stage. He ceremoniously wears three threads across his left shoulder, hanging on the right side of the waist. The three threads signify his three debts, the debts to the Gods (devas), sages (ṛiṣis) and ancestors (pitṛis). In the sacred thread ceremony of vivāha-saṃskāra (marriage ceremony) these threads are doubled, signifying the taking over the debts of the wife as well. The upanayana saṃskāra signifies the acceptance of the boy as a member of the group and of the spiritual life to which his forefathers belong and his initiation into the formal education of the sacred lore and his spiritual birth, entitling him to being called dvija (the twice born). The samāvartana saṃskāra celebrates the return of th student to his ancestral home and signifies his fitness to enter int and accept the responsibilities of family life. With the vivāh (marriage) saṃskāra the individual enters into the gṛihastha āśram and the antyeṣṭi or funeral rite, performed at death, marks th end of the earthly career of the individual and his entrance into th realms of the ancestors.[23]

As a Dharma and as an institution every āśrama enjoins a se of normative duties on the individual which are related to the goal of the āśrama. To acquire a knowledge of Dharma, to underg practical training in disciplining the body and organs, to lear self-restraint, non-stealing and non-violence in the Brahmachary āśrama the sons of rich and poor are to live and study under simila conditions and are to be subject to the same treatment. Th first aim of the vivāha (marriage) saṃskāra is the attainment c Dharma, the second to get progeny and the last to have sexua pleasure (rati). Without marriage and householding, life is in complete. The wife is a necessary companion in the pursuit c Dharma. If the husband is master of the house, the wife is it goddess of wealth. The relationship between husband and wife i determined by the ideals of Dharma, Artha and Kāma. Dutie toward the gṛiha (house) and the kula (family) are the basis of th gṛihastha āśrama Dharma. The householder is to protect an preserve the house which is the abode of the pitṛi (family ancestors and the putra (offspring, present and future).

The Gṛihasta has a twofold set of duties, one towards the pitṛ and putra, the other towards society as a whole. The concept of debts (ṛiṇas), penance (tapa), liberality (dāna) and sacrific (yajña) bring out the social obligation of the gṛihastha. Th gṛihastha āśrama is one wherein a person repays his debts to th Gods, sages or ancestors through penance, liberality and sacrifice Revering the Gods, Brahmin, guru and learned, being non-violen and honest, uttering the Truth and words pleasing and beneficia to others, practising scriptural injunctions, self-control and purit of thought without ulterior desire constitute the most desirabl penance. Dāna as liberality is the giving appropriately to sages ancestors, the Brahmin, Brahmachārin and sannyāsin. To giv without desire for reward or return is the true source of dāna an social obligation. In the spirit of dāna, tapa and karma-yajña th gṛihastha must perform five sacrifices to pay his debts—the stud and imparting of knowledge, offerings to the manes, offerings to the Gods, offering food to human beings and other living creatures, and looking after guests as well as possible. Thus viewed the gṛihastha is the trustee of the family and society. The object of his role as trustee is dharmasangriha (accumulation of Dharma) and loksangriha (welfare of the world). The gṛihastha āśrama is the basis of all other āśramas and the puruṣārthas. Its importance is reflected in the analogy that as all rivers flow into the sea, all āśramas flow into the gṛihastha.

The vānaprastha āśrama is undertaken on completion of the duties of the gṛihastha āśrama. Retiring to the forest with or without one's wife, after handing over care of the house to sons, is an important requirement of this āśrama. Others are giving up luxuries, sleeping on the ground, covering the body with bark, eating only fruit and roots, celebacy and suppressing worldly longings by canalizing them into a spiritual quest through studying the Vedas and Upaniṣads. One keeps his body and mind pure through meditation in order to consciously realize the unity of the soul.

The fourth āśrama (sannyāsa) requires a complete renunciation of worldly life. One must part company with his wife, perform his funeral rite, take a new name and give up even the tuft of hair on the head (śikhā) and sūtra (sacred thread). The sannyāsin is above varṇa and caste and is not to have a permanent abode. As a mark of complete renunciation, he becomes the mendicant wanderer, not entering the village except to beg alms and never resting in one place more than a night. He begs as much as he needs for a day, keeping nothing for tomorrow. His social obligations are the spiritual realization of the unity of man and God and the service and welfare of humanity. The sannyāsa āśrama has been and even now is the safety valve of society with its rigid and authoritarian stratification of caste. It has provided a social-cultural sanctuary to those too sensitive to submit to the authoritarian mores of caste.[24]

V The Varṇa System

Each āśrama is a Dharma and the Dharmas of all the āśramas together constitute āśrama-dharma which provides the individual-social basis for the ideology of the puruṣārthas, saṃskāras being the ritual means of achieving those goals. The socia basis of aśrama and saṃskāra lies in the varṇa system (the idea system of stratification). The saṃskāras provide a ritual basis fo the varṇāśrama-dharma which may be said to constitute the ver core of Indian social philosophy. The varṇāśrama-dharma, o the one hand, provides idealistic but dynamic moorings for the socia existence of man while on the other hand, it rationalizes inequality idealizes man's devotion to the duties that fall to his lot and provide an eternal hope of salvation in the future and thus ideologicall canalizes the social strain and conflict which inequality tends t generate. Everyone is not equally entitled to the idealized schem of saṃskāra and āśrama. It is available only to those who deserv it on the basis of their guṇa (quality) and śrama (endeavour). I is something one achieves either in this life on the basis of his guṇ and śrama or in the next life through the accumulation of Dharm and Karma (actions) in successive rebirths.

Such a scheme of life is based on the philosophical assumptio of an idealistic but eternal scheme of social stratification which rest on a broad dichotomy of the dvija (twice born) and the Śūdra Āśrama and saṃskāra are the privilege of the dvija—a privileg which is not equally available even to all the dvijas. The dvija i further divided into three hierarchical groups in ascending order— Vaiśya, Kṣatriya and Brāhmaṇa. With regard to spiritual an social rights and duties each of the three have differential status and corresponding rights, duties and saṃskāras. The Śūdra does no have any privileges whatsoever. Thus, saṃskāra-āśrama-dharma is a social (varṇa) privilege as well as the source of ritual power.

This fourfold hierarchical division of men is a varṇa system and each stratum of the hierarchy is a varṇa. Each varṇa is also a social grouping of those possessing an identical privilege in the availability of saṃskāra-āśrama-dharma and the power flowing therefrom. For example, the Brāhmaṇa receives the upnayana saṃskāra at eight years of age, the Kṣatriya eleven and the Vaiśya twelve. Not being entitled to upnayana saṃskāra, the Śūdra cannot study the Vedas. The orthodox view regarding limitations on studying the Vedas has not been universally accepted, however, Dayānanda, a Gujarat Brāhmin who founded the Ārya Samāj at Bombay in 1875, holding the Vedas are available to all and citing the second verse of the 26th chapter of the Yajurveda to prove it: "He has revealed the Vedas for all of them...."[24] Other examples of varṇa inequalities re such forms of marriage as anuloma and pratiloma[25] and differing naterials from which the sacred thread is made.[26]

Each varṇa, like each āśrama, has its Dharma or set of idealized ocial functions considered vital to the functioning of the social rganism and treated as ordained individual-social duties flowing rom the dominant disposition of members of the varṇa. Meditation, enance, forgiveness, uprightness, cultivation of spiritual and cientific knowledge and piety are some of the Brāhmin's karmas; rowess, fortitude, engaging in war and governing the Kṣatriya's; griculture, cow-protection and trade the Vaiśya's and service o the other three the Śūdra's. The functions of each varṇa, being atural to its members, constitute their Dharma. They conserve heir energy and promote their natural development and welfare long with the welfare of society. For every individual the Dharma f his varṇa is his svadharma which should never be given up.

The four types of social functions leading to the fourfold division f society result from variations in man's tendencies called guṇas in he Gītā.[27] Of the three guṇas (sattva, rajas and tamas), a person is lominantly possessed by one of them. Man, empirical reality, and ll things which flow from human action are manifestations of the uṇas. For example, from the sattva guṇa flow sāttvik jñana (know-edge of unity in diversity), sāttvik karmas (kind and unselfish action), he sāttvik actor (the unattached, non-egoistic person), sāttvik intel-ect (the equanimous and balanced mind), sāttvik contentment flowing from an unattached intellect) and sāttvik pleasure (spiritual appiness). Likewise rajas knowledge promotes awareness of liversity and rajas action egoistic action and desire for enjoyment. The rajas actor is attached to desire, the results of action, violence, vickedness, happiness and sorrow. The rajas intellect cannot listinguish between duty and non-duty, Dharma and non-dharma. Rajas contentment is tinged with longing and attachment to the re-ults of Dharma, Artha and Kāma. Rajas pleasure is mere ndulgence in physical pleasures. Similarly there is the tamas equivalents producing ignorance, blind indulgence in bodily pleasures, irrationality, laziness, obstinacy and complete worldly bondage.

In the process of the guṇas being manifested persons with the sattva guṇa becomes the Brāhmins, the rajas the Kṣatriyas, the tamas the Śūdras and the tamas and rajas combined with a tendency toward the rajas the Vaiśyas. By their very natures the Brāhmin,

Kṣatriya, Vaiśya and Śūdra are disposed toward the guṇas the must cultivate, conserve and promote as the basis of mokṣa. Goin against guṇa and karma would be going against nature, which bring neither happiness nor welfare to the individual and society. Th innateness of guṇa in a person is due to the cumulative effect of th karmas of previous births, for the accumulative effect of action dete mines the course of the jīva in the process of transmigration and th attainment of mokṣa. One's present birth as conditioned by one previous karmas approximate one's heredity. One's śrama is one potentiality, and one's saṃskāra, āśrama and varṇa constitute one environment. An individual's innate guṇa flowers through śram which, while not independent of is not totally conditioned by guṇa, fc śrama is effort as well. Dharma, āśrama and saṃskāra can refin guṇa in this as well as the next life. The attainment of human life already an achievement of past karmas (actions) and an opportunit for further refinement of guṇa and śrama on the way to mokṣa Therefore the best way to attain the highest ideal through the trans migration process is to perform the actions one's guṇa entails and t desirelessly devote oneself to the duties of his guṇa in this life.

Varṇa is neither a group nor a collectivity in the current socio logical senses of the terms but is a category of those identifiable a manifesting a guṇa in their psychical make-up and the karma-resultin therefrom. Conceptually the term varṇa-vyavasthā (the system of varṇas) stands for a fourfold categorization of societal member based on the classification of guṇa and karma placed on the idealisti scale of the precedence of the guṇas (sattva, rajas, tamas) which give rise to the corresponding scale of social precedence (Brāhmin Kṣatriya, Vaiśya and Śūdra). The social duties of these fou categories, scripturally ordained, are idealistically assumed to b flowing from what their respective natures in society require for thei highest fulfilment and for the integrated functioning of society In one of the explanations offered to emphasize it, organicism i mixed up with an allegorical and mystical world view: "from th mouth of the Creator (the Puruṣa) is created the Brāhmin, from th arms, the Kṣatriya, from the thighs, the Vaiśya and from the feet the Śūdra."[28] The four varṇas and their respective karmas hav such functional importance to society as the mouth (the Brāhmin) the arms (the Kṣatriya), the thighs (the Vaiśya) and the fee (the Śūdra) have to the organism (the society).

What is allegorically social-functional is mystical as well. Ma and Society and their variations are the manifestation of the guṇas which flow from Nature as created by That who is transcendental but in man as well. Man and society therefore transcend individuals that come and go as organic manifestations of the guṇas of Nature. Man, thus, has a dual base of his individual-social existence, the organic-social and the spiritual. The organic-social is the manifestation of the guṇa which binds the spiritual to the organic. The social placement of the individual is the societal manifestation of guṇa. Therefore, on the one hand, the individual must respond to the call of his guṇa which primarily shapes his svakarma (one's own action) and svadharma (one's own dharma) and, on the other hand, he must endeavour to rise to that stage (mokṣa) where the manifestation of the guṇas ceases to operate, the state of guṇātīta. This is possible only when the manifestation of guṇa is taken as mundane reality, as mere duty, without any attachment to and longing for the results of karma (duty).

Socially, the order of the varṇas is a stratified division of labour which is functional-historical but idealistic and symbolical as well, besides being mystical and allegorical. In the Mahābhārata the sage Bhṛigu tells Bharadwāj that "In fact, there is no difference between the varṇas. Previously, the whole of mankind belonged to the Brāhmin varṇa. Later on, because of differences in karma, different varṇas came into existence."[29] On the other hand, all along a differing view has persisted, laying emphasis on guṇa, karma and dharma in determining varṇa.[30]

As a theory of the double retribution of action, the karma theory occupies the key position in the grand theory of the varṇa system. It hinges on three concepts—karma, transmigration and mokṣa, and daiva (fate). As already stated, the karmas of one's previous births determine the guṇa of one's present life and bind one to certain potentialities setting the broad limits of one's endeavours. Right karma or karma as ordained on the basis of the guṇa, is called positive (niyat) karma, which enables one in his present life to attain spiritual evolution or heaven. They also determine one's birth. Niyat karma, therefore, can obliterate and improve upon the condition caused by the karmas of previous births.

The transmigration of one's soul continues until one attains mokṣa. For man, therefore, the way to salvation lies in attaining freedom from that transmigration by taking to positive karma whose criteria are guṇa, scriptural injunctions and time-place configuration.

Through either desirelessness and non-attachment to the results of action or surrender to God, or both, man frees himself, not from karma, but attachment to karma. Karma binds only when there is attachment to its results. Thus viewed, karma is neither bondage nor fate. Karma is fate inasmuch as it causes the guṇa of one's present life; but it includes also śrama, the effort one can make. Therefore, it is often said that fate is the field and karma is the seed. Karma is fate in the sense that man sows what he has already harvested; but, as positive karma, karma is also the source of attaining the stages of karmātīta (above and beyond karma) and guṇātīta (above and beyond guṇa). "Karma, thus, looks both ways; it glances back into the past and it also looks forward to a bright future," Gokhale states.[31] Or, as Tulsidās says: "It is only the lazy that invoke Fate."[32]

Varṇa is not class, race, caste or even tribe. As a concept, class is the product of materialistic-empirical thought whereas varṇa comes from idealistic thought. The varṇa system in Indian thought is the ideal social stratification of the ideal society, the ideological contrast of the caste-society Indian society has been through the ages. It is the ideal to be cultivated, conserved and promoted as Dharma, both by the citizen and the state. Varṇa also means colour; hence in Indian thought and literature varṇa and colour have been associated to explain the nature of varṇa. The four colours of the four varṇas symbolize the four gunas.[33] Sattva as white goes with knowledge and symbolizes purity. The rajas is red going with longing and attachment. The tamas is black symbolic of ignorance. The associating of a colour with a varṇa is a symbolic way of describing the guṇa of that varṇa. Sattva predominating in the Brāhmin makes him symbolically white and rajas in the Kṣatriya red. As partly rajas and partly tamas the Vaiśya is yellow and the Śūdra, being possessed completely of Tamas, symbolizes blackness.

In the evolution of social thought from Buddha to Gandhi there has been a continuing denouncement of jāti (caste) and an affirmation of the varṇa ideal. In earlier Sanskrit literature the word jāti does not occur. Somewhere two varṇas, Brāhmin and Kṣatriya, are referred to; elsewhere a third (Vaiśya) is added. The fourth is affixed in post-Vedic literature. In later texts the word jāti is used increasingly, meaning a social group whose social status is ascribed by birth. In contemporary India in actual living, one comes across jātis and tribes, not varṇas.

A caste as we find it today is a social group, a stratum with a traditionally ascribed social status based on birth, social and economic power and privileges and life chances and life styles. In it strict rules of endogamy (marrying within one's own group) prevail. A caste is also an occupational group. Specific occupations with accompanying rights and privileges are assigned by tradition to each caste thus eliminating competition and duplication of functions. As a traditionally defined endogamous, occupational and status group based on the notions of ritual pollution and purity, each caste also has its own traditionally ordained rituals and ritual roles as well as rules of intermingling and interdining which are partially sanctioned by scriptures but which derive their sanction mostly from tradition, operating as the customary law of the group. The power of ensuring that customary laws are carried out rests in a body of hereditary functionaries called that jāti panchāyat (a jury of five caste members). Caste becomes, then, a political group but without full political sovereignty. It is a semi-political group operating within and subject to the jurisdiction of the state.

Tribe in India has all the characteristics of the caste, except it is not occupationally specialized. When a tribe undergoes economic specialization and with a monopoly over an occupation integrates itself in the social economy of the village and adopts the general tenets of Hinduism, it becomes a caste. There is no word in Sanskrit equivalent to "tribal" as used in anthropology. The dichotomy of "tribal" and "Hindu" is of recent origin, a consequence of British political interests supported by the anthropologists of the Raj. India has had varṇa and jāti for, being endogamous, a tribe is virtually jāti in the sense jāti is understood in India. The tribe, as known today, is more of a political than social reality. However, in Indian society, tribe and caste merge into a sociocultural continuum on the idealized value of the varṇa system.

Socially, India does not have Brāhmin, Kṣatriya, Vaiśya or Śūdra jāti but rather jātis. This is because the jātis in each of the four jāti differ between themselves in regard to rules of endogamy, purificatory rituals, etc. Caste seems to have an origin in the system of tribes prevailing in pre-Aryan Indian society.[34] On the other hand, there is neither any organization of varṇa nor is varṇa bound up with any such rules of endogamy and interdining. The basis of caste is birth, whereas the basis of varṇa is karma.

There is a definite relationship between varṇa, caste and tribe. Every caste, as per its traditional status, would fall under a varṇa. All the castes of a village, a region or even of the country as a whole are classifiable under the four varṇas. In that case each varṇa would be an ideal type category of castes having an identical status and role. The Brāhmin varṇa would consist of all the castes which have traditionally been given the status and role of the Brāhmin and the same would be true of the three other varṇas. The varṇa status of a caste is never final. It is always changeable on the basis of the ideology of dharma-karma.[35] The karma that befalls one in this life is the consequence of the karmas of previous births. One should take up his present karma faithfully and desirelessly in order to attain the highest excellence in this and the next life. By following varṇa dharma, if not in this life, then in successive births one may improve one's lot. And many castes have been able to and even now are trying to do so by following the ideal of the Brāhmin varṇa or the other two next varṇas.[36]

While caste circumscribes the social and cultural life of the individual, it also provides economic security by allowing a monopoly over occupation and eliminating competition. The ideal of the varṇa system offers an eternal hope of social mobility and salvation to those presently having a low status. Those who are more sensitive to the authoritarian ways of caste and are ready to forego the advantages of the caste find a socio-cultural safety valve in the sannyāsa or in the ideology of varṇa or in both, and even more so if they become motivated to take up the role of religio-social reformer like Buddha, Rammohun Roy, Vivekananda and Gandhi. In the dynamics of Indian social thought, varṇa has grown as, and even now is, the ideal philosophy of social stratification. It is the traditional ideal to be upheld against the reality of caste which socially circumscribes individuals and groups, which is rigid and authoritarian and divides man from man on the basis of birth.

VI Dharma and Political Philosophy

The attainment of the state of uttamapuruṣa is possible only when there is order in society and the individual is able to follow the pursuit of the puruṣārthas and varṇāśrama dharma. Such order, along with its required social, economic and political aspects, is to follow from dharma itself. As maintained in the

Buddhistic texts, "dharma is the ruler of rulers". Here dharma is described as a composite tradition of justice, impartiality and benevolence and is related to the five distinct concepts of artha (economic good), dharma (ethics), kāla (time), mātrā (measure) and pariṣad (counsel).[37] No doubt, the king is divine and so is the state. But, divinity is associated with the person of the king only in a functional way. The king is divine so long as he acts according to the dictates of Dharma. Dharma is therefore higher than the king. Dharma moralizes the authority of the state and the rights and duties of the subjects. Gokhale states that "The right to revolution is one of the clearly recognized rights of individuals and groups in Indian political thought. The Mahābhārata recognizes it and Manu condones the overthrow of a wicked king as not sinful."[38] And the same theme continues up to Gandhi: "We must be content to die if we cannot live as free men and women."[39] Gandhi's concept of satyāgraha philosophizes the right to revolution.

The state, therefore, has to promote the three ideals of life—Dharma, Artha and Kāma. Mokṣa is beyond the jurisdiction of the state as the state cannot help an individual to attain it. Moreover, the exclusion of mokṣa from the funcitions of the state makes the state secular. The authority of the state to promote the three ideals flows from daṇḍa (coercive power, punishment) which according to Kauṭilya "is the law of punishment or science of government."[40] Daṇḍa enables a king to rule or to maintain order, provided the king bases daṇḍa on dharma. Daṇḍa without Dharma may destroy even the king. No doubt, the king is the guardian of Dharma but the king does not have the power to tamper with Dharma or to alter it substantially. For the king, the sources of Dharma are śruti (Vedic literature), smṛitis (the law codes), vyavahāra (custom or tradition) and royal edicts. Among these, custom, as the existing historical behaviour of the group, is of the greatest force. To rule his subjects according to their customs, to promote the preordained ideals of life and to preserve and protect varṇāśrama dharma constitutes the Dharma of the king. Being based on the tradition as given in the Koran and the Shariat, Islamic rule gave vent to the already existing force of custom which even the British recognized. And the legal force of custom continues even now.

Politically Dharma is the law and the duties of the king in relation to his subjects and the duties of the citizen in relation to the king, the state, his family, caste and village. It is also the law of inter-caste relations as entailed in the ordering of hierarchical relations between castes and of the ritual and economic rights and privileges of individual castes. Dharma is also the law of preservation and regulation of varṇāśrama dharma. Dharma, thus, enjoins on the king of a wide area of activity and control, though it also tends to check and limit the control of the state. That is why the king is likened to the father. Unlimited loyalty is expected towards the king but only as long as the king is functioning on the basis of Dharma. Thus arises, on the one hand, the expectation of fatherly behaviour from the state (which continues even now in the expectations from the state and which lies at the base of socialism as conceptualized in independent India) and, on the other hand, the function of the state as that of the father and the regulator of morals and customs. The Hindu kings of Vijayanagar assumed the title of the maintainer of castes and appointed officials to enforce and regulate the sva-dharma of each caste. The concept of law as Dharma emphasized the citizens' rights and duties.

VII Contemporary Society and Social Philosophy

The foregoing themes of thought, popularly known as varṇāśrama dharma, constitute the ideational nexus of the cultural continuum of India through the ages. Their reinterpreted affirmation and denouncement have been going on side by side through the renaissance movements following almost every political crisis in India.[41] The impact of the British Raj and the West gradually changed the conditions of villagism and, consequently, the nuances of the traditional thought and institutional complex.

The superior arms and military technology of the British fulfilled the historical ideal of political unity. Along with that, through the modern means of transportation and communication, followed administrative and economic unity. India sought that knowledge and technology which had already enabled Europe to achieve the cultural brilliance which dazzled and dominated the whole world. In her age-old tradition of imparting higher education and administration through unspoken language as a monopoly of the elite, India replaced Sanskrit and Persian with English. Since the introduction of European education through the medium of the English language, India has been standing face to face with post-Baconian science and philosophy. Consequently India has been feeling the impact of idealism, materialism, pragmatism and utilitarianism and along with that the impact of the dichotomies of capitalism vs. socialism, parliamentary democracy and liberalism vs. communism and sociologism vs. exitentialism. The authoritarian mores of caste society felt a greater impact of liberalism which India met by reviving the ideal of varṇa and pluralism.

Organized religion challenged the ideal of pluralism and democracy the traditional rule of consensus. The introduction of the printing press took from the Brahmin his monopoly over scriptures and their interpretation. With growing industrialization, land no longer remained the only source of wealth. This altered the traditional social economy based on village, caste, jajmānī system (monopoly of caste over occupation and the resultant system of fixed clientage with property right in it), joint family, agriculture as the mainstay of economic life and consumption-oriented production. A new occupational structure emerged in which allocation depended on educational achievement, economic resources and merit. The village lost its isolation as well as its socio-economic moorings. A national problem of social reconstruction resulted. Three levels of societal living developed—the village, town and big industrial city, each responding differently to the impinging imperatives of change.

The rule of secular law established by the British did not recognize any distinctions of caste and creed. On the other hand Indian jurisprudence, being custom-oriented even under the British, accorded legal recognition to caste and community based-custom, unless it contradicted state policy. The organization of legislature and judiciary, the formulation of the Indian Penal Code, the introduction of landlordism and the practice of realizing revenue in cash in place of kind, weakened caste and its panchāyat and led to the gradual disintegration of the village panchāyat in spite of official and non-official efforts to revive it. When all these changes rocked the social-philosophical moorings to India, the Europeans discovered "The Wonder that India was". This awakened India's national pride. The Indian elite felt the need for change, at least, for "social and political advantage."[42]

Through the efforts of the nineteenth century leader Rammohun Roy the custom of satī was banned. He opposed polygyny, the unification of Hindu and Muslim law, idolatry and Christian missions and staunchly supported widow remarriage and European education. Believing monotheism to be the natural, universal tendency in man, he advocated a revival of the impersonal monotheism of the Upaniṣads. He upheld the precepts but not practices of Jesus. The Brāhmo Samāj, the society of worshipppers of the One True God, which he founded in 1828, flowed into many channels, viz. orthodoxy vs. heterodoxy, catholicity vs. eclecticism and religious reform vs. social reform and nationalism and philanthropic social work. He pleaded for a revival of a modified village panchāyat as the Indian jury system.[43]

Keshub C. Sen, Roy's successor, continued the pluralistic tradition and viewed Christ as a prince among prophets, one revelation of God in history, a Vedāntist Hindu yogī and an Asiatic. Styling himself the Younger Son of the Father, Sen founded the New Dispensation. He espoused female education and temperance and encouraged inter-caste marriages, the last being legalized by the Special Marriage Act of 1872. Amended in 1954, it continues even now adding a ninth form (court marriage) to the scripturally prescribed eight forms of marriage. The Brāhmo Samāj streamlined rituals by dropping from them practices pertaining to polytheism, idolatry and ancestor worship.[44]

Dayānanda, the founder of the Ārya Samāj, did the same by compiling the saṃskāravidhi (a manual of rituals).[45] He denounced eclecticism and sounded an anti-Western and Puritan strain and philosophized a reformed revival of Vedism as the only national religion as well as the religion of man. Let everyone become Ārya (noble and respectable as well as faithful to the religion and laws of his country) by converting himself to Āryaism (Vedism). Āryaism stands for a belief in the infallibility of the Vedas as the only source of all true knowledge, one God both impersonal and merciful, karma-based social stratification, this worldliness, vegetarianism, teetotalism, rebirth, everyone's (women as well as śūdra) right to sacred and secular education and steadfast adherence to svadharma (one's own religion).

Co-education and the dissolution of marriage and widow-remarriage do not have any place in the social organization idealized by Dayānanda. As an answer to the problems of divorce and widow-remarriage, he advocates the revival of niyoga, the ancient practice of permitting a childless widow to have intercourse with the brother or any near kinsman of her deceased husband. He denounces astrology, polytheism, idolatry, desireful prayer, the concept of eternal salvation (sayujya mukti), vows, fasts, ancestor whorship and the Brahmin's supremacy based on birth. Jāti (caste) in the sense of species is natural. As a social group based on birth, it is man-made or artificial. Based on karma, the varṇa system is natural and ideal.

The concepts of svarāṣṭra (one's own country), svabhāṣa (one's own language), svadharma and svadeśī (patriotic love towards what belongs to one's own country) are patriotic tenets of Dayānanda's religious doctrine. Long before Gandhi he preached, "Self-government is better than foreign government howsoever good." He advocated the revival of the village panchāyat, the traditional system of inter-village organization and the ancient system of education through the medium of the Sanskrit language. Hence arose the Anglo-Vedic System of education which the Ārya Samāj evolved following in the footsteps of Christian missions. To save the poor and the destitute from falling into the hands of Christian missionaries, the Ārya Samāj undertook philanthropic social work among Harijans, tribals, widows and orphans. To reclaim and rehabilitate the Harijans it allowed them the right to gāyatrī mantra, the sacred thread and priestcraft. Failing to rehabilitate them as dvija (twice born), it evolved a programme of Harijan rehabilitation—the organization of schools and cooperative societies exclusive to Harijans, agitation for everyone's right to draw water from village wells and opposition to forced labour to which Harijans were traditionally condemned. Thus was paved the way for the Gandhian movement for Harijan uplift and the eradication of untouchability. The Ārya Samāj welcomed social legislation for social reform and appealed to the politically minded also.[47]

Vivekananda, elaborating the teachings of his spiritual Guru, Ramakrishna, propounded a vigorous social philosophy of fearlessness (abhaya), egalitarianism, individualism, religious pluralism and a synthesis of nativistic catholicity with the West.[48] He upheld the ideal of God being one in many and Absolute as well as Merciful. Idol, cross, and crescent are means to realize that Absolute. There is no one rigid path to realize unity in diversity. There is no conflict between dualism (dvaita), qualified monism (viśiṣṭādvaita) and monism (advaita). In the spiritual evolution of man, dualism leads to qualified monism and, ultimately, to monism.

Consequently Hinduism, based on Vedānta, could be the only true religion of man, as it does not believe in the ultimate redemption of Hindus alone. It treats religion as a means of attaining perfection. Polytheism is its aspect of faith and Vedānta that of philosophy. By not tying man to any one rigid path and exhorting man to realize unity in diversity, Hinduism saves man from religious prejudice, hypocrisy and proselytization. Not proselytization but religious tolerance is the way to religious unity. Therefore, let everyone seek his spiritual development in his own religion.

Lacking the spirit of serving the poor, the competitive social system of the West is unethical. Positivism and humanism, even scientific humanism, are perfectly valid if they do not reduce the human soul to a mere function of the environment or if they do not lead to the swamping of the spirit of man by what one may call "over-civilization". India has blundered in overemphasizing renunciation and mukti (spiritual renunciation) and the laws meant for the life of the sannyāsin (monk). The West neglects the soul, India the body. The asset of the West is manliness and of India saintliness and spirituality. The need is for the combining of the two, Vivekananda says.

Man can manifest the divine in him, by controlling nature, external (science, technology and socio-political processes) and internal (ethics and religion). This is to be done "either by work or workshop, or psychic control or philosophy—by one or more, or all of these." This is the whole of religion. Doctrines, dogmas, rituals, books, temples, or forms are but secondary details. . . . Anything, caste or class, creed, institution or nation that bars the power of free thought and action of an individual, so long as that power does not injure others is devilish and must go. Therefore, "the end of all training is man-making" and of education "the manifestation of the perfection already in man."

Trampling on women and grinding the poor through caste restrictions are two social evils of India. The present is "the age of the śūdras, the proletariat." Therefore, the well-being of the higher classes now lies in helping the lower castes to get their legitimate rights. Let a caste be called Brahmin if by doing so it can raise its status. Women have a right to education, to the knowledge of Vedānta and to sannyāsa. To serve society women have rights equal to men. Vivekananda founded the Ramakrishna Mission, an organization of sannyāsins (monks), to preach and initiate in Vedānta and to serve men, particularly the poor and the destitute. Thus he gave a modernistic orientation to the institution of sannyāsa

These themes of thought flow into the theological eclecticism of he Theosophical Society, the philosophy of the Superman of Aurobindo and in Gandhi's precepts and practices of combining reform with politics. Gandhi's precepts and practices had as a forerunner the philosophy and trends of social reform in Bengal and Maharashtra.[49] The social reformers of Bengal—Rammohun Roy, Ishwar Chandra Vidyasagar, Keshub Sen and Shashipada Mukerji—made many efforts to get the custom of satī legally banned and to obtain legal sanction for widow-remarriage (1856) and inter-caste marriage (1872). They advocated female education and opposed polygyny which is now legally banned among Hindus but not among Muslims.

Inheriting the legacy of social reform M. G. Ranade, founder of the Indian Social Reform Conference, argued that social reform was intrinsic to social reconstruction leading to development and nationalism. It is neither Westernization nor revival. He aimed at renovating Indian social institutions to suit the requirements of time. His efforts to increase social intercourse between sub-castes and to use caste panchāyats as a media of social reform tended to strengthen caste and ushered in a new role for the caste panchāyat. To impart social-political education for national reconstruction, G. K. Gokhale founded a secular missionary organization, The Servants of India Society, with a trained and paid cadre of social workers. Gokhale stood for combining social reform with social work to prepare for swarāj. Ranade stood for modernizing social institutions. Denouncing reform imposed through an alien government, Tilak opposed both. His commentary on the Gītā enunciated the ideal of action, valour, this-worldliness and an incessant fight against slavery. Necessary social reform would follow with freedom. He therefore exhorted Indians to fight for freedom as a birth-right. To rouse the masses politically he popularized the cult of Shiva and Ganesh (a God with the head of an elephant). Thus politics came to be combined with reform and culture, a legacy Gandhi could not disregard.

In this social milieu Gandhi combines eclecticism and liberalism with catholicity, modernism with conservatism, humanism with nationalism and social reform with the politics of mass agitation.[51] Women have a right to education and the service of society. Widows can remarry if they desire; otherwise the ideal of celibacy is best for them. His opposition to cow killing gets constitutional sanction as does his ideal of prohibition. Cow protection, prohibition the eradication of untouchability, the uplift of Harijans and th rehabilitation of the village on the traditional socio-economic moorings of self-sufficiency and the decentralized collective leadershi of the village panchāyat, Hindu-Muslim harmony, non-violenc and satyāgraha provided the ideological basis of his social philosoph for national liberation.

With Gandhi reform is reorganization from within society. Untouchability being a sin committed by higher castes against untouchables, its eradication lies in atonement. Caste is artificial Varṇadharma is as unalterable as the law of gravitation. Varṇadharma emphasizes duties against rights. It treats all occupation as equal and eliminates competition for profit. The concept o svadharma rules out inter-varṇa mobility. Competition fo occupational mobility cuts the root of equality. Holding the idea of equality of occupations and a living wage, varṇa promotes mor equality than even communism. The ideal of varṇa helps in th realization of unity in diversity and will ultimately free society fro untouchability.

Gandhi's ideal of varṇadharma combines a rationalization o the attributes of caste with the liberal tradition of the modern West In Gandhi's view one is best suited to his hereditary occupation Regarding intercaste commensality, a Hindu is not obliged to din even with his son. It is a problem of personal hygiene rather tha a social one. All are entitled to knowledge; yet a śūdra is mor suited to manual labour. However the śūdra alone is not born t suffer the inconveniences of physical labour. In society knowledg and manual labour are to be combined. Herein arose Gandhi' philosophy of basic education (a combination of primary educatio with training in handicrafts) which independent India adopte

In Gandhi's view swadeshi stands for the reform, revival an reorganization of social institutions. To render and take servic from one's immediate neighbour as a duty is the essence of swadesh It is a tacit affirmation of the jajamānī system underlying the trad tional rural social system. In Gandhi's ideal of the realizatio of mokṣa as the ultimate end by serving society through love an non-violence, one's role in society is that of a trustee. An increas in the power of the state may apparently do good by minimizin exploitation but it does greater harm to mankind by destroyin individuality. With Gandhi individuality lies at the root of a rogress. Gandhi restores a belief in Hinduism and affirms its hilosophy of pluralism which underlies his well-known philosophy f non-violence. He denounces the West and proselytization but ot the ethical philosophy of Jesus. Being only imperfect ways to ealize God, i.e. Truth, all religions are equal. God is perfect, ot religion. Morals are of greater concern than religion. Hence, eligion is something entirely personal.

The renaissance of modern India, thus, ideationally lies in a re-nterpreted and reformed revival of traditional thought under the mpact of the West. It mainly borders on varṇadharma, pluralism, illagism, puritanism and nativism. It protests against proselytiza-ion and the "over civilization" of the West but not against its cientific and liberal thought. It is a product of interaction and con-lict between Westernization and Sanskritization, villagism and rban industrialism and the principles of organized religion and luralism. It created the ideational-social milieu for institutional ontinuity and change and also for the dilemma of synthesis which ontemporary India faces.

The Preamble of the Constitution of India seeks to affirm the istorically inspiring ideals of social, economic and political justice, iberty of thought, expression, belief, faith and worship, equality of tatus and opportunity and a fraternity which assures the dignity of he individual and the unity of the nation. The Directive Principles f State Policy legislate the idealized contents of social reconstruction nodern India stands for, viz. the organization of village panchāyats, he formulation of a uniform civil code, the promotion of the ducational and economic interests of the scheduled castes, tribes nd other weaker sections, the endeavour to bring about prohibi-ion, the prohibition of the slaughter of cows and calves and the rganization of agriculture and animal husbandry on modern nd scientific lines. Behind the Directive Principle to secure a ocial order promoting of the welfare of the people lies the ideal of ājadharma.

The Fundamental Rights to equality, property and constitutional emedies of exploitation negate the traditional distinctions based on aste and creed. They restore to the individual his dignity and privileges. Cultural and educational rights and freedom of religion ssure the social expression of religious and secular convictions nd their continuance. The Fundamental Rights thus uphold and egislate the ideal of diversity in the legislated ideal of unity.

The philosophy of pluralism opens into a vista of limitless possibi lities and alternatives and of dynamic continuity in which nothin is final. What is right depends on the time-place configuration It is a philosophy of limited certainty and Fundamental Rights therefore, are not ultimate and over-riding the needs of histori cal circumstances. The Indian Parliament can change them i necessary.

This constitutional recognition of diversity drives India to seek he national unity in emotional integration in the way she has sough a conscious and emotional recognition of the unity of the Godhea along with a recognition of its diversity. This also forces India t synthesize contradictions. The ideal of pluralism negates pro selytization and conversion, but India does not ban them legall despite the demand for it. Employing a Russian model in planning India aims at gearing social change to economic policy through th institution of parliamentary democracy which tends to politiciz caste, religion and region. In planning, the state shall be the mai agency working and acting on behalf of the community. Its air is not to develop into a monolithic totalitarian state or to tie stat policy to any particularism. Therefore, the course of action in stat policy is left to historical circumstances—consequently, contemporar India experiments in synthesizing the coexistence of the "private" and the "public" for which the rules of the game are yet to evolve.[5]

In the law borrowed from the West, India is a unity. Being orient ed to custom personal law is diverse in spite of the Directive Principl that "the state shall endeavour to secure for the citizens a uniforn civil code throughout the territory of India." Consequently, alon with the accepted principle of monogamy, polyandry and polygyn are also valid but only where practised as custom.[53] The ritual o saptapadī (the taking of seven steps by the bridegroom and th bride jointly before the sacred fire) now carries legal force wher custom makes it a part of the marriage rites.[54] So is the case witl other aspects of marriage and provisions relating to the dissolutio of marriage. Along with the enacted provision for the dissolutio of marriage lifted from customary law, are also found customs relat ing to the dissolution of marriage of various castes and communities The dissolution of a marriage may be sought in a court or in th council of the caste or community of the parties seeking it. Diversity in the law of inheritance results in the diversity of family forms the unity of which lies in its being joint. Those marrying beyon caste and community are governed by the Special Marriage Act and the Indian Succession Act which are all India enactments. Marrying first in the secular form, a Hindu later may sanctify it through traditionally prescribed rituals. Even law permits this continuum and synthesis of tradition and modernity.

The renaissance in modern India started the process of simplifying and streamlining rituals by dropping from them idolatrous and animistic practices. By weakening the traditional bonds of kinship, caste, village and region, urbanization and industrialization, through the processes of migration and mobility, tended to weaken the social bases of rituals. For example, in the simple family in the city the observance of the traditional practice of segregating a woman in menstruation is not possible, for the husband does not have the time nor is any other woman available to do the household chores as in the village and extended joint family. Rituals relating to birth, marriage and death are ordinarily performed. Urban conditions of living, rising prices and objectification flowing from the growing use of money in rituals do not allow time and resources for the traditional elaborateness of rituals. However, the ruralite is more ritual-minded than the middle class city dweller. Urbanization has tended to enhance conspicuous consumption in the performance of rituals in the upper and the new-rich strata of society. Urbanization has also created the scope as well as motivation among lower castes to adopt rituals as a measure of social-ritual mobility which the renaissance made possible.[55]

The jointness of the Indian family, which Anglo-Roman interpretations of Indian law by British judges made proverbial, rests in coparcenary rights and obligations along with the individual's birth right to a share in the family property and to separation from the family.[56] Thus the coparcenary base of jointness has always been subjest to fission and formation. The conditions of villagism superimposed on it the ideal of the common roof, hearth, rituals and property and a premium on age which finds extension in the socially upheld principle of seniority. Like varṇa in stratification, the jointness of the family has tended to remain more of an ideal. Industrialization and urbanization tends to free the individual economically from the bonds of kinship and caste. The Gains of Learning Act saves an individual's income from being pooled in the income of his father or brother(s). The Special Marriage Act allows freedom from the family and caste in matrimony. Urban conditions of living, rising prices and a monetary economy wean the individual away from the ideal of joint-living and render the coparcenary base of jointness subject to more fission than it ever was.

Any assessment of jointness beyond the coparcenary base gets lost in sociological polemics. On the other hand, where the traditional base of an agricultural social-economy exists, as among the polyandrous Khasas, joint-living finds a stronger emphasis. In all Indian family types older traditions tend to continue.[57] It is a prerogative as well as obligation of the eldest son of a person to light his funeral pyre. Even now on the death of a person, his near consanguineous relations get their head shaved as a part of post-funeral rites. In times of need, in the absence of any comprehensive scheme of social security, the individual falls back upon his family of orientation for help which generalized roles in the family expect and anticipate.

The weakening of villagism tends to free the woman from her subordination to men. The education of women and the growing scope for women's economic independence have widened the horizon of the woman's social life beyond the traditional confines of hearth, matrimony, motherhood, ornamentation, rituals, fasts and festivals. The old notions of satī and pativrata may still sway the naivety of the illiterate and the conservative. Law now sanctions widow-remarriage and the dissolution of marriage among castes where custom did not permit them.[58] Among many lower castes and almost all the tribes, custom permits widow-remarriage and divorce. The observing of purdah has never been a universal custom. It is not observed among tribals or among the polyandrous Brahmins and Rajputs of Jaunsar Bawar. It came to be customarily sanctioned among the high castes in Northern India. Education and urbanization are now gradually eroding the custom of purdah. However, carrying religious sanction, it is increasing among Muslims as a phase of revivalism in spite of progressive Muslim women's protests against it. Many a tribe and caste are now adopting normative sanctions against widow-remarriage and divorce and for purdah as a short cut to social mobility. While a few highly westernized and sophisticated women may talk of women's liberation and the desirability of extra-marital relations in the columns of weeklies, the average high caste woman in the city may be found observing fasts, festivals and rituals magically aimed at her husband's longevity. In modern India, along with the traditional ideal of absolute devotion to one's usband, stand the tribal customs sanctioning pre-marital and extra-arital licenses.[59]

Urban-industrial living and working conditions, modern means of ransportation, restaurants and military and other modes of modern fe increasing contacts between members of different castes tend o weaken the rigidity of caste.[60] Courts, police and Penal Codes ave taken away from the caste panchāyat much of its traditional uthority. The legalizing of intercaste marriage strikes at caste ndogamy which, while continuing, is not as strong as it was. Re-ruitment in the new occupational structure on the basis of edu-ational achievement and merit tends to weaken the traditional elation between caste and occupation, especially where modern ducation has made its impact. The greater the freedom of an ndividual or a caste from the rural social economy and/or from he traditional occupation of the caste, the greater is the occupational eterogeneity of a caste and the weakening of its traditional social ttributes. That is why, relatively speaking, there is a greater weak-ning of the social attributes of caste in the city and among the igher castes and the middle class drawn from the lower castes. In he Indian pattern of city-ward migration an individual's family, is caste, religious brotherhood and region have also migrated o the city along with the individual. In the heterogeneous urban-ocial milieu the individual depends on his caste and kinship for natrimony, in searching for a job and for social belongingness in bserving rituals. Caste emerges as a primary group in the city. Social belongingness to caste as a group goes still deeper where the raditional correlation between caste and occupation continues and aste assumes the role of the trade union as well. Where caste and religious brotherhood coincide, the primary group character of caste becomes all the sharper.

Modern forces of change have tended to strengthen caste in other respects also. The movement to make caste a vehicle of social reform and of increasing intercourse between subcastes for that purpose strengthened caste horizontally. It found expression in all India caste organizations which the post and telegraph and modern means of transportation and printing facilitated. Promot-ing among caste members teetotalism, vegetarianism, modern education and philanthropic social work and discouraging dowry or bride-price, as the case may be, and urging caste member to give up a traditional occupation if it carried the stigma of untouchability, the caste panchāyat emerged as an organized social medium fo reform and mobility. The politics of protective discriminatio flowing from the impact of parliamentary democracy promoted th trend of solidarity among endogamous groups similar in status a among the chamār jātis.

In the caste system, every type of group—racial, linguistic, reli gious and cultural—is assured its identity in spite of being functiona ly related to society as a whole. Retaining their identity i endogamy, religion, rituals, language and social organization bu gradually integrating themselves in the Indian economy, th Tibetan refugees are already on the way to becoming a caste. A caste system thus underlies the continuous and simultaneou multiplicity of behavioural patterns. The ideational source an justification of it lies in Indian philosophy which upholds that "every thing being a manifestation of Brahmin has a right to exist. . . each i relative and each taken alone is false."[61] On the other hand, a already stated, varṇadharma lends a futuristic hope of redemptio to the lowly ascribed groups. Varṇadharma serves as a perennia source of ideational inspiration for any movement of reform revival and mobility. All such movements remained anchored i the reinterpreted revival of varṇadharma, the vedic traditio (nigama), to suit the requirements of time and to encompass an assimilate as much of the agama (non-vedic) tradition as historica circumstances demanded and permitted. The nearer a caste t the nigama tradition the higher is its status in caste hierarchy Consequently, such movement, often tends to cut across caste and in due course, becomes a caste in itself.

Under the impact of western technology and the institution o parliamentary democracy and western education this philosophica ethos created an unprecedented scope for freedom from the shackle of caste or for what Srinivas calls "the tendency of breaking of from caste". Being the custodian of the literary tradition, the Brahmin was first to westernize to the extent his adherence to Sanskritic values admitted. Where any other caste (as the Kāyastha in Bengal and the Khatri in Punjab) shared the literary tradition with the Brahmin, it westernized along with the Brahmin with a view to claiming a greater share in Sanskritic traditions. "The Brahmins, thus, interposed themselves between the British, the new Kṣatriyas, and the rest of the people. The Brahmins looked up to the British and rest of the people up to both the Brahmins and he British." This generated the processes of Westernization and anskritization for social and economic mobility.[62] Among the ower castes a swing towards the traits of Sanskritization developed, iz. vegetarianism, teetotalism, the worship of the Hindu pantheon nd the adoption of Vedic rituals with emphasis on donning the acred thread. Though opposed to Sanskritization, Westernizaion facilitated both it and the breaking off from caste for social nobility, particularly at the lower levels of caste. Failing to attain ecognition at the top, the breaking segment of a low caste turns o the modus operandi of group shift by Sanskritizing caste as a whole nd by building up political pressure in parliamentary democracy. Thus, both these processes promote as well as operate through the rocesses of intra-caste solidarity and dissociability.

There is another aspect as well. Benoy K. Sarkar writes: "It is not so much the varṇāśrama as the protests against varṇāśrama, not so much the law and order as the violations of law and order, not so much the alleged pure races or castes as the varṇasaṃskāras the mixed colours,' fusion of ethnic elements—or rather the simulaneous operations of these two sets of forces that constitute the norm of Hindu cultural evolution. . . . This is the eternal society naking process, the millennium-old metabolism, that has led to he vertical mobilization of groups from the lower to the higher trata."[63] In what is being conceived as a dichotomy of and conflict between Sanskritization and Westernization and/or between radition and modernity one may read a continuation of "the ternal society making process" in India.

Historically, with every political crisis that displaces the tradiional elites from the apex of power, this society making process gets a movement-like swing from the elites displaced from power. All such movements in India have been launched as a philosophy of he elect. In every political crisis resulting in a change in the power structure, India revived the philosophy of varṇadharma and pluralism to meet the challenge from her adversary with catholic radicalism. The displaced elites found it handy in rebuilding their ocial base of power to philosophically rationalize unity in diversity and karma against birth and to combine reform with politics. This enabled the elites to widen the avenues for Sanskritization. The philosophy of pluralism and varṇadharma has all along been an elitist philosophy of compromise with the emerging contenders of power. It enables the elite to adopt the posture of radicalism but only in profession, and thus to retain their privileges. Neithe Gandhi nor Dayānanda advocated interdining and intermarriag between castes in spite of the radical egalitarianism they preachec The Indian brand of socialism is making rich richer and poc poorer. European education through the medium of Englis helps the elites more than it helps the masses. It enables them t retain their hold on levers of powers and retain their exclusivenes. From pluralism flow ideological voidness and indecision. Th philosophy of synthesis negates any option for bold action aimed a social reconstruction. That is why, perhaps, the elites in cor temporary India have drifted, consciously or unconsciously, towarc building up what Gunnar Myrdal calls the "soft state" and to whic he attributes most of the ills of the political-economy of contemporar India.[64]

11

INDIAN ETHICS

I. C. SHARMA

I MAN, GOD AND THE PURUṢĀRTHAS

By Indian ethics I mean the ethical views expounded in the entire philosophical, religious and cultural tradition represented by the Vedas, Upaniṣads, Bhagavadgītā and the classical schools of Indian philosophy including Jainism and Buddhism. This survey deals both practically and theoretically with the basic values of Indian ethics, which may be designated as spiritual utilitarianism, and includes contemporary ethical thought as a continuous and consistent evolution of traditional Indian ethics. We need to indicate here that the word "traditional" is not being used in a derogatory sense. The traditional and modern are not poles apart. What is modern today will be traditional tomorrow.

In India especially there is a thread of continuity in the midst of change as far as the philosophy of life is concerned. Undoubtedly the true significance of numerous ethical and metaphysical concepts has been lost to modern man, even in India, the result being that many of the most significant, logical, philosophically sound and even scientifically verifiable concepts, ideals and practices in Indian culture have been and are being adopted by an overwhelming majority of Indians almost blindly.

However, the pragmatic value of the practice of these ideals and concepts is evident from the very fact that in spite of the lapse of time and the unprecedented attacks upon and foreign domination of India and its culture for thousands of years, this tradition has not died out. Not only this, but it has proved to be ever new and evolving in the changing historical, political, social and scientific environment. It may be said that the perennial nature of Indian philosophy is unique due to the fact that basically the Indian tradition is not static but dynamic, not instinctive but rational, not dogmatic but evolutionary, imbibing the new, modifying the ol ever renewing and ever giving a dynamic boost and new dimer sion to the individual and society.[1]

We also need to explain the term "spiritual" in this context. I does not stand here for some weird or mysterious ghost like realit There is no doubt that in the English language there is no alternativ to translating the word "Ātman" in any other way than "spiritu self". At the most it may be said that this word is metaphysica But even "metaphysical" is a very poor translation of the Sanskri equivalent "Tattvajñāna" or "knowledge of the core". Let us there fore use the word "Ātman" for the spiritual self or the core c human personality to avoid the western notion of the metaphysica self called soul or ghost like supernatural entity. When I say tha Indian ethics is a spiritual utilitarianism, I mean that it is concerne with the integrated development of the human personality whic aims at the manifestation of "Ātman".

This "Ātman" is not a mere metaphysical concept in the wester sense, but in the Indian sense stated above. It may be compare to the concept atom (possibly derived from Ātman) in physics whic was a metaphysical notion for thousands of years and which throug experimentation has now become a physical reality. In othe words, what is metaphysics today becomes physics tomorrow Metaphysics therefore is not something nonsensical, as many wester philosophers contend today, but a real existential, meaningfu pursuit of man. This is the Indian sense of metaphysics and th metaphysical meaning of Ātman, the core of human personality the truth of truths (Satyasya Satyam) and the centre of centre (Kendrasya Kendram) in man. It is the innermost aspect of man the most intense nature of man and hence is not supernatural, bu most naturally natural. The term self-realization means th awareness, the awakening and consciousness of the Ātman, th attainment of which is the goal of all ethics, the adoption of al values and the adherence to duty.[2] Such an attainment is not merel an ideal, but an actual state of existence—experiential, real and attainable in our empirical life.

If the goal of ethics is self-realization in the sense expressed above, the Dharma (law, righteousness or duty) is not something authori- tarian or imposed from above. If duty was something like the commandments forced on individuals either by society or by an organized institution or even by an external God, it would be educed to an external constraint on the human mind. Since very man has the Ātman, which is the source of his freedom and hich brings about an integral development of his personality, a ode of conduct imposed by an external authority is bound to be esented by him sooner or later for two reasons. First such an im-osition conflicts with individual freedom and the Ātman of man. econdly, man's reason would lead him to ask: "Why should I be noral and conform to an external, authoritarian code of conduct?" n the West, the very inquiry about the utility of ethics has led to the ontroversy between rationalism and materialism or intuitionism and tilitarianism and has ultimately brought about an annihilation f ethics. The controversy over the nature of an ethical judge-nent has been responsible for the confusion in contemporary vestern ethics. It, like contemporary theology, is in a state of onfusion. The external, personalistic and anthropomorphic notion f God has given birth to radical theology, which declares the death f God. Similarly authoritarian ethics devoid of the goal of self-ealization has been responsible for the emergence of positivistic nd emotive theories of ethics which declare ethical judgements to e nonsensical and exclamatory respectively. It is my contention hat spiritual utilitarianism is free from these flaws and deserves a letailed discussion in this context.

The controversy between rationalism and hedonism or intuitionism nd utilitarianism has no place in Indian ethics because the ultimate ood it accepts rises above all controversies and antinomies. This night appear to be an abstract idealism to the western mind ntrained in any spiritual discipline. But the title "Spiritual Jtilitarianism" should bring home to the reader that Indian ethics is ot abstractly metaphysical. The basis of this doctrine is psycho-hysical, anthropologically psychological or psychometaphysical nd not merely metaphysical. Hence even a logical positivist is nable to dismiss it as nonsensical.

Since ethics is essentially concerned with man as an organic unit f human society, it is necessary to explain the nature of man in his context. For want of space it is not possible to give a detailed ccount. It should be mentioned however that Vedic is the nshakable ground of all the subsequent schools of Indian philosophy. The Vedas declare man as an integrated whole made up of the physi-al body (Śarīra), sensitive mind (Manas), rational intellect Buddhi) and unitive soul or self (Ātman). Indian philosophy is unique in declaring, "Yathā Piṇḍe Tathā Brahmāṇḍe," i.e. "microcosm is macrocosm."[3] This statement is not a mere metaphysical conception or an abstract notion. This universal proposition was arrived at by the Vedic sages after centuries of continuous investigation into the nature of man and the cosmos. We are not concerned here with the method of their research which was summed up in "Ātmanam Viddhi," "know thyself". I have indicated in my book *Ethical Philosophies of India* that these findings of the Indian sages which are more than five thousand years old, are most scientific, consistent and not contrary to the discoveries and findings of contemporary science and technology. These conclusions summed up the nature of the constitution of all existence in a fourfold manner. For want of an appropriate equivalent term in the English language let me use the original term Brahman for the expression "entire existence" used above. Brahman has wrongly been translated as an absolute in the sense in which Hegal uses it in his idealistic philosophy. It has also been wrongly translated as an impersonal concept of God, thereby misinterpreting Indian philosophy as a kind of Spinozistic Pantheism. A philosophy of absolutism deprives the individual of his freedom and pantheism has no place for ethics. In order to avoid these misconceptions we will use the original term Brahman in this context.

Brahman as such has a fourfold nature which is simultaneous as far as our apprehension goes. We may designate this fourfold nature of Brahman, as the four aspects viz. (1) Avyaya Brahman, infinite or unnamable or unlimitable Brahman as the ground of the cosmos (Viśvādhāra); (2) The Akṣara Brahman or Indestructible Brahman, beyond subjectivity and objectivity, as the invisible uncaused cause of the cosmos (Viśva Kāraṇa); (3) the Ātmākṣara Brahman, the universal Agent or Supreme Self (Parama Puruṣa) not in the sense in which man is a self or person, but as one Absolute Self or potential with an unlimited energy and capable of splitting into a subjective and objective reality (Viśvakartā). In this sense Brahman is the creator of the cosmos. This is the state of uncaused motionless mover or absolute motion, which is also absolute rest as it is beyond the relativities of time, space and causality of the material world. This in fact is the psychical vital self, which in its fourth aspect sprouts forth into the pluralistic cosmos; (4) Viśvāśrita Brahman or the Brahman manifested in the pluralistic cosmos of motion, universes, galaxies, solar systems, planets, etc. all of which

.re the creation of the Ātmākṣara (universal self). This fourth .spect is the cosmic form or cosmic manifestation (Viśvarūpa). n this aspect Brahman is cosmically immanent in pluralistic notion and energy. Einstein tried to explain this aspect of Brahman n the equation $E=mc^2$. This is the real empirical pluralistic cosmos .nd is not a mere illusion, as many Indian and western scholars of Indian philosophy have most erroneously contended.

Man's fourfold nature corresponds to that of Brahman. His oul or self is the infinite ground of his being. His intellectual or ational aspect is the cause of his personal being. His mental aspect is the creator of his mental or physical processes and his physical aspect is the manifestation of his being in the material ense. However, in the case of man, body, mind and intellect are imited by time, space and causality. They are grounded on and hence unconsciously controlled by the extra spatio-temporal Ātman or self, which has been designated as the centre of centres. The physical, mental and intellectual aspects of man are all subject o time, space and causality. Man is not completely free at these hree levels, though he exercises his choice and performs voluntary actions. But these three aspects of his personality are real, pluralstic, conflicting and therefore need to be developed and integrated. But the integration, according to Indian ethics goes a step further and is consummated when body, mind and intellect are centralized, harmonized and organized by the unitive Ātman thereby bringing about a unity in diversity and harmony in discord. This is an actual experiential state of human existence and is called self-realization or Ātmānubhūti.

The term self-realization should not be confused here with any abstract idealistic theoretical conception based on some absolutistic philosophy like Bradley's. Self-realization in this context stands for an actual state of human existence which is attainable by every normal human being and which, once attained, lasts for ever. A person who attains this state is called Jīvanmukta or one who is liberated while alive. In other words, the goal of Indian ethics is the complete freedom of the individual. The problem of the freedom of will, which has engaged the attention of western thinkers for centuries and which still eludes their philosophic grasp, is experientially solved in Indian ethics. Man is potentially free and capable of achieving a state of mind in which the conflict between the opposite notions of right and wrong, relative good and evil and even of pleasure and pain, are perfectly resolved. The lev attained is that of equilibrium, balance and inner peace of min This very experiential level has been designated variously b various schools of Indian philosophy.

The Bhagvadgītā, the quintessence of Vedic and Upaniṣadi philosophy, calls this level Sthitaprajñatā or the level of the stabilit of intellect.[4] Nyāya and Vaiśeṣika (The logico-analytical school designate it as the state of Apavarga (complete freedom from a suffering). Jainism calls it Nirjarā. Buddhism terms it the lev of the Bodhisattva or enlightened entity. All the schools with th exception of the materialistic Cārvāka unanimously accept th expression Jīvanmukti. It may once again be emphasized tha Jīvanmukti, when attained, is a fact and not an approximation or conjecture. It is an ultra-empirical, highest, utilitarian good an not an elusive, transient gain. It is a real state of mental peac equilibrium and equanimity, which adds an ineffable joy and zes to every human activity, whether that activity is physical, emotiona connotative, intellectual. It is not a withdrawal from active life It does not consist in escapism but is an exhilarating, stimulating an dynamic attitude towards the total life of an individual as a membe of society. Not only this, it also lifts a person from the lower leve of renunciation to the loftiest height where all his desires, emotions ambitions and longings are harmonized. Being free from all tensions he attains real freedom from conflicts, because the right choice become spontaneous selections for him. This liberated Jīvanmukt person while living a normal life resorts neither to the supression o desires nor to their unlicensed gratification, but to their harmonization and consummation without any distraction whatsoever.

The liberated person does not crave for sensuous pleasures; bu pleasures automatically go toward him in the form of joy and bliss free from all frustration and fear of the inseparably attendant pai which a man without such an equilibrium of mind is bound to suffe from. Consciously or unconsciously, wittingly or unwittingly, ever normal individual makes a relentless effort to reach this level throughout his life. But unfortunately, the means he adopts for this end engage his limited attention to such an extent that he takes them to be the end in themselves. He gets attached to the instrumental, transitory, side effects of his original effort to achieve the highest goal of an unmixed happiness. He forgets his inherent dignity, his prerogative to rise above the means and to be free from the creation his body, mind and reason in the sense of having complete astery over them. This freedom is not limited only to the will, ut also includes freedom of feeling and thinking. In this freedom e relativities and the antinomies of empirical life and discursive inking are not negated but transcended in the sense of being inte-rated.

This however is not the be all and the end all of Indian ethics, r it also puts forward a scheme of practicable values. Since man an integrated whole of body, mind, intellect and soul, the scheme also fourfold. These values are called Puruṣārthas or goals. gain the semantic problem stands in our way. There cannot be ıy literal translation of the word Puruṣārtha in the English nguage. This word is a compound of the two Sanskrit words, uruṣa and Artha. Puruṣa means self or soul and Artha means m or goal. Thus Puruṣārtha may be translated as the effort ttain the spiritual goal. It is also translated as the meaning or the nplication of the soul, self, agent, doer, subject or man. In other ords, the very term man implies the fourfold values. Thus the ur values ultimately aim at the final goal of self-realization. These ur Puruṣārthas are: (1) Artha or economic value-wealth, (2) āma or the emotional value of the satisfaction of desires—love, 3) Dharma or the moral value of duty—virtue involving individual ffort to serve society for the general well-being, and (4) Mokṣa e spiritual value of liberation—self-realization.[5]

We have given this order to the four Puruṣārthas, though ormally they are arranged as Dharma, Artha, Kāma and Mokṣa spectively. This order has been chosen to bring home to the reader e fact that this fourfold scheme corresponds to the fourfold nature f man. The economic value or wealth is needed for the healthy evelopment of the human body. The satisfaction of desires, specially the fulfilment of sex in conjugal love, promotes a healthy nd balanced mind. Similarly the performance of one's moral duty, hich includes an individual's obligation to his society, state or ation, leads to the intellectual advancement of his personality. inally Mokṣa or spiritual value is the highest level of the spiritual elf. Hence, ethics is not an imposition, or virtue a terror of an angry od, but is an utilitarian value which brings about the intellectual volution of the individual by making him a free and useful member f human society. It is from this point of view that Dharma is eld higher than wealth and Kāma. Dharma, the intellectual evolute of human nature summed up in the virtues of truth, justic compassion, love, fellow-feeling, courage, wisdom, temperen and toleration, is the highest Puruṣārtha. It is so because it brin about the full utilization and enjoyment of the mundane values Artha and Kāma and also because it leads to Mokṣa or spiritu awakening and self-realization. It stands midway between tl material ambitions and achievements of man and the attainme of highest spirituality, which is the very core of human personalit Thus the four Puruṣārthas bridge the gulf between material ar spiritual realities. They give us an integrated view of the pluralisti material world of body, mind and intellect and the self or sou which is an emanation from and the spark of the spiritual sour of all existence—Brahman.

The identity of the microcosm and the macrocosm or the identit of man and God in the sense in which we have used the latter tern is again not a product of imagination. The pluralism of the cosmi existence of the universe, galaxie, inter-stellar systems, etc. undoubtedly the manifestation of an emanation from Brahma which a contemporary scientist may designate as an *X*. Similarl in man, the pluralistic existence of atomic body, emotive mind an discursive thinking or intellect etc. is the manifestation of and a emanation from the soul or self, the microcosmic centre. Wester ethics stops at the intellectual level and is bewildered at the plurali tic and conflicting commandments and principles, which woul always be relative and limited in their scope. Indian ethics go a step further and points out that a pluralistic ethics has its co summation in the unitive experience of self-realization. Henc for an integrated development of human personality, the adoptio of all the four Puruṣārthas is necessary.

There is no doubt that in the history of Indian culture there wer times when one or two of these Puruṣārthas were emphasized a the expense of others.[6] This resulted in a lopsided view bein adopted by individuals and society leading to an ethical degeneratio and social evils causing the deterioration of the entire Hindu cultur But there has always been exceptional personalities even durin periods of degeneration. Spiritual leaders and God-realized sou like Rāma, Kṛiṣṇa, Vyāsa, Mahāvīrā and the Buddha in the ancie past and Tulsidās, Nānak, Kabir, Rāmakrisha, Vivekanand Rāmtirtha, Tagore and Gandhi in the modern and contempora periods have again and again demonstrated the application

.tegrated ethics to practical life. Besides, hundreds of thousands ' other spiritually inclined souls have always adhered to the ıtegrated way of life.

Corresponding to the fourfold nature of Brahman and man a urfold path of Yoga has been propounded in Indian ethics. The ɔal of the four Yogas is the same. After an analysis of these ›ur paths, it will be clear that all the schools of Indian philosophy arring the Cārvāka have emphasized one, or more than one, of ıese Yogas in their own way. It is noteworthy that so far these ›ur Yogas have not been explained in the context in which they re being treated here. It may also be asserted that so far as an xposition of Indian ethics in the English language is concerned, ıost writers have depended on sources other than Sanskrit. They ave especially neglected the Brahmanic aspect of the Vedas, which ɔntains the key to the whole of Indian ethics. This drawback as been overcome in this essay.

Before giving a brief analysis of these four Yogas, let me name them ı the order of the fourfold nature of man and Brahman beginning 'om the gross to the subtle aspects. Corresponding to the body r the material aspect of man and Brahman, i.e. the Śarīra of ıan and the cosmic immanent aspect of Brahman in time, space nd causality, is the Yoga called Karma Yoga or the path of action. 'orresponding to the mind of man (the emotive aspect) and the .tmākṣara or the universal Supreme Self aspect of Brahman is ıe Bhakti Yoga or the path of devotion and love. Corresponding › the intellect of man and the beyond aspect, Akṣara or Brahman, the Jñāna Yoga or the path of knowledge. Finally corresponding › the spiritual aspect (Ātman) or man and the Infinite or Unnam-ble (avyaya) aspect of Brahman is the Buddhi Yoga or the path of ıe stabilized intellect or intuive intellect, which, incidently, is the ombination and consummation of the other three Yogas. In our reatment of these Yogas however we will not follow the order given bove. We shall begin with the Buddhi Yoga and end with 'hakti Yoga for our own convenience.

II Buddhi Yoga

Since the pluralistic, empirical universe is the manifestation ›f the unitive Brahman and man is a miniature cosmos, harmony in ndividual life can be brought about by realizing that the unitive principle, Ātman, is unaffected by the relativities of the manifeste universe. But at the same time the performance of all duties an the enjoyment of worldly pleasures should not be denied. This possible through the path of the stable intellect, which has bee beautifully depicted in the Bhagavadgītā in the following verse "Endowed with wisdom, being unattached to the consequences action, attaining self-realization and freedom from the bondage birth and death, the wise attain that level, which is free from evi When your understanding will cross the meshes of delusion, onl then you would have attained transcendence from that which heard."[7] It does not mean that one should disregard the impor ance of good and evil as opposities. The state of Yoga brings abo a reconciliation of empirical and spiritual experiences. The wor Yoga stands here for intuitive knowledge of the truth or the Buddl Yoga. A person whose knowledge is true, who performs actio without attachment to the consequences and who constantl meditates on God as the Supreme source of all love attains the sta of Sthitaprajña (stable intellect). In other words, the thre disciplines of knowledge, action and devotion followed in an int grated manner lead a person to the state of the established wisdom the intellect.[8]

The first prerequisite of Sthitaprajña is the giving up of th desires of the mind (sensual or base animal desires) and delight i one's own self (Ātman). This latter characteristic should not b misunderstood as selfishness. On the contrary a person delighte in the self knows that the self is not his body, mind or intellect, bu the universal Brahman, which resides in all and which promp him to love and be just to all.

The second characteristic of Sthitaprajña is forbearance, whic means courage to stand against all the odds of life. According to th Bhagavadgītā, "That sage is said to be a person with establishe intellect, who is not disturbed in misery, who is not elated amid pleasures and who is free from all attachment, fear and anger.'

The third prerequisite is similar to forbearance because it requir him to be free from attraction towards pleasure and free fro distraction in the presence of pain. This quality of freedom fro affection and from hatred or rather from favour or jealousy has bee explained in the following manner. "One who behaves the sam when compliments are paid to him, who does not retaliate fo injury done to him, or flatter those who do good to him is a perso vith stable intellect."[10]

The fourth and the most essential characteristic of the person with teady wisdom is self-control. This quality is explained fully in he Bhagavadgītā with illustrations and with the warning that the bsence of self-control leads to the total destruction of an individual. elf-control leading to equanimity is regarded as the most vital rerequisite of a Sthitaprajña, because without it not only would here be no spiritual outlook, but, on the contrary, there will occur gradual deterioration of the mind of the person ultimately ending n mental chaos and intellectual disintegration.

Serenity and calmness of mind is not possible without the exercise f self-control. One who has no control over his senses and mind an neither have knowledge nor resort to meditation; a person levoid of meditation can have no peace; and a person who has lost eace of mind must constantly be miserable. Psychologically nd logically, it is commonly accepted that once a person yields o animal instincts and relaxes control over mind and senses, he is ound to lose the power of discrimination and fall to the level of a rute. Hence, it is emphasized constantly that only a person whose enses are completely under control can be said to have a stable ntellect or wisdom. Such a person follows the mean between the wo extremes of asceticism or self-mortification and licentiousness r self-indulgence. A Sthitaprajña therefore is one who synthesizes ction and knowledge, passion and reason, psychology and logic, ntellect and intuition, thereby systematizing all desires, instead f either supressing them or becoming a slave to them.

It is evident that the ideal of Sthitaprajña is nothing but the ractice of spiritual utilitarianism. The heart of a man with nental equilibrium overflows with love and compassion for all iving beings irrespective of friend or foe. Hence, such a person can ever retaliate even when he is victimized by the aggressor.[11] The ublimation of the emotions attained through self-control enriches ife and promotes harmony, bringing about the healthy development f the individual and happiness of family life. Modern psychologists ave pointed out repeatedly that the emotions of anger and fear are ot only harmful for bodily health but may even prove fatal when ncontrolled. The emphasis on self-control, indifference to depressing and elating situations and freedom from the emotions of fear nd anger advocated as the characteristic of the Sthitaprajña are ndoubtedly useful from the point of view of maintaining the bodily health and cheerfulness necessary for success in practical life. Bu the combination of the paths of knowledge, action and devotior which is the characteristic of Sthitaprajña, leads to spiritual awaken ing or self-realization without which the integrated developmen of the material-pluralistic aspects of human personality and i unitive spiritual aspect is impossible.

III Jñāna Yoga

Though we are treating Jñāna Yoga, Karma Yoga an Bhakti Yoga separately because they are indicative of the differen types of people to whom they are suited, yet it would be wron to consider them mutually exclusive.[12] Knowing, feeling and willin are the basic constituents of human nature, and the paths of know ledge, devotion and action respectively correspond to them. Th very word Jñāna Yoga indicates that this path requires true know ledge which discriminates between the permanent and impermanen But the path of knowledge shows that this knowledge should b regarded as the redeeming feature of man's nature. When onc a person has come to know or rather to see intuitively that neithe his body, mind nor intellect is Ātman, or the abiding principle, h must rid himself of the ego feeling. He must give up the fals notion that he is the doer or the subject, because his real self is abov the activities of the body, senses, mind and intellect. Howeve this higher knowledge does not abolish the existence of those fou Rather, it makes one aware that Ātman transcends duality an manyness in its real state of self luminous existence. The ego is manifestation of the unmanifest soul, and so are the body, senses mind and intellect. Although these are intimately related, and th grosser depends upon the subtler, yet the subtlest of all is the sou (Ātman), the central and pivotal element in human personality.

This supreme knowledge causes a person to give up ordinar attachments and to perform actions without any expectations o its fruits. The goal of the path of knowledge is self-realization, o the identity of the self with Brahman. Hence, a knowledge of th transcendental nature of the self which is to be realized makes a individual indifferent to selfish desires and eliminates all impuritie of mind. One who has this knowledge is free from all evil con sequences of action which bind the ignorant. The nineteent verse of the fourth discourse entitled "Path of Knowledge" states

He whose actions are all free from the hankering for desires, whose ;tions have been burnt by the fire of knowledge, him the wise call sage." Though engaged in action, such a person is in fact not oing anything, because he is always contented and does not worry oout the consequences. His actions are like the offerings of a person the fire of knowledge. Such a person is said to be engaged in erforming the sacrifice of knowledge (Jñāna Yajña). It has ierefore been said that "He who is devoid of attachment, free, hose mind is established in knowledge, and who does work as a crifice (for the Lord)—his entire action melts away." We should eep in mind that the melting away of action does not mean the epudiation of action or resorting to inactivity but stands for the estruction of the evil consequences of action.

The path of knowledge might appear to be a mere ideal at first ght, and one might very well say that giving up the notion of being doer, which amounts to eschewing personal responsibility, at least piritually, is not what we require today. But a study of con-emporary problems would reveal that the path of knowledge is a olution to many of the problems of suffering humanity.

The present age is one of psychological maladjustment, divided amilies, disillusionment and disintegrated societies which suggests hat man has lost his balance of mind and that scientific knowledge as become a handicap in the march towards peace and prosperity. Our argument has suggested that what is missing in all this is true nowledge of the underlying oneness of the universe. What we ack today is not scientific knowledge of the plurality of the physical niverse but intuitive knowledge of the monistic and non-dualistic Brahman. This deficiency cannot be made up by overemphasizing cience, overasserting egoism, and giving unlicensed freedom to man n every walk of life. On the contrary, our emphasis today should e on self-control, duty and self-realization, which makes the ocialization, nay, even the divinization of man possible, and nfuses in him love not only for his fellow beings, but for all living creatures and even for the entire cosmos. This is possible only when he path of knowledge leads the individual to realize that in spite of being physically insignificant in the vast cosmos, where his native planet is comparatively less than an atom in space, he is the miniature cosmos and virtual Absolute, because the indwelling spirit of the uni-verse is most truly manifested in his personality alone.

There is little doubt that the path of knowledge fulfils the needs of contemporary crises. In the domestic, social, national or inter-national areas of life there is dire need for enlightened persons, awakened souls and balanced minds who can infuse the spirit of self-devotion and self-sacrifice in each and every individual by imparting this true knowledge to satisfy the urgent craving for self-control, duty and social well-being instead of the clamour for unlimited freedom and individual rights. The path of knowledge would not deny the rights of man, but would dignify them and make man cap-able of enjoying these rights with greater zest than ever before. It would not crush freedom or political equality, but it would give man an insight into the nature of real freedom, which is liberation and genuine spiritual equality.[13] How this path brings about a synthesis of material progress and the spiritual development of human personality will be evident in showing that the Niṣkāma Karma Mārga, or the path of renunciation in action, which prompts man to be most actively engaged in social and empirical pursuits, is in fact the necessary corollary of the path of knowledge.

IV Karma Yoga

To avoid confusing the significance of the path of knowledge and the path of action, which are ultimately inseparable though distinguishable, it may be pointed out that the path of knowledge is meant for the followers of Saṃkhya (persons whose minds have been prepared by true knowledge of self-control) and the path of action is meant for the Yogins (persons who attain true knowledge through action or duty performed without any selfish end). Both paths aim at self-purification and lead to the same goal. The two paths may be adopted by persons with different bents of mind; but, just as disinterested action as a spiritual discipline leads to true knowledge, similarly true knowledge of Brahman and also of the world prompts the wise man not to give up action, but to give up attachment towards action.

If a person thinks that by giving up activity or by renouncing duty one reaches a state of inactivity, he is deluded. The mere renunciation of activity can never make a person attain perfection. The fact is that inactivity is not at all possible as long as man exists physically, because the physical world, which is generated by Prakṛiti (nature), is continuously active in view of the constant inter-action of the three Guṇas belonging to the Prakṛiti. No one can xist even for a moment without performing activity of some kind r other. Hence, a person who gives up activity altogether is inferior the Karma Yogin, who, in spite of adopting self-control, continues perform all actions through his organs of action without being ttached to those actions. Performing one's daily duties is regarded s unavoidable both for the attainment of gradual liberation and for ie maintenance of one's bodily existence.

In order to support the unavoidability of performing action for ie successful conduct of life in the pluralistic physical world, the hagavadgītā quotes the Vedic injunction which requires man to erive all physical benefits from the gods (i.e. the physical elements), y performing sacrifices, i.e. by analysing the physical phenomena nd by yoking nature to enjoy physical pleasures. When the Bhaavadgītā urges that men and gods should both attain the supreme ood by mutual give and take, what is meant is that man, being ntelligent, should utilize scientific knowledge about the material vorld for the ultimate purpose of attaining perfection. It has een mentioned that man should enjoy the benefits he receives from ature by engaging in activity and by rendering service and selfacrifice. If a person enjoys worldly pleasures without performing is duties and sacrifices towards gods, i.e. without making offerings f his action towards nature, he should be considered a thief.

The performance of sacrifice towards the gods also means sharing he benefits received from natural forces with our fellow-men. A spiritual communism was accepted by the Indian sages, who delared that a person who does not share his meals with others, and vho cooks only for filling his own belly, was a criminal and sinful. This utilitarianism is beautifully expressed in the following verse of he Bhagavadgītā: "The good who partake of the remnant of a acrifice are freed from all sins; but those sinful persons, who cook for their own sake, partake of sin."[14] By declaring selfishness sin, the Bhagavadgītā advocates an ethics which favours cooperation and humanitarianism. The recognition of the necessity of performing constant action, with a view to producing wealth and food to bring about material prosperity for the human race, shows that non-attachment to action means the performance of one's duty, not merely for the sake of duty, but for social well-being also. This aspect of Niṣkāma Karma Yoga indicates that unattached action is not to be identified with Kant's 'will that wills nothing', but that it has a wider motive and a nobler purpose to be fulfilled than the selfish motive of satisfying sensual desires. Niṣkāma Karma Yog does not advocate the renunciation of action. It simply propounc renunciation in action.[15]

This ideal exhorts us not to have any motive of future benefit whi performing an action, and not to bother about the good or ba consequences of the action. This, however, does not falsify huma psychology, according to which no action can be motiveless. Wha it commands is that one should give up attachment to the motiv in the sense of remaining unperturbed by the success or the failu of the action. It should be remembered that Karma Yoga ha two motives, one of which must be tacitly accepted by the agen The first is Ātmasuddhi, or self-purification; the second is subservin the purpose of God. The aim of the first motive is self-conques and that of the latter is self-surrender to God, to become free fro all fears (Abhaya). If a person accepts the first motive, he mus sacrifice his personal interest for that of society as a whole and brin about social well-being even at the cost of his own life. If th second motive is accepted, the aspirant must go on working for th well-being of all living creatures, taking himself to be an instrumen in the hands of God. Thus self-realization and God-realization ar the two goals, one of which is accepted by the aspirant when h performs actions without any selfish motive.

V Bhakti Yoga

However critical and pragmatically fanatic modern ma may be towards God or religion, he cannot, even on intellectua grounds, discard and disprove the existence of God and the spiritua power centred and magnificiently manifested in man's mind Scientists, sages, and philosophers in all ages and climes have asserted and experienced the presence of the Divine in man as well as in nature.

This spiritual potentiality in man can be made manifest and actual by following the path of knowledge, action and devotion. The threefold path is the spiritual discipline by which the unlimited power of the soul can be experienced by the individual. Thus the experience of religious conscious can be had by a common man, provided he chooses to have it. God, therefore, is not a theoretical concept, but an actual empirical reality, the Divine presence, which can be felt by a sincere devotee. There is no need of ɔrmalities, but instead an attitude of mind, an honest urge and rm conviction in the Power, Presence and Potentiality of the Divine. This conviction can be aroused by a certain ethical discipline, by knowledge of the Supreme Being, and by the Grace of God, which showers forth when a person surrenders himself to the Almighty and dedicates all his thoughts, feelings and actions to Him, making himself an instrument for the fulfilment of the Divine purpose.

Those who deny the existence of God or ridicule the ideas of Divine Grace are generally those who have never made any effort to experience the potential power which resides not outside, but inside their own hearts. They forget that we cannot have a direct experience of any potentiality without bringing that potentiality under some striking or drastic conditions. As laymen we believe and take it for granted that water is liquid, but science tells us that it is only a combination of gases. Now the gaseous nature of the water is its potentiality. If the scientist is challenged with regard to the gaseous nature of water, he would take the doubter to the laboratory, pass an electric current through the water, and we would see with our own eyes how the liquid is changed into gases. Similarly, the infinitude, transcendence, immanence, indestructivility and omnipresence of the soul are the potentialities which can be made manifest when spiritual discipline is practically followed. Unless a person submits himself to the discipline and the conditions of the path of knowledge, action and devotion, he will not experience the Divinity in his own self. He will never know the reality of the immanence and the transcendence of the spirit. But he has no right to deny the existence of the Supreme Power, or God, just as a person, who has never witnessed the change of water into gases in a laboratory has no right to deny that fact. One who says that he does not believe in the existence of God or would not adopt the spiritual discipline required and yet would like to know or see God, would be acting like a man who wants to learn the art of swimming without actually entering the water.

That is the reason for the great emphasis on conviction in Bhakti Yoga. A firm conviction (Śradhā) is an unavoidable pre-condition of God-realization. The Bhagavadgītā clearly says in this regard that only a man with firm conviction attains true knowledge, whereas a doubter perishes. Once a person is firmly intent upon following the spiritual path, he makes spiritual progress; and the power acquired by him during the course of his effort (Sādhanā) expels his doubt. A Yogin (aspirant) is he who worships God with full faith and devotion. The best Yogins are those who are ever devoted and are ever endowed with supreme faith. But at the same time, those who worship the indestructible, indescribable unmanifest, inconceivable, changeless, immovable and eternal Brahman by self-control, are also regarded as devotees who attain God. Since meditation on the unmanifested Brahman is tedious and difficult, the followers of the Niṣkāma Karma Yoga, who are attached to God instead of being attached to the fruits of action, do attain God.[16] A person not able to meditate should practise Niṣkāma Karma with full faith in God and in that manner would attain God. Self-surrender to God makes Niṣkāma Karma psychologically justified and practisable. Without the aim of God-realization the path of action would either turn into an empty doctrine or lead the individual to indulge in sensual pleasures. Similarly the central object of Jñāna Yoga, which requires an aspirant to give up the notion of a doer, would not be possible to attain if a man were not to accept the will of God as supreme and his personal will as the instrument to fulfil the Divine purpose. Hence we find that the path of devotion makes possible the success of the path of knowledge and also the path of action because of the faith in the Supreme God, which is necessary for the execution of Yoga, or the uniting of oneself with the Supreme Reality.

We have used the word "God-realization" because it is not only the personal God who is the object of devotion but also the Infinite Brahman. The Personalness of God is not denied, but his real nature is explained in Indian philosophy as we have done earlier. He is accepted as the creator, preserver and destroyer, where creation, preservation and destruction are the three functions of God as Ātmākṣara or Supreme Self. God as a personal being is worshipped and propitiated, because the omnipotence of God or Brahman does not deny the possibility of the appearance of the personal God to the devotee. Bhakti Yoga does advocate deep love and devotion to God. But it clearly points out that this Father, Doer and Maker, Almighty God is all pervasive, and as such resides in every individual. God-realization therefore means the actualization of the Divine potentiality of man. The words Paramadhāma, the supreme place of the refuge of the devotee, indicate that the state reached by the devotee ultimately is the Divine State. However, hen a devotee strongly desires to see God face to face and remains ear Him for worship and meditation, deriving utmost joy, power nd inspiration, he is granted that choice by the Almighty. Thus ne goal of Indian ethics, which does not deny the greatest good of umanity even in the material sense, is spiritual utilitarianism, which dds an extra zest to all the pursuits of man in the world.

12

CONCEPTS OF MAN

V. N. K. Reddy

I The Epic View of Man

In this survey we shall begin with the Purāṇas and Itihāsas, continue with the Epics and heterodox and orthodox schools and conclude with three recent thinkers and their views of man.

The people of the Itihāsas and Purāṇas (c. A.D. 100) believed man's ultimate goal to be beyond this world, although they emphasized at the same time man's life here and now. A wise man was considered a boon to society, for he had experienced and overcome suffering. Suffering was not considered inherent in the world but was due mainly to man's wrong adjustment in life. To escape it, a person need not renounce the world and stop all activity.[1] Instead he must work within the world and learn how to overcome suffering through determined effort.

The life-span alloted to man by the Gods was believed to be a long one. Vālmīki, author of the Rāmāyaṇa, stated that man lived for a hundred years; and in the Classical (Gupta) Age man supposedly lived for a thousand years or more. According to the poet and dramatist Bharata (c. first century B.C.) man has two qualities, sṛingāra (beauty or splendour) and vīra (valour or heroism). Poets influenced the concept of man in the Itihāsas and Purāṇas more than priests. The ideal man was a blend of internal and external virtues. He was believed to be the maker of his own destiny and the destiny of one involved that of all.

The epics, written either by the Śaivites (worshippers of Śiva) or Vaiṣṇavites (devotees of Viṣṇu), describe the everyday life of the people and thus present a more popular concept of man than the Vedas and Upaniṣads. The epics Rāmāyaṇa and Mahābhārata prescribe a philosophy of action (Karmayoga), although they occasionally advocate the ways of jñāna and bhakti. Three major oncepts—Dharma (virtue), Mokṣa (liberation) and Vairāgya renunciation) were recognized by almost all epic writers. Desire-ess action (niṣkāma-karma) was lauded especially in the Rāmāyaṇa and Mahābhārata. The Gītā view of man is based on the concept of Yoga, a spiritual discipline stressing the identity of the Ātman and the Paramātman. The epics advocated the major yogas but he Patañjali, Sāṃkhya, Mantra and other yogas had their own pecific influences on the concept of Man. The Haṭa-yoga says man can attain salvation by controlling the vital processes, the Laya-yoga by dissolving one's ego in the Supreme Being, the Auṣadha-yoga by taking certain herbs and the Mantra-yoga through uttering acred syllables or mantras. The Purāṇas' and Epics' conception of man is a classical one, interpreted mainly through Yoga.[2] It is also natural, humanistic, synthetic and constructive in implication.

The concept of man in the Mahākāvya or Grand Epic is mainly metaphysical. Aśvaghoṣa (c. first century A.D.) wrote two poems, Buddha-Carita and Saundara-Nanda. One depicts the life of Buddha, the other the ascendence to the throne by his half-brother Nanda. In the latter, Aśvaghoṣa clearly shows the insignificance of man's worldly life. The first poem concentrates mainly on human feelings, especially compassion. Buddha's and Nanda's attitudes toward life vary sharply. Buddha straightway transcended worldly luxuries and prepared himself for final renunciation; Nanda wavers between the ascetic ideal and worldly life.

Kālidāsa, India's greatest poet (c. fifth century A.D.) presented man as a valiant hero with all the emotions, cravings and failings of human beings. Man is happy in this life. There is no room for sin and suffering, if man realizes his inner potentialities. In the drama Vikramorvaśī, Kālidāsa glorifies man's place in nature. He is not separate from the cosmos or the living forces of religion. Pure human love is never separate from Divine love. In the poem Ṛitusaṃhāra, the Lord of Love, Kāmadeva, with his trusted companion approaches God to make him realize man's importance. Kālidāsa views man as of significance and value, the apex of all beauty and glory.[3]

For Kālidāsa, man's main aim is to lift himself out of ignorance and entanglement to an awareness and enlightenment beyond all spatio-temporal relationships. The cultured man of the poem Raghuvaṃśa cannot be enclosed within categories, confined to images or contained in verbal structures. He maintains a balance between the four ends of life. History, liberty and creativity a all expressions of man's inner spirit. The truly enlightened ma lives the supreme life of contemplation. Kālidāsa's concept of ma is a universal one in that it includes the social, ethical and met physical, as seen in the works noted above and others.

The destruction of avidyā (delusion) is a central theme of India most popular epic, the Bhagavadgītā.[4] The Gītā asserts tl universe is based on a moral order which is declining because man's infatuation; hence man's duty is to re-establish that orde Whenever the forces of evil gain an upper hand, the Divine appea on earth in human form. The Gītā declares that man mu surrender everything to God and that he undergoes a complet transformation through work done in a spirit of dedication. Wor not based on sacrifice and dedication results in bondage. Th Gītā is opposed to both vikarma (wrong action) and akarm (inaction) and prescribes niṣkāma-karma (detached action). Ma is to never waver in performing such action and in dischargin ordained duties. In actuality, God is the doer, while man is onl an instrument of action.

The Gītā identifies the individual self with the self of all. Also there is no antagonism between the natural and spiritual.[5] Th natural man of the Gītā has many qualities of Yoga—self knowledge control and surrender, equanimity, devotion, service and con templation. Man is born in a body; so he carries his saṃskāras o character-impressions with him. Though subject to apparen change, there is something unchanging in man, namely his immorta self or prakṛiti. Thus man is viewed as fashioned in God's imag and an instrument of the Divine on earth. According to the Gītā all man's actions are determined by the three guṇas (attributes)— sattva, rajas and tamas. The three cardinal virtues—sacrifice austerity and charity—are acquired through hard struggle. Righ knowledge is self-knowledge. Deluded by the senses man think he is the doer, but all his actions are based on the guṇas of th Prakṛiti. The ideal man of the Gītā is not easily swayed by likes an dislikes. The man of faith gains knowledge and all that comes fro it. A man not attached to any selfish purpose seeks to scale th heights of the knowledge of Yoga. The Gītā's concept of man is both ethical and practical. It is based on devotion, knowledge and action with more emphasis on action than the other two.

In Hindu psychology, man is viewed in terms of a succession o ates of consciousness or stream of consciousness which connects ast, present and future.[6] Man is governed by certain mental forces alled saṃskāras. They are the conscious strivings of personality, ot blind impulses of the unconscious. The will-to-power has no lace in Hindu psychology. The conscious self of man is a unity nd his activities are meaningful and purposeful. The mind's greatess is measured by its capacity for integration and unification, ot its ability to reason out.

Indian psychology recognizes four states of consciousness—ışupti, svapna, jāgrat and turīya.[7] The first two states of sleeping nd dreaming are included under the category of the unconscious. n this way the sleeping, waking and aspiring states correspond to he Unconscious, Conscious and Superconscious levels. Man's nind (Antaḥkaraṇa) integrates the above states into one stream of onsciousness. Antaḥkaraṇa, or the inner instrument, has four unctions—manas (rational knowledge), buddhi (intuitive knowedge), ahaṃkāra (self-knowledge) and chitta (self-consciousness). 'hus the whole personality of man becomes a sākṣi-chaitanya, a vitness of the conscious apart from its dynamic role.

The search for external reality and the abiding spirit in man go and-in-hand in Indian psychology. The object of psychology is elf-analysis, which implies restoring man to mental wholeness hrough spiritual discipline. Indian psychology does not stop at he discovery of past saṃskāras but believes a man can change his ourse of life if he has full self-understanding. He can create a new et of saṃskāras. Hindus believe that individual minds are but parts of the universal mind. Each man is potentially divine and levelopes according to his nature. The concept of man is both deational and practical in Indian psychology, which is deeply eligious but highly scientific in its method. Man is not a product f association; nor is he a structural being or a functional medium. Ie is not a reflex mechanism or an instinctive action. He is a dynanic whole, a potential reality and an eternal seeker.

II Jain and Buddhist Views of Man

While in Vedic literature self-realization is achieved through acrifices, in Jainism it is accomplished through personal purity and renunciation.[8] Jainism considers man a wanderer and wayfarer. There is little regard for worldly life and its accomplishments.

Emphasis is more on man's inward life. Spiritual life is isolate from the social life of man and a high code of spiritual disciplir is encouraged. Austerity and self-mortification is the Jaina's (tł conqueror) method of realizing Jīva (self-hood).

The Jain concept of man is one of common sense realism an pluralism. Man or Jīva is a substance possessing extension. Jīva is also a soul and so as conscious substance. A perfect Jīv has the highest consciousness. It shows things, performs activitie suffers pain and illumines itself and other objects. But bad passio like anger, pride and greed cause bondage or karma pudgala whic can be gotten rid of through two processes—saṃvara (stoppin the influence of new karma) and niyarā (wearing out the existin karma in one).[9] Man can attain Mokṣa when he practises the thre jewels (tri-ratna) and accepts the five great vows (pañcha-mahā vrata).

The concept of man in Jainism is both ascetic and pessimisti The goal of life is the restoration of the pristine purity of the sou so that man may attain pure knowledge. Jainism prescrib "manaḥsuddhi" or purity of mind as the only mārga of salvatio Such purity is based on the control of the senses. One mu struggle against the four kaṣāyas of anger, mind, illusion and gree Equilibrium leads to the conquest of anger and ennui. Man mu inculcate universal friendship (maitrī) and emphasize the goo traits of others. Although man is constantly subjected to the influ of karma pudgala, he has an infinite power for right action in hin Man's hope of salvation rests on his own efforts to drive away th old-karma and protect the entry of new-karma into his Jīva or sou The saying that Jainism is a religion of self help is a result of th emphasis on individual effort.

The liberated soul in Jainism is a "siddha" who possesses God-lik qualities and serves as a beacon light for the rest of creation. He free from the influx of karma and is in a state of eternal blessednes Such a person is also called a Jina (victor) and vīra (hero). H is intrinsically good, positively detached, actively self-controlled an self-purified, having achieved salvation through an inner proces

Buddhist schools of thought vary in their views of man. Th Mādhyamika school holds man is "śūnyatā" or voidness, meanin his real nature cannot be explained or described. The Yogācār school is idealistic, emphasizing consciousness and mind as th important factor. Man is a combination of mental and externa eality according to the Sautrāntika and Vaibhāsika schools. According to one interpretation man is a momentary aggregate of kāyā, manas and cit (body, mind and consciousness). According to another he is a combination of five changing elements—rūpa (body), vedanā (sensation), sajñā (perception), saṃskāras (aggregates) and vijñāna (consciousness). In either case no one is permanent as nothing exists for more than one moment.

Buddhism begins with the view that life is full of sorrow and suffering. Attachment, hatred and infatuation (rāga, dveṣa and moha) obstruct man's action. However, man's higher action, based on perfect insight into the real nature of the universe, comes into play, saving man from the evil influence of karma. All actions are products of our past karmas. No one can claim a new life free from accumulated action. However, one can overcome past karmas and attain Nirvāṇa. Nirvāṇa is not the extinction of existence but the cessation of misery and rebirth. It also means the reaching of perfect peace through selfless action. Nirvāṇa can only be experienced, not described. Buddha prescribed an eightfold path to it, of which self-control is a key factor. The Bodhisattva of the Mahāyāna school is the fully-realized man striving for others' salvation. He is not satisfied until the last man is liberated and postpones his own salvation for the sake of other sentient beings. In the Hīnayāna school, Arhatship, the working out of one's own salvation, is the ideal projected.[10]

III The Orthodox School

The concept of man in the Sāṃkhya school is nearer to that found in the Kaṭha than Taittīriya Upaniṣad. Man is the centre of creation and the nucleus of the external world of reality. The ahaṃkāra or ego transcends both man and the world. It is one of the three aspects of the inner self, spirit and mind being the others. Prakṛiti is the ground or ultimate principle of the world of objects, including man. It is the eternal and ubiquitous unconscious and unintelligent principle, forming the basis for all and the first cause of all objects. Thus it is called the "mūla-prakṛiti", the causal matrix of the world. It is made up of three guṇas, sattva, rajas and tamas, which are either in constant conflict or cooperation with each other. Each tries to dominate the other two.[11]

The Puruṣa or Self is a conscious spirit and subject of knowledge.

It has the nature of eternal and all-pervading consciousness. Th Sāṃkhya school preaches the plurality of selves unlike the Advait Vedānta of Śaṅkara. The evolution of the world, including man has its starting point in the union of Puruṣa and Prakṛiti. Prakṛit is primal matter, an active principle; Puruṣa is the conscious spirit inactive but intelligent. Their active conjunction results in th evolution of Mahat, Ahaṃkāra, Manas, Gñāna-Indriyas, Kāma Indriyas, Tanmātras and Mahābhūtas. The Ahaṃkāra or ego o the individual is sattvic, rajic or tamic, depending on the pre dominance of the particular guṇa over the other two.

Human life is a blend of joys and sorrows. Man cannot escap decay and death. Man ordinarily is a victim of three kinds of pain that produced by physical disorders and mental afflictions, by beast and thorns and by demons and ghosts. Every person wants to ge rid of pain and can do so only by escaping the hedonistic ideal o pleasure. The summum bonum of life is the complete cessation o all pain. Man attains knowledge of reality when he is free fron aviveka (ignorance). Aviveka is the failure to discriminate self fron non-self. Salvation results from renouncing the material world.[1]

Sāṃkhya-Yoga believes in transmigration.[13] The subtle bod transmigrates, not the real self, because it is all-pervading. Th Linga-śarīra consists of eleven sense-organs, the buddhi, ahaṃkār and the five tanmātras. The subtle body is permanent while the gros body changes at death and birth. The subtle body carries all th traces of thoughts and actions from the past life. The Sāṃkhy begins with a provisional detachment leading to a permanent o final one. The latter implies complete knowledge. Asceti preparation precedes yogic training. The yogi ideal is kaivaly (independence) through samādhi (contemplation). In the fina stage of samādhi man becomes one with the object of realization thus achieving life's goal.

The Sāṃkhya further preaches spiritual independence as th goal of life. Man's judgements must not be either too subjective o objective in explaining the facts of experience. Man can attai his ideal of freedom under given environmental circumstances Nature is a "good mother" to man, so it cannot enslave his spirit Puruṣa (pure spirituality) is the end of normal evolution, mar reaching it through the four puruṣārthas. The first two (kāma artha) are worldly values and the second two (dharma, mokṣa) other worldly. Man follows eight disciplines to attain the latter 'hose disciplines assist him in his ascent to the larger vision of the vorld of reality. Thus Sāṃkhya-Yoga is concerned with two aspects f self-realization, the first being the purification of the body partikaraṇa) and the second the purification of the mind (dhyāna) ading to union with Īsvara (the Lord).

In Patañjali-Yoga man's bondage is believed due to the identifica-ion of his self with mental modifications. Their cessation is beration, a state in which all forms of conscious activity are fully isciplined. Among the five levels or stages of the mind (Citta), he first three (Kṣipta—distracted, Mudhva—infatuated, Vikṣipta—ccasionally steady) are not conducive to man's yoga, while the last wo (ekāgra—one-pointed, niruddha—restrained) are. Ekāgra is rolonged concentration revealing the true nature of Citta and pre-aring the way for the cessation of all mental modifications. Jiruddha ends with the ceasing of all mental functions.[14] The ast two are governed by the sattva element and so are most helpful a attaining liberation. In the first of the last two there is a clear nowledge of the object contemplated while in the second, nothing s known about the mind or object due to the cessation of all mental unctions. Ekāgra prepares for the cessation of mental functions; iruddha ends in their complete cessation. Thus both are classed inder samādhi-yoga.

Samādhi-Yoga is a yoga of concentration and meditation based on he eight means of self-realization called aids to yoga (yogāṅgas). They are yama (morality), niyama (self-culture), āsana (good osture), prāṇāyāma (breath-control), pratyāhāra (control of the enses), dharṇā (concentration), dhyāna (meditation) and samādhi complete union). According to Patañjali-Yoga, man consists of physical body, vital energy and the psychic principles in addition o the primary self or puruṣa. Man is not a mechanical entity out the ideal medium for the expression of spiritual life.[15] The organic aspect of man is only an accompaniment to the subtle self. Man's inner self is called antaraṅga and the external bahikaraṅga. Patanjali-Yoga emphasizes human sympathy, imperturbability and erenity of mind. While hating sin, man must not hate the sinner. The concept of man in Patañjali-Yoga is ethical, humanistic, altrus-ic and ascetic; and the chief characteristics of a yoga are vairāgya (detachment), śraddhā (composure of mind), vīrya (endurance), prajñā (insight) and abhyāsa (repeated yogic practice). The Sāṃkhya and Patañjali-Yoga concepts of man are similar and complement each other except for the latter's extreme emphasis o training and control of the body and mind.

The concept of man in another orthodox system, the Nyāya founded by Gotama (c. 200 B.C.), is a traditional one. Liberatio is the cessation of all pain and suffering. Man must not be misle by wrong knowledge based on passions and impulses but shoul learn to acquire true knowledge. In order to rise above worldl life man must inculcate in himself an absolute freedom unaffecte by fear, decay, change and death. As the body is related to self so is man to God. Man is a mārgayāyin, a way-farer, and th process of the world is from outward to inward in the Nyāya as i many of the orthodox systems.

To act according to one's own essential nature is one of man' basic demands according to most orthodox systems and the Nyāy is no exception. Man must know himself and search his own sou The life of reason is not separate from the life of spirit. The ātma or self in its pure state is beyond the reach of mind or intellect Nyāya exhorts man to realize his inner self. Man is a unique an privileged being, able to realize the Divine on the one hand and t resolve himself into matter on the other. The Nyāya concept o man is somewhat pessimistic.[17] It does not deny the reality o pleasure as a positive experience; but avoiding pain implies avoidin pleasure as well. One should seek escape from the life of pleasur which is evanascent and transient. The ideal of life lies not so muc in the attaining of happiness as the resignation of pleasure. As wit other orthodox schools, the Nyāya emphasizes cultivating a spiri of detachment. For much of the world's misery is due to man' selfishness coming from his seeking pleasure. The adherent o Nyāya is not an Epicurean; nor is he a hedonist like the Cārvākas

The Vaiśeṣika school founded by Kaṇāda accepts a view of ma which is in accord with the general spiritual outlook of India philosophy. The world is created by God according to the mora deserts of man and God's destructive will is responsible for th dissolution of the objective world.[18] Man is determined by th adṛiṣṭa, the merits and demerits of the karmas of the individual souls which guide the creation of the world. Man is viewed as pheno-menal consciousness present in the world of objective reality a distinct from noumenal consciousness, which is essential reality or th transcendent God. The mind is an atomistic quality of man actin like an inner instrument. The ātman is pure existence (Sat), thu liffering from the phenominal consciousness of the mind. The tman again is different from Buddhi or reason. Buddhi is a quality he ātman acquires now and then. Even ānanda (bliss) is not tman though an ātman experiences bliss. Manas, cit and ānanda re the adventitious qualities of man while the ātman is his essential ttribute.

In Vaiśeṣika thought man is bound by karma and adṛiṣṭa. He is aught up in Saṃsāra, the state of enjoyment leading to continuous leath and rebirth. Moha or ignorance prevents his release and keeps him from experiencing the highest pleasure of the wise based on the universal duties of anupadha-bhāva-suddhi (self-purification). Man's ultimate goal is mokṣa, a state beyond pain and pleasure. It is neither liberation from misery nor attainment of bliss, but a final release of the self from all pain and pleasure and their specific qualities of thought, feeling and will. The liberation of man implies a state of perfect qualitylessness in which the self remains in itself, in its own purity. The liberated man does not merge in God to share his glory, as there is no internal relation between man and God. The atoms, soul and God are externally related. For this reason Śrīhara condemns Vaiśeṣika, calling it the "owl philosophy."

The Sāṃkhya, Yoga, Nyāya and Vaiśeṣika schools base their views on independent grounds while the Mīmāṃsā and Vedānta schools accept the Vedas as authoritative. Mīmāṃsā views were developed to elucidate and justify the ritualistic aspect of the Vedas and the Vedānta the speculative. According to Jaimini, the founder of Mīmāṃsā, man's physical body is an aggregate of atoms brought together by the law of karma and man's essence is in the intrinsic nature of the soul.[19] It has a potentiality for consciousness, though it is independent of all consciousness. The summum bonum of life is liberation from the bondage of flesh.[20] Salvation comes when one exhausts the enjoyment of the fruits of his good and bad actions. Once liberated a man is free from all attachments of the body including the mind, all karma-ties and the bondage of rebirth.[21]

To gain salvation man must perform required rites (nitya-karmas).[22] He must never expect any reward for their performance, as the disinterested performance of duties alone can liberate man. By repeating the vidhis (formulas) of the Vedas man attains salvation, for the injunctions of the Vedas are eternal. A virtuous life is one of absolute faith in the Vedic commandments.[23] The reality of the Vedas excels every other reality, even God.

Man's position is central in Vedānta which is grounded in the Vedas and Upaniṣads.[24] The Vedas were devoted to a study of God and man. They never view man as a separate entity but as the companion of God, as a part of the whole Being and as an instrument of the Divine. In the Ṛig-veda there is a description of Gods who have both human forms and emotions. They are not beings superior to man; superior companions perhaps, but not beings. As God is a superior companion to man, so man is to the "fauna and flora". Man's pride, love of freedom, attachment to his country, realization of values in life and other such features are very prominent in the poetry of the Ṛig-veda.[25] Man is highly esteemed. He is a free thinker who would exert himself to lead a free life and allow others to lead the same.

There are two views in the Vedas regarding man's creation, one that he is made from matter, the other out of spirit, the latter being predominant. Man is not determined by his physical environment though he may be conditioned by its relations. Man is controlled by his actions and will and partly by past karmas. Dharma (supreme righteousness) alone sustains man and the universe. It and Ṛita, the universal law of right, are co-eternal realities. Man is the abode of Gods;[26] for if man was not born, the Gods would be without an abode. Man is the integral unity of all bodies or ātmans.[27] Man's consciousness is not limited to his life or body; it extends beyond them. Thus it is well said that "he was created as the centre of the activities of the cosmic Gods." For this reason man is the ātman, a part of the Supreme Ātman or Paramātman. Freedom from bondage is a major theme in Vedic texts. Man's highest good is the breaking of fetters barring him from ultimate reality. This is accomplished through ceremony and ritual.

According to the Upaniṣads man has no existence independent of God.[28] Man is composed of body and self or soul. The self is identical with Brahman. Man is a form of pure consciousness and God is its essence. "That Thou Art" indicates an inherent relationship between Man and Brahman. That stands for God and Thou stands for God in the form of man. The ātman is identified with the paramātman, the self with the Universal Self. The realization of the ātman is man's supreme good.

Avidyā (ignorance) leads to māyā or illusion, which is the cause of man's misery and suffering. He can be free from them and realize imself by cultivating detachment and acquiring knowledge. 'airāgya (renunciation) and Jñāna (knowledge) transform man 'om a lower to higher state of existence. A study of Vedānta elps man overcome his deep-rooted ignorance.[29] On the other and, he who delights in ritualism and ritualistic knowledge is even vorse than he who worships blind ignorance. Worldly life is ıcompatible to a wise man; he rejects, also, a life devoted to mere ıeditation without dedication or dedicated acts.[30] Those one vith the form of prayer ever remain as rājasik; those one with its ontent are bound to become sāttvik.

Man attains emancipation through discriminating the eternal 'om the non-eternal. A man with an egoistic conception of the ody, caste and life is ignorant (mūḍha), while he who has recognized ıe true self latent in him is the learned seeker (vidvān). The xperience of realization is not a consciousness of objects perceived ut is the knowing and seeing in oneself the being of all beings. Ian is the ectype; Brahman is the archetype. Thus God, the world nd man are all based on one ultimate consciousness.

There are two ways of human action, that of knowledge and truth 'hich brings eternal salvation to man, and that of sensual satis-ıction leading to momentary happiness. If one chooses the latter, e will not achieve his ultimate goal. The wise man prefers the ood to the pleasant. He who worships knowledge is never satis-ed with wealth. The wise one is above avarice and attachment. Ie meditates on the inner self and relinquishes both joy and sorrow. Ie becomes free through the purification of the senses and mind nd attains immortality. A person desiring emancipation must ave a guru in whom he has complete faith.[31] The Guru must be roficient in the Vedas, scripture-loving, straightforward, interested n the welfare of all beings and all-compassionate. A man wishing o realize himself must study all 108 Upaniṣads. A cessation of ıis three bodies and complete emancipation will result. He who as given up all caste duties and good and bad actions is the real scetic person. He practises nirvikalpa-samādhi; he is a Yogin, an Avadhūta, a Paramahaṃsa; he alone is the Brahmin.

IV Contemporary Views of Man

Gandhi calls himself a follower of Advaita; thus man and God are not separate in his view. Man's self or soul is nothing but

Brahman; so man is a part of the one Ultimate Reality. Man i limited and finite because of his ignorance. God is the maste (Prabhu); man is His servant (dāsa).[32] Gandhi speaks of man a a "spark of the divine fire", a part of God.

Gandhi believes as much in the absolute oneness of man as of God If one wants to serve God, he must serve man. Man is the centr of the world; thus a person must work in that centre, expandin the finite into the infinite through the service of man. Gandhi' is like Tagore's views on man and service. Also man is the sol maker of his destiny and so must rely on his reason and conscience.[3] Gandhi extols man to raise himself by himself. Man is ma because of his self-restraint. Man as a whole is progressing fron generation to generation. God is helping and guiding man throug reason and love. At the same time God has given man freedom t mould and improve himself by himself. Man is above all institu tions, for he is a living institution in himself. Gandhi stresses th oneness of man on the one hand and service to God on the other.

Gandhi's successor, Binoba Bhave, stressed an egalitarian concep of man. Man is a symbol of good, emblem of virtue, embodimen of value and living image of God. Man's wholeness represents th total goodness of man and his perfection implies his devotion t the moral self, intuitive reason and spiritual conscience. Man i a life-principle and generic ideal. He is the animating hiatus o altruistic impulses. There is a constant and dialectical struggl in him and a deeper desire for a creative synthesis. In Sarvoday (the ideal of the well-being of all) this is called a "humanitaria metaphysics". Thus, the concept of man in both Gandhi an Vinoba is a happy combination of thought and action.

Tagore views human existence as a polarity.[34] In one aspect ma is part and parcel of nature, a last link in the evolutionary chain an thus bound by the natural laws of necessity. On the other hand man is unique in all creation. He is a break with nature; evolutio seems to have taken a new turn in his creation. On this level o creation mind is above body, as physical needs are subordinate t mental functions. Man is a creative being, able to know an transform himself. "For after all, man is a spiritual being, an not a mere living money-bag, jumping from profit to profit, and breaking the backbone of human races in its financial leaping," Tagore wrote. There is a "personal man" in him, higher than body and mind, above the expedient and useful. Man is potentially divine and so essentially good.[35] He is characterized by freedom, creative activity, virtue and universal love.

Tagore declares the essence of man is his soul-consciousness. What is inherently and universally real is the unity of the soul. "To find out this One is to possess the all," Tagore says. Soul-consciousness leads to God-consciousness, which is itself Cosmic-consciousness. There is a fundamental unity between the individual (ātman) and universal (paramātman) soul. The One in man seeks for the unity in knowledge, love and will. This unity reconciles all contradictions of life and distinctions of self, and the One in man becomes one with God. The miseries and anxieties of life impede man's self-realization. He must not become pessimistic over them but must feel they are only meant to improve his lot. Tagore draws a parallel to a river whose banks are not its limitations and a poem whose rhyme and metre are no obstructions to its central theme. They stimulate rather than obstruct their flow. Tagore views man in terms of a rarified and purified transcendentalism. "Life is immortal youthfulness," endlessly new and eternally beautiful. There is an intense yearning for the Divine in men's hearts. Tagore never searches temples or scriptures, but only man, for the Divine. All through his works he speaks of love and sympathy, unity and harmony, joy and delight in the affairs of man.

Radhakrishnan, too, believes there is "an incommunicable uniqueness" about man.[36] Moreover man is not only conscious but self-conscious and thus free. This freedom gives him a new dimension. The man whose fate is governed by environment and whose nature is moulded according to circumstances is no man, for he has no power in him to resist the evil around him. He is an animal, not a human being. Individual purification and social realization go hand in hand, according to Radhakrishnan. Man is not a product of environment but makes himself and also participates in the "creative intensions of the Cosmos." Man is a microcosm of the great macrocosm or God.

Man consists of matter, life, mind, consciousness and self-consciousness and in addition has an inner and more abiding psychic reality called the soul. Thus, man is a spiritual being, and the same spirit runs through every being and object in this world. The religion of man is the perfecting of the truly human.[37] Man is a being straining towards infinity but his finite, limited, temporal and mortal existence causes suffering. When he attains integrality, there is harmony and joy in his life. All great men are manifestations of the Spirit and an inspiration for the masses. Man has the capacity to rise above himself and transform the world around him. Man is a part of both this world and the other world above this one. Man is actually human but potentially divine.

Twentieth-century man is glorifying the importance of matter and relegating the spiritual into the background. Radhakrishnan is not content with this and pleads for the creating of a "new man," exclaiming, "Let us all fight and suffer for the cause of man."[38] No distinction should be made between East and West in this regard for all are faced with the same problems. Radhakrishnan believes it is never too late to strive for man's spiritual recovery. Man has to grow into a regenerate being to permit the currents of universal life to flow through him. Radhakrishnan believes man is rising higher and higher. He has the determination to go beyond his present life and stand on the truth of his being. "Man-making" and "soul-making" go hand-in-hand, according to Radhakrishnan. He has an implicit faith in the working of the spirit in man and says that an integrated development of the different dimensions of man which leads to his highest fulfilment is the only remedy for his lost recovery: "The human spirit when lit by the divine fire is mightier than the most mighty weapon."[39]

Aurobindo's integral philosophy holds that man is the apex of the cosmic evolutionary process. Man is a mind in a living body. Mind is finite, with only limited powers of consciousness. The nature of evolution indicates that mind is to be followed by a higher or supra-mental consciousness. Thus contemporary man is a stage in and not the end of evolution. Not being the highest power of consciousness, the mind does not possess full truth. Beyond it is the Supermind, the Gnostic power of consciousness, in eternal possession of Truth.

Aurobindo claims the Supermind is the Superman. Such a concept gives new hope and perspectives to present man and adds to his individuality and dignity. Aurobindo accepts the traditional Sāṃkhya and Gītā view that man is a blend of the physical, vital and mental (tamas, rajas, sattva). They are in constant conflict; the last is the stronger of the three. Ironically, the vital is fast tending to dominate today.[40] Man is not destined to languish in darkness for long, however. He has a divine purpose to perform. Aurbindo believes in the potential divinity of man.[41] Man's divine ature is opposed to his "desire-soul". Man must awaken to the divine person" (chaitya-puruṣa) within and overthrow the yrannical rule of the desire-soul. Man has to brace himself against ll forces and evolve his capacities of knowledge with greater nastery over them.[42] Aurobindo calls this an "extension of consiousness."

Aurobindo places much emphasis on man's conscious will. It is ar superior to the blind instinct of animals. There are three levels f existence—being, being and non-being, and non-being. Man s born into the world on the second level. Non-being is described s the process of becoming. History and man are involved in that rocess. Man's glory consists in his will and aspiration to transcend imself and to complete the process of becoming.

Aurobindo's Integral Yoga stresses the transformation of man into uperman. This will be accomplished in part by man's ascension hrough his will and efforts and in part by the descending of the upra-phenomenal, the Super-conscient or the Higher Nature. Natural man has to evolve himself into the divine man and at the ame time the Spirit descends participating in that transformation.[43] The "new-man" resulting will be the perfect consummation of the sychical and spiritual.[44] He will manifest the inherent unity of the hree principal categories of Man, Nature and God. He will be naster of himself and the forces of nature, not for the purpose of xploiting but perfecting the latter, however. He will be the entinel of a "new race." At first only a few individuals who are nore open will reach that height. Gradually their number grows ntil the "Gnostic Community" or "Spiritualized Society" of mankind is realized.

Traditional forms of knowledge—rational, conceptual and sense lerived—do not avail in the process of transformation. They are 'bad witnesses" and cannot serve man as the media of higher volution. Rational knowledge is necessary to a certain extent. It illumines experience, gives man new faith and so enlarges one's onsciousness; but it cannot reach the final truth. It is known hrough direct apprehension. The faculty of intuition characterizes he new man. It is the direct perception of knowledge, the total pprehension of reality. Paradoxically, it includes and at the same ime excludes all other levels and types of knowledge. It is both 'parā" and "aparā".

While influenced by Nietzche, Aurobindo's superman is a

spiritualized, divine being. Similarly, Aurobindo's superman as ad vancer of gnostic consciousness differs from the philosopher-kings o Plato's Republic who are guardians of intellectual culture Aurobindo's differ from early Vedic views in that he projects a transformation of the natural or mother-earth and not just the vitalist tic and mental. Both mundane nature and man will be divinized in Aurobindo's view. Thus, Aurobindo's philosophy is unique in that he believes spiritualization will reach a maximum; it will be all-inclusive.

V Summary

While there are differences between the schools and amongst individuals over the nature of man, we might conclude this chapter by indicating points on which there is fairly general agreement, the Cārvāka excepted. An initial and obvious one is an acceptance o the fact of man's finiteness. Man, as he is, is a limited, imperfect incomplete being. His present existence is tenuous, circumscribed and fleeting, a view the Buddhists carry to its ultimate when they say the individual is but a momentary aggregate of five embodied qualities. At the same time man's goal is to attain or reach the opposite condition, the state of completeness, fulfilment, perfection Indian thinkers are concerned with seeing man not only as he is bu as he might or will be. Man should be viewed in terms of poten tiality as well as actuality. His journey is from imperfection to perfection, finiteness to infiniteness. The "realized" man is one who has completed that journey.

It would be timely at this point to add that the journey is made o goal is arrived at through self-effort. Perfection is achieved no granted man by some external, gracious Deity. Of course, some schools emphasize the latter but even they insist that man's effor as well as God's grace are required for salvation. The large emphasis is upon self-discipline and self-effort. Man is responsible for his own salvation, and self-responsibility implies or necessitate self-effort. The Dhammapada states this succintly: "By onesel evil is done; by oneself one suffers; by oneself evil is left undone by oneself one is purified. Purity and impurity belong to oneself no one can purify another." Moreover, added to "You yoursel must make an effort" is the statement: "The Tathāgatas are only preachers." The Tathāgata, or the Guru to use a Hindu correlate a guide, helper or aid; but ultimately attaining the end is up to ach person himself. The same is true of religious scriptures. .s Radhakrishnan says: "The scriptures could point out the road ut each man must travel it by himself."[45] This emphasis on self-alvation is one major source of the concept and practice of Yoga 1 the Indian tradition. Yoga as a method is systematic physical nd mental discipline, its goal being mokṣa and union with 'rahman.

The basic premise of Yoga and Indian thought in general is that nan is good. He is capable of self-effort. He can know the right .nd the true. He does have the will to act in terms of such know-edge. This positive view of man is affirmed by innumerable ndian thinkers past and present. In the Laws of Manu we read: 'Of created beings the most excellent are said to be those which are ınimated; of the animated, those which subsist by intelligence; f the intelligent, mankind, and of men, the Brāhmaṇas."[46] A :ontemporary philosopher, T. R. V. Murti, states: "Indian religious hought...definitely and most emphatically asserts that man can)vercome his predicament and that he can attain freedom and the 'ullness of his being."[47] Radhakrishnan declares: "The Hindu ideal ıffirms that man can attain his immortal destiny here and now. The Kingdom of God is within us and we need not wait for its attain-nent till some undated future or look for an apocalyptic display n the sky.[48] And Gandhi reiterates the theme of man's goodness when he said: "I refuse to suspect human nature. It will, it is bound :o respond to any noble and friendly action."[49]

It is important to underline that, from the Indian perspective, man s a being not an animal or thing. Man is not an object like other material objects. He is not to be viewed or understood by the same categories as one looks at material reality. Indian thought affirms a non-Darwinian view of man. Man is more than matter. He is a vibrant, living being. He occupies time and space; at the same time he transcends them. While subject to the past, he is not a helpless victim of it; and in his present existence he can do some-thing to determine his future existence. He is in essence a spiritual being. As Kalidas Battacharya points out, what is "common to the different Indian views of the individual" is that "every individual has a spiritual side" and that "his spiritual side is, form the valuation-al point of view, more essential than his material side."[50] Indian thinkers uphold the value of the individual on both humanistic and theistic ground. Gandhi objected to the dominance of technology because the machine dehumanizes man. Contemporary religiou humanism is reflected in D. M. Datta's statement that "Every individual, every living being, thus comes to be regarded as a sacred centre of potential value, deserving of respect and possessing freedom for unhampered progress towards its goal."[51] The Upaniṣad contain many statements portraying a theistic view of man: "The self-luminous Lord. . . has entered into the whole world. . . ;" "The Supreme Lord. . . is vast and is hidden in the bodies of all living beings;" "The Self. . . is hidden in the hearts of creatures." The Bhagavad Gītā contains the same view: "Who sees his Lord within every creature, deathlessly dwelling amidst the mortal, that man sees truly."

The explaining of an individual in terms of inherent tendencie has had wide acceptance also. The guṇa theory provides a rational explanation of individual differences. While the three guṇas are present in all, people vary in accordance with the guṇa or tendency which predominates in each. At the same time, the individual is not bound by his dominant guṇa. Through his own efforts he can to some extent at least, overcome undesirable tendencies so that eventually the sāttvik will predominate. Such a view gives hope to the individual. It leads him to realize that he can transcend and need not be a victim of inheritance. Another important aspect of the guṇa theory is that, because individuals are different, there will be a variation in means. All people have the same general biological, psychological, social and religious ends or needs. How they are met will vary, depending on the particular preferences and tendencies of each individual. This approach to individual differences is one source of the attitude of tolerance which characterizes the Indian scene.

The emphasis on individualism or individual differences is not carried to an extreme in Indian thought. The larger emphasis is upon men's similarities or the things they have in common which make social unity and harmony possible. The general belief is that man's similarities outweigh their differences and, whenever the good of the group conflicts with the good of the individual, the former is to have precedence. This may account in part for the strong emphasis one finds in Indian thought upon minimizing the self or ego. Self-renunciation rather than self-assertion has been the basic theme. A classical example of this is in the Bhagavad Gītā ı which we are urged to "renounce attachment" to the fruits of ur work. One must give up the "I and mine" attitude, for only y so doing can one attain inner peace, rise to cosmic consciousness nd become a part of the Supreme One. If one is detached from he fruits of one's labour, he can more easily dedicate them to the ord. One can "perform every action with your heart fixed on the upreme Lord." The emphasis on renunciation is especially rominent in Jainism. We see it in a number of passages: "Live n a way as though you felt, nothing is mine;" "Dost thou not know hat the happiness lies in subduing the demon of desires?"; "He vho grasps at even a little, whether living or lifeless, or consents o another doing so, will never be freed from sorrow;" and "Oh nan, refrain from evil, for life must come to an end."[52] And a nodern proponent of renunciation is Gandhi who declared: "The luty of renunciation differentiates mankind from the beast."

From the Indian view there is a natural order and rhythm to life. ife is patterned. It follows a natural course of growth and develop-nent. This is seen in the emphasis on the four stages of life. Each erson goes through them although the duration of each stage nay vary with individuals. Each one must first learn, then apply is learning to making a livelihood. Once the responsibilities f family and work are discharged, one then turns with greater ntensity to cultivating the spiritual and the ultimate.

Similarly the four ends of life are common to all. They are a part f man's natural inheritance. Everyone has material, emotional nd spiritual needs to be fulfilled. It is true of course that some eople will spend more of their energies on one pursuit. The rahmins will devote more time to spiritual ends. But they cannot ispense with the others entirely. This view of life is based on a oncept of man as a composite of supplementary not conflicting lements. He does not consist of sets or pairs of attributes diametri-ally opposed to each other. In such a non-dualistic view of man he material is not antagonistic to the spiritual or the emotional to he moral. Each has its rightful place in the scheme of things, ach its natural role to be played out.

It should be mentioned, however, that the four ends are ranked ierarchically, especially in regard to the material and spiritual. ife is a journey from the material to the spiritual, the lower to the igher. Material well-being and ends are not denegated. They re simply conceived of as a part of the relative world or existence, the transcendence of which is man's ultimate goal. This life is shadow of the next. Human love is but a foretaste of divine lov Earthly joys are but a prelude to heavenly bliss or ānanda. Ma in his earthly existence is a compatriot of others, but in his final sta he is a companion of God. In Indian thought true self-realizatic is associated with the attainment of spiritual rather than materi ends, for man's real self is the spiritual not physical self. Th material exists not to be denied but to be gone through an beyond.

Finally, we might point out that the Indian tradition holds u as the ideal man the "purified" man. Such a person is an embod ment of the sensitive not the acquisitive virtues. To the India mind the hero, for instance, is one who renounces rather tha asserts himself. "The greatness of the great is humility," a Jai scripture declares. The purified man is self-restrained, free fro greed, rancour and other harmful attitudes. In the Dhammapad the Arhat is described as one who is content, thoughtful, seren "tolerant of the world". He "finds no fault with other beings, "does not kill or cause slaughter," "utters true speech," "does nc offend by body, word or thought," and "has cut all fetters." A attribute of the purified man found in the Gītā is equanimity. Th ideal man "must accept pleasure and pain with equal tranquillity. He "does not desire or rejoice in what is pleasant." Nor does h "dread what is unpleasant, or grieve over it." He "rests in th inner calm of the Ātman, regarding happiness and suffering as one. He "pays no attention to praise or to blame. His behaviour is th same when he is honoured and when he is insulted."

Because the Indian concept of the ideal man is primarily a mora one, anyone can be a purified man, regardless of caste. And on can find in Indian history many people of various castes who hav become such. Moreover, withdrawal from the world is nc necessary either, as is often thought. One need not be an asceti to be purified. Rather, the opposite has been emphasized muc more in the Indian tradition. The symbolism of the lotus i Buddhism is a classical example of this. To his followers Buddh said:

> "Whatever men do, whether they remain in the world as artisan merchants, and officers of the kind, or retire from the worl and devote themselves to a life of religious meditation, let the

put their whole heart into their task; let them be diligent and energetic, and, if they are like the lotus, which, although it grows in the water, yet remains untouched by the water, if they struggle in life without cherishing envy or hatred, if they live in the world not a life of self but a life of truth, then surely joy, peace and bliss will dwell in their minds."[53]

PART FOUR

The Medieval Period

INTRODUCTION

The Medieval Period was one of both continuity and change. The influence of the older philosophies—Nyāya, Vaiśeṣika, Mīmāṃsā, Sāṃkhya and Yoga—remained; yet new schools arose such as the Advaita of Śaṅkara, the Dvaita of Madhva and the Viśiṣṭādvaita of Rāmānuja. Śaṅkara's philosophy is monistic; Madhva's is dualistic and pluralistic and Rāmānuja's is a qualified non-dualism. They may be distinguished further by saying Śaṅkara's outlook is absolutistic and idealistic while Madhva's and Rāmānuja's is theistic.

Śaṅkara followed the Nyāya school's predilection toward epistemology and the Yoga's emphasis on psychic training as the chief means of salvation. Thought in its highest and purest stages is the means to the highest bliss or state. He agreed with the Jains and Sāṃkhya, emphasizing even more than they, that ignorance is the cause of bondage. Because avidyā causes men to see only in part, to mistake the empirically experienced for the real and to view reality as dualistic and pluralistic, it must be overcome. Śaṅkara rejected both the Jain notion of an independent jīva and the atomic view of reality held by Jain and Vaiśeṣika alike. They were a hindrance to a totalistic or integral view of reality. For the same reason as well as others, he disclaimed the dualism of earlier schools, the Prakṛiti-puruṣa distinction of the Sāṃkhya, the jīva-ajīva of Jainism and the matter-soul dichotomy of the Vaiśeṣika. Nor could he fully accept the Mīmāṃsā position regarding karma.

Śaṅkara, Madhva and Rāmānuja alike were concerned about man's ultimate destiny. Each viewed religion and ethics as inseparable. They agreed that the moral law cannot exist by itself. The greatest difference between them was that the latter two conceived of God as personal rather than impersonal. Madhva and Rāmānuja considered God as central, not peripheral, as Nyāya thinkers and Patañjali did. They conceived of God as having attributes, but not the three guṇas of Sāṃkhya. While separate from the world God has specific functions in regard to it. Creation is not, for example, what the Sāṃkhya believed it to be. Unlike Śaṅkara Madhva and Rāmānuja asserted the reality of the empirical world. They believed, with the Sāṃkhya, that phenomenal plurality is ground in a single reality, Prakṛiti. Prakṛiti, however, is not self-existent. Individual selves, like the phenomenal world, are real and the individual's goal is not the extinction but full realization of personality or self. The self is, to one degree or another, both a constant and a separate entity from God. Madhva and Rāmānuja both rejected fatalism or any complete determinism also.

Madhva and Rāmānuja were concerned with the masses of people and what forms of religion would be most meaningful to them. As a result they brought the God of Yoga much closer to men, personalizing Him and thus making him much more meaningful. While differences between the two will be considered subsequently, faith, love and devotion to a personal God emerged as the archstone of their philosophies.

In considering the Medieval Period as a whole several dominating tendencies may be noted. One is the trend toward monism and monotheism. A second is the status given reason or reasoning. Śaṅkara is an obvious example of both. A third is the continued acceptance of the authority of early writings such as the Vedas. New interpretations were given, as had been done previously, but the Vedas' prerogative was not denied. The belief in incarnations persisted unabated. Avatāras were still held to be visible manifestations of the Supreme on whom people could shower their faith, love and devotion. In fact these attributes, emphasized especially by the Bhakti schools, became so much a part of the times that the Medieval Period in India, as in Europe, may well be called the Age of Faith and Devotion.

The belief in reincarnation continued to be accepted in the Medieval Period also. This life is still set within the context and perspective of a series of lives whose final destination is union with Brahman. That religion entails certain prescribed rituals, practices and duties was not questioned in general, although some objected as we shall see. It was generally agreed that one needs a guru or spiritual preceptor as a guide on the path to truth and salvation.

The need to distinguish between the changing, and the permanent, the temporal and the eternal, the relative and the absolute was recognized. In fact speculation about Māyā undoubtedly increased in this period, mainly due to the influence of Vedāntism. The classical virtues were upheld—kindness, forgiveness, renunciation, compassion, generosity and humbleness. Finally, there was common agreement that the goal of the religious and philosophical quest is salvation and liberation or freedom from suffering and the bondage of rebirth. Moreover, there is more than one path to that end.

Thinking in the Medieval Period centred around a number of basic questions. For example, how can we overcome Māyā or distinguish between the real world and the world of appearances? What is the relationship between faith and reason? Are they antagonistic, mutually exclusive, supplementary, or what? Of course, a basic problem was that of the nature of reality. What is the nature of causation, for example, and the cause-effect relation? An associated question was that of the nature of God. Is the Deity personal or impersonal, immanet or transcendent, perfect or imperfect? Furthermore, what is the nature of man and man's relationship to God? How may that relation be best expressed? How are the World Soul (Paramātman) and the individual soul (ātman) associated?

Though there was agreement as to the goal, the question of the best means to the goal of Mokṣa or union with Brahman continued to be debated. The place of works, rituals and God's grace was often discussed. The emphasis on Māyā or illusion stimulated greater reflection on the question of real knowledge and how it is attained. The problem of evil—its nature, source and eradication—continued to obsess men's minds. Finally, thinking in this period had to take into account as a major factor the Islamic world-view resting on a basic dualism or dichotomizing of reality which was quite alien to most Indian ways of thinking.

The Bhakti schools of south India in the early Medieval Period will be discussed subsequently. The Bhakti movement in the north came later in the fifteenth and sixteenth centuries. Typical of its leaders is Chaitanya, a native of Bengal. Chaitanya was noted for his gentle character and pure life. He was born in 1485. He was a very studious youth. At sixteen he opened his own school at Navadwip and soon became famous as "one of the greatest teachers of grammar and logic." When twenty-two, he visited Gaya where the Buddha had attained enlightenment. While worshipping in a Viṣṇu temple he "received a sudden illumination that transformed his being." Two years after returning to Navadwip he began his great renunciation. Leaving his students, family and friends he was initiated into the monastic order by Keśava Bhāratī. He then went to Puri, a well-known place of pilgrimage, where he spent most of his remaining life.

Chaitanya believed in God not as an object of knowledge but of love and devotion. Prabhavananda writes that "In Sri Chaitanya is to be found the culmination and fulfilment of the philosophy and the religion of love." Religion requires complete love and devotion to whatever manifestation of the Supreme one chooses to worship, Chaitanya declared. Kriṣṇa was the embodiment of God which he chose for himself. Chaitanya was little concerned about speculative or theoretical religious questions. To him God was Kriṣṇa, the God of love. Kṛiṣṇa is the great lover, the embodiment of love. He loves all men and it is his unbounded love which draws men to him.

Chaitanya believed that love is not acquired by man or given him. It is already in his being, but is covered over or hidden by ignorance and sensual attachment. When ignorance and sensuality have been dispelled, man becomes aware of the love within him and begins to cultivate and fructify it. When his love becomes universal and complete, he has realized God. This natural love in man is brought to fruition through various practices—japa or chanting the name of God, hearing and singing his praises, or through meditation. Reflecting may lead one into a state of samādhi in which one attains complete union with God. Most, however, do not reach such a level of consciousness. Instead they remain on the dualistic level in which, though separate, man and God are brought into spiritual union through love and devotion.

Chaitanya taught that, because men are united in love to God and therefore to each other, there should be no distinctions between them. Thus Chaitanya became an opponent of caste and would not allow it among his followers. Love also compels kindness and compassion, and this led Chaitanya to become an ardent advocate and practitioner of ahiṃsā as well.

Kabir, the Moslem weaver who lived from 1440 to 1518, is in many ways an exception to the general characteristics of the Medieval Period indicated previously. He was a disciple of Rāmānanda, a worshipper of Rāma, one of the important incarnations of Viṣṇu. At the same time he was strongly attracted to the Sufi mystics. However he finally declared that he would be neither a Moslem nor Hindu exclusively, and he initiated a sect or movement of his own.

Like other mystics, the only authority Kabir would accept was his own inner visions and experiences. Neither Vedas nor Koran would he permit to compel him. To him religion was personal experience and realization. God is to be seen and experienced directly and immediately. "If thou art a true seeker, thou shalt at once see Me; thou shalt meet Me in a moment of time," he wrote. Through love and joy one experiences the Ultimate who is everywhere. Disputation, theorizing, argumentation will neither save nor lead one to God. Instead "...he who has seen the radiance of love, he is saved." All men seek God and will find Him through love and virtuous living. Kabir emphasizes that ethical purity is a prerequisite for God-realization. "The man who is kind and who practises righteousness...who considers all creatures on earth as his own self, he attains the Immortal Being....He attains the true Name whose words are pure, and who is free from pride and conceit."

Kabir believed in the efficacy of repeating the name of Rāma, his God, in an attitude of love and devotion. He refused the use of idols as aids in worship. The traditional rituals and ceremonies he felt were of no avail. Renunciation and asceticism do not help. "I do not ring the temple bell: I do not set the idol on the throne: I do not worship the image with flowers." "It is not the austerities that mortify the flesh which are pleasing to the Lord," the reason being that "I am neither in temple nor mosque....Neither am I in rites and ceremonies, nor in Yoga and renunciation." Kabir did not believe that Brahman or God manifests himself in Avatāras either. There is no need to, for he is already here everywhere. "God is the breath of all breath," Kabir declared. One only needs to look within to discover him: "Hari is in the East: Allah is in the West. Look within your heart, for there you will find both Karim and Rām."

Kabir like Chaitanya recognized no caste distinctions among his followers, for all are divine and cannot be reduced to a caste. "All the men and women of the world are His living forms," Kabir wrote. This view along with the stress on God's immanence which meant that God can be realized anywhere—in one's home or at work—and the emphasis on love and purity as the means to God—means

13

ŚAṄKARA

T. M. P. Mahadevan

I Life

Saṅkara came not to destroy, but to fulfil; and his Advaita is not a rival to the other systems of thought, but their crowning glory and consummation. In subtlety of logic, clarity of thought, and lucidity of expression, few can equal him, for his magnetic personality brought about a spiritual revolution and a cultural revival in India. The foundations on which Śaṅkara built the edifice of his thought are the Upaniṣads, the Bhagavad-gītā and the Brahma-sūtra, the triple texts recognized as basic for Vedānta.

The age which saw the advent of Śaṅkara was not unlike our own. It was one of unrest and strife, of spiritual bankruptcy and social discord. Śaṅkara describes in his commentary on the Brahma-sūtra the sorry state of affairs as follows: "He who upholds that the poeple of old were no more capable of conversing with the gods than people are at the present might as well hold that because there is at present no ruler paramount, there were no such sovereign rulers even in the former times; or he might argue that in former times the vocations and duties pertaining to the different classes and stations in life were as generally unsettled as they are now."[1] At Śaṅkara's time there were literalists and ritualists who were holding on to the letter of the scriptures, missing their spirit, and there were nihilists and iconoclasts who were out to destroy all that was sacred and old. It was an age of conflict among the different schools of philosophy and hostility among the religious sects. People had given up the performance of duties relating to their class (varṇa) and stage (āśrama). The leaders as well as followers of the various faiths used religion as a weapon of aggression instead of finding in it the solace of life. Neglecting the central teaching of the eternal scriptures, people thought that performing ritual-acts for gaining prosperity here and happiness in a hereafter was the purport of the Veda. This led to a spiritual egotism which is more dangerous than secular aggressiveness.

It was in such an age of crisis and confusion that Śaṅkara was born at Kāladi about six miles from Alwaye in Kerala. Tradition has it that he was an incarnation of Śiva. Śaṅkara was a child prodigy, displaying a remarkable intelligence and capaciousness of heart even in his earliest years. The landmarks in the life of Śaṅkara are mentioned in a Sanskrit verse thus: "At the age of eight he had mastered the four Vedas; at twelve he was versed in all scriptures; at sixteen he completed writing his Bhāṣya; and at thirty-two he departed this world."

It is extremely difficult to determine the exact date of Śaṅkara. According to tradition based on the records of the Dvārkā, Purī, Kāñcī maṭhas, Śaṅkara must have lived in the fifth century B.C. Western oriental scholars and others fix Śaṅkara's date as A.D. 788-820. Though there are difficulties in establishing the date, we can certainly determine the period when Śaṅkara should have lived from internal literary evidences. He was conversant with Kumārila Bhaṭṭa's views and criticized them. Kumārila Bhaṭṭa quotes from Kālidāsa's Śākuntalā. Vācaspatimiśra wrote a commentary called the Bhāmatī on Śaṅkara's Brahma-sūtra-bhāṣya. From this data we may conclude that Śaṅkara must be assigned to a date posterior to Kālidāsa and Kumārila Bhaṭṭa and prior to Vācaspati.

As a boy of eight, Śaṅkara travelled northwards in search of a preceptor. Govinda Bhagavadpāda, a disciple of Gauḍapāda, was living in a cave on the banks of the Narmadā. Pleased with the profound knowledge of Advaita which Śaṅkara possessed even at that tender age, Govinda accepted Śaṅkara as his disciple, initiated him into sannyāsāśrama in conformity with convention, and imparted to him the purport of the major texts of the Upaniṣads which teach the truth of non-duality. Śaṅkara then proceeded to Banaras where Padmapāda, Hastāmalka, and Toṭaka became his disciples. After his trip to Badarikāśrama in the Himalayas he returned to Banaras, and wrote his commentaries on the Upaniṣads, the Bhagavad-gītā, and the Brahma-sūtra, as also his commentary on the Viṣṇu-sahasranāma and other independent manuals.

In his travels Śaṅkara had many discussions with adherents of the different cults and practices both within and outside the orthodox fold, as well as schools of philosophy, and converted them to the way of the Veda and the Vedānta. Mention may be made, in this onnection, of the debate he had with Maṇḍanamiśra. Śaṅkara vanted to correct the lopsided view of the teaching of the Veda eld by the followers of Mīmāṃsā. He sought out and engaged Aaṇḍanamiśra, a doughty champion of the Mīmāṃsā school, in a rolonged debate lasting for several days, defeated him, initiated him nto sannyāsāśrama, and gave him the name "Sureśvara". Orthodox nd heterodox schools alike gained by Śaṅkara's helpful criticism, for is mission was not only to establish the non-duality of Brahman but lso the ultimate identity of the systems (darśanādvaita). Religion, ike philosophy, profited by his teachings. While he sought to remove he excrescences that had crept into the faiths and their institutions, e wished to conserve them in their purity as but various modes of pproach to God. On account of the diversity of mental modes, the ne Reality is spoken of in many ways as Brahmā, Viṣṇu, Rudra, gni, etc. The substance of religion is the same, though its ex-ressions vary. Śaṅkara professed and practised true spiritual niversalism. The cults of Hinduism were purified and consolidated y him. To safeguard India's cultural unity based on Advaita and o hold aloft the ideal of spirituality, Śaṅkara established monastic entres in different parts of the country and charged his principal isciples to head them so that in each there could come into being n unbroken succession of Advaita preceptors.

According to Ānandagiri and some others, the last days of Śaṅkara vere spent in Kāñcī, where he discarded his body. There is nothing ike an end for him even in the empirical sense. He lives and will ontinue to live in human memory. Among the path-finders to the ternal, he stands pre-eminent. He spent his entire life, short though t was, in urging his fellowmen to turn from the ephemeral to the biding, from the fleeting panorama of temporal life to the spiritual elicity of the life eternal.

II Advaita

Śaṅkara's Advaita is based on the Upaniṣads. At a time vhen false doctrines were misguiding the people and orthodoxy had othing better to offer than a barren and outmoded ritualism to ounteract the atheism of the heterodox, Śaṅkara expounded the hilosophy of the Upaniṣads for the benefit of humanity. Great s was his logical skill, it was not logic alone that crowned his mission vith success, but a conviction and authority born of living experience.

It was out of his own self-evidencing plenary experience that Śaṅkar poured forth his philosophy which bears the name "Advaita" Although disclaiming originality, he wrought a revolution in th minds of men, the salutary effects of which can be felt today. H set up a model in thinking and exposition which subsequent philos ophers in India have striven to follow. His works are characterize by penetrating insight and analytical skill. He wrote stupendou works both in prose and verse; and all of them are marked by lucidit of language and depth of thought. Among his major works are th great commentaries on what are known as the three canons o Vedānta, viz. the principal Upaniṣads, the Bhagavad-gītā, and th Brahma-sūtra, and such independent manuals as the Upadeśasāhasr and the Vivekacūḍāmaṇi.

The quintessence of the philosophy of Advaita is stated by Śaṅkar in a half-verse thus: "Brahman is real, the world is illusory; and th individual soul (jīva) is Brahman itself and no other."[2] Advaita i non-dualism. The ultimate reality, according to Advaita, is non dual. Advaita does not profess to formulate conceptually wha reality is. It is not, therefore, a system of thought, an "ism". I is not a school among schools of philosophy. It does not reject any view of reality. It only seeks to transcend all views, since these ar by their very nature restricted and one-sided. The pluralistic school theistic or otherwise, imagine that they are opposed to Advait but Advaita is not opposed to any of them. It recognizes that ther is truth in each of them, but insists that the truth in each is not th whole. Hostility arises out of partial vision. When the whol truth is known, there can be no hostility.[3] Gauḍapāda, Śaṅkara' preceptor's preceptor makes this clear when he says: "The dualist (i.e. pluralists) are conclusively firm in regard to the status of thei respective opinions. They are in conflict with one another. Bu Advaita is in no conflict with them."[4] Again, he says: "Advaita verily, is the supreme truth; dvaita is a variant thereof. For th dualists, there is duality either way (i.e. both in the Absolute and in the phenomenal manifold). With that (duality) this (non-duality) is not in conflict."[5]

In his commentary on these verses of Gauḍapāda, Śaṅkara argue that Advaita which is established through Scripture and reasoning is the true philosophy, and that the rest which are external theretc are non-true philosophies. He writes: "The philosophy of th dualists is non-true, because it gives room for defects such as attach-nent and aversion. How? The dualists who follow the philosophies of Kapila (Sāṃkhya), Kaṇāda (Vaiśeṣika), Buddha (Buddhism), Arhat (Jainism) and others, hold firmly to their own convictions thus: 'The supreme truth is thus and thus alone, not otherwise.' Therefore they become attached to their own schools and hate the others which they consider to be opposed to them; thus they are endowed with attachment and aversion, and are in mutual conflict on account of their respective convictions. With those mutually conflicting philosophies, our view of the oneness of Self which is in accordance with the teachings of the Veda is not in conflict because it is not exclusive of any of those schools, even as one's own hands and feet are not in conflict (with oneself)."[6]

The roots of the Advaita insight into the nature of the ultimate reality as non-dual Spirit can be traced to the Vedic mantras and the Upaniṣads. In some hymns of the Ṛigveda the ultimate reality is referred to in the neuter gender, and its non-duality is taught. Even where the masculine gender is employed, it is clear that no anthropomorphism is meant. The Puruṣasūkta, which gives a description of the Puruṣa both in its immanent and transcendent aspects, speaks of the Puruṣa as thousand-headed, thousand-eyed, and thousand-footed. It says: "Puruṣa is this all—all that has been and that will be. And he is the lord of immortality, which he grows beyond through food. Such is his greatness, and more than that is Puruṣa. A fourth of him is all beings, three-fourths of him are what is immortal in Heaven."[7] In one striking verse the gods are characterized as but different names for one and the same reality. "They call him Indra, Mitra, Varuṇa, Agni, and he is heavenly nobly-winged Garutman. To what is one, sages give many a title; they call it Agni, Yama, Mātarivan."[8] The well-known Nāsadīya hymn containing the central thesis of Advaita traces all things to one principle. Opposites like being and non-being, life and death, night and day, are shown to be the self-unfoldment of this One. How from the distinctionless principle which is "neither aught nor naught" the world of opposites and distinctions arose no one can tell. "That one" (tad ekam) which the hymn does not name is the ground of the universe. How the one appears as many is a mystery.

The Advaita that is incipient in the Vedic hymns becomes pronounced in the Upaniṣads. Reference may be made here to Yājñavalkya's teaching in the Bṛihadāraṇyaka-upaniṣad. When called upon to explain the nature of Brahman which is immediate and direct, and the self within all, Yājñavalkya replied that Brahman Ātman which is within all is the life of all. When pressed to be more definite, he said: "You cannot see the seer of the seeing. You cannot know the knower of the knowing. This is the Self of yours which is within all. Whatever is other than this is mutable."[9] The Self which is dearer than the son, dearer than wealth, dearer than everything else and is innermost should be seen, heard, thought about and meditated on.[10] Since the Self is all, there can be nothing left unknown, after the Self has been known. But the Self cannot be known as objects are known. That is why Yājñavalkya said that the Self is to be described as "not this, not this."[11] All determination is limitation. The Self is infinite. There are no limits to it. Therefore it cannot be characterized as this or that.

The knower-known relation is tenable only in the sphere of duality. "Where there is duality as it were," said Yājñavalkya, "there one knows another. Where, indeed, for one everything has become the self, there through whom and who, is one to know? Him through whom one knows all this, through whom is one to know? Lo, through whom is one to know the knower?" Brahman-Ātman, which is immutable, is the support of all-that-is. It is eternal consciousness. It is constant and unchanging through the changing states of waking and dreaming. In the states of waking and dreaming, the Self neither thinks nor moves. But it thinks as it were, and moves as it were.[13] In the state of deep sleep where all distinctions vanish, there is nothing but consciousness; for consciousness which is the Self can never be lost.

III Brahman

It should be evident from the teachings of Yājñavalkya that he is an advocate of the acosmic view of ultimate reality. The Self, according to him, is Brahman. It is the seat of supreme happiness. It is light and love. It is the life of life. It is not an object of experience per se. It is not possible to determine its nature in a specific way. All contradictions vanish when the Self is realized. The pluralistic universe is an illusory appearance, for there is no plurality in truth. This, in short, is Yājñavalkya's teaching. And this is the substantial teaching of the Upaniṣads in general. Śaṅkara's Advaita is based on the teaching of the Upaniṣads.

The Upaniṣadic terms Brahman and Ātman, according to

aṅkara, indicate the highest reality which is non-dual. As the
ature of Brahman-Ātman cannot be defined in terms of any
ategory, the Upaniṣads refer to it as "not this, not this" (neti neti).
'his does not mean Brahman, the absolute, is a night of nothingness,
contentless void. In some texts of the Upaniṣads, positive ex-
ressions such as real (satyam), knowledge (jñānam), infinite
anantam)[14] and bliss (ānandam)[15] are used with reference to Brah-
ıan. But these, too, make us understand Brahman by telling us
vhat it is not, viz. that it is not unreal, not insentient, not finite, and
ıot that which is related to sorrow. To define a thing is to limit
t, to finitize it. The infinite and the unlimited cannot be characteriz-
d in terms of finite categories. Śaṅkara argues that Brahman
annot be denoted by any word. "Brahman does not belong to
species of existents, and so it cannot be referred to as an existent,
tc. It does not have qualities, because it is qualityless, and so
annot be expressed in terms of any quality. Nor can it be indicated
y any word expressing action, because it is actionless."[16] Brahman
s nirguṇa, without characteristics, and so the Upaniṣads resorts
o the negative characterization of Brahman as "not-gross", etc.[17]
Even to say that it is one is not strictly true, for the category of number
s inapplicable to the Absolute. That is why Śaṅkara calls his philosophy "Advaita", the doctrine of the not-two, or non-dualism.

There are scriptural passages which characterize Brahman as the
ause of the world,[18] and the home of all auspicious qualities.[19]
If so, how does Śaṅkara reconcile the two views—the view of Brah-
nan as the Absolute, without characteristics, and the view which
haracterizes it as the cause of the world, and as endowed with attri-
outes? Śaṅkara solves this problem by postulating two standpoints,
he absolute (pāramārthika) and the relative (vyāvahārika). The
upreme truth is that Brahman is non-dual and relationless. It
ılone is; there is nothing real besides it. But from the empirical,
elative standpoint which we adopt when we speak of Brahman, it
ppears as God, the cause of the universe, as what is related, and as
ndowed with attributes. According to Śaṅkara, there is no real
ausation. The world is but an illusory appearance in Brahman,
even as the snake is in the rope. Śaṅkara accounts for the illusory
appearance of the world in Brahman by means of vivartavāda
(the theory of illusory appearance), which is to be distinguished
from pariṇāma-vāda (the theory of transformation).

It is on account of Avidyā (nescience) that the non-dual Brahman appears as many, that what is infinite and unconditioned appear as finite and conditioned and what is free from attributes appear as endowed with attributes. Śaṅkara writes: "That omniscient omnipotent cause from which do occur the origination, sustentation and destruction of this world which is manifest as name and form which is associated with many agents and enjoyers, which is the abod of fruits regulated in accordance with place, time, and action, and th structure of which is my mind inconceivable—that is Brahman."[2] The following passage is also significant: "The omnipresent Sel which is free from all characteristics, of transmigration, remain unchanged by its own unconditioned nature, but appears to th dullwitted, ignorant people as if experiencing all the changes c transmigration caused by the conditioning adjuncts, and as if many one in each body."[21]

The ultimate reality, Brahman, which is unconditioned, and i without attributes and qualifications, is called God when viewed i relation to the empirical world and empirical souls. Brahman i the same as nirguṇa (attributeless) and saguṇa (with attributes) There are not two Brahmans, as wrongly alleged by some critics Śaṅkara says: "Brahman, verily, is known to be of two forms, an that which, on the contrary, is devoid of all adjuncts. . . . Althoug Brahman is one, it is taught in the Vedānta texts as what is to b meditated upon as being related to assumed adjuncts, and as what i to be known as being devoid of any relation to adjuncts."[22]

When God is referred to as the lower (apara) Brahman, what i meant is not that Brahman has become lower in status as God, bu that God is Brahman looked at from the lower level of relativ experience. These are two forms (dvirūpa) of Brahman and no two Brahmans, Brahman as-it-is-in-itself, and Brahman as-it-is-in relation-to-the-world. The former is the unconditioned Brahman, th latter Brahman as conditioned by nomenclature, configuration, an change. God, thus, is conditioned Brahman; and the conditionin principle is māyā. As māyā is not a reality alongside or apart fron Brahman, it does not make for the introduction of any real duality All that the Godhead requires for its status is assumed duality, and no real duality. Either is spoken of as either-at-large in relation to not either, though there is no difference in either as such. Similarly God is said to possess omniscience, omnipotence, etc., as distinguish ed from the soul which is parviscient, with limited power, etc. I itself, the Godhead knows no distinction and cannot be categorized

IV Māyā

It is necessary at this stage to refer to the nature and work of māyā before we explain how God or Īśvara is the cause of the universe. If Brahman is one and non-dual, immutable and partless, how is it that there is a manifestation of the world of plurality? Since Brahman is immutable, it cannot give rise to or originate the world or get itself transformed into the host of phenomena. In short, Brahman, according to Śaṅkara, is neither the originating cause nor the transformed cause of the world. But it illusorily appears as the world in the same way as a rope illusorily appears as a serpent. It suffers nothing by such appearance. Not all the faults and foibles of the world can affect the purity of Brahman. The attributes of a serpent do not really belong to the rope. The rope remains in its own nature even when it is mistaken for a serpent. The principle which accounts for the appearance of the world of plurality in the non-dual Brahman is māyā or avidyā. To quote Śaṅkara: "That which is supremely real is non-duality: through māyā it appears as diverse, even as the plurality of moons on account of defective eyesight, or the rope appearing as a snake, water-streak, etc., and not in reality, for the Self is partless. . . . The partless, unborn reality can by no means become different. This is the meaning. If what is immortal, unborn, and non-dual were to become really different, then it would become mortal, like fire becoming cool. But this is not acceptable, for a change of one's nature into its contrary is opposed to all evidence. The unborn non-dual Self becomes different only through māyā, not in reality."[23] Śaṅkara refers to this principle, which makes the one appear as many, by different terms such as māyā, avidyā, prakṛiti, avyakta. "The seed-power (responsible for creation)," says Śaṅkara, "is of the nature of nescience (avidyā); it is designated by the word avyakta (the unmanifest); it is dependent on God, is of the form of māyā, the great sleep. In it the transmigrating souls sleep, being devoid of the knowledge of the Self. The unmanifest, indeed, is māyā."[24]

Māyā-avidyā is beginningless, indeterminable, and of the nature of the existent. It is said to be beginningless[25] because, if a beginning is predicted of it, there would be something antecedent to it, and this would lead to infinite regress. But māyā-avidyā is not beginningless in the sense in which Brahman-Ātman is. If it were really beginningless, there would be no end to it. So the beginninglessness of māyā is like that of a perennial stream. To the questioning intellec māyā-avidyā is a riddle. It cannot be defined as being either tru or untrue, and so it is said to be indeterminable. It is calle māyā, according to Śaṅkara, because it is not possible to define i in terms of known categories.[26] It cannot be said to be real; for if i were real, it has to be reckoned as an entity in addition to Brahman and this would be in conflict with the scriptural declaration of non duality. Since it accounts for the appearance of the world, it canno be unreal either. Nor can it be both real and unreal because c contradiction. It has, therefore, to be regarded as indeterminabl It is considered to be of the nature of an existent because non existence cannot be the ground of even illusion or appearanc Though it is an existent, it is not real, beacuse it is sublated by th knowledge of Brahman.[27] From the standpoint of Brahman, ther is no such thing as māyā. But we have to admit its existence so lon as we view Brahman in relation to the world form the relative, em pirical point of view. The pluralistic universe, which is a produc of māyā, is also denoted by the word māyā because it is not real.

V Īśvara

God, or Īśvara, as already stated, is only Brahman conditione by māyā. The place of God in Advaita is neither pernicious nc precarious. On the contrary, the concept of God is quite pertinen to and precious for Advaita-experience. The place of God may b understood from the standpoints of both metaphysics and axiology God is to be regarded as the ground of the universe, and as the goa of meditation. In relation to the world, God is basic existence; i relation to the soul, He is the supreme value.

According to Śaṅkara, neither Brahman nor māyā can indepen dently be the material cause of the world. Brahman-in-itself trans cends the cause-effect relation, and so cannot be the material caus of the world. Māyā which is insentient cannot by itself be the caus of the world. It is Brahman which is conditioned by, or in associatio with, māyā that is the cause of the world. God or Īśvara is no a cause among causes producing the world; He is the whole and th sole cause. God, according to Śaṅkara, is both the material an efficient cause of the world. Godhead or Brahman is that fron which beings arise, in which they reside after arising, and into whicl they disappear at the end.[28] The Universe is differentiated b names and forms: it includes many agents and enjoyers; its constituents are regulated in respect to place, time, cause, action, and fruit; the design which it reveals cannot be even conceived by the mind. For an infinitely ordered and variegated universe no other cause or ground could be postulated than the omniscient and omnipotent God.[29] This and other similar arguments should not be regarded as proofs for the existence of God. God is not the end-result of syllogistic reasoning. The arguments are useful only as aids that render intelligible the intuitively discerned and scripturally declared truth.

God is not only the world-ground but also the moral governor. The law of karma which operates in the moral realm has God for its guide. If souls reap the consequences of their actions, good for good, and ill for ill, it is because of God's dispensation expressed in the form of the karmic law. To the Mīmāṃsaka's contention that karma can and does function by itself, the Vedāntin's reply is that karma, which is inert, does require an intelligent controller for its operation. No finite intelligent agent can be the controller of karma. In fact, the agent-souls are the victims of karma, although this statement should not be taken to mean that the souls are playthings in the hands of fate. Each soul certainly deserves the fruits of his own deeds. And the dispenser of justice, the inner immortal ruler, is God. He is both the Law-giver and the Law. He resides within souls and rules them. His rulership has for its ultimate aim the liberation of souls. The world which He has projected out of Himself is the vale of soul-making.

The ends that man seeks are prosperity and the supreme good. Prosperity, whether in this world or in the next, is temporal; the supreme good, which is release from bondage to the temporal process, is eternal. In the gaining of either of these ends, it is necessary to crave for the grace of God. Four categories of devotees are mentioned in the Bhagavad-gītā: people in distress, those who desire to accumulate wealth, the seekers of metaphysical knowledge, and the knowers of Self. Of these, the first may strive for the removal of distress or accumulation of wealth without calling on God. But if one waits on God for the fulfilment of even these limited objects, then these very successes will prepare the person concerned for wanting to pursue the higher path which leads to Self-knowledge. And it is by gaining knowledge that comes through God's grace that one gets released from bondage.[30]

The devotee worships God in various forms and under different names. It is the same God that takes on a variety of forms and names through His power of māyā. He assumes the form which the devotee chooses and responds to the name by which He is called. Whenever dharma is threatened, God incarnates Himself in order to preserve it for the world. Although unborn and without body He appears to be born, to be embodied as it were. In order to shower His grace on the devotees in the most concrete mode, He makes the images that are made for Him alive with Divinity. It is true that the highest way of worship is to see God everywhere, as all in all. But for most people, limited as they are, unevolved as they are, this becomes difficult, if not impossible. For their sake God assumes limited forms and definite names.

While it is true that Advaita seeks to go beyond theism, it is not to be confused with atheism or antitheism. The supreme Reality is absolutely unconditioned; it is superpersonal. But it appears as if personal in order to serve as the ground of the universe and the object of adoration for man. It is not that Brahman is degraded into Īśvara (God); on the contrary, it is Īśvara that is realized to be Brahman in plenary experience. It is God that the Absolute becomes the pivot of the universe and the paradigm of perfection for the soul.

Any attempt to explain the creation of the world is bound to fail. On the phenomenal level, the intellect seeks to inquire into the nature of the world and does not succeed in its attempt. When the final intuition of Brahman is gained, it will be realized that the world was never created, that it is an illusory appearance (mithyā). Brahman-Ātman alone is: the world is a misreading thereof, even as the illusory snake is of the rope. It must be borne in mind that Śaṅkara does not deny the empirical reality of the world. So long as Brahman is not realized, the world is real to the ignorant man. But to the enlightened person (vidvān) who has realized Brahman, Brahman alone is. The Upaniṣadic texts which speak of creation have no purport of their own. They are to be interpreted figuratively. They serve to introduce the truth of non-duality (advaita).[31]

VI The Jīva

According to Śaṅkara, the individual soul (Jīva) in its essential nature is no other than Brahman; but, due to avidyā, it appears o be different. The jīva is a conscious living being. There are everal grades of conscious living beings, from a blade of grass to Brahma (the first to be created). These may be grouped under hree heads—sub-human (e.g. animals), human, and superhuman (e.g. gods). Among the conscious living beings, man is unique because he alone is eligible for action and knowledge.[32] In justification of this, Śaṅkara quotes a passage from the Aitareya Āraṇyaka[33] which runs thus: "The Ātman is expanded only in man. He, indeed, is most endowed with intelligence. He gives expression to what is known. He sees what is known. He knows what is to come. He knows the visible and invisible world. He perceives the immortal through the mortal. Thus is he endowed. But with the other animals, eating and drinking alone constitute the sphere of their knowledge."

The individual soul is not what is created, according to Advaita; only its empirical outfit consisting of body and mind is. The body-mind complex and its cause (avidyā) constitute the soul's transmigratory life (saṃsāra). The jīva is said to possess three bodies—causal, subtle, and gross. The causal body is avidyā. It is also known as the sheath of bliss (ānandamaya-kośa). The subtle body is composed of three sheaths—that of intellect (vijñānamaya-kośa), mind (manomaya-kośa), and vitality (prāṇamaya-kośa). The gross or physical body is the sheath of food (annamaya-kośa). What happens at death is only a change of the physical body. The subtle body, however, continues with incidental alterations, and also the causal body, till the onset of release. The inward Self which is identical with Brahman must be distinguished from all these five sheaths (pañca-kośa), which are not-Self. So long as one fails to distinguish the Self from the not-Self, mistakes the characteristics of the one for those of the other, and thinks, "This is mine", "I am stout", "I am blind", "I am happy", etc., he is caught up in the wheel of bondage.

Man's experience is distinguishable into three states—waking, dream, and sleep. Man experiences the external world in the state of waking. In dream, he creates an inner world of images and imagines that he is a denizen thereof. He is not conscious of anything, outside or inside, in sleep: there is just awareness without awareness of anything. The inquiry into the three states helps one to realize that the Self is pure consciousness uneffected by accidents such as the body, the mind, and the world which change and pass.

VII Jñāna

Since avidyā is the cause of bondage, knowledge alone, dec lares Śaṅkara, is the means to release. According to Advaita, th realization of the non-dual Brahman is release. Brahman which i to be realized is ever-existent, and is not what is to be accomplishe by an act. Though it is one and non-dual, eternal, ever-free an identical with the inward Self, it is not realized to be such, du to avidyā, which veils it. So what is required for attaining Brahman realization, which is release, is knowledge (jñāna) and not ritua action (karma). To quote Śaṅkara: "On account of ignorance th Self appears conditioned as it were; when that is destroyed, the pur Self, verily, shines of its own accord, like the sun when the cloud i dispelled."[34]

Śaṅkara rejects the Mīmāṃsā view that release can be obtaine through ritual action (karma) alone as prescribed by Scripture. I is the contention of the Mīmāṃsaka that, like prosperity here i this life and in a hereafter, release is what-is-to-be-accomplished, and what-is-accomplished requires action for its accomplishment. The Mīmāṃsā view is not acceptable to Śaṅkara, as it is based on a thorough misunderstanding of the nature of release and also of the nature and competence of karma.

The fruit of karma is prosperity (abhyudaya) which is what-is-to-be-accomplished and is impermanent. The goal of Vedānta as taught in the Upaniṣads is release (mokṣa) which is not what-is-accomplished, but is eternal. If we speak of the "attainment" of release, it is only in a figurative sense. The truth is that release is the eternal nature of Self. What stands in the way of realizing this truth is ignorance. When ignorance is removed through knowledge, there is release. This is not a new acquisition; it is the realization of what eternally is.

Śaṅkara argues that anything that is caused by karma is bound to perish. Through action one of the four results may be obtained—origination, attainment, purification, and modification. Release is different from these. The Self, which is of the nature of release, is not what is originated, attained, purified, or modified. And so karma is not the means to release, which is eternal.

Śaṅkara is not in favour of the view that release can be obtained by combining karma with jñāna, in whatever way the combination between the two is explained. If jñāna is understood in the sense of Brahman-knowledge, there can be no combination between karma and jñāna as the means to release. The reason is that the content and fruit of the one are different from those of the other. The Self which is the content of jñāna is one, independent, and eternal, whereas the rites that constitute the theme of the ritual-section of the Veda are many, dependent on causal correlates, and emphemeral. The fruit of knowledge is release, while the enjoyment that is the fruit of action only confirms the jīva all the more in bondage. Since karma and jñāna are mutually exclusive, they cannot be combined. Śaṅkara says: "The opposition between knowledge (jñāna) and works (karma) is unshakable, like a mountain. Bhagavān Vyāsa, the great Vedic teacher, taught his son conclusively after much reflection, thus: "These two paths are taught in the Veda, one called the path of activity (pravṛitti) and the other of renunciation (nivṛitti)'."[35] Knowledge does not require the help of karma as its subsidiary, because by itself it is competent to remove ignorance, the cause of bondage. Karma which involves distinctions based on avidyā cannot be of any use, either as the principal or as a subsidiary, for removing avidyā. That is why Śaṅkara observes: "Action does not remove ignorance, as it is not opposed to it; knowledge does destroy ignorance, as light (destroys) dense (darkness)."[36] "He who regards Brahman as the self-complete end," declares Śaṅkara, "will not see any use in action. And no one will engage himself in action that is known to be futile."[37]

We should not think that Śaṅkara has not recognized the utility of karma in the scheme of discipline leading to liberation. According to him, the competence to tread the path of knowledge is gained only when one's mind has become pure; and for the purification of the mind, karma-yoga (the performance of one's duties without attachment to results) is necessary. Śaṅkara says: "All karma and knowledge (relating to ritual), when well observed by the one who is free from desires, but longs to gain release, make for the purification of the mind."[38] Since disinterested action (niṣkāma-karma) performed in a spirit of dedication to God serves to purify the mind, Śaṅkara holds that karma is a remote aid to the path of knowledge. Bhakti which is devotion to, and worship of God is equally important for a spiritual aspirant. It is only through the grace of God that one becomes interested in the study of Vedānta and develops a longing for the knowledge of the non-dual Absolute. Śaṅkara lays down four conditions to be fulfilled by a spiritual aspirant in order to become eligible for the path of knowledge, which is the path of self-inquiry: (1) discrimination of the eternal from the non-eternal, (2) non-attachment to the enjoyment of fruits either of this or the other world, (3) possession in abundance of six virtues—calmness, equanimity, turning away from sense-objects, forbearance, concentration, and faith, and (4) an intense longing for liberation.[39]

The discipline prescribed for one who is eligible for the path of knowledge consists of learning or study, reflection, and contemplation. Hearing or study stands for the proper understanding of the meaning of Upaniṣadic statements. The statements are of two kinds: intermediary texts and major texts. The former relate to the nature of the world, the individual soul, the non-dual self, etc. The major texts impart the supreme knowledge of identity. From the intermediary texts, only mediate knowledge of the truth is gained. It is only from the major texts that one can obtain direct experience of the plenary reality. In the case of the supremely competent inquirer, even a single hearing of the major text, "That thou art", will do to effect release. In the case of others this does not happen because of the impediments of long-established false beliefs, the belief that the teaching of the Vedānta is impossible and the belief that the contrary is the truth. While rational reflection (manana) serves to remove the first of these, the practice of contemplation (nididhyāsana) overcomes the second. When the impediments have been removed, the intuitive experience of the non-dual Brahman-Ātman results.

VIII The Highest End

The highest human end is release, which must be distinguished from others such as wealth, pleasure and moral goodness, which are only instrumental values. Release, according to Śaṅkara, is not a post-mortem experience to be achieved in another world. It is the supreme felicity which is the eternal nature of the Self; and so one need not go elsewhere in search of it. The Kaṭha-upaniṣad declares: "Higher than the Self there is nothing whatever. That is the end. That is the final goal."[40] To Śaṅkara, Ātman and mokṣa are synonyms. The Self is ever free; freedom is its very nature. Only this truth is not realized because of avidyā. The removal of avidyā alone is required for the attainment of release. Śaṅkara says: "Being Brahman is release. . . . Release is of the nature of Brahman which is eternal and pure."[41] Again, "The Self, although always attained, is unattained, as it were, on account of ignorance; when that (ignorance) is destroyed, it becomes manifest, as if attained, like the ornament round one's own neck."[42]

It is true that release is said to be "attained" and bondage "destroyed" when avidyā is removed. But the expressions "attainment" and "destruction" should be understood here in a figurative sense. There are two kinds of attainment and two of destruction—attainment of the unattained, and attainment of the already attained; destruction of what has not been destroyed, and destruction of the already destroyed. For the first kind in each, action is necessary, but not for the second variety of attainment and destruction. For getting an ornament made of gold action is essential; and it is a case of attaining what has not been attained. But no action is required for attaining the gold chain which a deluded person imagines to have been lost, though all the time he is wearing it round his neck. When a passer-by tells him that the chain is round his neck, it is a case of attaining what is already attained. What is required here is the knowledge of the fact that the chain was not lost. Though for destroying a real serpent action such as beating with a stick is required, for destroying the rope-serpent, the serpent which is imagined in a rope, what is required is sufficient light or the information to the deluded person that the object is not a serpent, but a rope. The "attainment" of release and the "destruction" of bondage are in the second of the two senses, which is the figurative sense. Śaṅkara explains the position as follows: "The souls are never under the veil of bondage, imposed by avidyā; they are ever free from bondage. They are pure by nature, enlightened, and liberated from the very beginning. So they are of the nature of the eternally pure, enlightened, and free reality. 'If this be so, why is it said by the teachers who know that they are liberated?' It is replied thus: Just as the sun, although ever of the nature of illumination, is said to be shining, and just as the hills, although ever devoid of movement, are said to be standing, even so here."[43]

According to Śaṅkara, release can be attained here and now. As release is the eternal nature of the Self, one need not wait for realizing it till death overtakes the physical body. Even while tenanting a body, one is released at the onset of knowledge. Such a one is called a jīvanmukta—released even while living in the body. The continuance of the body is in no way incompatible with the status of release. What happens when release is gained is a change in perspective. Before release, one took the world of which the body is a part to be real; after gaining Self-knowledge, one realizes that the world is an illusory appearance. If the body were real, then release could come only after the destruction of the body. But, since the body is not real, its continued appearance is of no consequence. The present body is the result of prārabdha-karma, i.e. that part of the past karma which has begun to fructify. It is only when the fruit of prārabdha is exhausted that the body will fall. But the continuance of the body does not in any way affect the state of wisdom of the released. Śaṅkara observes: "Being endowed with a body is due to illusory knowledge. So it is established that for the wise there is no body even while living.... For the one who has Brahman-knowledge there is no subjection to transmigration as before."[44] The explanation that is given for the continuance of the body in terms of prārabdha in the case of the jīvanmukta is from the standpoint of others who are released. For the jīvanmukta there is no body at all, and so there is no need either for explaining the continuance of the body.

The jīvanmukta has nothing to achieve, no ends to gain. The satisfaction that is his is without any limit and determination. He is devoid of any kind of activity, good or bad. Even the activities like eating, drinking and bathing, which are attributed as indispensable to him, do not exist before his vision. For him, there is not even the obligation of study and reflection, since they are intended for those who do not know the truth. He has neither the sense of agency nor that of enjoyership. He does good to society, but without any sense of egoity. His actions are not born of constraint; they are the spontaneous expression of his innate goodness. The very existence of such a person is a blessing to the world. Such a one, having attained Brahma-nirvāṇa, the freedom that is the Absolute, is not born again. In his case, there is no return to duality, which is bondage.

In breadth of vision and depth of understanding Śaṅkara stands unparalleled in the history of philosophy and religious thought. In speculative daring and subtlety of logic, convincingness of style and clarity of expression, few can equal him, and none has surpassed him. Narrowness and bigotry are entirely foreign to his philosophy. He gave India back her soul which she had almost lost and infused into the body politic a sense of unity and strength. His Advaita is not the creed of a limited sect or the possession of an exclusive group. It is the gospel of fearlessness and freedom to which every one has a claim.

14

ŚAIVA-SIDDHĀNTA, VIŚIṢṬADVAITA, DVAITA

S. S. Raghavachar

I Theism, the Third Phase of Indian Thought

One who attempts to give an account of the Indian Theistic Systems cannot help noting three striking phases of Indian religious thought. First of all comes the period of scriptures—the Vedas, Upaniṣads, Epics inclusive of the Bhagavadgītā, purāṇas and early Āgamas. This is conspicuously the period of original inspiration, profound and many-sided. This is followed by the age of rationalistic systems of thought, heterodox and orthodox, culminating in the Advaita Vedānta of Śaṅkara. Though theism is not absent in the second phase, as some form of it, halting and incomplete, is found in Nyāya-Vaiśeṣika, the yoga system of Patañjali, the Absolutism of Śaṅkara and also in the Purāṇas and Āgamas, it is remarkable that developed Theism in all its glory is not a creation of this period of Indian philosophy. It is in the third period from about the tenth century that we have the great Schools of Theism in Indian philosophy.

The bases of this movement are certainly laid in the first phase and it runs somewhat through the second, but it grows into comprehensive philosophical and religious structures of thought in the third. The older, unsystematized inspirations are gathered up and moulded into elaborate and completed systems of religious philosophy. It is significant that the three formulations of Theism, Śaiva-Siddhānta, Viśiṣṭādvaita and Dvaita, took shape in South India and roughly in the period from the tenth to the fifteenth century. They endeavoured to maintain the semi-poetical products of the first phase and developed the technique of ratiocination characteristic of the second phase.

II Common Features of the Three Schools

There are some common traits of the three schools. The struggled beyond two prominent and prevailing trends of though They cleared themselves of the naturalistic bias found in earl Buddhism, Jainism, Sāṃkhya and even Vaiśeṣika and Mīmāṃsā They clearly longed for the transcendent. They also discarde the acosmic monism of the later idealistic Buddhism and Advait Vedānta. It is with considerable heat that these three schools c Theism seek to refute the naturalistic denial of God and the monisti denial of the empirical world. They affirm the reality of the world In other words, these theisms build up a monotheism combined witl a realistic acceptance of the world. They find no contradictio between these two affirmations; on the contrary they perceiv contradiction in a world-denying monism and an atheistic realism

The one supreme God is named Śiva in Śaiva-Siddhānta anc Viṣṇu in the other two. This sectarian difference is due to differen mythological traditions, symbols and modes of ritual worship. Bu the Śiva of Śaiva-Siddhānta is no longer the terror-God of the Ṛigveda and is sublimated beyond recognition. The Viṣṇu o Rāmānuja and Madhva is no longer a minor solar deity but a powerful representation of the infinite. Thus the line of sectarian demarcation tends to disappear in the ampler dimensions of the new epoch.

The Ultimate Spirit, conceived as the central reality in these schools is looked upon as personal and as a Being, rather than as the impersonal principle of being; and communion, adoration and surrender come to be adopted as the right approach to this supreme reality. It is this approach that comes to be called Bhakti. The God-head is also regarded as infinitely responsive and as overflowing with grace. It is not merely an object for contemplation but a living presence to be invoked in worship, a presence as infinite in love as in existence.

This element of love becomes irrepressible in these movements and it overflows into social relations with the consequence that the old rigid social order of castes is subjected to a revolutionary levelling-up process. One of the singular effects of these movements is the systematic belittling of caste distinctions in the realm of devotion. Hinduism becomes humanized and democratised in the religion of Bhakti. Non-violence or Ahiṃsā becomes a cardinal ethical principle in the cult of Bhakti. Animal sacrifice disappears leaving no trace.

III Epistemology

Having considered these general aspects of the three schools let us now look at them in detail. We shall consider them as a whole rather than separately because of their large measure of agreement on fundamentals. At the same time the unique points of each will be specified. The systems devote themselves fully to epistemological questions, thus indicating their philosophical maturity. The tenets propounded are supported by methods of proof, defined, clarified and established by the basic epistemological investigations of the schools. Consistent with the realistic temper, all the schools contend that knowledge of reality is intrinsic to thought and that errors arise when thought is impeded by extrinsic factors. In this view of Svataḥ prāmāṇya (intrinsic validity) there is agreement between the Mīmāṃsā and Advaita systems. The truth of a judgment or proposition is generated by the very factors that generate the judgment or proposition, and the fact of their truthfulness is cognized by the very process of cognizing they constitute. Errors arise through external interference and come to be cognized through contradiction from other instances of knowledge. True to the spirit of extreme opposition to subjectivism, all error is looked upon as a case of incomplete apprehension by Viśiṣṭādvaita; while Śaiva-Siddhānta and Dvaita adopt the moderately realistic explanation of error as misconstruction. Thus Satkhyāti (true apprehension) and Anyathā-Khyāti (misapprehension) are the two favoured explanations of errors and illusions.

The three systems recognize only three modes of knowledge as pramāṇas-perception (pratyakṣa), Anumāna (inference) and verbal testimony (Śabda). They do not further reduce the number as the Cārvāka, Buddhist and Vaiśeṣika schools try to do. They subsume under the three all the other pramāṇas such as Upamāna (comparision or analogy), Arthāpatti (postulation) and Anupalabdhi (non-perception) which are admitted by the Nyāya and Mīmāṃsā systems. Elucidation of the pramāṇas largely follows the Nyāya method in practice with characteristic corrections dictated by fuller consideration and the individual philosophical directions of the school. For instance, indeterminate perception is declared by Viśiṣṭādvaita as merely insufficiently determinate. Reasoning by pure negative concomitance is not countenanced. Inference from another is not given such importance and the rigidity of its form is relaxed by Dvaita. Śabda pramāṇa is of paramount importan and the scriptures are the outstanding examples of this pramāṇ

All three schools are unanimous in proclaiming the philosophic ultimacy of the contents of the Śāstra. They do not interpret tl Śāstra as purely of ethical value as the Prabhākaras maintai but attribute to it primary metaphysical import. The actu identification of what constitutes Śāstra varies from school to schoo For both Dvaita and Viśiṣṭādvaita, the Śruti, meaning the Veda inclusive of the Upaniṣads, is the eternal fountain-head of know ledge. It is supplemented by the recorded spiritual experienc of sages and saints. These later are embodied in the Itihāsa Purāṇas, and Dharma-Śāstras. For Viśiṣṭādvaita, the works the Tamil saints named Aḷwars are also highly venerated authoritie The Vaiṣṇava Āgama named Pāñcharātra is Viṣṇu's own promu gation of ultimate truths for both Dvaita and Viśiṣṭādvaita. I Śaiva-Siddhānta, the Śruti is somewhat replaced by the Āgam though it too is admitted. The Śaiva Āgama are accepted as comin from Śiva himself. His saints, the Nayanmars, the Tamil devote of Śiva, have left the weightiest records of Śiva's revelation to then They are also primarily authoritative. The parts of ruti such Śa the Śvetāśvatara Upaniṣad are also primeval as sources of know ledge. It is evident, thus, that these schools appropriate as thei fundamental source of knowledge the entire theistic heritage i Sanskrit and also inspired mystical poetry of the God-intoxicate saints, Aḷwars and Nayanmars. It is noteworthy that these saint precede the systematic philosophers in Śaiva-Siddhānta and Viśiṣṭā dvaita, while they succeed them in Dvaita. In the body of th Śāstra so broadly conceived we have both dogma and mysticism In Indian Theism there has never been a radical contradictio between dogma and mysticism and this harmony is certainly due t the philosophical largeness of the dogma and the integrity of th mystics in seeing in their exalted experiences only a re-discovery o the Divine.

IV Proofs of God's Existence

The crucial doctrine of the three schools we are considerin is the idea of God as the ultimate reality. They refute schools tha degrade God as an appearance or being in God, as Patañjali and th Nyāya philosophers do, or as a supplementary category not formin the centre of the ontological scheme. God is not duly admitted if He is not admitted as the central and foundational verity. Rightly is He characterized as 'Pati' in Śaivism ; He is the Puruṣottama or Vāsudeva of the Gītā, the Nārāyaṇa of Pāñcharātra and the Paramabrahman of the Upaniṣads.

The schools have an exact understanding of the problem of proving the existence of God. Śaiva-Śiddhānta offers the cosmological and moral proofs, more or less on the pattern of Nyāya Theism. God is the first cause, the ultimate ground, the creative source of the world. It is easy to amuse oneself with the difficulties of the principle of causation. But how does one go about comprehending a finite empirical presentation except by integrating it with an explanatory ground? The idea of a first cause is bound up with a causal explanation itself. It is meaningless to affirm secondary causes or a sequence of causes without a first cause just as some ultimate ground of intelligibility is necessary for all intelligibility.

Why should there be only one first cause instead of many? Causation is a process of differentiation, as the Sāṃkhya philosophers maintained; and there is no possibility of reaching any finality of explanation except in one really first cause. Analysis can proceed endlessly but integration is an attainable objective. The very fact that the cause is first also implies that it must be spiritual in character, for spontaneity or intrinsic creativity is intelligible only as the operation of will and is not ascribable to matter. Matter that exercises creativity of this character can hardly be mere matter. Such self-initiated creativity can be characteristic of only a perfect spirit, for liability to external impulse is an aspect of imperfection.

In addition to the cosmological proof, the moral argument is also used in the specific context of the doctrine of Karma. If the world is ruled by a moral law as both Jainism and Pūrva Mīmāṃsā affirm, the fundamental fact of the cosmic situation must be a moral power, a power for which moral values are of importance and demand conservation. The Universe can be a field of the moral evolution of the finite self only if it is itself an expression of a reality for which that evolution is a matter of compelling concern. The metaphysics of Theism is a presupposition or completion of the doctrine of Karma.

Dvaita and Viśiṣṭādvaita do not offer positively any rationalistic proof for the existence of God. They are content to rest the case on the deliverance of the Śāstra. But they do engage in a great deal of speculative thinking in order to answer rationalistic objections to Theism, for refuting the positive tenets of the Godless philosophies and for exhibiting the internal coherence of the Theistic position. When such a vast range of non-contradiction is secured, they contend it is sheer irrationality to distrust Śāstra, which stands vindicated by its own Svataḥ-pramāṇa.

V The Nature of God

The God of these schools is intensely personal, the supreme personality. In reality the category of personality finds its utmost realization in God. He is the Parama-puruṣa. The connotation of personality is not finitude but self-identity, or self-affirmation. The non-self is excluded by finite personality but in the infinite personality it is appropriated as a dimension, even as the meaning of a poet assimilates into itself the expression. A dualism of God and the world is conquered through assimilation and the world puts on the splendour of being the garment of the Deity.

The God of these schools is not an attributeless or indeterminate principle. He is, no doubt, without the so-called Guṇas of Prakṛiti, but he abounds in the attributes of intelligence, power and grace. To be a bare something undifferentiated by quality is to be virtually nothing. Śaivism names some fundamental attributes. They are infinite bliss, consciousness, desire, knowledge and force of action. They reduce themselves to omnipotence and omniscience. The defining attributes posited by Viśiṣṭādvaita are reality, knowledge, infinity, purity, and bliss. In Dvaita also a similar list of Sat, Chit, Ānanda and Ātmatva or self-hood is given (Sūtra Bhāṣya-3-3-2). Flowing from these are inexhaustible lists of attributes each conceived as inherent, eternal and unsurpassed. In fact to be infite means to be the substratum of infinite attributes. This is almost a definition of God.

How is the substantive being of God related to the attributes? Dvaita advances a special concept here. The attributes are essentially identical with the substance of God's being, though they are distinguished in thought and language. This is the Dvaita conception of Viśeṣa. The attributes are classified into those that signify the majesty of God-head, and those that signify His accessibility. His grace is a pivotal attribute for Śaiva-Siddhānta and in reality all other attributes are instrumental to the working out of Grace. Grace is the supreme power behind the effectuation of man's redemption and God as Ānanda constitutes the supreme object of endeavour. He is the basal reality, the basic omniscient power and the final object of desire and adoration. One of the perennial attractions of these schools of Theism is their unending rapture over the aesthetic absoluteness of God.

God is the cause of the world. In both Dvaita and Śaiva-Siddhānta God is the efficient cause only and the material cause consists of Prakṛiti or Māyā. In this way the transcendence and immutability of God are upheld. In Viśiṣṭādvaita He is regarded as both the material and efficient cause. The point is that the rudimentary material principle also belongs to God and carries Him as its inner Ruler in all its status. To say that it is the material cause is the same thing as saying that its Antaryāmin (inner controller) furnishes the material cause for the world's creation through its instrumentality. He is the material cause mediately (Sadvaraka). The difference is not radical, for the Dvaitin and Śaiva-Siddhāntin also concede that the material cause, unlike the Prakṛiti of the Seśvara-Sāṃkhya and the Atoms of Nyāya-Vaiśeṣika, does not enjoy autonomous existence even in its pre-cosmic stage. When the material cause is so wholly dependent on God in all its states and God, in Viśiṣṭādvaita, exercises only Sadvaraka Upādānatva (indirect material causality) the distinction between the two views boils down to a matter of terminology.

The functions of God in relation to the world are enumerated as five in Śaiva-Siddhānta. They are the causation of being or existence, continuance, dissolution of the world, self-concealment and gracious self-revelation. The last two relate to God's concern for the individual self and they seem to be behind the first three also. The cosmic role of God is through and through teleological and that teleology is governed by the paramount principle of divine grace. In Dvaita the functions enumerated are eight. They are creation, preservation, and dissolution and control on the one hand and concealment, self-revelation, bondage and release on the other. It is to be noted that creation is just release into manifestation of the physical universe out of its rudimentary unmanifested condition and dissolution is relapse into non-manifestation. Even individual souls are subject to creation insofar as they are brought into the state of gross-embodiment, and dissolution is the suspension of this embodiment. This goes on for them as long as they are in the state of transmigration. The last four functions relate to the responses of God toward their spiritual lapses and merits.

The Viśiṣṭādvaita asserts only a variation on the same theme They are creation, maintenance, dissolution, indwelling and control As far as individual selves are concerned, there are the additiona functions of Upāyatva and Prāpyatva, the first being the means fo self-perfection and the second being the end to be sought in perfection. We may sum up in the terminology of Viśiṣṭādvaita. God i is Ubhayaliṅga (has a twofold character). He is free from all the imperfections characteristic of matter and finite souls, and He abounds in infinite positive perfections such as knowledge, power compassion and beauty. He is Ubhaya-Vibhūti (has a twofolc glory), as He holds the mundane world of ours as a realm of Hi temporal splendour and the Supra-mundane world to which the released souls enter as the realm of His eternal splendour. He i Śiva (holy) and Viṣṇu (all embracing).

VI The Individual Self

All the schools endeavour to prove the existence of individua selves through speculative proofs and also through the authority o scriptures. Souls are uncreated and indestructible in their substantive being. But in the state in which we find ourselves we are caught up in material embodiment. This impurity is analysed by Śaiva-Siddhānta in its doctrine of the three defilements—Ānava Karma and Māyā. Anava brings about a shrinkage of powers Karma impells action within the plane of worldly career and Māyā covers up the light of knowledge. These impurities bring abou embodiment. This is the law of Karma. Karma explains man' present lot in terms of his own past conduct and man's present conduct will determine his future status. There is a kind of self-determination here but no fatalism, as the future has to be shaped by present effort. This vicious cycle can be ended through the intervention of Divine grace. That Grace is not arbitrary but is to be earned through the liberating mode of conduct characterized by Bhakti.

Thus there is self-determinism, necessity and a way of escape through Grace. The schools maintain that individual souls have a static-dynamic character. The essential self is enduring and unchanging but the attributes and active experiences undergo alterations. In other words, finite personality is not all change as early Buddhism asserted, nor is it wholly immutable as the Sāṃkhya contended. It exercises the power of knowing, volition and affective experiences. Jñātṛitwa, Dartṛitwa and Bhoktṛitwa (enjoyership) are genuine aspects of personalities held together by the self-identical core of self-consciousness. The substance-attribute manner of conceiving is appropriate here also. Viśiṣṭādvaita posits a dual consciousness, Dharmaswarūpa-Jñāna and Dharma-Bhuta-Jñāna (attribute consciousness). Dvaita operates its principle of Viśeṣa in explaining this dual aspect.

As the self has this dual nature, at once eternal and dynamic and exercising the various operations of consciousness in feeling, knowing and volition, the diversities characterizing the selves are intrinsic to them. Thus there is a real plurality of individual selves. Likeness in essential attributes may be there but that does not take away numerical plurality. Each self is a persistent individual. This self-conscious individuality persists even in release; or rather it reaches its effective fullness of life only in that state. In relation to God it is a 'paśu', a subordinate being drawing all its being and worth and joy from Him. This conception of Śiva being the 'pati' or 'Lord' and Jīva being the 'paśu' is fundamental to Śaiva-Siddhānta and also to Viśiṣṭādvaita and Dvaita. The individual self is both eternal and absolutely paratantra (dependent) in relation to God. This latter relation is not a disaster but the only real life and delight for the individual. He lives insofar as he lives in subservience to His Supreme Lord. He loses himself in virtual nothingness when he defies this life-giving subordination.

There is a specific doctrine of a natural hierarchy and gradation of souls in Dvaita Vedānta. It is called Tāratamya. This gradation implies on the one hand the possibility of some selves resisting the emancipating grace of the Lord and on the other the continuance of gradation in the state of release also. The souls are many and are also of many levels of natural potency. Within the limits of nature determined thereby the free initiative of the Jīvas operates. This doctrine of Tāratamya combines in Dvaita with the doctrine of Karma to explain the riddle of evil. Śaiva-Siddhānta and Viśiṣṭādvaita have to rely only on the law of Karma to meet the problem of evil. Grace is inherent in the Divine nature and its possibility is infinite but its actualization in the direction of working out human salvation requires the fulfilment of the secondary condition of human aspiration and effort in that direction. We must choose to be chosen.

VII Nature

The philosophy of nature outlined in these schools follows the Sāṃkhya pattern insofar as it traces the diversified world of phenomenal reality to a single root-principle, Avyakta, Prakṛiti or Māyā, regards causation as the continuity of substance passing through variations of forms or states, utilizes the doctrine of guṇas for explaining the cosmic evolution of diverse effects and does not adopt an indiscriminating attitude of rejection or acceptance of nature. Nature is no illusion; nor is it a self-sufficient and self-explanatory system. So much is common ground for all the three systems. Common is also the account of the five gross elements, their subtle bases, the ten senses and the mind, and the apparatus of Ahaṃkāra (ego-hood) and Mahāt (cosmic intellect). There are certainly minor differences from Sāṃkhya and also among the systems in details but they do not amount to a deviation from the fundamental mould of Seśvara-Sāṃkhya.

But the Śaiva-Siddhānta makes an advance beyond this structure and it is to be noted that all schools of Śaivism and even the original Śaiva Āgamas contain this completing supplement. They maintain that the Sāṃkhya view is an account of the lower order of creation and that there is a higher order which is also more basic.

The highest reality is Paramaśiva and in Him are housed all divine perfections, such as Chit, Ānanda, Jñāna, Kriyā, Icchā. He bursts forth into formations such as Śiva, Śakti, Sadāśiva, Īśvara and Vidyā. The subjectivity of Parama-Śiva thus takes on objectivity through a gradual process of self-exercise. The external 'this' (Idam) thereby comes to be shaped into existence.

Perhaps, this doctrine of Śaivism corresponds to the four Vyuhas posited by Pāñcharātra. There we have Vāsudeva manifesting all His six attributes of Jñāna (knowledge), Bala (power), Aiśvarya (Lordship), Vīrya (energy), Śakti (potency), and Tejas (radiance). Vāsudeva is also the exalted object of the adoration of the liberated Jīvas. He partially suppresses the other attributes and exercises only Jñāna and Bala and becomes Saṃkarṣaṇa. Saṃkarṣaṇa, presides over dissolution and sleep and imparts Śāstra for the next creation. With Aiśvarya and Vīrya as dominant attributes, he becomes Pradyumna and creates the world and maintains Dharma. He is the presiding Deity of Dreams. As Aniruddha He exercises predominantly Śakti and Tejas, presides over waking, conducts the world-process and leads the Jīvas towards emancipation. The three later Vyuhas are also associated in a special manner with the psychic entities, the Jīva, the manas and Ahaṃkāra. But the Pāñcharātra thesis relates to the cosmic process and the moulding of souls, while the Śaiva scheme is pre-cosmic in its idea.

To continue with Śaivism, there is a next plane of descent for Parama-Śiva after Vidyā (knowledge). He gives rise to Māyā, Kala, Niyati, Rāga, and Avidyā. Māyā emerges in this stage as the inscrutable principle making for ignorance and misapprehension. Time introduces the phenomenon of sequence. Kala brings about partial exercise of spiritual powers. Niyati sets up the causal law. Rāga is mundane desire and Avidyā is plain nescience. In this plane the individual self is clothed with the attributes of Saṃsāra and is covered by a sixfold sheath.

The next phase of descent is the Sāṃkhyan scheme starting from prakṛiti. Altogether, apart from the primordial and supreme Śiva, we have thirty-six principles or levels of His self-manifestation including the jīva in his state of bondage. This entire realm of the phenomenal universe from Māyā downwards effectively ties up the individual soul in his career of transmigration. Hence it is fittingly called 'pāśa', the rope, tying up the 'paśu'—the Jīva, who has turned away from his great Master overflowing with Grace, the 'pati'. At its roots the 'pāśa' functions through three defilements in the Jīva. They are 'Anava', the factor of self-contraction, Māyā, the factor of nescience and Karma, the factor of wrong-doing.

VIII God and the Cosmos

It is time that we considered in a definitive manner the relation between God and the world of finite selves and nature in these theistic systems. In the first place the systems are positive that the two finite categories are real and not projections of Māyā. They differentiate their position sharply from the illusionism of Yogāchāra Buddhism, Mādhyamika Nihilism and Advaita Vedānta. They are also positive that the finite reals are not identical or one in substance with the ultimate principle. It is in this connection that the Dvaita Vedānta formulates its famous doctrine of fivefold difference (Pañcha-Bheda). Each Jīva differs from other Jīvas, from God and from physical nature. Physical nature differs from God and from the Jīvas, and also each physical entity differs from other physical entities. God transcends both; and within Himself in respect to his form, attributes, manifestations, activities and essential substance, He is an indivisible unity. This sharply stated pluralism is considerably mitigated by the theory that the world is utterly dependent on God in respect of existence, function and knowability. This relation of dependence applies to selves also and selves are further spoken of as reflections or images of God. They are pratibimbas, and the term is defined as signifying dependence and similarity. The image in this context does not connote either transitoriness or illusoriness. Madhva gives the glorious analogy of the Sun and the rainbow to bring out the relation of Brahman to the cosmos. This status of reality, of distinctness and dependence, characterizes the finite soul in the state of release also. The only difference is that in that ideal condition there is a conscious enjoyment of that status by the perfect spirit.

In Viśiṣṭādvaita and Śaiva-Siddhānta an additional imagery is brought in to throw light on the relation. This is one of the happiest concurrences in the philosophy of Theism. The universe inclusive of the finite selves is conceived of as the body of God and God is the ultimate soul of the cosmic totality. This concept is presented grandly in the Bṛihadāraṇyaka Upaniṣad and Rāmānuja elaborates it to perfection. Śaiva-Siddhānta adopts it. Śrī Kaṇṭha in his commentary on the Brahma-Sūtras uses it as a foundation. The body is defined as that which is supported, operated and used by the soul. It loses its being and intelligibility apart from the soul. The soul pervades, sustains, functions through and appropriates the body to its own ends. This is perhaps one of the richest notions contributed by Indian Theism to Theistic thought in general. It duly preserves the centrality of God and attaches finite realities to Him in organic inseparability. Dvaita too, as it accepts the Bṛihadāraṇyaka Upaniṣad, does accept this fundamental thought with its own refinements of meaning.

It is interesting that in Vālmīki's Rāmāyaṇa, in Parāśara's Viṣṇu Purāṇa and in Kālidāsa's invocatory verses we find definite anticipations of this illuminating thought. Kālidāsa seems to be simply adopting a well-known Śaivite thought of antiquity when he utilizes it in his great prayers. At one stroke Theism is rescued by this thesis from Illusionism, Pantheism, and Deism and the outcome is a Monistic Theism.

IX The Ultimate Good

A great deal has already been hinted at with regard to the supreme goal of life propounded in these theistic systems. It is not Nirvāṇa understood as extinction of personality; nor is it just freedom from pāśa, the source and mechanism of bondage. It is a positive life of conscious realization. The characteristic of this consciousness is that it is positive Ānanda. But this consciousness and bliss are not just the fruits of self-recovery, the individual self attaining to a possession of its own fundamental nature. It lies fundamentally in the attainment of God, the Pati, by way of direct experience, love and service. It is fullness of life attained in and through self-integration with God.

This integration is no dissolution of the individual in God. It is not his shedding of individuality and the passing away of his essence into the substance of the universal spirit. Nor is it just the rectification of the error and illusion of individuality as against universal being. Individuality is no accidental state of the self and it is no illusion either. The self is ineradicably a self-identity, a uniquely individual entity. The attainment of God carries to perfection its individuality, and its powers of thought, will and feeling reach fullness of actualization in the beatific vision of God. It is a union by way of apprehension, adoration and loving service that the soul's integration with God signifies. There is self-recovery through self-dedication.

X The Pathways to Salvation

It is remarkable that these are the schools of Indian thought in which the concept of divine grace receives utmost valuation. It is true that the older religious literature does contain the doctrine of grace. A slight introduction of it into philosophical thought takes place in Yoga, Nyāyavaiśeṣika, Advaita Vedānta and even Mahāyāna Buddhism. But a full doctrine of grace and grace exalted as the supreme and ultimate power making for man's liberation has blossomed only in these Theistic schools. It is admitted by all the three systems that grace is the principal means of salvation and whatever a man does by way of spiritual effort is just a contributory factor, facilitating the unimpeded operation of grace. Man is to be freed ultimately by the abundance of God's compassion. In

Śaivism, a special concept is fashioned for the purpose and it is 'Śakti-pat'. In Dvaita and Viśiṣṭādvaita the ordinary notion of 'Anugraha' or 'Prasāda' meets the need.

It is characteristic of these doctrines that they conceive of grace as coming into effective operation in response to human aspiration and endeavour. These subserve a condition for the flow of grace although they do not bring it into being. Grace has been waiting for all eternity and for it to function a yearning invocation is necessary. It is that subsidiary condition that human Sādhanā accomplishes. That condition is what makes grace a factor that fulfils and not what negates. Autonomy is required of the aspirant if his liberation is not a matter of coercion but a consummation of his quest. Thus a fine reconciliation of grace and human effort is worked out.

The effort in its turn is manifold and shapes itself through many stages. In its ultimate phase it is characterized as self-surrendering love. It is Bhakti and Prapatti. Viśiṣṭādvaita elaborates this element of surrender immensly and to the point of making it a means independent of Bhakti itself. But the normal procedure is Bhakti terminating in or growing out of surrender and always containing it. It is love duly subordinating the lover to the beloved.

The characteristic of the highest type of Bhakti is that it is founded on knowledge. Madhva insists that it must spring from an understanding of the majesty of God (Māhātyma-Jñāna-pūrva). For Rāmānuja Bhakti is a form of knowledge (Jñāna-viśeṣa). In Śaiva-Siddhānta, among the elements of Sādhanā, Charyā, Kriyā, Yoga and Jñāna, the last is the climax. So the three schools are inherently free from the emotional excess and ritualistic aberrations of the popular sentiment of Bhakti. The exaltation of Jñānī Bhakta recorded in the Gītā stands firm and strong. In reality love can ascend to its greatest heights only when founded on clarity of vision.

The introduction of the factor of Jñāna gives rise to some conventional conflicts. Jñāna dissociated from Karma is the standard Advaitic notion of Sādhanā. This would be natural for a school which adheres to the belief in the unreality of the world in which Karma has to be performed. The world of action is a world of change and plurality. But the Theistic schools discard that view of the illusoriness of the world. Action does bind the agent when he puts himself as the sovereign factor into his action. But when he effaces his ego and puts God in its place, the same way of work can acilitate his inward spiritual progress.

The theistic schools accord to moral endeavour by way of works . decidedly higher place in the scheme of spiritual life. The Gītā urnishes the framework. The Karma in that context includes ituals but is not exhausted by them. Some older Vedic rituals re dropped, and new ones inculated in Śaiva and Vaiṣṇava levotionalism find their way into the field. All activity, even that upposedly secular in common parlance, goes into the composition of the Karma under consideration. Only the inner aspect of Karma, he Bhāva rather than the Kriyā, is of value. If the source of action n the heart and soul is undefiled by egoism and is oriented God-vard, it supplies the necessary strength to Jñāna. Thus the Bhakti of these advanced Theisms is no mere contemplation indifferent o ethics or morality. Jñāna built up on the basis of Karma, and ising to self-surrendering Bhakti is the complete pathway to God. No wonder the God of Grace fosters, accepts and fulfils this lofty and ntegral devotion. The inclusion of Karma and Jñāna in Bhakti loes not reduce or minimize the fervour or magnitude of love. Karma is great insofar as it issues in the illumination of knowledge and knowledge justifies and amplifies itself in the height of love it can lead to, and such love reaches the peak. Love including and emerging beyond these does not minimize the role of divine grace but rather creates conditions for its unlimited operation. The greater the love of man to God, the greater is the space for God's self-imparting grace. The last word in the journey to God is 'Arul', Compassion and Grace'.

PART FIVE

The Modern Period

INTRODUCTION

People and movements offer two foci for the study of Indian hought in the Modern Period. The chapters in this section include ne on Aurobindo, a modern counterpart of the ancient riṣis and ounder of a noted aśram at Pondicherry. Another is on Rabindra-ath Tagore, the most prominent leader of the nineteenth century enaissance in the Arts. A third deals with Gandhi, the social and olitical leader and reformer whose life ended tragically in 1948. n addition we have a chapter on Ramakrishna and the Ramkrishna Iovement which typifies in many ways theological and practical hanges occurring in Hinduism in the nineteenth and twentieth enturies.

A major characteristic of the Modern Period was the impingement n India of western ideologies and institutions. In politics demo-racy became the basic philosophy and form of government. In ocial philosophy equalitarianism and freedom were rallying cries round which reforms were organized. In academic circles a study f western philosophies and philosophers was introduced into the hilosophy curriculums of many Indian universities in the 1800's nd 1900's as illustrated by the book, *Chief Currents of Contemporary hilosophy* by D. M. Datta published in 1950. While some of it eals with Indian thought the main portion is concerned with such ems as Hegelianism and Neo-Hegelianism, T. H. Green's Idealism, he Absolute Idealism of F. H. Bradley along with Bosanquet's, oyce's and Hocking's, Italian Idealism in the person of Croce, ergson's Process Philosophy, the Pragmatism of Pierce, James and ewey, Realism and the Neo-Realism of G. E. Moore, Bertrand ussell and American Realists, British Empiricism and the Sense-atum School, C. L. Morgan and Samuel Alexander, the philos-phers of Emergent Evolution, Whitehead's philosophy of Organism,

Logical Positivism and the Analysis Movement, Existentialism ar finally the Japanese philosophy of Zen and Mu.

Jadunath Sinha's book, *Introduction to Philosophy*, which appear at about the same time illustrates the penchant for wester philosophy also. It was "... intended to serve as an Introductic to Contemporary Philosophy" and "... was adopted to the ne syllabus of the B. A. Honours Examination of Calcutta University It deals with the same persons and topics listed in Datta's book an in addition discusses Descartes, Locke, Hume, Leibniz, Kant, Herbe Spencer, Berkeley, Schilling, J. S. Mill, Nietzsche, Sartre, Evolutio Teleology, Empiricism, Personal Idealism, Naturalism, Mechanism Primary and Secondary Qualities, Lamarck, Materialism, Atomism Gestaltism, and Freud. The result of such studies was that India thinkers were pressed to consider new problems posed by wester philosophers which the new science, positivism and empiricism ha stimulated, and also to rethink their own philosophical and religio traditions, the latter having gained greater prominence recentl One consequence has been the development of "integral" philo ophies, Aurobindo's being an outstanding example.

In religion the Samājs illustrate two ways Indians reacted to th penetration of western views. One response of Indian thought wa withdrawal into itself or a turning back to earlier traditions an concepts. The Arya Samāj founded by Swāmī Dayānanda in 187 was representative in several ways of this alternative. Dayānand attempted to revive the pure "Aryan faith" of the past. One que tion raised by Christianity in India was that of authority. Orthodo Christians adjudicated their claims on the authority of the Bibl It was the sole source of universal religious truth and offered a men the way of salvation. Dayānanda stoutly opposed this view He admitted the need for an authority but asserted that for the Hind there is only one, namely, the Vedas. He, as Sarma points ou "took his stand on the infallible authority of the Vedas." The are the "word of God" and are "absolutely free from error and ar an authority unto themselves."[1]

Other tenets of Hinduism criticized by Christians were its doctrin of Karma and rebirth. Dayānanda staunchly upheld them, nc only in the face of Christian opposition but of Indian laxity as wel for many Indians, especially among the intellectuals, had simpl become agnostics, professing nothing, Indian or Western. H asserted that salvation consists in freeing oneself from Māyā an becoming one with Brahman and that this is primarily a process of self-effort requiring several lives for its accomplishment. Man must save himself instead of being saved by an incarnation sent from God.

Dayānanda opposed an English type education in the schools and urged Sanskrit and the Vedas as the core of the curriculum. He stressed the ancient ideals of brahmacharya (chastity) and sannyāsa (renunciation). He upheld the sixteen traditional Saṃskāras (ritual practices), claiming "their due and proper observance is obligatory on all," and also insisted on the old rites of upāsanā (communion with Brahman through Yoga) and Agnihotra (fire offering). While nationalistic and traditional and thus an exponent of the Indian way, Dayānanda was critical, nevertheless, of some aspects of that way. He reacted positively to western influence in his supporting of important social reforms such as the abolishing of suttee (widow-burning), child-marriages, and the ban against widows remarrying. Furthermore, like many other reformers, he was opposed to both idol worship and the caste system, declaring that neither had any sanction in the Vedas.

The parent Brāhmo Samāj founded by Rammohun Roy in 1828 and its protege set up by Keshub C. Sen in 1866 illustrates a second reaction to western thought, namely assimilation and eclectism. Sen's method was to fuse certain aspects of Christianity and Hinduism into a new religion, "a sort of conglomerate of Brahmo rationalism, Vaiṣṇava emotionalism, Christian super-naturalism and Vedāntic mysticism,"[2] as one author rather disparagingly put it.

Sen rejected the central claim of Christianity that Christ is God's incarnation sent to save all mankind and held instead that Christ is but one of a series of saviours or prophets appearing in history, whose coming will be climaxed by a new religion. This "New Dispensation," as he called it, will grow out of and combine elements of past and present religions, but will not be like any one of them. It will accept and use in its religious services the best of the scriptures of all religions. It will incorporate in its rituals only practices which give dignity and demurity to worship.

The new Faith will include all mankind and unite all men in a close brotherhood. This will be readily accomplished because God resides in every person and not outside of the world. When men recognize God in themselves and each other, they will come together in a world of fellowship. The new religion will not countenance idol worship since such aids are not necessary. All one needs to do is to look within himself and see God and realize him in practice. Love is the chief attribute of God and the basis for the brotherhood of man. The social correlate of such love is a classless society. Sen staunchly opposed caste as a denial of the true practice of religion. The ideal of universal love compelled him to advocate and through his efforts legislation was actually brought about 1872 which sanctioned civil marriage, legalized inter-caste marriage, abolished child-marriage, prohibited bigamy and permitted remarriage of widows. In addition Sen supported temperance reforms, the education of women and the printing of religious tracts in the vernacular. He also opposed Zenana (the seclusion of women) and in the Brāhmo Samāj churches women were not made to sit behind screens, apart from the congregation, during public worship.

Thus on the one hand we have in both the Ārya and the Brāhmo Samājs an acceptance of western social concepts such as equality and freedom and attempts to implement them in Indian society. On the other hand we find in them two different reactions, rejection and assimilation, as far as western religious beliefs and practices are concerned. Ramakrishna offered a third alternative which will be discussed in a subsequent chapter.

Although chapters on them could not be included, persons such as Sarvepalli Radhakrishnan and K. C. Bhattacharya should be noted as influential twentieth-century Indian thinkers. Radhakrishnan was both philosopher and statesman. He was well versed in western and Indian thought and one of his major goals was to elucidate and synthesize both. His numerous writings are widely read and influential among large numbers of people, East and West.

Bhattacharya's influence, on the other hand, has been primarily in intellectual circles. He took as his chief concern the nature of the Absolute and began with Kant's question of its knowability. Bhattacharya does not believe it is unknowable, as Kant asserts; but then, one must first determine what is meant by knowable or in what senses we use the term knowable. Bhattacharya did not write extensively. But his is a profound philosophy and, of it, Datta writes: "...to Bhattacharya lies the credit of conceiving an entire scheme of logic, metaphysics, philosophy of secular spirit, of religion and of the absolute in the light of the indefinite, and assigning a place to each of the apparently conflicting systems of logic, metaphysics and philosophy, justifying its claim to truth in the light of his conception of truth as manifold, i.e. as the possible alternative revelations of the indefinite absolute."[3]

In characterizing recent philosophy in India one must note that the twentieth-century British Analytical Movement and, more specifically, Language Analysis, has been an influence, although not as dominant a one as in the United States and Britain. Diversity has continued in India. P. T. Raju notes that "Besides the above trends, one can come across, among the younger generation of philosophers, varieties of Marxists, logical positivists, linguistic analysts, different kinds of realists and idealists, and followers of several other recent western traditions."[4]

There are those who would say that the Analytical Movement is not necessarily a desirable legacy and that it has been a major factor in making contemporary philosophy trivial and in-grown. One hears students in American colleges and universities often say that the philosophy being taught is meaningless and irrelevant. The editor recalls such a sentiment being echoed in India too. Perhaps a problem beginning to confront Indian philosophers is the one which American philosophers already face, namely that of revelance, or whether what they talk about is meaningful to the lives of students and the world in which they live. What will happen to philosophy, if it is not?

15

AUROBINDO

R. R. DIWAKAR

I HIS LIFE

In India philosophy is called Darśana of which there may b said to be two types, one derived mainly from an intellectua perception of things based on sense-data, the other grounded pri marily in intuition and/or mystic experience. There are also tw types of philosophers, those who spin out and are satisfied with systematic and logical theory of reality, and others who are intent o applying their philosophy to their own and others' lives. In Indi most philosophers are of the latter type. For instance Śaṅkara Rāmānuja and Madhva were intensely occupied with spiritua disciplines and practices aimed at attaining the highest kind relationship between themselves and the Divinity. While the ap proach of the first type of philosopher strikes one as intellectual abstract and impersonal, the latter's is not less intellectual but is more practical, personal, warm and human approach.

Aurobindo, while relentlessly logical, is intuitionistic and mystica in his method. Mystic here does not mean mysterious or secret bu refers to an experience one undergoes with one's whole being. Suc an experience is final for that person, convincing to the mind an satisfying to the heart. Not only are the senses, intellect and cons cious self involved, but the emotional self, the subconscious and th total integrated personality are also. The result is that the tota being of the person concerned is imbued and becomes one with th experience which is indubitable and unquestionable.

Aurobindo was born in Calcutta in 1872. His father was quit anglicized in habit and outlook. Determined that his childre be schooled in English ways and institutions, he sent Aurobind when seven with two elder brothers to England. Aurobind lived in an English clergyman's family in Manchester, went t

t. Paul's School in London in 1885 and to King's College, ambridge, in 1890 for two years. Passing the competition for the adian Civil Service in 1890, he did not care to present himself for ding test and was disqualified for I. C. S. Meanwhile he met the aekwar of the state of Baroda, then visiting London, and obtained a appointment in the Baroda Service from him.

Aurobindo was in that Service from 1893 to 1906, first in the evenue Department and secretariat work, then as Professor of nglish and French and finally, Vice Principal of Baroda College. iving in England from his seventh to twenty-first years Aurobindo ecame well acquainted with ancient, medieval and modern western ulture but was ignorant of his own. He made up that deficiency t Baroda, learning Sanskrit and several modern Indian languages, nd assimilating the spirit of Indian civilization. These were years f self-culture, literary activity and preparation for future work. Much of the latter part of this period was spent on leave in silent olitical activity, Aurobindo's official position debarring him from ublic activity. The Swadeshi Movement against the partition of engal in 1905 provided an opportunity to give up the Baroda Service nd to engage openly in politics. He left Baroda in 1906 and went to Calcutta as Principal of the newly-founded National College.

Aurobindo's political career was a stormy one. At Cambridge he poke occasionally at the Indian Majlis and toyed with a revolu-ionary secret society, the Lotus and the Dagger. When in Baroda ervice he wrote anonymous articles in *Indu-prakash* advocating xtremist action and praising popular political heroes. In 1902 he oined a revolutionary society in Maharashtra and secretly en-ouraged similar activity in Bengal. After the Alipore Bomb ase in 1908, in which he was acquitted, his views began to change. Aurobindo then wrote that Brahmatej is greater than Kshatratej—he moral power of truth and purity, the power of the tapas is greater han the mere power of arms. "My Last Will and Testament" in *Karmayogin*, written on the eve of his departure to Pondicherry in 1910 advocates substantially the non-cooperation method Gandhi ater used successfully. While in Pondicherry until his death in 1950 Aurobindo was approached a number of times to return to politics but he replied he was seeking a higher spiritual centre from which to act, and he saw no reason to abandon that quest for any immediate political results.

II His Philosophical Background

Philosophy is as natural to man as poetry. While poetry stems mainly from man's emotions and imagination, philosophy is the result primarily of reason. The two overlap however. Since they are both products of the body, life and mind of man, and the myriad experiences he goes through, they cannot be exclusive of each other. This is especially true in the case of Aurobindo. He was as great a poet as a philosopher. He worked for several decades on *Savitri*, his magnum opus in poetry. During those years his philosophy was formulated in many writings, culminating in the two volumes *Life Divine*. Its very title is more poetical than philosophical. So is the title *Savitri*, a saga of the human soul, through which his philosophy runs like an ever present undercurrent. We may understand Aurobindo's thought more readily if we realize that in him the poetic and philosophic, the emotional and rational are blended into one.

His views will be more easily understood also, if we recognize that he studied western philosophy first and then eastern, and especially Indian, thought. Thus Indian philosophy was superimposed on the western thought he had already imbibed, before both intermingled and blended into a single flow. This sequence has left its mark on his writing method, as when he struggles hard to express his thoughts in English and then suddenly quotes in Sanskrit from Indian sources. The English words and idioms he uses fall short of expressing his full meaning so he falls back on Sanskrit terms. While the assimilation of western with eastern thought is there, the final mould emerging is a digest with the full and original impress of his own thinking and experience.

The earlier western influences on Aurobindo include the historical and scientific approach, a recognition of the powerful, inclusive evolutionary principle and the relentless pursuit of the truth of existence. Aurobindo approached Indian thought and spiritual ideals with that background. This gave him an unusual opportunity of viewing the traditional thought, wisdom and yogic discipline of India and the East in the light of a western perspective. Endowed with an imaginative power freed from orthodoxy, he could burrow deeply into the history and development of human consciousness and with equal ease behold a future vision of evolving humanity on all levels. Equally familiar with the ancient and modern philosophies and mysticism of the West, he delved deeply into the mystic regions of the soul familiar to the Vedic and Upaniṣadic Ṛiṣiṣ. He mastered the coordinating effort of the Gītā and practised the profound yoga of total human perfection. All these and many more similarly significant things enabled Aurobindo to reach certain heights and from there pour forth effortlessly in flowing torrents of limpid English, in prose and poetry, in interviews and conversations, in letters and wordless guidance, a wisdom which is neither eastern nor western but embraces both, a philosophy of thought and action which is a total, integral philosophy of life and being, a synthesis of material and spiritual existence which goes beyond the dualities of being and becoming but which involves a simultaneity of both, initially and eternally.

While the idea of evolution influenced Aurobindo strongly, his originality consists in giving it a new meaning, namely that it is a psychical as well as biological evolution with the capacity to mould matter itself, giving it a new capacity and deeper meaning. Thus we find in his philosophy not a superman as usually conceived but a being who uses matter not as it is but as it has been transformed into a far more plastic and subtler material. It is almost a new world being used by a new man. It is not like a child who grows in the same body of flesh, blood and bone but a spirit which moulds out of existing material a subtler and nobler instrument for a higher existence.

Another aspect of Aurobindo's thought is that it is both an intellectual structure and a philosophy to be lived and tested in experience. This is because his Yogic Sādhanā of spiritual practices and experiences and his philosophical views developed simultaneously. Aurobindo's primary urge and purpose was not merely to see and know but "to be". To him knowing was but a means to being. In one sense knowledge is power and knowing is being, just as means are ends. But the most important link between them, the will, must be there to pursue to the last till the ends are achieved. In Aurobindo it was his will to utilize every opportunity of accumulating knowledge to make the corresponding effort to attain the highest poise indicated by knowledge, that took him from stage to stage for fulfilment.

Like other philosophers Aurobindo sought the Truth of being and becoming through an examination of the material and the instruments for it available to him in his own consciousness. In Aurobindo the whole field of total consciousness is before his mind, not just that part of it which we are conscious of. Our conscious life is but a small part of what we call consciousness just as the visible part of an iceberg is only one-seventh of the whole, the rest being submerged in and one with the vast ocean of cosmic existence. Jung calls it the "unconscious"; but Aurobindo thinks more in terms of the "superconscious". He says that what may be unconscious in our eyes is supremely conscious, being the matrix which contains everything pertaining to consciousness.

Though we frequently use the words objective and subjective, there is really nothing strictly objective, as no object can be cognized or characterized unless there is a subject to do so; and, as soon as there is a subject to cognize, the object is subjectivized, so to speak. No subject can perceive or cognize any object except by his own consciousness; and, as soon as the object is a part of the subject's consciousness, it ceases to be an object. Thus no one can go out of and beyond his own consciousness. Whatever is experienced in one's own consciousness is already an integral part of that consciousness. It is only from the point of view of purposive action that we use the words subjective and objective. Philosophers through the ages have sought the truth in and through their own consciousness. "I think, therefore I am" is a universally experienced truth. But the thought itself is part of oneself and no longer outside one's consciousness!

What is called becoming or change is an eternal process, as eternal as "being" itself. Man's effort is to become aware of it and to bring to bear that awareness into our conscious life so that we can consciously participate in our evolution to the fullest extent possible. This has become possible because man is becoming more and more self-conscious and is conscious of his self-consciousness and thus has developed the faculty of introspection. He is now aware of the direction in which his evolution lies and is capable of participating in his own evolution to the extent of his awareness and his will to hasten that evolution. That is why Aurobindo says for man "Yoga is conscious evolution". If we constantly remember that, in his view "All life is Yoga," we shall be able to understand better his philosophy and action.

III Poorna Yoga

Aurobindo, as he himself said, was not a philosopher in that

He did not deliberately attempt to found a school of philosophy. Instead, as he proceeded with his spiritual Sādhanā he percieved certain truths, experienced particular conditions of consciousness, penetrated beyond the multiple veils of psychic phenomena and found himself in the presence of the eternally evolving Spiritual Person in His infinite power and superabundant joyful play. The laws which he discovered operating in that Divine Play and sought to express are what may be called Aurobindo's philosophy. The discipline and practices which he followed in experiencing the instant and constant presence of the Spiritual Person, the Puruṣottama within and around him, may be called Aurobindo's yoga. Yoga is the science of the eternal communion of the individual with the Universal Self. It deals with the method or means leading to that communion and to living in that ecstatic delight of integral union.

In that sense Aurobindo was more of a Mahāyogī than a philosopher, more a path-finder to what he called Poorna or Integral Yoga than a follower of any existing Yoga schools. His Integral Yoga is not the Yogic discipline of an individual yogi who would merge his self in the Universal Self in supernal bliss, but is one which attempts the collective or social salvation of all humanity, present and future, by a process of conscious evolution. Aurobindo's yoga is integral also in embracing Spirit and Matter as two nodes of the same Reality; and its ambition is to spiritualize all matter and divinize all life. His yoga is not an escape of the soul from matter, life and mind as inferior modes of Spirit manifestation; rather it strives to attain the highest consciousness in order to see that material, vital and mental existence is transformed into a higher instrument for ever higher transcendence. Thus Aurobindo's yoga accepts everything as coming from the Supreme Person. So evil is but a negative aspect of good; darkness is want of light, having no positive content. All that exists is on an eternal march of spiritual evolution which is without beginning or end. How can eternity end and infinity conclude its course? Such perception, when matured and perfected, will make way for the realization of the eternal pilgrimage of the self to the Supreme Person and His constant presence in everything and everywhere.

Apart from breath control (prāṇāyāma) and concentration Aurobindo began a serious practice of Yoga in 1905. His first step was to gather into it the essential elements of the spiritual experiences of religious leaders everywhere. He then continued in search of a more complete experience, uniting and harmonizing the two mode of existence, Matter and Spirit. Most ways of Yoga are paths to the Beyond leading to the Spirit and away from active life. Aurobindo's Integral Yoga rises to the Spirit to descend again bringing its light, power and bliss into the life of the world to transform it. Man's present existence in the material world, according to Aurobindo, is a life of ignorance with inconscience at its base; but even in its darkness and nescience the presence and possibilities of the Divine are involved. The created world is not a mistake or illusion to be cast aside by the soul returning to Heaven or Nirvāna but the scene of a spiritual evolution by which out of this material inconscience is to emerge progressively the Divine Consciousness in things.

Mind is the highest dimension yet reached in the spiral of the present cycle of evolution, but it is not the highest of which existence is capable. Above it is a Supermind or eternal Truth-Consciousness which is in its nature the self-aware and self-determining light and power of Divine Knowledge. Mind is an ignorance seeking after Truth, but this Supermind is a self-existent knowledge harmoniously manifesting the play of its forms and forces. It is only by the descent of this Supermind that the perfection dreamed of by all that is highest in humanity can come. It is possible for man by opening himself to a greater divine consciousness to rise to this power of light and bliss, discover his true self, remain in constant union with the Divine and bring down the Supramental Force for the transformation of mind, life and body. Its realization was the aim of Aurobindo's Yoga.

IV Involution, Evolution, the Absolute, Supermind

Aurobindo begins by observing his own self as cognizer on the one hand and the other-than-self on the other. His next step is to find the relationship between the two. But that is not all. One must know from whence, why, and how are the self, non-self, their relationship and the causus causa of all these? Finally, what is the relationship between the self, non-self and the ultimate cause?

The three apparently ultimate categories of self, non-self and ultimate cause are not static but in constant motion, Aurobindo says. Even matter, supposedly inert, is tremendously active. Each atom has a nucleus round which electron, protons and what not revolve swiftly. Thus movement is the essence of phenomena; and, unless we take into consideration its nature and cause, our search is incomplete. If matter is evolving or changing every moment, the observing self cannot be static either. A philosophy of things cannot, therefore, be static but must move with the discoveries of science. Aurobindo's philosophy is thus dynamic because it takes evolution fully into account. But evolution from where and towards what is the question again.

From Aurobindo's view time cannot be split into periods, whether seconds, centuries or eons. Existence cannot convert itself into non-existence. Instead we are dealing with an infinity and eternity which has neither beginnig nor end. Infinity of space, meaning transcendence of space, and eternity of time, meaning transcendence of time, are what philosophy deals with. Even the categories we start with are not separate, isolated existents with lives and laws of their own but are integrated into a totality, a whole which alone exists fundamentally. Relativities are creations of our limited minds and are necessary for action. In philosophy we go beyond those limitation in order to glimpse the totality and basic truth of things. This is the perspective from which Aurobindo looks at things, questions evolution and arrives at the answer that involution precedes evolution. It is only initial involution which can call for evolution. They are the two inseparable aspects of the truth of existence.

Aurobindo conceives of the order of involution (the process of higher to lower) as Existence (sat), Consciousness-force (chit), Bliss (Ānanda), Supermind, Mind, Psyche (soul), Life, Matter. Involution starts, if what is eternal can have a start, as a result of the will of the Absolute. We call it "will" because we have no other word to use. However, it is neither will nor non-will, being beyond the power of man to know. Nevertheless, we begin with involution and try to know the how of the evolution which follows it.

Aurobindo's view of evolution is that at the present stage matter, life, psyche, and mind have been evolving and the next step would be the Supermind leading to Bliss or Life Divine. Here Aurobindo has introduced a new idea, the conscious participation of man in the present and coming stages of evolution. The dawn of the Supermind is already on the horizon; but, since man has become self-conscious and capable of understanding evolution, he can and must hasten the process by his efforts and keep himself ready for the stage when Supermind replaces Mind. Man as the advance guard of higher humanity has transcended geospheric and biospheric existence and is now in the psychospheric. The next step is supremely important as the psychospheric is full of limitations and weaknesses. Man is limited by egoistic urges. His mind is incapable of knowing truth directly, his joy often mixed with sorrow. Of promise, however, is his urge for pure joy, his appreciation of selfless love, and his desire for transcendence.

All that can follow when the Supermind predominates. It is capable of truth-consciousness, unbounding joy, and unselfish, pure love. Aurobindo's view, unlike others, is that transcendence is not a leaving behind of mind, life and matter as they are and assuming new garb but a transformation or even a transmutation of mind, life and matter. He envisions even earthly immortality as a possibility, since matter and life can be transformed by the power of the Supermind to yield richer dividends by becoming purer, subtler and capable of sustaining life in the material body indefinitely.

Evolution therefore for Aurobindo means both a higher stage of mind and all consciousness and a simultaneous transformation of matter itself. Thus Heaven or higher levels of existence do not mean merely an escape of the soul to higher regions but the transformation of gross matter and our bodies and faculties into nobler instruments of life divine. Aurobindo says this is the duty and function of man, now awakened to the possibility of the Supermind possessing and sublimating the whole of terrestrial life pertaining to man.

Aurobindo's view of evolution allows no positive existence to evil, ignorance or darkness. They are negative and temporary. What is happening is that the involved is being evolved. As higher stages are reached, the lower are eliminated without any trace left behind, because the whole process of evolution is the transcending of all by its transformation and transmutation. Aurobindo does not hold that a soul goes successively through bodies of flesh and blood keeping them where they were; rather, in the course of evolution, the gross is transformed into the subtle in order to be an adequate instrument for higher ascension. That ascension Aurobindo calls upon humanity to expedite by the discipline of Yoga. That Yoga has to be integral and whole so that the ascension is total, of body, mind and vital powers. There is not to be a yoga of one faculty only. Man consists of all three together. He is to evolve or ascend in his psyche or soul by invoking the Supermind for transforming the instruments as well, so that the transformation is total. Aurobindo denies the alternate path of escapism from matter into spirit or of individual salvation to the exclusion of humanity. His is the idea of total transcendence, not of one but all, by transformation. The Absolute which is whole and integral cannot consist of bits and pieces and individuals who save themselves alone. To spiritualize and not escape from matter must be the aim of evolution.

Aurobindo arrived at his concept of the Absolute after much meditation on man's life and mind. Normally man is baffled by the dualities and pluralities of his daily experiences and the thought processes which his intellect and logic take him through. Spirit and matter, one and many, black and white, good and evil are all true of human experience. But man's mind is not satisfied with this experience of duality. It wants to discover a unity which it conceives as the basic truth. Aurobindo eliminates this duality by asserting that spirit is matter in intension and matter is spirit in extension. The Absolute is beyond this duality but has the capacity to be both without losing its own absoluteness.

Aurobindo points out that physics has already concluded that what exists in essence is energy, and all we experience is the varied formations of one single, indivisible energy in its infinite and eternal manifestation. This energy cannot be mechanical in its process of manifestation, since infinite variety without mechanical repetition is the characteristic of this manifestation. This indeterminateness and variety is exactly attributable to the "will" of the Absolute which cannot be explained further. This is where the Puruṣottam, the Supreme Person of Aurobindo's, comes in. The manifestation is the Divine Play in which the player, play and witness of the play are all from, in and not beyond, behind or above the Absolute. Here some of the Śānti Mantra of the Ishāvāsya Upaniṣad may be profitably quoted: "Poornamadah poornamidam poornāt poornamudachyate" (From what is whole and complete and perfect eternally and infinitely emerges this cosmos which too is whole, complete and perfect at each moment of its existence). Thus, while duality and plurality are truths of our experience because of the limitations of relativity, everything at every moment of its life is whole and perfect, seen from the point of view of the Absolute and of total reality.

While the Absolute is the fundamental reality, dynamism or movement is also real. Being and becoming, seemingly contradictory, are both there; but both are synthesized in the Absolute which is beyond both. Man must realize that escape from "becoming" is but a partial way. Egoless, passionless, detached existence in "becoming", which is ever evolving in a spiral without losing sight of "being" which is the ground of all "becoming", is the perception which is real spiritual perception and spontaneous "being-becoming" is the final philosophy.

Aurobindo believed that his perception of the Absolute, of which being-becoming are the relative aspects, and which are there because of pure bliss or Ānanda which is the basic characteristic of the Absolute, is confirmed by the Upaniads.ṣ He recognized that we experience evil, sorrow and imperfection. The soul of man longing for pure good, unmixed joys and perfection is hampered by the contradictories of their opposites. Here again, rising above dualities is the way to perceive truth. Matter is not all matter. Spirit is in matter and will transform it into subtler forms. So too, evil, sorrow and imperfection are not totally or finally so. They are only negatively so in the course of involution. The evolution of the human psyche is the remedy which will make us realize the temporariness and negative nature of evil, sorrow and imperfection. Aurobindo is one with other idealists in this matter. The highest condition of the human psyche is "beyond good and evil", the highest joy beyond joy and sorrow. Pleasure and pain are experienced as they are while man is in the lower rungs of the evolutionary ladder. The widening and deepening of consciousness will carry man to a height where pleasure and pain would be equally enjoyable as aspects of essential joyful being. Man has already gone beyond animals in knowing and experiencing evil and sorrow in a different way and from a higher standpoint. His nervous system, his brain power too are capable of experiencing far greater and subtler forms of these things and their contradictions. At the same time man realizes he can go beyond the dualities. Hence his conscious attempts at total bliss which can transcend the dualities and partake of the Ānanda of the Absolute.

Our finite minds and present stage of evolution are responsible for our experiencing of evil, sorrow and imperfection. What can bridge the gulf between such negative aspects of experience and the positive ones of good, joy and perfection? Involved we are; evolve we must. But how or by what force? Aurobindo answers, the Supermind. It is the inherent truth-conscious force of the evolutionary urge. As truth-conscious it is necessarily good, joy and perfection-conscious. While man carries with him all the egative forces and burdens of involution in his subconscious and is hus clogged in his path of evolution, the Supermind in the super-onscious region is carrying man beyond the dualities to the new world f goodness, joyfulness, and perfection. Self-consciousness is but a mall part of man's consciousness. In fact, man cannot be said to e completely conscious of himself even during the whole of his vaking day, not to speak of his hours of sleeping, dreaming and magining. His conscious self is sandwiched between his sub-onsciousness and what is called unconsciousness on the one hand, nd the superconsciousness on the other. Nature seems to have eld together in juxtaposition in man the forces of involution and volution, since man alone among animals is conscious of both involu-ion and evolution. It is man's privilege to know both and to cons-iously participate in the epic adventure of evolution towards higher evels of nobler living in truth-consciousness.

As Supermind is a new concept, it should be characterized. Auro-bindo describes mind as that power of consciousness which tries to nterpret the truth of universal existence for practical uses. It is not he power which either guides existence or which created or mani-ested existence. It is instead the Real-Idea, the Ṛita-chit of the Ṛig-veda. It is "a power of conscious Force expressive of real being, nd partaking of its nature, and neither a child of the void nor a weav-r of fiction. It is conscious Reality throwing itself into mutable orms of its own imperishable and immutable substance." In ubstance, Supermind is the Creative force, power and will to evolve hrough involution to higher and higher levels. Mind is essentially power to analyse and think only in terms of parts and almost lways with a view to action. It is beyond its depths in the realm f conceiving things in their totality. Even when it does, the totality s an aggregate and not an integral whole. The communication etween Supermind and the mind is sometimes through intuition. Aurobindo calls it communication from "above". He says: "Intui-ion brings to man those brilliant messages which are the beginnings f his higher knowledge." But in the course of communication ntuition is often weakened because of the reasoning process.

The conception of the Supermind as the vital link between involu-ion and evolution completes the basic structure of Aurobindo's hilosophy. It cannot be called a pure philosophy or metaphysics s the terms are used normally. What he has stated in his writings his thought and the structure of existence as it presented itself to him. He began with himself as a conscious human being with a the limitations imposed by nature at the present stage of evolutio He takes man's universal inner aspiration to joy, harmony, in mortality and perfection in knowledge and action as the bas urges of evolution from the involution which has taken place. Sin man is conscious of all these and has his conscience pointing to high levels of existence as distinct from lower ones, Aurobindo asks ma to participate consciously in the evolutionary march in the preser cycle. The eternal spiral of ascent is there but what is relevar and immediate is the present cycle.

To sum up, the Absolute is self-existent, eternal, infinite. I nature is Sat (Reality-Truth-Existence), Chit (Consciousness-Forc and Ānanda (Bliss-Joy abounding). Out of Joy and Ānanda an for joy there is creation which is necessarily an involution, a kind lessening of reality or extension of conscious force. In the involutio process Existence, Consciousness-Force, Bliss, Supermind, Min Psyche, Life and Matter is the descending order. In evolutio there must be an ascending order since one cycle has to be complet for the next and higher cycle to begin. The Supermind, the creativ Force, provides the power of ascension. Evolution in Aurobindo' view is not the abandoning of the lower orders of existence but thei transformation and transmutation as evolution proceeds. Man' soul or psyche, when evolving to a higher level is also transformin life and matter to a higher level, thus making them better instrumen of ascension. Here Aurobindo calls upon humanity to participat consciously by Yoga in the evolution already occurring. Yoga the science and art of purifying and developing all man's energi with a view to canalizing them as instruments of illumination an evolution. Since man is self-conscious and has developed the powe to know the good and eschew the evil, he is responsible for helping h own evolution to higher levels. When doing so, he is to transfor his mind, life and matter, and also take the whole of humanity wit him. Evolution is not just the escape of the individual soul to highe levels but is a transformation of the totality of human beings. N doubt Aurobindo has added a new chapter to current ideas of Ve dānta and Yoga. To that extent his is a call for new thought an valuation.

16

RABINDRANATH TAGORE

B. G. Ray

I Tagore and the Indian Tradition

Broadly speaking, Indian thought admits of two main facets. One affirms worldly values and finds their fulfilment in this life and the life beyond, the other affirms spiritual values which can be realized only in the life beyond. According to the second, worldly values are not finally real and a pursuit of them lands us in the realm of mere appearance which falls short of reality. The second one is concerned with spiritual values apart from worldly ones. The Upaniṣads affirm both the personal God and the impersonal Absolute and teach both life-affirmation and life-negation. Advaitin Śaṅkarāchārya attributes final reality only to Brahman or the impersonal Absolute while some Vaiṣṇava sects hold that the personal God and the world constitute ultimate reality.

The poet Rabindranath Tagore's philosophical writings have been deeply influenced by the teachings of the Upaniṣads. All of his philosophical discourses in *Santiniketan, Dharma, Sadhana, Creative Unity, Sanchay, Manuser Dharma, Man, The Religion of Man* and *Personality* have been built on the bedrock of the Upaniṣads. In addition, some of his lyrics and philosophical dramas reflect Upaniṣadic wisdom. In the preface to *Sadhana* Rabindranath confesses: "The writer has been brought up in a family where texts of the Upaniṣads are used in daily worship; and he has had before him the example of his father who lived his long life in the closest communion with God while not neglecting his duties to the world or allowing his keen interest in all human affairs to suffer any abatement." Again, somewhat later he observes: "To me the verses of the Upaniṣads and the teahings of Buddha have ever been things of the spirit and therefore endowed with boundless vital growth." To Rabindranath, that aspect of the Upaniṣadic teaching which treats God as positive, personal, adorable and realizable in love, appeals most. A Vaiṣṇava-ideal is more acceptable to him than a Śaṅkara-goal. Man belongs to God with his soul and the relation between man and God is the relation of love. World and life affirmation leads him to announce:

> "Deliverance is not for me in renunciation. I feel the embrace of freedom in a thousand bonds of delight
> Thou ever pourest for me the fresh draught of thy wine
> of various colours and fragrance, filling this earthen vessel to the brim.
> My world will light its hundred different lamps with thy flame
> and place them before the altar of thy temple.
> No, I will never shut the doors of my senses. The delights of sight and hearing and touch will bear thy delight.
> Yes, all my illusions will turn into the illumination of Joy,
> and all my desires ripen into fruits of love."[1]

When we speak of Vaiṣṇava influence on Rabindranath we must not identify him as an out and out Vaiṣṇava. A Vaiṣṇava does not dismiss the world as Māyā or illusion. He holds that finite individuals and the world are all real. Without them the Godhead is not complete. And man can realize God in pure love. Rabindranath would agree with a Vaiṣṇava on these points. But, according to a Vaiṣṇava, God can be realized only in a supernatural order of existence. Rabindranath, however, thinks that the love-drama between him and his God is being enacted in this sensible world of colour, sound and touch. Salvation is being realized here on this earth of ours. The game of hide-and-seek between the Deity and the devotee is being played in this human life of pleasure and pain, hazard and hardship. Through the portals of death the finite devotee passes from one life to another but every life is a human life radiant with the beauty and harmony of nature. A Vaiṣṇava is ever eager to divinize man but Rabindranath's mission is twofold, the divinizing of man and the humanizing of God.

II God

Rabindranath's God, whom he calls Jīvandevatā, is a great lover. The poet-philosopher says: "There is One and the One says shall become many. The One wanted to appreciate its unity in diversity, so the creation began."[2] God is eternal, man is eternal and love too. In a poem[3] in *Mānasi* he expresses the truth that the lover and the beloved have been loving each other through all eternity. At every birth this love-drama is being enacted anew. God and man are bound up in an indissoluble tie and the truth of the one lies in that of the other. God has separated man from Him so that He can feel the pangs of separation. Though God is one yet He creates within Him a plurality of souls from whom He receives love and adoration. It is undoubtedly a limitation of God but the limitation is self-imposed. There is an eternal thirst in Him for the company of finites. In *Fruit Gathering*:[4]

> "Day after day you buy you sunrise from my heart and you find your love craven into the image of my life."

Again in *Gitanjali*:[5]

> "Thus it is that thy Joy in me is so full. Thus it is that thou hast come down to me. O thou Lord of all heavens, where would be thy love if I were not? Thou hast taken me as thy partner of all this wealth. In my heart is the endless play of thy delight. In my life thy will is ever taking shape. And for this, thou who are the King of kings has decked thyself in beauty to captivate my heart. And for this thy love loses itself in the love of thy lover, and there art thou seen in the perfect union of two."

God (Jīvandevatā) is the Supreme Person. He is goodness (Śiva), beauty (sundara) and truth (satya). Also He is bliss (ānandam). In this world man is engaged in cultivating intrinsic values which are completely and finally realized in God. Rabindranath firmly believes that such values are not the subjective creations of man. They are rooted in an objective reality. Again intrinsic values are all the expressions of one grand value which is bliss (ānandam). Beauty is beauty because of bliss. Truth is truth, or goodness is goodness because of bliss. Intrinsic values are eternally realized in God and man can cultivate them according to his limited capacity.

III Evil

If God is all good, why is there evil and suffering? Rabindranath tackles this age-old problem in his own way. At the very outset it must be admitted that he does not treat evil as an illusion. Rather he accepts the factual existence of evil in the finite world. The question for him is not whether there is evil but is it permanent and absolute? He writes: "Pain which is the feeling of finiteness is not a fixture in our life. It is not an end in itself as Joy is. To meet with it is to know that it has no part in the true permanence of creation."[6] Again he says: "Evil cannot altogether arrest the course of life on the highway and rob it of its possessions. For the evil has to pass on, it has to grow into good; it cannot stand and give battle to All."[7] From the above it is clear that Rabindranath accords to evil a temporary existence in the scheme of the real. The question naturally comes up. Why then should there be evil? Tagore does not believe it is due to some inherent depravity of man. He writes: "This age must be described as the darkest age in human civilization, but I do not despair. As the first bird, when the dawn is still dark, proclaims the rising of the sun, so my heart sings the coming of a great future which is near. We must be ready to welcome this new age. There are some people, who are proud and wise and practical, who say it is not in human nature to be generous, that men will always fight one another, that the strong will conquer the weak, and that there can be no real moral foundation for man's civilization. We cannot deny the facts of their assertion that the strong have power in the human world, but I refuse to accept this as a revelation of truth...."[8]

Tagore answers the problem of evil by saying that the finite self has to attain his true personality, and attainment of true soulhood or personality entails evil and suffering. "It is pain which is our true wealth as imperfect beings, and has made us great and worthy to take our seat with the perfect. He (the true man) knows that we are not beggars; that it is the hard coin which must be paid for everything valuable in this life, for our power, our wisdom, our love; that in pain is symbolized the infinite possibility of perfection, the eternal unfolding of Joy..."[9] The finite self has to realize his own soulhood and this is why he has to walk through pain and suffering. The Mighty God has been leading mankind from untruth to truth, darkness to light and mortality to immortality but the path of alvation is strewn with evils.[10] Rabindranath welcomes the advent of pain as a corrective:

"Thou hast done well, my lover, thou hast done well
to send me thy fire of pain.
For my incense never yields its perfume till it burns,
and my lamp is blind till it is lighted.
When my mind is numb, its torpor must be
stricken by thy love's lightning;
And the very darkness that blots my world burns
like a torch when set afire by thy thunder."[11]

How to face evil? When evil threatens us, we should not fly away n cowardice. Rabindranath suggests: "Come what may, have a trong mooring in your own self. Evils and pains will come and hake the foundation of life but never, never lose confidence."[12] n *Gitanjali* he prays:

"Where the mind is without fear and the head
is held high; where knowledge is free; where the
world has not been broken up into fragments by narrow domestic
walls;
Where words come out from the depth of truth;
Where tireless striving stretches its arms toward perfection;
Where the clear stream of reason has not lost its way
into the dreary desert sand of dead habit;
Where the mind is led forward by thee into ever-widening thought
and action; Into that heaven of freedom, my Father, let my country
awake."[13]

IV Contemporary Ills

The social, political and technological evils of the modern age attracted the notice of the poet-philosopher. He carefully studied their causes and suggested remedies. One cause of contemporary ills is the undue status and effects of science. Tagore's poetic nature leads him to be cautious of science and reason or cold intellect. Tagore does not berate them completely: "Our scientific world is our world of reasoning. It has its greatness and uses and attractions. We are ready to pay the homage due it." However,

"...when it claims to have discovered the real world for us..., the we must say it is like a general grown intoxicated with his powe usurping the throne of his king. For the reality of the world belong to the personality of man and not to reasoning, which is useful an great but which is not the man himself."[14] Tagore believes tha one of the most unfortunate mistakes we make is to transfer ou scientific attitude toward nature over toward men as well. We be come habituated to viewing the material world analytically and wit a utilitarian attitude and we carry that tendency over in viewin man also. No wonder we see others as objects to be used for ou own ends!

Selfishness and narrowness are root causes that lead to many ar evil of our times. Most of the evils arise when we try to live only ir the individual and not in the Universal. There is no happiness ir the little; bliss resides in the Great. The narrow bigoted perspectiv of selfishness has blinded many nations of the world. Suc nationalism is dehumanizing, violent and terrible. Being disguste by the narrow nationalism of the West Rabindranath raised hi voice of protest and warning: "The West must not make herself a curse to the world by using her power for her own selfish needs, bu by teaching the ignorant and helping the weak; she should save her- self, from the worst danger that the strong is liable to incur by making the feeble acquire power enough to resist her intrusion. And als she must not make her materialism to be the final thing, but mus realize that she is doing a service in freeing the spiritual being from the tyranny of matter."[15] He does not like to do away with al nationalism. What he wants is that each nation should respec the personality of the other in a spirit of love and sympathy. Thi principle forms the nucleus of his idea of internationalism.

Tagore's ideal is not that of a closed, bellicose world but an open pluralistic one in which each nation seeks to retain its own identity and at the same time does not let differences come between itself and others. Of the present world he asks: "...does it not still represent night in the human world, a world sleeping while individual races are shut up within their own limits, calling themselves nations, barri- cading themselves, as these sleeping cottages were barricaded, with closed doors, bolts and bars, and prohibitions of all kinds. Does not all this represent the dark age of civilization...."[16] Tagore points out that "neither the colourless vagueness of cosmopolitanism, nor the fierce self-idolatry of nation-worship is the goal of human history."[17] For, "The world-wide problem today is not how to unite by wiping out all differences, but to unite with all differences intact."[18] Tagore goes on to say that "All over the world today we find every nation striving hard to preserve its separate self. At the same time we find each getting to be conscious of its link with humanity at large. Thanks to that consciousness, all are shaking off the forms of individualism which are peculiarly their own, and which stand in the way of contact with the outside world. Each nationality is offering all its belongings to the scrutiny of the universe. There is no satisfaction any longer in beating the drum of one's individuality in the seclusion of one's own room. There is an urge in the soul to make one's individuality an adornment for all mankind."[19]

Tagore was very much aware of and concerned over the effects of industrialization and urbanization in India and elsewhere. They tend to discourage cooperation and stimulate competition and selfish individualism. He writes: "...cities are in the main a competitive field and here the urge for mutual help is not suitably encouraged. Individualism and competition are necessary for the generation of power, but danger comes when the proper limits are exceeded. Modern civilization has indeed gone beyond the limits."[20] Evils stemming from selfishness are also found in any society in which the good of all is not the basic concern. In an individualistically oriented society one's own good and not that of his group takes precedent. The good of all should be primary, however. "The heart of a country lies wherever the people's welfare is centred,"[21] Tagore writes.

V The Good

Evil and suffering vanish when goodness is cultivated. Good is that which is desirable for our greater self. In every individual reside the lesser and the greater man. The lesser is occupied with selfish interests but the greater man lives in the universal. The lesser man engages himself in the pursuit of ego-centric wishes while the greater man's duty lies in cultivating the true will of the universal. Only when the selfish individual expands himself into the selfless universal, do evils cease as evils and grow into good. Rabindranath lays stress on Sarvānubhūti or the feeling of at-homeness in the whole. Sarvānubhūti is not merely a feeling; it is also an attitude. At-homeness entails harmony with all created objects.

"Man loses his true station when he fails to unite fully with hi fellows. A complete man is one who has this capacity for union a lone individual is a fragmented being,"[22] Tagore writes. Th basis of unity is unbounded love. The attitude of a man possessing true love is Brahma Vihāra. What is Brahma Vihāra? Rabindranath answers: "With everything whether it is above or below remote or near, visible of invisible, thou shalt presume a relatio of unlimited love without any animosity or without a desire to kill To live in such a consciousness while standing or walking, sitting or lying down till you are asleep, is Brahma Vihāra, or in othe words, is living and moving and having your Joy in the spirit o Brahma."[23]

Love implies the negation of all egoism. So long as the 'I' is prominent in a man, love cannot dawn in him. Ego-consciousness blurs our vision and makes us narrow and bigoted. Hence Rabindranath's prayer is: "Sink all my egoism in tears." He is ashamed to take his little egoistic self to God.

"I came out alone on my way to my tryst.
But who is this that follows me in the silent dark?
He is my own little self, my Lord, he knows no shame;
but I am ashamed to come to thy door in his company."[24]

What is wanted is a selfless soul and only such a soul is blessed by God. When Yāgñavalkya asked Maitreyī to receive her share of earthly possessions she replied: "What shall I do with material riches? They cannot grant me immortality." Material possessions bind our soul with fetters and the egoistic self assumes mastery over the unblemished soul. Lord Jesus said: "a rich man can never attain salvation." Here riches do not mean only money, it means all our earthly possessions, our near and dear ones and our fame. The little self is an obstacle of salvation. The central idea of Rabindranath's drama—*The King of the Dark Chamber*—is that egoism, pride and vanity prevent the queen, Sudarśanā, from seeing the King. The proud queen only sees darkness, deep and cruel. But when her mind is chastened by humility and selflessness she sees the King in front of her. When the 'I' in her is effaced, she sees the King in her own heart.

Rabindranath's view of love reminds us of the teachings of Jesus Christ. The son of God preaches fatherly love towards God and brotherly love towards man. Love of God means the giving of oneself to Him in joyful surrender. True Christianity lies in loving friends and foes alike. Rabindranath's *Gītāñjali* and *Naivedya* are filled with devotional poems that speak of self-surrender and love to the Infinite. Man's total peace lies in doing His will. The love of man led the poet-philosopher to formulate the Religion of man, a religion grounded in humanism. In *Sonār Tarī* he writes: "Whatever I can offer to God I offer to man and to God I give whatever I can give to man. I make God man and man God."[25] His concept of humanism is not anthropocentric but Godcentric. Anthropocentric humanism lays undue emphasis on man's ego. Soon it is faced with dualism and opposition—opposition between self and non-self, reason and faith. Man's loneliness, anxiety and fear are all due to his estrangement from God. Divine humanism which speaks of man's rootedness in God guarantees peace and true happiness.

One may raise the question: What is the end of this all-embracing love? In love, does the finite individual become God? Rabindranath does not uphold Śaṅkara's view that in Mokṣa or emancipation man becomes Brahman or the Absolute. We have seen that love forms the nature of God and without love godhood is a nullity. In order that the eternal love-drama between God and man may go on uninterrupted, the lover and the beloved must maintain their individual distinctness. This does not mean that Rabindranath believes in anything like dualism. The finites are in the Infinite but they have their own distinctness just as waves are in the sea but they are distinct from the sea. God or Jīvandevata has the supreme need of finite persons to love and receive from them love in return. At every birth man takes part in the divine love-drama and attains some perfection. Through every death man becomes more and more perfect and hence his destiny is only perfectivity. The aim of human existence lies in the process of perfection and not in perfection itself. Rabindranath believes that if man attains complete perfection, he becomes God and in that case the divine love-drama comes to an end and godhood becomes meaningless. This is why he accords to man more and more perfection but not complete perfection.[26]

17

RAMAKRISHNA

Pritibhushan Chatterji

I Life and Experiences

India in the eighteenth century was passing through an intellectual crisis. British Raj having been established, waves of thought came from the West challenging India's traditional value systems. In the ensuing conflict of ideas Ramakrishna came to India. Born on February 28, 1863 in Kamarpukur, Bengal, to pious parents, he was named Gadādhar after a temple deity in Gaya where his father had gone on a pilgrimage and received a vision about the child's birth.

Gadādhar's birth was not unusual and his childhood was sheltered. From about six he began to have ecstatic experiences. Once on passing through a paddyfield, he was enchanted by the sight of snow-white cranes flying in the sky covered by a dark cloud. The colour-contrast made a sudden impact on his mind and he fell into a swoon. When nine while playing the role of Lord Śiva in a village drama, he fell into an ecstatic fit, seemingly possessed of the spirit of Śiva himself.

Gadādhar was not attracted by village games like other boys but preferred the company of monks and pilgrims at the village rest house. Their religious discussions and chanting enthralled him. He was not inclined toward academic life and had little formal schooling. Supposedly he developed an aversion toward arithmetic when taught subtraction, although he cheerfully learned addition. Perhaps even in boyhood his mind loved to dwell on the notion of cosmic expansion; hence anything smacking of diminution had no appeal to him!

Concerned over Gadādhar's apathy toward education in the village and having opened a school for Sanskrit studies, Rāmakumār, his eldest brother, brought Gadādhar to Calcutta. Even then at seventeen, he showed no eagerness for formal study. Disappointed, Rāmakumār sought work for Gadādhar, eventually getting him appointed as priest to several families. In 1855 Rāmakumār became chief priest of a temple dedicated to Kālī, newly constructed by Rānī Rāshmani, a rich Hindu widow, at Daksineswar on the Ganges outside Calcutta. On being brought there by his brother, Gadādhar reluctantly accepted some duties connected with the worship of the Deity. Unfortunately Rāmakumār died within a year and the burden of the priestly office fell entirely on Gadādhar's shoulders. Since then the temple at Daksineswar became the scene of his sādhanā.

Thereafter the getting of a direct vision of the Divine Mother dominated Gadādhar's mind. Determined as a priest to feel the actual presence of the Deity to whom he prayed, he continued for days asking the Divine Kālī: "Mother, you showed yourself to Rāmprasād and other devotees in the past. Why won't you show yourself to me? Why won't you grant my prayer?"[1] Gadādhar spent many sleepless nights passionately desiring to see God face to face. He gave up food, forgot to perform his priestly duties, first sat motionless for hours meditating deeply on the Deity and then broke out in passionate appeals, tears rolling down his cheeks. One day, giving up all hope of the Divine vision and wishing to end his life, a frenzy seized him. His eyes fell on a sword hanging in the sanctuary. As he caught hold of it, surrounding objects disappeared and a dazzling ocean of Spirit seemed to engulf him. Losing all contact with the outer world, the real form of the Divine Mother appeared and blessed him. Indeed, Gadādhar now saw God!

After that each time he envisioned the Divine Mother he was on wings of ecstacy for several hours. He made the food offerings to the image of the Deity in unusual ways. He uttered no prescribed mantram, observed no formalities of worship and showed his love for the Divine Mother in whatever manner he pleased. Outsiders, not understanding his behaviour, believed him mad; and fastidious temple officials interpreted his actions as sacrilegious. Blessed with visions of the Divine Mother, Gadādhar wished to see God in other forms such as Kṛiṣṇa and Rāma, his family's deity, which he was able to do. Physically and mentally exhausted during this period, Gadādhar found attending his priestly duties difficult. Being sympathetic and wishing to grant him rest, Rānī Rāshmani sent Gadādhar back to his native village.

After a few months Gadādhar recovered somewhat. To cure him fully it was decided he be married. Finding parents who would give their daughter to Gadādhar proved difficult; however a five year old girl named Sāradāmani was finally secured and the marriage solemnized. After a year and a half in his village Gadādhar returned to his duties at Daksineswar. Ramakrishna's marriage is a striking phenomenon in his life.[2] Unlike the typical sannyāsin, he retained his connections with his family and even willingly gave his consent to marriage. He wished not to run away from but to rise above the world. Moreover, Ramakrishna's marriage, unlike others, was without copulation. Ramakrishna looked at his wife from two viewpoints. Since she was much younger, he wanted to train her in the spiritual field; and, as he looked upon every woman as an expression of the Divine Mother, he could not think of any woman, even his wife, in sexual terms.

On returning to Daksineswar the old desire for the Divine Mother haunted Ramakrishna. His distress could not be smoothed until he had some vision while absorbed in deep, self-forgetting meditation. Having already overcome the sexual obstacle to spirituality, Ramakrishna now wanted to transcend any attachment to money. He therefore took a few coins in one hand and some earth in the other, saying to himself that money is no better than earth. Then, mixing both, he threw them in the Ganges. By repeating this several times his renunciation of money became so great that he could not even bear the touch of any coin or valuable metal. Ramakrishna also realized spiritual progress would be impossible unless he could look on all men equally as manifestations of the same Universal Spirit. A Brahmin himself, Ramakrishna washed the latrines of houses of sweeper caste members in order to banish any vestige of caste, egoism or sense of superiority in himself.

Thus far Ramakrishna had not followed any traditional path in his spiritual journey but had educated himself according to his own light. Now he came into contact with several spiritual guides, the first being a female ascetic of the Tāntrika school named Bhairavī, who claimed God had ordained her to deliver a message. Looking for someone fit to receive it, she saw Ramakrishna, and recognized him as the sought-for disciple. He told her of his intense thirst for Divine vision. She realized that Ramakrishna was passing through the highest phase of ecstatic love and under her direction he performed all the rites necessary for Tāntrika sādhanā.

One feature of that sādhanā is the devotee's enjoying of sense-objects so as to overcome the desire for enjoyment.[3] Ramakrishna performed the sādhanā successfully, not falling victim to enjoyment, as sometimes happens; for through self-education he had already conquered all desires for sensual pleasures. Highly impressed, Bhairavī realized that Ramakrishna was an incarnation of God; and, proving her case, an assembly of highly learned men accepted her verdict that Ramakrishna indeed had all the marks of an incarnation.

After the Tāntrika path of action Ramakrishna was drawn to the Vaiṣṇava way of bhakti. Jatādhāri, an itinerant Vaiṣṇava monk and ardent devotee of Rāma, then appeared at Daksineswar with a metal image of the child Rāma. Ramakrishna poured his love on the image, as if it were a living child, and also identified himself with the legendary milkmaid girls, the female associates of Lord Kṛiṣṇa. Finally, in an ecstatic mood, he received a vision of the Lord.

Tāntrika and Vaiṣṇava sādhanās are dualistic, the seeker maintaining a relative distinction from the object of concentration. Ramakrishna now undertook the monistic path of jñānam under the direction of Totā Puri. Completely withdrawn from the world, he realized it was a product of cosmic māyā. In detached meditation on the nature of the true self, he sank into nirvikalpa samādhi, a state in which subject-object dualism vanishes and the self as pure subject is realized. In this state for several weeks, he had a vision of the Divine Mother who asked him to remain on the level of relative not pure consciousness for the benefit of humanity at large.

His mind now able to move freely and alternately on the planes of knowledge, devotion and action, Ramakrishna declared of God as personal or impersonal: "When I think of the Supreme Being as inactive, neither creating, preserving, nor destroying, I call Him Brahman or Puruṣa, the Impersonal God. When I think of Him as active, creating, preserving, destroying, I call Him Śakti, or Māyā or Prakṛiti, the Personal God. The distinction between them does not mean difference. The Personal and Impersonal are the same thing, like milk and its whiteness."[4] Having actually followed the three important sādhanās, Ramakrishna found no conflict between them.

Concluding that ultimate spiritual Truth cannot be the prerogative of any one religion Ramakrishna now began realizing Truth as followers of other faiths did. In 1866, impressed by the earnest prayers and humility of a Muslim saint, Ramakrishna behaved like a Moslem, remaining outside the Hindu temple. He then had a vision of the Prophet and realized the nature of the formless God as described in Islamic texts. Feeling that, in regard to the transcendent Absolute, Hinduism and Islam agree, Ramakrishna returned to Hinduism. In 1874 he developed a desire to know Christianity directly. Listening intently to a disciple reading the Bible and seeing a picture of the Madonna with the baby Christ in her arms made Ramakrishna an enthralled devotee of Christ. Dominated by the Christian concept of love, he had a vision of Christ in all his effulgent glory and fell into a swoon. Ramakrishna also had great respect for Buddha, openly declaring he was an incarnation of God. Moreover, he found no difference between Buddhist theories and the doctrines of the jñāna-kānda of the Vedas.

Thus of all recent religious leaders only Ramakrishna underwent the full gamut of spiritual experiences. He concluded that each religion is true and leads to the same God. Just as a chamelon appears in different colours—red, green, yellow and sometimes is colourless—so the Supreme Reality presents itself in different forms to different persons and sometimes in a formless fashion. Ramakrishna thus opposed religious quarrels and the condemning of a particular religion as false. The special significance of Ramakrishna's view of the basic unity of all religions is that he spoke from his own experience.

II His Teachings

Ramakrishna's life is important as an inspiring book of instruction. No author or professional philosopher, he lived the philosophy he believed and preached in a simple manner through anecdote and parable. His teachings appealed directly and spontaneously to his listeners.[5]

Ramakrishna was a monist and simple-hearted believer in God. He held that any one determined to see God could see Him. God has many names and infinite forms; by whatever name addessed or form sought, in that very name and form man will see him. Only ignorance leads some to say there is no God. If God is one, it is the same God who is worshipped in different religions. Why, then should followers of different religions quarrel among themselves? Ramakrishna answers it is due to their failure to understand the ssence of religion. All religions lead to the same goal. As different rnaments may be made out of the same gold, so the same God is vorshipped in different countries and ages under different names nd forms. Our view of God varies also, some loving him as father, thers as mother. Some call Him friend and others beloved. ome pray to Him as the innermost treasure of their hearts and call Iim their child; but it is the same God being worshipped in all these elations and modes.

Ramakrishna's answer to whether God is with or without form is hat He is both. As fire which has no form itself assumes certain orms in glowing embers, so the formless God sometimes converts Iimself into certain forms. Ramakrishna drew a parallel with vater and ice when answering the question of the personality f God. Water becomes ice when congealed. In much the same vay the personal God is the condensed form of the formless bsolute. Though condensed, ice remains a part of water and also nelts in it. Similarly the personal God is part and parcel of the mpersonal Absolute or is a condensed form of the Absolute. He ises from the Absolute, or remains in and ultimately merges in the bsolute. Indeed, having a form or not is an irrelevant question n reference to the Absolute, as Brahman, strictly speaking, transends form and formlessness.

Although the Absolute is unchanging in itself, Māyā is the name of s changing or manifested form. Māyā may be compared to a snake ctive and moving, while Brahman is the snake absolutely still. The rouble is that the notion of Brahman cannot be described adequately y words. One may realize Him but be unable to narrate fully is experience of Brahman. It is like a person who, overwhelmed vhen seeing an ocean for the first time, describes it as "a vast heet of water—water, water all round." Similarly, a man who has ealized Brahman cannot portray it but simply says: "It is Brahman, Brahman everywhere." The devotee of God can never comprehend Iim fully. Indeed it would be futile for the finite to grasp the Innite. In attempting this he would experience the same result as doll of salt trying to fathom the depths of an ocean. It is dissolved nd lost. Similarly, the finite self in trying to measure God loses is individuality and becomes one with Him. As a piece of lead hrown into mercury dissolves, so the individual soul loses its limitaions as soon as it falls in the ocean of Brahman.

The finite self, Ramakrishna says, though from ignorance thinking itself independent, has no independent status of its own. A bubbles originate in water, float on and are ultimately dissolved ir it, so the individual and Supreme selves are basically one and the same. The difference between them is in degree—one being finite the other infinite; one small, the other immeasurable; one dependent the other independent. The idea of duality is traceable to Māyā The union of the finite and infinite selves is like the union of the hou and minute hands of a clock at noon or midnight.

Tragically, though God is in all men, all men are not God-orientec or in God. Is this because God does not attract men? No, Goc is related to man as a magnet is to iron. But when deeply embeddec in mud, the iron is not attracted by a magnet. Similarly, when en meshed in Māyā, the individual feels no impulse to move to God A genuine yearning for God is necessary; whoever shows such wil not be disappointed. While the seeker should meditate deeply or God, meditation will not yield quick results in every case; a continuec and unflinching meditation is required. Ramakrishna concede that in this iron age a person cannot constantly meditate and con template. Hence he advises bare repetition of the name of Goc for the masses. Taking the name of the Lord always, not elaborat observances, are needed. Whenever one utters God's name, con sciously or unconsciously, one acquires the merit of such an utterance Ramakrishna adds that, for God-realization, Divine Grace is als necessary. No one can realize God, unless God wills to reveal Him self. As a nightguard can see everyone he flashes his torch on, bu no one clearly see him until he turns the light on himself, so God see everyone; but no one can see Him until He is his infinite mercy re veals Himself.

The man who is able to realize God is blessed and so changed tha evil cannot touch him any more. Free from all worldly cares anc anxieties, nothing can bind him again. Living in the world, it imperfections do not affect him; and mixing with innumerable un regenerates does not effect him adversely. He is like milk which i readily mixed with water but, when converted into butter, no longe mixes but floats on it. Or, as a piece of uncared-for iron gets rust but does not when converted into gold by the magic touch of the so called philosopher's stone, so nothing will contaminate the man Goc has granted a vision of Himself.

The truly religious man, recognizing the truth found in differen religions and not holding a dogmatic view of his own, is unlike th roverbial frog in the well. Realizing the essence of religion is sing above all disputes and engaging in silent meditation, he does ot resort to vain discussions and sophistries. As the bee humming nd hovering round the petals becomes silent once inside the flower icking honey, so he who has a vision of supreme Truth becomes uiet, no longer resorting to flippant arguments and delighting 1 noisy quarrels. The true worshipper talks little and practises eligion in all humility. As Ramakrishna says: "A common man alks bagfuls of religion, but acts not a grain of it; while the wise man peaks little, but his whole life is a religion acted out."[6]

Because living a spiritual life is an art to be practised, men should e persuaded to adopt the spiritual ideal when young. The young hould guard against falling prey to worldy temptations. When hey grow strong in faith, no evil can vitiate them and they may be piritual guides for others. Ramakrishna also stressed developing he spirit of renunciation, for Divine Truth can be impressed only n the mind filled with devotion and not worldly affairs.

From the above we see that, for Ramakrishna, Brahman alone is he ultimate reality; yet Ramakrishna does not view the world as ompletely unreal. When an aspirant seeks to realize the Absoulte s ultimate reality, he may approach it by the principle 'neti,' 'neti' 'not this,' 'not this'). When he reaches the Absolute and loses himself in It by the process of negation, the Absolute alone is realized s true and all else as false. Yet when he comes out of his state f absorption, he feels the empirical world is what it is because of the Absolute, because of its Śakti or Māyā. Thus by interpreting Māyā s the creative aspect of Brahman and not simply an illusion-producing power, Ramakrishna's approach to the world is more positive than negative. Using the analogy of a woodapple, he says he fruit consists of kernel, seeds, sticky juice and shell. Anyone nterested in knowing the essence of the fruit refers to the kernel and gnores its seeds, etc. If he wishes to know the totality of the fruit, he must take into account not only its kernel but the rest also. In nuch the same way the absolute and relative together constitute the whole of reality, while the Absolute constitutes its kernel. So whether the Absolute minus the world or plus it is reality can be determined only in the light of what the aspirant wants to know about the Absolute and to what level of sādhanā he is able to rise. However, what the aspirant will be able to attain finally depends on the Grace of God.

III Ramakrishna and Today

However Ramakrishna's teachings may be interpreted philoso phically, they undeniably make a direct appeal to the hearts common men and women, inspiring them spiritually. He represen the spirit of religion at its highest and best. Of the many lesso we may learn from his life, one is the value of renunciation as a prep ration for religious training. He showed by his own actions how o can conquer and become detached from egoism and sexual an monetary temptations.

A worldly man's heart is like a moist match which does not catc fire however much rubbed; while the heart of a devotee, like a dr match-stick, is kindled immediately by the slightest mention of th Lord's name. The worldly man is not entirely unregenerate; hi conversion is difficult, however, Ramakrishna says, as pure mil when mixed with double the quantity of water takes a long tim and labour to make into condensed milk, so "the mind of a worldl man is largely diluted with the water of evil and impure though and it requires a long time and labour to purify it."[7] Asceti renunciation is not necessary. Though living in the world, the worl should not live in the man of the world, just as a boat is to float i water without water entering it. By keeping company with th holy the minds of ordinary persons are purified and invigorate Ramakrishna declares. And those having spiritual knowledg already are duty-bound to communicate their experience and wisdo to their less fortunate brethren, uplifting them spiritually.

Ramakrishna follows the liberal Hindu tradition in believing in number of Divine Incarnations such as Rāma, Kṛiṣna, Buddh and Christ. They are related to God as the waves of an ocean ar related to the ocean. An incarnation moves the minds of and bring individuals to God. As a saviour he draws a multitude of me laden with sin into the presence of the Almighty, just as a locomotiv engine, while itself moving toward its destination, brings a lon train of loaded wagons with it. Though being in the world, the in carnate's mind is constantly attuned to God. His life has bot historical and spiritual aspects. As the elephant has two sets of teet —external tusks and internal grinders—so the incarnation lives a a common man in the view of all, while his soul rests far away withi the Divine fold. Ramakrishna is himself looked upon as an incarna tion by modern Hindus, having come into the world to save mankin by his life and teaching. Hindus believe God appeared as Rāma and Kṛiṣṇa long ago, and He who was Rāma and Kṛiṣna appeared again in recent times as Ramakrishna.

Ramakrishna's philosophy is primarily Vedāntic, leaning toward the Advaita of Śaṇkara though not a mere repetition of it. Śaṇkara taught that the Supreme Reality or Brahman is totally indeterminate or qualityless, while for Ramakrishna it is determinate and indeterminate. For Śaṇkara, Brahman looked at from the empirical point of view appears as Īśvara; but, since from the ultimate standpoint creation itself is false, the notion of God as the Creator is also false. Ramakrishna does not hold that creation is false; he says the world is real, though not eternal. He identifies God with the Absolute as Śakti, and Śakti is engaged in creation as the līlā-rūpa of Brahman. Ramakrishna's advaitism is thus reconciled with the Dvaita and Viśiṣṭādvaita world-views.

Whether the Absolute is purely indeterminate or not is controversial and in such matters Ramakrishna speaks from personal experience, not relying simply on theoretical discussions. He declared that God appeared to him as both indeterminate and determinate, impersonal and personal; and the truly wise man (vijñānin) realizes God in his meditation (samādhi) as both. Samādhi is of two types—savikalpa and nirvikalpa. In the latter Reality is realized in its formless aspect and in the former as God or as a Personal Being with qualities. Also there are two types of spiritual aspirants—those realizing the Absolute in its formless aspect and losing their ego in it and others who, even after having realized the Absolute, recover a semblance of the ego and live again on the worldly plane, recognizing the things and beings of the world as manifestations of the Infinite. For them Reality is both undifferentiated and differentiated. Also, the Absolute is not now determinate and now indeterminate; rather He is both at once, though he transcends the personal and impersonal aspects, as they do not exhaust His nature and being. No one can say what He is in Himself. A second is that religion is not mere theoretical discussion but is intensely pragmatic. It is more to be lived and practised than speculated about, a view Ramakrishna's disciple Vivekananda effected by setting up the Ramakrishna Math and Mission. Agnostic and sceptic claim that God can neither be seen nor proved logically. Ramakrishna took up their challenge, proving by his own experience that through passionate devotion anyone can see God as he himself had. Moreover he believed that religious experience obtained through sādhanā should be communicated and shared, not kept as a private treasure. To experience Divine Love is not simply to be lost in it but to invite others to taste it also.

Another lesson from Ramakrishna's life is that we should rise above conflict and seek harmony in philosophy and religion. He realized through his own experience that on the ultimate plane conflicting theories of Reality meet and agree. Different philosophies represent different aspects of Reality, and each of them is partially true. Even within a particular system of philosophy there are different schools; Vedānta is divided into Advaita, Viśiṣṭādvaita, Dvaita, etc.; but, as they approach Reality from different levels of experience, they do not conflict from an ultimate view. Similarly quarrels among adherents of different religions appeared meaningless to Ramakrishna, for he had realized the same God by actually following different religions. Hinduism is also divided into sects. But Ramakrishna told us from his own experience Kālī, Śiva and Viṣṇu are only different forms of the same reality. Thus even while a worshipper of Kālī, the goddess of the Śāktas, he could in ecstasy contemplate Lord Kṛiṣṇa; and he saw God in the form of Kṛiṣna even as in the form of Kālī. Ramakrishna's life thus teaches us the harmony of all religions.

Ramakrishna's experience does not imply that we should make a new religion out of the old ones; nor should we follow all religions at the same time. He spoke in favour, not of eclecticism, but of a religious democracy in which each religion freely follows its own course, ultimately reaching the same goal thereby. Harmony is the keynote of Ramakrishna's vision.[8] His message to the world as Vivekananda interpreted it is: "Do not care for doctrines . . . sects or churches or temples; they count for little compared with the essence of existence in each man which is spirituality. . . . Earn that first . . . criticise no one, for all doctrines and creeds have some good in them. Show by your lives that religion . . . means spiritual realization. Only those who have attained to spirituality can communicate it to others, can be great teachers of mankind. They alone are the powers of light."[9]

18

GANDHI—A MODERNIST HERESY

T. K. MAHADEVAN

I His Eclecticism

Mohandas Karamchand Gandhi (1869-1948), more familiarly known as Mahātmā Gandhi, was not an Indian philosopher in the same sense as Śaṅkara, Rāmānuja or other mediaeval ācāryas. That is to say, he was not an interpreter of the śruti and the smṛiti, the major scriptural texts which form the common ground of the orthodox schools of Indian philosophy. Nor was Gandhi a system-builder or the founder of a school of philosophy in any strict sense or in a sense acceptable to orthodox opinion in India. Indeed some of his more pronounced philosophical biases are un-Indian.

Could we then relate Gandhi to some of the heterodox traditions in Indian philosophy, such as the jaina and bauddha schools? I do not think so. Except in a marginal sense, the jaina elements in Gandhi's thought are in no way more important than those coming from the vedānta. Gandhi is thus something of a freak in the realm of Indian thought. Unclassifiable in terms of known Indian categories, it yet remains true that no book on Indian thought would be complete without a chapter on Gandhi. Why this is so will be apparent in the sequel.

There are two schools of thought regarding the status of Gandhi's ideas in the field of philosophy in general. One holds that since Gandhi never formulated his ideas in any systematic manner, their philosophical significance can only be marginal. This school abhors the notion that there is anything like a philosophy of Gandhi. It is a view which seems to me too dogmatic and extreme. The other school, taking a more pragmatic view, argues that, although Gandhi's ideas are scattered over a long period of essentially journalistic writing, there is a perceptible thread of consistency running through the entire corpus of his work. With some effort his thought can be neatly systematized into a coherent philosophy.

In a general sense, this second view may indeed be the right one. But when we try to place gandhian thought within the mainstream of Indian philosophy and to procure for it a habitation and a name, we run into difficulties. Superficially, Gandhi seems to be saying, at different times, precisely what one or the other ācārya had said in the past. On a closer look, however, one finds that although he is using more or less identical terminology, he is giving his words new and unconventional meanings. Therefore, any attempt to systematize his thought must, first of all, guard against this semantic trap.

For example, when Gandhi speaks of Brahman, he is not referring to the unconditioned absolute of the upaniṣads but to something that, in his mind, is the same as īśvara—God as creator. Indeed he uses the terms interchangeably, as when he says: "I have defined brahmacharya as that correct way of life which leads to brahman, i.e. God."

Similarly, Gandhi's "advaita" is not the non-duality expressed in such upaniṣadic texts as "ahaṃ brahma asmi" (I am brahman) or "tat tvam asi" (you are brahman). Nor is it the same thing as the sage Vāmadeva's identification of himself, in a mystical flight, with everything that existed in the past and which exists now. When Gandhi speaks of advaita, it is simply a way of affirming that "God alone is" or that all life is one and indivisible, as when he says: "I believe in advaita, in the essential unity of man. If one man gains spiritually, the whole world gains with him; and if one man falls, the whole world falls to that extent."

One should not infer from this that Gandhi's thinking suffers from a certain laxity. Imprecise though he is, the nature of his thought can best be understood if we look upon it as an attempt to achieve, by eclectic means, an acceptable synthesis of the basic ideas of the Indian tradition. Thus does he say: "I am an advaitin and yet I can support dvaita. The world is changing every moment and is therefore unreal. But it has something about it which persists and to that extent it is real. I have no objection to calling it real and unreal and being called a syādvādī. But my syādvāda is not that of the learned; it is peculiarly my own." Or again: "I believe God to be creative as well as non-creative. From the platform of the Jains I prove the non-creative aspect of God and from that of Rāmānuja the creative aspect."

II Faith and Reason

In a manner of speaking, this eclecticism in Gandhi is part and parcel of his basic unconventionality and a certain ingrained rebelliousness in him towards received doctrine. From these to the modern notion of rationality is only a short step. But Gandhi's rationality, again, is a thing apart. A man of great faith, he yet subjugated his faith to the demands of reason. He would accept no idea, however well-established and sacred, unless it appealed to his reason. How he succeeded in reconciling reason with faith is a piece of legerdemain characteristic of Gandhi. I think he did it by rephrasing his faith in rational terms. He turned faith into what he called a workable assumption. In this manner he thought faith would help to correct the faults of reason and reason would help to correct the faults of faith.

This gandhian emphasis on reason constitutes, within the meaning of Indian philosophy, a heresy. Once when asked about the source of his knowledge, Gandhi pointed to his breast. "It lies here," he said. "I exercise my judgement about every scripture, including the Gītā. I cannot let a scriptural text supersede my reason." Elsewhere he mollified the force of his heresy by arguing that "Whilst I subscribe to divine revelation I cannot surrender my reason." Explaining his cautious approach to received texts, he says that they "suffer from a process of double distillation. Firstly they come through a human prophet and then through the commentaries of interpreters." And he asks students of the śāstras to "reject whatever is contrary to truth and nonviolence."

All this is the purest heresy—mitigated only by the fact that it is to a large extent unconscious. The unconscious nature of Gandhi's heresy comes out clearly in his celebrated saying: "I have nothing new to teach the world. Truth and non-violence are as old as the hills." In fact, the truth and non-violence that he was propounding were not as old as the hills. They were an innovation. Gandhi's thought not only did not derive from India's ancient traditions; in significant ways it went counter to them. And yet—for political or psychological reasons, one cannot tell—Gandhi took it for granted that his ideas had their roots in the texts. This unawareness probably sprang from his early unfamiliarity with the nuances of Indian philosophical thinking. Clearly he was being innovative without knowing it, heretical without realizing it.

The essence of the Hindu philosophical tradition, on the other hand, consists in the primacy not of reason but of scriptural truth. What the texts say is final and inarguable. It is beyond the pale of reason. It is a priori. Neither pratyakṣa (perception) nor anumāna (inference) can dare challenge what the text says. It is often the trump card in Indian philosophical disquisition. "For the text says so" (śruti-pramāṇatvāt) is the final clinching argument. It can be refuted, if at all, only by another text equally authentic.

It has been widely argued that this tradition of textual evidence is a blight on the free growth of Indian philosophy and should be done away with. It is said that the tyranny of the text has reduced Indian philosophy to nothing more than an exercise in exegesis. If the final evidence for philosophical truth is the scripture, what (it is asked) is left for philosophers except to split scriptural hairs? Some have even contended that Indian philosophy is theology pure and simple.

How much of all this is justified? Was Gandhi consistent in subjecting scriptural evidence to the evidence of what he called reason? In thus questioning the supremacy of the received text, did he come within the meaning of a nāstika? But then Gandhi is not denying the validity of scripture in the same way as the heterodox schools do. He is merely downgrading it—a deviation of another and novel kind.

The "tyranny of the text" and the "heresy of reason"—these two phrases conveniently provide an epitome of what differentiates philosophy as understood in India from philosophy as understood outside India. They point to the existence of two epistemologies, mistakenly assumed to be mutually exclusive. In fact, what may be called the vedic epistemology comprehends and subsumes the modern epistemology of science and reason. The tests are apauruṣeya—that is to say, they are trans-human in origin (which is not the same as saying that they are a divine revelation, a concept wholly foreign to vedic thinking). They deal with matters which are beyond the ken of reason (which again is not the same as saying that they deal with divinity). One may say that they are based on another kind of reason.

In settling this abstruse (and, to modern minds, exotic) philosophical point, one can do no better than consult the Brahma-sūtra—the aphoristic tour de force attributed to the sage Bādarāyana. In his monumental commentary on the work, Śaṅkara describes the purpose of the Brahma-sūtra as the "ascertainment of the meaning of upaniṣadic texts, with the help of reasoning not running counter to them." He says further that "the realization of brahman results from the firm conviction that comes from deliberating on upaniṣadic texts and not from other means of knowledge."

Now the third aphorism of the Brahma-sūtra makes the laconic statement: "śāstra-yonitvāt." This can mean either (a) that brahman is the source of the scriptures or (b) that brahman is known only from the scriptures. Significantly, Śaṅkara prefers the second meaning, thereby underlining the supremacy of scripture as evidence for philosophical truth. In the same vein, commenting on the third aphorism, Śaṅkara refutes the notion that the origin of the universe is to be traced to the insentient pradhāna of the Sāṃkhya system on the ground that the pradhāna is nowhere mentioned in the upaniṣads. The Bṛihadāraṇyaka-upaniṣad, a amajor text, says: "I ask you of that puruṣa which is to be known only from the upaniṣads. "The Brahma-sūtra ends with the declaration, "anāvṛittiḥ śabdāt": "The liberated one never more returns to the cycle of births and deaths—because the upaniṣads say so."

Although the weight of textual evidence is overwhelming—and I have only adduced a mere sprinkle—the modern mind, when brought into contact with Indian philosophy, refuses to come to terms with its central pillar of śabda-pramāṇa. The resulting communication block is not one that is easy to surmount. When I say "modern mind" I mean also Indian professors of philosophy and not only their western counterparts. They sin in common. As for Gandhi, he is a downright modern insofar as Indian philosophical tenets and conventions are concerned. The notion that he is a traditionalist is one of those evergreen fallacies which often surround the life of a celebrity. His politics might have been archaic but his philosophy is ultra-modern. One may simplify the whole question by saying that where modern knowledge is a posteriori, vedic knowledge is a priori; and it is thus that the professor fails to understand the pandit —or, as is more often the case, misunderstands him.

Some have tried to bridge this serious communication gap by equating śruti with the cumulative human wisdom that is to be found in the teaching of world sages, whether semitic, Aryan or Chinese. Others have tried to do so by extending the meaning of śruti to include non-vedic scriptural texts, such as the Bible, the Koran, the Avesta, etc. These attempts are syncretistic in a way which is wholly repugnant to vedic tradition. Śruti has nothing whatever to do with the insights or mystical intimations of great men, whether vedic or any other. Śruti in its purest sense denotes a completely independent means of cognition for the perception of philosophic truth.

The Brahma-sūtra makes this point abundantly clear when it says: "śāstra-dṛiṣṭvā tu upadeśaḥ vāmadevavat." That is to say, "to be authentic, a seer's vision, such as Vāmadeva's, must agree with the śruti." This contrasts, interestingly, with Gandhi's equally categorical assertion that he will accept no śāstra unless it "appealed to his heart"! Whom shall we accept—Bādarāyana or Gandhi? Nevertheless, the traditional Indian position is, clearly, that no human insight, however profound, is in the same class as a vedic precept which is apauruṣeya (non-anthropic).

Śaṅkara, in his commentary on the Brahma-sūtra, employs two different approaches when he attempts a clarification of this crucial issue. There is, first of all, the goal of human endeavour, which obviously is the creation of a just, peaceful and happy social order. He says: "kartavye hi viṣaye na anubhava-apekṣā asti; śrutyādīnām eva prāmāṇyaṃ syāt." "Not human experience, but the śruti and smṛiti alone provide the right criteria when it comes to organizing human conduct." Secondly, he approaches the question by distinguishing between sensuous and non-sensuous knowledge. Says he: "na ca atīndriyān arthān śrutim antarena kaścid upalabhyate." "Non-sensuous knowledge does not come from any other source but that of the śruti." Even more forthright than Śaṅkara is Kumārila Bhaṭṭa, the celebrated exponent of pūrva-mīmāṃsā, who clinches the issue in a manner hard to challenge.

In sum, the position simply is that vedic knowledge is sui generis because it aims at attuning human life to its cosmic environment (or eco-system, in the modern jargon)—a field in which all other philosophies, including those deriving from modern science, have been total failures. Alas, by rejecting śabda-pramāṇa, gandhian thought appears to sail in the same leaking boat.

In partial extenuation of Gandhi's extraordinary heresy, one may bring up the excuse that, after all, he was more in the line of the bhaktas than in that of the ācāryas. There is certainly much plausibility here, provided that one confines oneself to Gandhi's numerous, and often profound, statements on God and the undertone of God-centredness that marked an otherwise hectic political life, and leaves out of account his frequent referenes to "advaita" and such other metaphysical notions alien to a bhakta's cast of mind.

But then, will Gandhi be accepted as a bhakta by the defenders of Indian tradition? I do not think so. He carried with him none of the stigmata, so to speak, of bhakti so dear to the Indian religious mind. He was nowhere near being God-intoxicated in the way Ramakrishna was. Gandhi's Rāma was never the ubiquitous physical presence that Ramakrishna's Kālī was. Moreover, one suspects that Gandhi's relationship to the deity was more Judaic than Hindu. His was a God that he loved with fear and feared with love. It was a master-servant relationship touching no more than the fringe of Indian bhakti and miles away from the exquisite sexual-sensual spectrum of emotions that characterizes a Mīrābāi or a Chaitanya.

One cannot do better than conclude this brief essay—which incidentally covers ground not hitherto attempted in any published work on Gandhi—by accepting his own view of his philosophy. A Swamy Yogānanda once asked him the question: "Sir, why is there evil in the world?" Here is how Gandhi answered:

> "It is a difficult question to answer. I can only give what I may call a villager's answer. If there is good there must also be evil, just as where there is light there is also darkness. But it is true only so far as we human mortals are concerned. Before God there is nothing good, nothing evil.
>
> "The vedānta says that the world is Māyā. Even that explanation is a babbling of imperfect humanity. I therefore say that I am not going to bother my head about it. Even if I was allowed to peep into the innermost recess of God's chamber I should not care to do it. For I should not know what to do there. It is enough for our spiritual growth to know that God is always with the doer of good. That again is a villager's explanation."

And yet, as I said at the beginning, no study of Indian thought would be complete unless one gave this villager's philosophy its due place in the history of Indian ideas—if only for its quaintness. For despite Gandhi's courageous heresy, the battle between non-anthropic text and anthropic reason still remains an open issue in Indian philosophy.

19

EPILOGUE

Donald H. Bishop

I The Illusions of Contemporary Man

In this concluding essay our major task will be the elucidating and summarizing of insights from the Indian tradition of special relevance and value to us today. We live in a restless and divided world. What can Indian thought offer to guide us toward a more sane and happy existence?

One answer is that India's greatest contribution may be her insistence on our need for overcoming Māyā or certain illusions. One is separation or particularism. In metaphysics this illusion leads us to deny universals or wholes and to believe that only individual entities or parts exist. Reality is simply a plurality of unrelated or, at best, loosely connected particulars. In epistemology we are led to conceive of knowledge as simply a collection of disparate impressions or the sum total of the discrete impressions coming from the interaction of the senses and physical objects. It induces us to believe that one knows only in terms of his own particular experiences. Thus man's knowledge is fragmented and limited. The individual sees things only from his point of view. Truth is what is true for each one; there are no universal truths.

Regarding concepts of man, the illusion of separateness leads to a philosophy of excessive individualism. Each sees himself as undisputed master of himself and all he surveys. Persons think of themselves as self-made and self-dependent. Each views himself as unique and different. It stimulates a "rights" view of life wherein the individual sees himself in a context against which he must assert himself to protect, maintain and realize his individuality and certain supposedly "inalienable" rights. Thus each visualizes himself as alone in and against the world. Others are a threat to his existence and authenticity. He lives in an alien world against which he must constantly struggle to maintain and realize himself.

In ethics the illusion of separatism gives rise to ethical relativism and egocentrism. The good is whatever is good for each individual or what each declares it to be. Because individuals supposedly differ, right and wrong will vary from one to another. Also it will vary from one situation to another. There is no universal good or right remaining constant from person to person or situation to situation. In fact there are no moral principles; there are only moral particulars. Another significant implication is that the individual is concerned first and foremost with his own interests and well being. He sees little or no connection between his good and others. His only or major concern as an isolated individual is for himself.

In social philosophy the illusion of separateness leads us to a Hobbesian picture of society as a tenuous aggregate of independent, self-contained individuals held together by self-interest. Men form societies only because it is the best way to insure their interests. By doing so the egoistic impulses of individuals can be curbed sufficiently to allow each individual to live a somewhat less precarious existence. The illusion of separateness is also at the root of nationalism and nations' insistence on absolute national sovereignty. Each nation like each individual thinks of itself as an entity unto itself, responsible only to itself, master of its own destiny, concerned only for its own good and unwilling to submit to any higher authority.

A second illusion is the illusion of materiality. It leads to the metaphysical view that there is only material reality. Physical objects or things are all that exist. Reality can be explained in terms of matter and motion. There is only material cause. In epistemology it tempts us to believe this day the one day of it. We can only know what we know at this moment. The truth is what is true for this particular instant. The immediate is the sole good we need pursue. The individual's existence is fleeting and precarious. It may end at any moment. Societies are but temporary coagulations of people which may be dissolved at any time by unforeseen and uncontrollable forces. Nations have come and gone; they will in the future.

We see at least two reactions to the illusion of momentariness. There are those who adopt the attitude of getting all they can out of the present without thought of the future. As this is the only life there is, cram it with as much pleasure as possible. Fatalism is the other. Nothing is permanent, why create anything of value?

Events are beyond our control. Life has no real meaning and one may as well give up in despair.

The fourth illusion is that of dualism, especially the dialectical Darwinian type. It induces us to view reality as consisting of two opposite forces eternally struggling with each other. It results in a concept of man as dichotomized into body and spirit, the demands and drives of the two being incompatible and at odds with each other. Moreover the individual is not only at odds with himself but his fellowmen as well.

Dialectical dualism leads to a social philosophy which sees society as cauldron of conflicting interests. There are the haves and have-nots, the in and out-groups, the powerful and powerless. Their interests differ, and one is constantly at battle with the other. The illusion of dualism in epistemology leads us to set up the law of exclusion and a two-value logic system. It is a matter of either *A* or not *A*, this or that, true or false. Furthermore it leads up to place the knowing process in a dualistic context of subject-object or knower-known, making direct or immediate knowledge impossible.

In ethics the illusion of dualism leads to the viewing of an act as either right or wrong, good or bad. Means and ends are separated. Being that all we can know is the material world as perceived through the senses. Truth is limited to material truths or truths of this world. In ethics the illusion of materiality leads to the adoption of hedonistic, utilitarian and quantitative criteria of value. Sensual pleasures are man's greatest concern. The good is associated with the acquisition of things. Happiness comes from their possession and use. A thing is good to the degree that it is useful in producing pleasure. The better is associated with the bigger; bigness is a mark of greatness.

As far as social thought is concerned, the illusion of materiality leads us to measure a society's or nation's greatness by such quantitative standards as gross national product, the amount of territory a nation controls, the standard of living enjoyed or the military might it can marshall. It produces a philosophy which asserts the economic factor as the major determinant of beliefs and actions. It leads nations to adopt a foreign policy of expediency and political realism. Nations are concerned primarily with protecting their national interests throughout the world and force is the most expedient means of doing so.

Further, the illusion of materiality leads to a biological view of man. He is but one of an infinite number of organisms whose physical needs are primary. The difference between man and other organisms is a quantitative one, man simply being more complex in structure. From a materialist standpoint man is a product of his environment as evolution demonstrates. His major concern is his biological well-being and his worth is measured by how much he produces.

The illusion of momentariness is a third one. It is the view that everything is constantly changing. Nothing is permanent or remains the same. All there is, is what there is at this moment. The illusion of momentariness engenders the attitude that this is the only life we can be certain of and thought of as two distinct entities, we conclude that evil means may be used legitimately to attain good ends. In religion we distinguish between saved and unsaved, redeemed and unredeemed. A religious belief is either valid or invalid. A religion is either true or false. Since truth and falsehood are always at odds with each other, conflict between religions is inevitable. The principle of exclusion requires one winning out in the end.

The last illusion to be noted here is the illusion of rationality. It leads to the view that reason is highest in man. We believe that reason is a reliable tool of knowledge or that reason can give us true and complete understanding. It makes us think that the rational man will be inevitably virtuous, i.e. reasonable man. It leads us to the faith that through reason man's problems will be solved and the Utopia reached.

II The Indian View

What is the Indian view regarding these illusions? First we need to clarify the meaning of illusion. A person is illuded when he takes as real or true something which is neither. The illusion may be complete or partial. The Indian generally uses the term in the latter sense. The person mistaking a rope for a snake is not completely illuded. He sees something but misinterprets what he sees. He declares something to be other than what it really is. It is only a rope, not a snake. Similarly, Indian thinkers do not declare the material world unreal in the sense that it does not exist. It is unreal only in that it is not ultimate or true reality.

For example, regarding the illusion of rationality, the Indian thinker does not deny rational knowledge. Rather he claims that reason does not necessarily or always give us valid knowledge and there are other types of knowledge which may give us greater certitude. Thus the person who claims reason is the only source of true and full knowledge is under the spell of an illusion.

Indian thinkers remind us that reason is simply a means to an end. Thus it is in the category of the relative rather than the absolute. That is to say, there is nothing in reason per se to guarantee its being used objectively, i.e. truthfully, rather than for the selfish ends of the reasoner. A superb statement to that effect has already been quoted in the chapter on Buddhism. Radhakrishnan makes a parallel point that reason is often used to separate rather than unite people: "Though the triumphs of intellect are great, its failures are not less great. . . . Even in this artificial world, where intellect has imposed on us the restrictions of tribe, race, and nation, the fundamental humanity of man wells up on occasions. . . . It is our intellectual consciousness that breeds in us the feeling of separatist individuality. . . . Our anxieties are bound up with our intellectuality, whose emergence at the human level causes a fissure or cleavage in our life. The break in the normal and natural order of things in human life is directly traceable to man's intellectuality. . . ."[1]

Radhakrishnan's view is that, in the contemporary West especially, reasoning is a process of minutely analysing and dissecting in which differences are discovered and magnified, resulting in separatism and disunion. His position, typical of Indian thought, is that genuine knowledge is synthetic, comprehensive and unitive. It is knowledge of the whole, not just parts. A composite view takes into account similarities which are believed to far outnumber and outweigh differences. Thus true knowledge unites rather than divides people. Indian thought, as noted in the chapter on Epistemology, emphasizes a "cosmocentric" point of view in which egocentric or man-made distinctions are rejected as being ultimately valid. They are an illusion we must get over.

Indian thinkers criticize the West for setting the knowing process in a dualistic context. In both empirical and rational knowledge a subject-object dichotomy is presupposed. What we know in such a situation is "always characterized by some limitation," as noted in the chapter on Epistemology. One does not know the object directly; he has only his perceptions of it. From the Indian view we should set the knowing process in a monistic context in which the viewer and viewed become one, so to speak. The Indian believes this can be done because the object or thing being perceived or known is in an active not just passive state. Thus the statements in the chapter on Epistemology that ". . . knowing is not something that a knower does. The thing shows itself" and "The objects of our perception and the one that perceives touch one another" make sense. The knowing relationship, to the Indian, is a triad; that which is to be known is an agent also.

Another sense in which the Indian emphasizes a monistic epistemological context is expressed in the phrase "knowing by becoming". In the chapter on the Upaniṣads the author writes "to know Brahman is to be Brahman"; and the author of the chapter on Epistemology states that knowledge of Brahman is gained when the seeker "no more knows it (Brahman) but becomes it." Knowing thus has an ontological status. It is a matter of being, not just doing. Being accompanies or precedes knowing. Thus genuine knowledge is of a unitive not separative type. And the Indian emphasizes we should set all knowledge in a monistic context. We should try to know other persons, just as we do Brahman, by becoming one with them. Doing so we would not treat them as objects but as "I's" and "thou's."

The emphasis on monism may seem strange to those brought up in a dualistic epistemological tradition. The point is that the Indian wishes to somehow overcome the subject-object dichotomy. He wants to know directly or immediately. He believes that only by doing so can we have true knowledge. This may be one reason the Indian associates knowing with vision or illumination. For example, the Vedic seers claimed to have visualized directly or received an inner illumination. Such illumination is a higher form of knowledge than rational. The West sometimes refers to it as intuitive. It is trans-rational or a-rational, not irrational. It is not contrary to reason; yet it is not provable or demonstrable by reason.

The Indian emphasizes a psychological factor important for epistemology also. It is reflected in the view that knowing is discovery. Truth is not something we create but come upon. It already exists; we simply discover it. This may be a blow to our egos but to think otherwise is illusory. This accounts also for the insistence on the close relationship of ethics and epistemology. Only the virtuous man can have full knowledge, for he does not seek knowledge for selfish gain. ". . . You must never exploit truth for your personal aggrandizement," Tagore wrote.[2] Further, the virtuous man will not confuse prejudice or bias with knowledge. In this sense virtue is higher than knowledge or is a prerequisite to the proper use of reason. Morality not reason is, then, the highest in man. Only when reason is in the hands of a virtuous man will it be used for good not evil ends.

Indian thinkers suggest also that epistemological dualisms such as the true-false dichotomy and the principle of exclusion be left behind. For example, from a monistic standpoint we should use a single scale and recognize that truth is a matter of degree. Seldom do we find a situation in which truth is all on one side and falsehood on the other. They are usually shared. Most assertions contain portions of both. No one person knows the whole truth. Our views are always subject to error to some extent. The concepts of absolute truth and falsehood are rational constructs and may lead to unfortunate results. Combined with the exclusion principle they often lead us to think that our views are right and others' wrong. This does not mean we can absolve ourselves from choosing whether we shall go in the direction of truth or falsehood. We can and must make that kind of choice; but this does not mean we shall never stray off in the opposite direction. While it may sound paradoxical, the Indian says we should attempt to transcend both truth and falsehood. The latter is obvious. What he means by transcending the former is, however, that we should not seek truth to use it for our own advantage. We should transcend such a motive. Furthermore, we should rise gradually to that state of being in which we search for and do the truth without even being aware of it. We must seek knowledge or know unknowingly.

The illusion of dualism needs to be overcome in ethics as well. From the Indian viewpoint it is invalid to divide people into the categories of good-bad, friend-foe, acquaintance-stranger; and it often leads to most unfortunate results. One reason is because it overlooks potentiality. Gandhi believed every so-called enemy to be a potential friend and therefore not an enemy in any absolute sense. It leads to such a false distinction as means and ends and the willingness to use evil means to attain good ends. Again Gandhi declared means and ends cannot be separated, that only through good means can good ends be realized. Dualism, further, may tempt us to false projections, to, for example, "espy an enemy in every stranger," in Tagore's words. Such unfortunate results would not occur if these dualisms were not presupposed.

From the Indian perspective a better alternative would be to view man in terms of a single category, in this case the good. Thus it would not be a matter of some men being good and others bad. Rather all are basically good or have the potential for goodness. Some have realized this potential more than others. Some have more obstacles blocking their paths than others. All are trying to realize their essential goodness and have realized it in varying degrees. From such a viewpoint evil is not the opposite but a lesser degree or absence of the good. In fact, in this system the concept of evil would be non-existent. Life is not a matter of going from evil to good but from lesser to higher good.

The Indian tendency toward monism is carried over into metaphysics and other areas as well. As has been noted many times in this volume, the Indian view generally is that reality is one. It has but a single ground. All reality evolves or emanates from one source of being, Brahman. Even in a material sense it is one, for all things are but differentiations of Prakṛiti. Having a single ground, reality does not consist of dialectically related sets. Thus a valid social philosophy, for example, emphasizes the natural oneness or unity of man. Classes are not natural to man; nor is class-conflict inevitable. Nothing in the nature of things makes it so. Societies need not be divided into antagonistic groups. It is not their natural condition. Whoever claims so does not see rightly because he is illuded by dualism.

The same is true in religion. The dichotomies dualistic type religions are based on are false. Such distinctions as saved-unsaved, redeemed-unredeemed, pagan-civilized, true-false are invalid. A person is not either saved or unsaved but is in a process of "going on to salvation" or realization. Some have gone only a little way, others farther; others have neared the end or completed the journey. A religion is not pagan or civilized. It is simply a matter of the degree to which a religion at a particular time in its history has purified itself of undesirable elements. Similarly religions are not true or false but rather in every religion elements of each exist, to a greater extent in one religion than another perhaps, or to a greater extent at one time than another in a religion's history. Likewise a rejection of dialecticalism enables one to see that conflict between religions is not inevitable, that cooperation is quite possible and should be worked toward. Ridding ourselves of the illusion of dualism will give rise to an amazingly different and much more positive world view. It will being in its train practical consequences almost beyond our imagination.

Indian thinkers claim that ridding ourselves of the illusion of separateness will produce identical results also. We need to recognize that reality is an integral whole. It is an interrelated, interdependent totality and true knowledge is knowledge of the whole. Differences are relative not absolute. They are "only matters of names and forms".[3] Differences are accidental not essential; for in essence reality is one. The difference between matter and spirit or material and immaterial is not a substantial one. Rather it is like water which is a liquid under one condition and a gas or vapour under others.

Indian philosophers would emphasize, generally, there is only one category we arrive at finally. Call it what you may—Consciousness, Existence, Being, Brahman, the Absolute—reality simply consists of many manifestations of it. Differences, then, are of degree, not kind. The difference between a person and an animal or tree is the degree of consciousness each exhibits. Man exhibits a much higher degree than a tree; however, they have sentiency as a common characteristic. Reality is one in its basic nature; differences are extrinsic or extraneous. While a great multiplicity of things exist, they exist not as isolated particulars but as particular manifestations of a single reality. From a metaphysical standpoint every particular is set within a context. That context is both a part of and apart from the particular. Thus the particular is both a particular and more than a particular; it is an irreducible part of a whole. From a religious viewpoint everything which exists is a particular emmanation of that One which is behind all, Brahman.

Thus while there is diversity, there is also oneness. All particulars are manifestations of the one Absolute, the one Universal. This view affirms both the particular and the universal. One need not be denied to affirm the other. As Tagore says: "The true universal finds its manifestation in the individual which is also true."[4] The allowance of diversity yet insistence on unity is a major theme of Indian thought. As pointed out in that chapter, it is a basic thesis of the Vedas: "Reality is one; sages call it variously." The Gītā asserts it: "Who sees the separate lives of all creatures, united in

3rahman, brought forth from Brahman, himself finds Brahman." ;aṅkara was its primary medieval exponent. Many assert it in the nodern period. Tagore wrote: "The inmost creed of India is to ind the one in the many, unity in diversity. India does not admit lifference to be conflict . . ."[5] "Unity in variety is the plan of he universe," Vivekananda told an America audience; and Auro-)indo wrote: "In nature, therefore, all things that exist, animate or nanimate, are becomings of the one Self of all. All these different :reatures are one indivisible existence."[6]

It is not to be wondered, then, that Indian thinkers generally 'eject not only a dualistic and dialectical but a positivistic, particu-aristic epistemology as well. For them true knowledge is not solely he knowing of particulars. It does not consist of the isolated per-:eptions we have of particular objects. Perceptual knowledge s not denied but viewed as only one and a limited way of knowing. Гrue knowledge is knowledge by identification and encompasses all 'eality. It is a vision of the parts, the whole and the interrelations naking the parts into a whole. It is a recognition of the entities ıniting reality and a realization of their greater importance. Lower :nowledge is knowledge of parts, higher of the whole. Inclusiveness s a criterion of truth. The more inclusive one's knowledge, the ıigher it is. Man has a natural capacity to see as a whole; he ıeed only exercise it. He can transcend his own limited experiences ınd incorporate those of others into a comprehensive view of reality. Liberation and perfection result. Aurobindo wrote: "When this ınity has been realized by the individual in every part of his being, ıe becomes perfect, pure, liberated from ego and the dualities,)ossessed of the entire divine felicity."[7]

Both broader and sympathetic understanding is required today. We must put much more effort into seeing things from others')oint of view. We need a greater understanding of how people n other nations think and feel; and our understanding must be empathetic, not simply objective. Empathy is the projecting of our-selves into others in order to understand and feel as they do. The objective, analytical type of thinking, dominant today in the West especially, lacks this. It is based on dualism and separatism rather than the identification of knower and known. Is it to be wondered there is much disunity and conflict in the world?

The practical implications of the rejection of separateness, the assertion of monism and the insistence on unity in plurality are especially momentous for us today. They offer a way to religious reconciliation, social harmony and world unity. They provide a natural foundation for such because they begin with the premise that man's natural feeling is of oneness with his fellows and the universe. Man's "primary patriotism," Radhakrishnan declared, "is the love of humanity."[8] From an Indian non-dialectical, non-Darwinian view the universe and others are friendly, not alien to us. It is not natural or inevitable that we view the stranger as an enemy for, as Radhakrishnan says: "Left to himself, man feels kinship with the whole universe, especially with living things and human beings. The sense of community is latent in the hearts of men" and man need not feel "himself at enmity with . . . the cosmic process" of which he was born.[9]

From the Indian viewpoint every individual is a part of a larger context, mankind; just as every particular is a member of a universal. Nor should we let anything come between the particular and the universal, i.e. the individual and mankind. Every individual is a manifestation of that which is greater than himself. The Upaniṣads declare: "There is one Supreme Ruler, the inmost Self of all beings, who makes His one form manifold. Eternal happiness belongs to the wise, who perceive Him within themselves."[10] In the twentieth century Gandhi reflects this view in his statement: "I believe in the essential unity of man and for that mater of all that lives. . . . I believe in the absolute oneness of God and therefore also of humanity."[11] The Indian believes the recognition that all are one under God is the initial step toward self-realization. "The first movement of self-realization is the sense of unity with other existences in the universe," Aurobindo wrote.[12] Or, as the Gītā indicates, liberation is living at peace in the universal or in a universal relationship. All are liberated when each sees his fellows as himself, as having the same feelings, needs, concerns, doubts and longings.

Oneness does not deny diversity. Unity does not mean individual differences are stifled. As a matter of fact they are encouraged. At the same time it is asserted that self-fulfilment takes place within and not apart from the group or whole; and self fulfilment is not to be carried out at the expense of others. "Man becomes great," Gandhi said, "exactly in the degree in which he works for the welfare of his fellow-man."[13] This is a "duties" not "rights" oriented philosophy. Being part of a whole entails duties to all as well as to oneself.

From an Indian viewpoint harmony within a society is more likely if duties are emphasized, if not more, at least as much as rights are. A peaceful society results not from individuals always bellicosely asserting their rights but from their willingly fulfilling their obligations toward each other. This is especially true of relations between the weak and the strong, the less and the more talented, the more and the less able. The classical Indian view is that the more highly one is endowed the greater his responsibilities toward others. It is immoral for one to use his greater capacities for his own gain only. They should be used in addition or primarily for the benefit of others. This outlook is based on a non-separatist view of man. The separatist view leads to the attitude that a person has no responsibility toward others and that his major concern is only for himself. It leads to the fallacious view that society's good is insured by each one being concerned for his welfare only.

Indian philosophers claim that the metaphysical concepts of oneness and plurality imply in social philosophy the view of society as an organism. A society is not a collection of individuals loosely joined by self-interest but an integral unit like an organism made up of many different but interrelated and mutually dependent parts. Their interests are ameliorative not antagonistic because they have basic needs and goals in common. Interdependence and harmony are therefore natural. Each part or group contributes to and receives from the whole. The good of one is tied up with the good of all.

From the organic view what is true for individual societies is also true for the world as a whole. As reality is an organic totality, so is mankind. Each person is a citizen not only of a nation but of the world. Nations are not independent, isolated, self-contained units free to assert their rights and act as they please. Such an attitude leads to division and conflict and denies the oneness of mankind. Tagore advocated "the advaita of humanity", replace "the bondage of nationalism" and "the egotistic spirit of separation and self assertion" which false nationalism stimulates.[14] The oneness of reality and mankind makes bellicose nationalism invalid and fruitless. Again monism does not rule out national any more than individual differences. It only means, as Tagore points out, that nations should not stress their uniqueness to the point of becoming a barrier to world brotherhood. Tagore's ideal was a pluralistic world in which each nation contributes to the world in its own particular way. Radhakrishnan points out that a world of independent nations, in which national sovereignty has some "mystical" significance is outdated. He believes such an outlook "is in dissolution and will soon be a past chapter in man's history."[15] As the world becomes more crowded and constricted, the significance and relevance of the "organicist" social philosophy of mutual dependence, unity within diversity, a pluralistic yet peaceful world will become more apparent and one people in increasing numbers will assent to.

Regarding the philosophy of separatism and ethics, Indian thinkers claim that only by denying separateness can one rise to the level of true virtue, the level of the universal. Separatism implies the individual is concerned only for his own good, but the virtuous man is concerned with the good of all. Such a criterion means that even concern for the good of the majority is not enough. Gandhi declared: "A votary of Ahiṃsā cannot subscribe to the utilitarian formula of the greatest good of the greatest number. He will strive for the greatest good of all and die in the attempt to realize the ideal. . . Not the good of the few, not even the good of the many but it is the good of all that we are made to promote, if we are 'made in His own image'."[16]

A separatist philosophy tends also to lead to the willing use of others as means to one's own good and this is stoutly denied in Indian thought. Buddha's statement, "Exalt not thyself by trampling down others", is an outstanding example of this. Utilitarianism as an ethical principle is generally opposed in the Indian tradition. To do the good because it is to our advantage or because it is useful for us to do so is not acting ethically but only expediently. Furthermore, while the utilitarion criterion may be valid for things—we can base the worth of a shovel on its degree of usefulness—it is not for people. The worth of a person is intrinsic in him and is not determined by how useful he is, especially as a means to another's ends. Indian thinkers have generally rejected ethical relativism as being simply egoism and therefore not an ethical philosophy at all. To say that the good is what is good for me and not necessarily for someone else is to take a very self-centred view of the good. In so much as we are extensions of each other, the good of one cannot be sharply separated, nor can it be completely different from that of others. There is such a reality as the common good. There are universal rights and wrongs. To say, therefore, there is only my good or the good is whatever is good for me is egoistic, contrary to reality and conductive to unfortunate results.

The Indian claims that the analogy between the individual and group or nation is valid in this instance too. Nations acting only in terms of their own interests are, likewise, not acting virtuously but only expediently. They act morally only when they are concerned over the good of other nations as much as their own. Nations, like individuals, act ethically when they act on the level of the universal, that is in terms of the good of mankind and not their separate good. Nations like individuals must transcend the illusion of "I and mine" which separatism perpetuates and rise to the level of "we and ours" in their thinking and actions.

The Indian emphasizes the need for overcoming the illusion of separatism and accepting a monistic-pluralistic view especially in the realm of religion. For one reason, the function of religion is to unite, not separate people. Religion becomes sectarianism if this primary task is not performed. Radhakrishnan stated that "It is the function of religion to reaffirm the intuitive loyalty to life and solidarity of human nature, to lift us out of the illusion of isolation and take us back to reality."[17] Vivekananda lamented that ". . . nothing has engendered fiercer hatred than religion"[18] and agreed with Keshub C. Sen that "The true object of religion is to bind mankind together, and to bind them all to God."[19]

The Indian declares religions become divisive when they accept a dualistic rather than monistic metaphysics. Dualistic type religions divide reality into dialectically related sets—man and God, true and false, the natural and supernatural. The Indian mind with its monistic world view rejects such dualities. This is seen in its definition of religion as realization based on the view that God and man are not separate entities but that God is within each man, or God is each man, and being religious is a recognition of and growing in the light of that truth. It is also based on the willingness of Indian thinkers to go beyond the view that "the nature of ultimate reality can be apprehended only as an object of reason."[20] Ultimate reality is "supra-rational". It is not "in its ultimate nature accessible to conceptual understanding" but is experienced directly in a kind of experience which "transcends all forms, all images, and all concepts."[21] Reason is not contradictory to religion. Rather religion simply transcends the dualities and separatism reason engenders.

Classical Indian thought rejects the true-false dichotomy in religion and asserts that all religions are true or there is truth in all religions, and by the same token, error also. Gandhi stated: "All faiths constitute a relevation of Truth, but all are imperfect and liable to error,"[22] and K. C. Sen declared: "Each sect in this world, each nation, each race, in my humble view, represents truth partially. The whole truth has not yet been revealed to any one of us . . ."[23] The Indian rejects the true-false and superior-inferior dichotomies for three reasons. They yield undesirable results. Gandhi asserted: "It is a travesty of true religion to consider one's own religion as superior and other's as inferior"[24] and the result, K. C. Sen said, is that "Men hate each other . . . because they believe that there is no truth beyond the pale of their own denominations and churches."[25] The true-false dichotomy is invalid, secondly, because it does not recognize the finite context in which religions are set. It assumes a perfect revelation and perfect recipients. Such an assumption is in error, Gahdhi believed, because all religions "have been received and interpreted through human instruments" who are imperfect. Vivekananda expressed that view somewhat differently: "All religions are but applications of the one religion adapted to meet the requirements of different nations" and every religion "is determined by the conditions of its birth."

The true-false dichotomy is invalid also because it does not take into account the truth that, while there is only one God, that Being can or has expressed or revealed itself not in just one but many ways. D. M. Datta states one of the major characteristics of Indian thought is "its conviction that Ultimate Reality manifests itself, or can be conceived in different ways. . . ."[26] The acceptance of such a metaphysics enabled Keshub C. Sen to say "God manifests Himself to us through external nature, through the inner spirit, and through moral greatness impersonated in man. . . . Thus we see there is One God, but there are three modes of revelation,"[27] and for Ramakrishna to claim "Many are the names of God, and infinite the forms that lead us to know him."[28] The view being upheld here is what might be called a monistic pluralism. It is quite different from the western religious view of only one revelation and one true religion.

Monistic pluralism in Indian religious thought is reflected also in its belief in many incarnations rather than one. The Bhagavad Gītā statement to that effect has been quoted already. From such a viewpoint a number of avatāras or saviours have appeared in history —Kṛiṣṇa, Buddha, Christ, Mohammed, Caitanya, Ramakrishna. They all come from Brahman and have an identical task, to rid the world of evil. Thus we cannot validly claim one of them the true saviour and the others imposters or the revelation associated with one as valid and the others invalid. Each is but a different revelation in a different time and place of the one ground of all being, Brahman.

From a monistic pluralism standpoint there is a natural affinity between religions which we would recognize if we could get beyond the illusions of dualism and separatism. It is a correlate of the unity and diversity in reality as a whole. "Unity in variety is the plan of the universe," Vivekananda declared. And Gandhi stated: "In Nature, there is a fundamental unity running through all the diversity we see about us. Religions are no exception to this natural law. They are given to mankind so as to accelerate the process of realization of fundamental unity."[29] The natural affinity of religions is a result of their having a single source and a common goal. That affinity makes it possible to affirm each religion is but a different means to the same end, a different path to the same vantage point. Ramakrishna declared that "As one can ascend to the top of a house by means of a ladder or a bamboo or a staircase or a rope, so diverse also are the ways and means to approach God, and every religion in the world shows one of these ways" and "As the same sugar is made into various figures of birds and beasts, so one sweet Divine Mother is worshipped in various climes and ages under various names and forms. Different creeds are but different paths to reach the Almighty."[30] Gandhi, drawing on nature, said that "Just as a tree has many branches but one root, similarly the various religions are the leaves and branches of the same tree." Vivekananda wrote: "My idea, therefore, is that all these religions are different forces in the economy of God, working for the good of mankind."[31]

Indian thinkers emphasize the many positive results of accepting a monistic pluralism in religion. A significant one is its provision of a theistic basis necessary for world brotherhood. If we are to have a "one world", it must be grounded in religion. An economic or political basis is not strong enough for they are rooted in self-interest, which is not conducive to lasting relations. A monistic pluralism makes possible and encourages the attitudes necessary for the unity of mankind. It stimulates tolerance and respect. Ramakrishna said: "A truly religious man should think that other religions also are paths leading to the truth. We should maintain an attitude of respect toward other religions."[32] Gandhi noted two results of such an attitude: "One must, therefore, entertain the same respect for the religious faiths of others as one accords to one's own. Where such tolerance becomes a law of life, conflict between faiths becomes impossible, and so does all effort to convert other people to one's own faith."[33]

One result of tolerance and respect is that a person is no longer concerned about converting others. The rejection of the true-false dichotomy reinforces that attitude. Instead each is anxious about improving his own religion, living up to the best of it and encouraging others to do the same in regard to theirs. Ramakrishna's advice to Moslem, Hindu and Christian was: "Remain always strong and steadfast in thine own faith but eschew all bigotry and intolerance."[34] Asked how religious quarrels might be resolved, Gandhi replied: "The key to the solution of the tangle lies in everyone following the best in his own religion and entertaining equal regard for other religions and their followers."[35] D. S. Sarma asserted that contemporary education should be set up to meet that end: "As we Hindus believe in the truth of all religions, it is our duty to strengthen the faith of each student in his own religion."[36]

A second result of tolerance is that it would minimize and eventually eliminate much religious conflict. The Indian attitude is that conflict between various sects within a particular religion is not inevitable because each simply emphasizes a particular aspect of religion and is an expression of but one of many ways to God. Since individuals vary, their approach to religion will also vary, and sectarianism is an outgrowth of these individual differences. Moreover, the different sects represent different levels of religious maturation. Sarma points out, for example, that "Dvaita, Viśiṣṭādvaita and Advaita are three stages in the spiritual growth of man."[37]

Conflict between religions is not inevitable either. One reason, Vivekananda said, is that "religions are not contradictory but supplementary." Moreover, from the non-dualistic perspective, other religions are not enemies to be defeated but allies to work with toward common goals. P. T. Raju expresses this catholic view as follows: "We have more important objectives to work and fight for than ideologies, religious or political. The welfare of humanity, a fuller and deeper life for man on earth, is a more urgent problem than is the spread of one's own religion or philosophy and defeat of all others."[38]

Actually, to the Indian, tolerance is not enough. Acceptance, Vivekananda asserted, should be the "watchword". The attitude of tolerance is too negative and implies one does not believe there is any truth or value to other religions and one merely lets them exist until they disappear by default. This is contrary to the Indian view of truth in all religions. It implies, D. S. Sarma says, that "our policy should not be one of absorption, but of fraternization."[39] Acceptance and fraternization is much more positive and will facilitate reaching the goal all religions seek, the realization of God.

Acceptance does not imply or lead to religious syncretism. The syncretist is one who would have a single religion for the entire world. It might be a combination of the best in existing religions or an entirely new religion with no roots whatever in present ones. All people would accept and practise it. As mentioned already, this alternative took shape in nineteenth-century India in the Samajs and the Theosophical Societies. After an initial surge, they waned however; primarily because they were contrary to the monistic pluralism in which Indian religious thought is grounded. The monism they emphasized was an artificial or forced one. It had no room for the variety which is an inevitable part of all reality. It was contrary to the ideal of peaceful coexistence, the logical implication of monistic pluralism, which Indian thought has traditionally upheld.

As to the illusion of materiality, Indian thought does not deny the existence of the material world, as is often supposed. Instead it simply attributes a relative, not absolute, status or worth to it. The spiritual or immaterial is prior or first, and whatever worth the material has is derived from the spiritual. To the Indian material reality is characterized by a finitude and limitation which man seeks to transcend or transform. Giving greater status, existence, significance or worth to material reality is, then, an illusion which must be overcome, for true reality is of the nature of the immaterial.

A similar position is taken in ethics. Indian thinkers do not assert that no time or effort should be given to the acquisition of material things, as many non-Indians believe. Radhakrishnan states that "There was never in India a national ideal of poverty or squalor."[40] And Artha has always been one of the four legitimate ends of life, as noted several times in this volume. The image of asceticism has often been associated with India; it should be pointed out that asceticism has in actuality been practised only by a few. It has been held up as an ideal, but moderation is the accepted rule in practice.

What the Indian asserts is that Artha should not be indulged in excessively and it should not become the single end of one's life. This attitude is found in the Bhagavad Gītā wherein we are urged not to become so attached to material things that they overwhelm us. The Buddhist says we should be like the lotus which, while growing in mud, is not stained by it. The acquisition of material things is held up as the primary end in a materialistic culture. The Indian would give them a second rather than first preference. He points out that in materialistic cultures a person's self-image is associated with the things he owns. Thus one views himself in terms of what he has. His worth is in proportion to what he possesses. From the Indian view this is erroneous, for one's worth comes from being, not having. A person's true measure is what he is, not what he has. The illusion of materialism leads us to substitute a false quantitative for a true qualitative standard in determining a person's worth.

The Indian asserts that in this respect what is true on the individual is also true on the social or national level. Radhakrishnan said that "Nations, like individuals, are made, not only by what they acquire, but by what they resign."[41] Tagore stated that no "nation in the world can be great and yet be materialistic." He added: "The great societies are the creation not of profiteers, but of dreamers. The millionaires who produce bales of merchandise in enormous quantities have never yet built a great civilization; it is they who are about to destroy what others have built."[42] Sarma wrote that "we should measure our progress as a nation, not in terms of the weapons of destruction we can forge or of the factories of production we can erect, but in terms of the degree of non-violence and spirituality that we can put into practice."[43] The danger he is referring to is that a materialistic society or nation is prone to turn toward a quantitative solution to both its internal and external problems. It is apt to be misled into believing that force can solve problems right wrongs. Tagore's comment was that "Power is intrinsically a-social" and "When greed and the worship of might grow unrestrained in social life, it becomes impossible for man to devote himself to the development of his humanity."[44] Gandhi, of course, is the best known recent Indian leader to deny the use of force and to uphold non-violence as a solution to national and international conflicts. He believed neither nations nor individuals realize or save themselves through force. To the Indian man's basic problem is an ethical and spiritual one requiring a qualitative not quantitative solution. This will be realized only when the illusion of materiality is overcome.

Let us conclude by reminding ourselves of the basic theme of this epilogue. A major contribution Indian thought can make today is to remind the world of the illusions it must overcome. Our present crisis results from living by illusions. Indian thought would call us back to the real.

REFERENCES AND BIBLIOGRAPHIES

Chapter 1: Prologue

REFERENCES

1. Charles A. Moore, *The Indian Mind,* Honolulu, 1967, p. 12
2. M. Hiriyanna, *Outlines of Indian Philosophy,* London, 1951, p. 17
3. Jadunath Sinha, *Introduction to Philosophy,* Calcutta, 1964, p. 16
4. Surendranath Dasgupta, *Indian Idealism,* Cambridge, 1962, p. 27
5. Moore, op. cit., p. 11
6. S. V. Venkateswara, *Indian Culture Through the Ages,* London, 1928, Vol. I, p. 32
7. Sinha, op. cit., p. 1
8. S. Radhakrishnan, *Indian Philosophy,* London, 1948, Vol. I, p. 32
9. M. Hiriyanna, *Essentials of Indian Philosophy,* London, 1967, p. 25
10. Dhirendra M. Datta, *The Chief Currents of Contemporary Philosophy,* Calcutta, 1961, p. 578
11. Moore, op. cit., p. 10
12. Radhakrishnan, op. cit., Vol. I, p. 28
13. Moore, op. cit., p. 25
14. Sinha, op. cit., pp. 1-2
15. S. C. Chatterjee and D. M. Datta, *An Introduction to Indian Philosophy,* Calcutta, 1960, p. 3
16. Datta, op. cit., pp. 577-8
17. Sinha, op. cit., p. 20
18. Datta, op. cit., p. 568
19. Radhakrishnan, op. cit., p. 25
20. Hiriyanna, op. cit., p. 18
21. Datta, ibid.
22. Hiriyanna, op. cit., p. 25
23. Venkateswara, op. cit., p. 32
24. Hiriyanna, op. cit., p. 18
25. Radhakrishnan, op. cit., p. 44
26. Radhakrishnan, op. cit., p. 46
27. Datta, op. cit., p. 578
28. Chandradhar Sharma, *Indian Philosophy: A Critical Survey,* London, 1960, p. 1
29. Radhakrishnan, op. cit., p. 28
30. Paul Carus, *The Gospel of Buddha,* Chicago, 1915, p. 131
31. Moore, op. cit., p. 15
32. H. Nakamura, *Ways of Thinking of Eastern People,* Honolulu, 1964, p. 154
33. Moore, op. cit., p. 15
34. Radhakrishnan, op. cit., p. 33

35. Radhakrishnan, op. cit., p. 34
36. Venkateswara, op. cit., p. 41
37. Sri Aurobindo Centre Saukati, *Magural Number,* Pondicherry, 1951, pp. 57-8
38. Radhakrishnan, op. cit., p. 174
39. Radhakrishnan, op. cit., p. 34
40. Sinha, op. cit., p. 1
41. Sharma, ibid.
42. Sinha, op. cit., p. 366
43. Hiriyanna, op. cit., p. 22
44. Hiriyanna, op. cit., p. 24
45. Hiriyanna, ibid.
46. S. Radhakrishnan, *Eastern Religions and Western Thought,* New York, 1959, p. 103

PART I: EARLY INDIAN LITERATURE AND THOUGHT

REFERENCES

1. Swami Prabhavananda and Frederick Manchester, *The Spiritual Heritage of India,* New York, 1963, p. 139
2. Chandradhar Sharma, *Indian Philosophy: A Critical Survey,* London, 1960, p. 2
3. Sharma, ibid.
4. Prabhavananda and Manchester, op. cit., p. 72
5. D. S. Sarma, *What Is Hinduism?*, Mylapore, 1941, p. 18
6. M. Hiriyanna, *Essentials of Indian Philosophy,* London, 1967, p. 42
7. D. S. Sarma, *Hinduism Through the Ages*, Bombay, 1967, p. 31
8. Sarma, op. cit., p. 39
9. Prabhavananda and Manchester, op. cit., p. 139
10. Prabhavananda and Manchester, op. cit., p. XIX
11. Sarma, op. cit., p. 28
12. Dhirendra M. Datta, *The Chief Currents of Contemporary Philosophy,* Calcutta, 1961, p. 568

Chapter 2: THE VEDAS

REFERENCES

1. Sri Aurobindo, *On the Vedas,* Pondicherry, 1956, p. 5
2. Haridas Bhattacharyya, *The Cultural Heritage of India,* Calcutta, 1953, Vol. I, p. 182
3. Sri Aurobindo, op. cit., p. 6
4. Rig-veda, X 164.46
5. Datta and Chatterjee, *An Introduction to Indian Philosophy,* Calcutta, 1960, p. 352
6. T. V. Kapali Sastry, *Lights on the Veda,* 1947, p. 20
7. Sri Aurobindo, *Bankim-Tilak-Dayananda,* 1947, p. 61
8. See Vedanta I 1.3 and Vaishesika I 1.3
9. Yajur-veda 22.1; see also Rig-veda I 164.46 and Atharva-veda V 13.4.16
10. Sri Aurobindo, op. cit., p. 61
11. For examples see Rig-veda III 54.8 and Rig Veda V 58.2

12. A. C. Bose, *The Call of the Vedas,* Bombay, 1960, p. 2
13. Bose, ibid., p. 4
14. Rig-veda I 164.46
15. Rig-veda III 62.9
16. Atharva-veda XIII 4
17. Rig-veda VIII 58.2, see also Rig-veda I 89.10 and Atharva-veda IV 163
18. Rig-veda VIII 43.24
19. Atharva-veda XII 1.1
20. T. V. Kapali Sastry, *Further Lights: The Veda and the Tantra,* Pondicherry, 1951, pp. 14-15
21. Sastry, op. cit., p. 32
22. Rig-veda, Mandala IX (Aurobindo's translation)
23. Rig-veda, X 129

BIBLIOGRAPHY

1. Bloomfield, Maurice, tr., F. Max Müller, ed., Hymns of the Atharva-Veda, Vol. XLII, *Sacred Books of the East,* Oxford, 1897
2. Bose, Abinash Chandra, *Hymns from the Vedas,* Bombay and New York, 1966
3. Edgerton, Franklin, *The Beginnings of Indian Philosophy, Selections from Rig Veda, Atharva Veda, Upanishads and Mahabharata,* Cambridge, 1965
4. Gonda, J., *The Vedic God Mitra,* Leiden, 1972
5. Griffity, Ralph T. H., *The Hymns of the Rigveda,* Varanasi, 1963
6. Hiriyanna, M., *The Essentials of Indian Philosophy,* London, 1948, Ch. 1
7. Macdonnell, A. A., *The Vedic Mythology,* Varanasi and Delhi, 1971
8. Müller, F. Max, tr. and ed., Vedic Hymns, Vols. XXXII, XLVI, *Sacred Books of the East,* Oxford, 1897
9. Prabhavananda and Frederick Manchester, *The Spiritual Heritage of India,* New York, 1963, Ch. 1
10. Radhakrishnan, S., Chairman, Editorial Board, *History of Philosophy, Eastern and Western,* London, 1954, Vol. I, Ch. II
11. Renou, Louis, *The Destiny of the Veda in India,* Delhi, 1965
12. Renou, Louis, *Religions of Ancient India,* New York, 1968
13. Smith, H. Daniel, *Selections from Vedic Hymns,* Berkeley, 1968

Chapter 3: THE UPANIṢADS AND UPANIṢADIC THOUGHT

REFERENCES

1. Chāndogya 4-9-3
2. Muṇḍaka 1-2-13
3. Chāndogya 7-8-1
4. *The Concordance of Upaniṣadic Sentences,* by G. S. Sadhale, contains references to as many as 239 Upaniṣads many of which are obviously unpublished.
5. Muṇḍaka 1-1-3
6. Kena 1-1
7. Śvetāśvatara 1-1
8. Bṛihadāraṇyaka 4-5-4

9. Muṇḍaka 1-1-4, 5
10. Īśa 11
11. Muṇḍaka 1-1-1
12. Kena 2-5
13. Kaṭha 1-2-2
14. Bṛihadāraṇyaka 1-3-28
15. Bṛihadāraṇyaka 4-5-6; cf. Śvet, 1-12
16. Māṇḍukya 2
17. Taittirīya 2-8
18. Īśa 16
19. Bṛihadāraṇyaka 1-4-10
20. Chāndogya 6-8-7, 6-9-4, 6-14-3
21. Kena 1-2
22. Kena 1-4
23. Praśna 4-9
24. Māṇḍukya 7
25. Taittirīya 3-1. cf. the whole of ch. 3
26. Taittirīya 3-6
27. cf. Khaṇḍa 3
28. Ṛigveda I, 164.46. See also X 114.5
29. Kaṭha 4-12
30. Kaṭha 6-3
31. Muṇḍaka 2-2-5
32. Taittirīya 2-4
33. Muṇḍaka 2-2-11
34. Īśa 1
35. Chāndogya 3-14-11
36. Kaṭha 5-15; Muṇḍaka 2-2-10; Śvetāśvatara 6-14
37. Aitareya 5-3
38. Taittirīya 2-1
39. Bṛihadāraṇyaka 5-1
40. Īśa 5
41. Śvetāśvatara 3-20
42. It is also spelled AUM
43. Māṇḍukya 1
44. Taittirīya 1-8, also Kaṭha 2-15, 16
45. Taittirīya 3-6
46. Taittirīya 2-7, 2-9
47. Kaṭha 5-14
48. Bṛihadāraṇyaka 2-5
49. Chāndogya 3-1 to 11
50. Bṛihadāraṇyaka 2-5-14
51. Chāndogya 3-1 to 11
52. Muṇḍaka 1-1-7
53. Bṛihadāraṇyaka, 2-1-20, Muṇḍaka 2-1-1

54. Kaṭha 5-9
55. Bṛihadāraṇyaka 5-1
56. Bṛihadāraṇyaka 3-8
57. Śvetāśvatara 3-18
58. Bṛihadāraṇyaka 4-4-19
59. Chāndogya 6-1-4
60. Śvetāśvatara 3-14, 15, 16; Ṛigveda 10-90, 1, 2, 3. The whole sūkta is called "Puruṣa Sūkta" cf. Muṇḍaka 2-1-10
61. Muṇḍaka 3-2-9
62. Praśna 4-10
63. Bṛihadāraṇyaka 4-5-6
64. Kena 4-8
65. Muṇḍaka 3-2-3, also Kaṭha 1-2-23
66. Chāndogya 7-22, 7-23-25
67. Bṛihadāraṇyaka 4-3-32
68. Kaṭha 4-10-11, also Bṛihadāraṇyaka 4-4-19
69. Kaṭha 6-9, also Śvetāśvatara 3-13, 4-17
70. Kaṭha 2-12
71. Kaṭha 3-12
72. Kaṭha 6-10
73. Kaṭha 2-24
74. Kaṭha 6-14
75. Kaṭha 3-13, 14
76. Īśa 2
77. Īśa 1, 5
78. Kaṭha 1-27
79. Bṛihadāraṇyaka 4-5-3
80. Īśa 6, 7
81. Taittirīya 2-9
82. Bṛihadāraṇyaka 4-4-22, 23
83. Bṛihadāraṇyaka 4-5-6
84. Taittirīya 1-6

BIBLIOGRAPHY

1. Deussen, Paul, *The Philosophy of the Upanishads*
2. Hume, R. E., *The Thirteen Principal Upanishads,* Oxford, 1931
3. Maccaro, Juan, *The Upanishads,* Baltimore, 1965
4. Müller, F. Max, tr. and ed., *The Upanishads,* Vol. I, XV, *Sacred Books of The East,* Oxford, 1884
5. Nikhilananda, *The Upanishads,* New York, 1949, Four Volumes
6. Pandit, M. P., *Guide to the Upanishads,* Pondicherry, 1967
7. Prabhavananda and Frederick Manchester, *The Spiritual Heritage of India,* New York, 1963, Ch. 3
8. Prabhavananda and Frederick Manchester, trs., *The Upanishads*
9. Radhakrishnan, S.. *The Philosophy of the Upanishads,* London

10. Radhakrishnan, S., *The Principal Upanishads,* London, 1953
11. Raju, P. T., *The Philosophical Traditions of India,* London, 1971, Ch. 3
12. Ranade, R. D., *A Constructive Survey of Upanishadic Philosophy,* Bombay
13. Rao, K. B. Ramakrishna, *Advaita As Philosophy and Religion,* Mysore, 1969
14. Rao, K. B. Ramakrishna, *Ontology of Advaita,* Mulki, 1965
15. Sinha, Jadunath, *Outlines of Indian Philosophy,* Calcutta, 1963, Ch. 2

Chapter 4: The Bhagavad Gītā

References

1. Swami Prabhavananda and Christopher Isherwood, trs., *The Bhagavad-Gītā,* Mentor Books, New York, 1954, pp. 88, 104, 67. Subsequent references are to this edition.
2. Georg Bühler, tr., The Laws of Manu, *Sacred Books of The East,* Vol. XXV, Dover Publications, New York, 1969, p. 503
3. Swami Nikhilananda, *The Upanishads,* Harper Torchbooks, New York, 1964, p. 90
4. The Gītā, p. 67
5. The Gītā, p. 99
6. Nirmal Kumar Bose, *Selections from Gandhi,* Ahmedabad, 1950, p. 7
7. The Gītā, p. 40
8. The Gītā, p. 42
9. The Gītā, p. 45
10. The Gītā, p. 58
11. Moses Hadas, *Essential Works of Stoicism,* Bantam Books, New York, 1961, p. 86
12. S. C. Chatterjee and D. C. Datta, *An Introduction to Indian Philosophy,* Calcutta, 1960, p. 17
13. The Gītā, p. 97
14. The Gītā, p. 99
15. Moses Hadas, op. cit., p. 67
16. Wm. De Bary, *Sources of the Indian Tradition,* New York, 1958, Vol. II, p. 378
17. The Gītā, p. 119
18. W. T. Jones, *Approaches to Ethics,* New York, 1962, p. 261
19. Bühler, op. cit., p. 416
20. The Gītā, p. 125
21. The Gītā, p. 62
22. De Bary, op. cit., p. 243 and John Yale, *What Religion Is,* London, 1962, p. 203
23. The Gītā, p. 127
24. The Gītā, p. 85
25. The Gītā, p. 50
26. Swami Prabhavananda and Frederick Manchester, *The Spiritual Heritage of India,* New York, 1964, p. 418
27. The Gītā, p. 99
28. Prabhavananda and Manchester, op. cit., p. 419

29. Prabhavananda and Manchester, op. cit., p. 93
30. The Gītā, p. 86
31. The Gītā, p. 95
32. The Gītā, p. 88
33. The Gītā, p. 89
34. The Gītā, p. 102
35. The Gītā, pp. 91, 95
36. A. C. McGiffert, *A History of Christian Thought,* New York, 1954, Vol. II, p. 362
37. Khalil Gibran, *The Prophet,* New York, 1923, p. 79
38. See Josiah Royce, *The Religious Aspect of Philosophy,* Cambridge, 1885
39. The Gītā, p. 92
40. W. T. Jones, op. cit., p. 95
41. Walter Stace, *The Teachings of the Mystics,* New York, 1960, p. 215
42. The Gītā, p. 111
43. The Gītā, pp. 103, 112
44. The Gītā, p. 103
45. The Gītā, p. 51
46. The Gītā, p. 73
47. The Gītā, p. 98
48. Ibid.
49. Ibid.
50. S. Radhakrishnan, *History of Philosophy, Eastern and Western,* London, 1957, p. 120
51. The Gītā, p. 59
52. The Gītā, p. 85
53. The Gītā, p. 69

BIBLIOGRAPHY

1. Chidbhavananda, *The Bhagavad Gītā,* Tiruppanatturai, 1965
2. Date, V. H., *Brahma-Yoga of the Gītā,* New Delhi, 1971
3. Deutsch, Eliot, *The Bhagavad Gītā,* New York, 1968
4. Paradkar, M. D., *Studies in the Gītā,* Bombay, 1970
5. Prabhavananda and Christopher Isherwood, trs., *The Song of God: The Bhagavad-Gītā,* Hollywood, 1944
6. Prabhavananda and Frederick Manchester, *The Spiritual Heritage of India,* New York, 1963, Ch. 5
7. Raju, P. T., *The Philosophical Traditions of India,* London, 1971, Ch. XIII
8. Sinha, Jadunath, *Outlines of Indian Philosophy,* Calcutta, 1965, Ch. III
9. Zimmer, Heinrich, *Philosophies of India,* Princeton, 1951

Chapter 5: JAINISM

REFERENCES

1. F. Max Müller, ed., *Sacred Books of the East,* Delhi, 1964 (reprinted) Vol. XLV, p. 256
2. S. Radhakrishnan, *History of Philosophy, Eastern and Western,* 1957, p. 148

3. A. L. Basham, *The Wonder That Was India,* Bombay, 1963, p. 239
4. E. R. Pike, *Encyclopaedia of Religion and Religions,* New York, 1958, p. 204
5. S. Radhakrishnan and C. A. Moore, *A Sourcebook in Indian Philosophy,* Princeton, 1957, p. 251
6. S. Radhakrishnan, *History,* p. 139
7. Sacred Books, Vol. XXII pp. 28, 31, 61
8. W. Theodore De Bary, *Sources of Indian Tradition,* New York, 1958, p. 67
9. Sacred Books, Vol. XXII, p. 36
10. Sacred Books, Vol. XXII, p. 61
11. Sacred Books, Vol. XXII, p. 202
12. Radhakrishnan and Moore, op. cit., p. 258
13. Sacred Books, Vol. XXII, p. 203
14. S. Radhakrishnan, *History,* p. 139
15. De Bary, op. cit., p. 61
16. Radhakrishnan and Moore, op. cit., p. 258
17. Sacred Books, Vol. XLV, p. 61
18. Sacred Books, Vol. XXII, p. 25
19. Sacred Books, Vol. XLV, p. 58
20. De Bary, op.cit., p. 67
21. Sacred Books, Vol. XXII, pp. 29, 39
22. Sacred Books, Vol. XXII, pp. 20, 22, 37, 187
23. Sacred Books, Vol. XLV, pp. 187-8
24. See De Bary, op. cit., p. 64 and Sacred Books, Vol. XXII, p. 34 and Vol. XLV, p. 141
25. De Bary, op. cit., p. 65
26. De Bary, op. cit., p. 67
27. Sacred Books, Vol. XXII, pp. 25, 171
28. Sacred Books, Vol. XXII, p. 186
29. Swami Prabhavananda and Frederick Manchester, *The Spiritual Heritage of India,* New York, 1963, p. 170
30. S. Radhakrishnan, *History,* p. 150
31. Sacred Books, Vol. XLV, pp. 259, 260; Vol. XXII, pp. 49, 59
32. Sacred Books, Vol. XXII, pp. 97, 160, 163
33. Sacred Books, Vol. XXII, pp. 158, 166, 167
34. Sacred Books, Vol. XLV, p. 257
35. Sacred Books, Vol. XLV, p. 205; Vol. XXII, pp. 25, 36
36. Sacred Books, Vol. XXII, pp. 84-5
37. Sacred Books, Vol. XLV, p. 255; Vol. XXII, p. 44
38. De Bary, op. cit., pp. 61, 65
39. Sacred Books, Vol. XLV, p. 46
40. Sacred Books, Vol. XLV, p. 257
41. John A. Hutchinson, *Paths of Faith,* New York, 1969, p. 100
42. Radhakrishnan and Moore, op. cit., p. 270
43. Chandradhar Sharma, *Indian Philosophy: A Critical Survey,* New York, 1962, pp. 36-7

44. Heinrich Zimmer, *Philosophies of India,* Princeton, 1971, p. 270
45. S. C. Chatterjee and D. M. Datta, *An Introduction to Indian Philosophy,* Calcutta, 1960, p. 98
46. Sacred Books, Vol. XLV, pp. 250, 260
47. Sacred Books, Vol. XXII, p. 77
48. De Bary, op. cit., p. 76
49. Sacred Books, Vol. XXII, p. 152
50. Basham, op. cit., p. 290
51. Basham, op. cit., p. 297
52. Basham, op. cit., p. 295

BIBLIOGRAPHY

1. Bhattacharyya, Haridas, ed., *The Cultural Heritage of India,* Vol. I, Calcutta, 1953
2. Chatterjee, S. C. and D. M. Datta, *An Introduction to Indian Philosophy,* Calcutta, 1960, Ch. 3
3. De Bary, Wm. T., *Sources of the Indian Tradition,* New York, 1958, Chs. IV, V
4. Hiriyanna, M., *The Essentials of Indian Philosophy,* London, 1948, Ch. 3
5. Hume, Robert E., *The World's Living Religions,* New York, 1959
6. Hutchinson, John A., *Paths of Faith,* New York, 1969, Ch. 4
7. Jacobi, Hermann, tr., F. Max Müller, ed., Jaina Sutras, Vol. XXII, XLV, *Sacred Books of the East,* Oxford, 1895
8. Prabhavananda and Frederick Manchester, *The Spiritual Heritage of India,* New York, 1963, Ch. 7
9. Radhakrishnan, S., Chairman, Editorial Board, *History of Philosophy, Eastern and Western,* London, 1954, Vol. I, Ch. 8
10. Radhakrishnan, S. and Charles A. Moore, *A Sourcebook in Indian Philosophy,* Princeton, 1957, Ch. 8
11. Renou, Louis, *Religions of Ancient India,* New York, 1968
12. Stevenson, Mrs Sinclair, *The Heart of Jainism,* New Delhi, 1970
13. Sinha, Jadunath, *Outlines of Indian Philosophy,* Calcutta, 1963, Ch. 7
14. Zimmer, Heinrich, *Philosophies of India,* Princeton, 1951

Chapter 6: LOKĀYATA MATERIALISM

BIBLIOGRAPHY

1. Chatterjee, S. C. and D. M. Datta, *An Introduction to Indian Philosophy,* Calcutta, 1960, pp. 53-70
2. Chattopadhyaya, D., *Lokāyata: A Study in Ancient Indian Materialism,* New Delhi, 1959
3. Chattopadhyaya, D., *What Is Living and What Is Dead in Indian Philosophy,* New Delhi, in press
4. Dasgupta, S. N., *History of Indian Philosophy,* Cambridge, 1952, Vol. III, pp. 512-50
5. Frauwallner, E., *History of Indian Philosophy,* New Delhi, 1973, Vol. II, pp. 215-26

6. Raju, P. T., *The Philosophical Traditions of India,* London, 1971, pp. 86-93
7. Sharma, C., *Indian Philosophy: A Critical Survey,* London, 1960, pp. 28-36
8. Sinha, J., *Outlines of Indian Philosophy,* Calcutta, 1963, pp. 61-78

Chapter 7: Buddhism

References

1. Paul Carus, *The Gospel of Buddha,* Chicago, 1915, p. 9
2. Kenneth W. Morgan, *The Path of the Buddha,* New York, 1956, p. 373
3. P. V. Bapat, *2500 Years of Buddhism,* Delhi, 1956, p. vii
4. Carus, op.cit., p. 210
5. Edward Conze, ed., *Buddhist Texts through the Ages,* New York, 1964, p. 285
6. Carus, op. cit., p. 133
7. Carus, op. cit., pp. 167-8
8. F. Max Müller, tr., The Dhammapada, *Sacred Books of the East,* Oxford, 1881, Vol. X, p. 18
9. G. Champion and D. Short, *Readings from World Religions,* New York, 1959, p. 165
10. Ibid.
11. S. C. Chatterjee and D. M. Datta, *An Introduction to Indian Philosophy,* Calcutta, 1960, p. 128
12. Carus, op. cit., p. 132
13. Carus, op. cit., p. 131
14. Carus, op. cit., p. 176; see also Thera, *The Buddha's Ancient Path,* pp. 208-9
15. Carus, op. cit., p. 178
16. Thera, op. cit., p. 111ff
17. Carus, op. cit., p. 49
18. E. A. Burtt, *The Teachings of the Compassionate Buddha,* New York, 1955, p. 66
19. Carus, op. cit., p. 134
20. The Bible, *New Testament,* I Timothy, Ch. 6, vs. 10
21. Carus, op. cit., p. 51
22. F. Max Müller, op. cit., p. 51
23. W. T. Jones, *Approaches to Ethics,* New York, 1962, p. 88
24. T. W. Rhys Davids, tr., Buddhist Suttas, *Sacred Books of the East,* Vol. XI, p. 147
25. Carus, op. cit., p. 133
26. Melvin Rader, *The Enduring Questions,* New York, 1956, p. 356
27. Carus, op. cit., pp. 5, 41
28. Rhys Davids, op. cit., p. 273
29. Thera, op. cit., p. 115
30. Thera, op. cit., p. 111
31. Marion L. Matics, tr., Santideva, *Entering the Path of Enlightenment,* New York, 1970, p. 178
32. Conze, op. cit., p. 180
33. Moses Hadas, ed., *The Essential Works of Stoicism,* New York, 1961, p. 85

34. Conze, op. cit., p. 186
35. Carus, op. cit., p. 73
36. The Bible, *New Testament,* Matthew, Ch. 5, vs. 5
37. Carus, op. cit., p. 131
38. Carus, op. cit., p. 136
39. Lewis Browne, *The World's Great Scriptures,* New York, 1961, p. 126
40. Carus, op. cit., p. 137
41. Champion and Short, op. cit., p. 174
42. Carus, op. cit., p. 132
43. Ibid.
44. Müller, op. cit., p. 80
45. Burtt, op. cit., p. 60
46. Carus, op. cit., p. 131
47. Carus, op. cit., p. 103
48. S. Radhakrishnan and Charles A. Moore, *A Source Book in Indian Philosophy,* Princeton, 1957
49. Carus, op. cit., p. 137
50. Carus, op. cit., p. 67
51. Carus, op. cit., p. 126
52. Santideva, op. cit., p. 174
53. Phra Khantipalo, *Tolerance: A Study from Buddhist Sources,* London, 1964, p. 88
54. Champion and Short, op. cit., p. 164
55. Carus, op. cit., p. 217
56. Carus, op. cit., p. 139
57. Thera, op. cit., p. 119
58. Khantipalo, op. cit., p. 181
59. Khantipalo, op. cit., p. 184
60. Rader, op. cit., p. 358
61. Wm. T. De Bary, *Sources of the Indian Tradition,* New York, 1958, Vol. I, p. 174
62. Müller, op. cit., p. 90
63. Thera, op. cit., p. 199
64. Carus, op. cit., p. 3
65. Carus, op. cit., p. 115
66. Carus, op. cit., p. 33
67. Carus, op. cit., p. 4
68. De Bary, op. cit., p. 175
69. Alan W. Watts, *The Way of Zen,* New York ,1957, p. 117
70. Carus, op. cit., p. 160
71. Carus, op. cit., p. 155
72. Müller, op. cit., p. 36
73. Wm. T. De Bary, *Sources of the Chinese Tradition,* New York, 1960, Vol. I, p. 469
74. D. T. Suzuki, *Outlines of Mahayana Buddhism,* New York, 1963, p. 369
75. De Bary, *The Chinese Tradition,* p. 91

76. Rader, op. cit., p. 365
77. John Donne, *Devotions Upon Emergent Occasions,* Cambridge, 1923, p. 98
78. Franklin Le Van Baumer, *Main Currents of Western Thought,* New York, 1961, p. 356
79. Hajime Nakamura, *Ways of Thinking of Eastern People,* Honolulu, 1964, p. 95
80. Carus, op. cit., p. 164
81. Walter R. Houghton, ed., *Neely's History of the Parliament of Religions,* Chicago, 1894, p. 323
82. T. R. V. Murti, *The Central Philosophy of Buddhism,* London, 1955, p. 10
83. Burtt, op. cit., p. 19
84. Burtt, op. cit., p. 66
85. Jadunath Sinha, *Outlines of Indian Philosophy,* Calcutta, 1962, p. 87
86. S. Radhakrishnan, *Indian Philosophy,* London, 1948, Vol. I, p. 370
87. Radhakrishnan, op. cit., p. 371
88. Ananda K. Coomaraswamy, *Buddha and The Gospel of Buddhism,* New York, 1964, p. 96
89. Harold L. Parsons, The Value of Gautama Buddha for The Modern World, *The Eastern Buddhist,* Vol. II, No. 2, p. 34
90. Parsons, op. cit., pp. 59-60
91. Carus, op. cit., p. 164
92. Kenneth K. S. Ch'en, *Buddhism, The Light of Asia,* Woodbury, 1968, p. 5
93. Carus, op. cit., p. 164
94. Burtt, op. cit., p. 19
95. Parsons, op. cit., p. 47
96. Burtt, op. cit., p. 53
97. Parsons, op. cit., p. 69
98. Suzuki, op. cit., p. 342
99. Browne, op. cit., p. 195
100. Carus, op. cit., p. 123
101. Edwin Burtt, *Man Seeks the Divine,* New York, 1957, p. 235
102. Carus, op. cit., p. 163
103. Coomaraswamy, op. cit., p. 116
104. Houghton, op. cit., p. 805
105. Suzuki, op. cit., p. 345
106. Coomaraswamy, op. cit., p. 123
107. Carus, op. cit., p. 173
108. Ch'en, op. cit., p. 70
109. Ibid.
110. Burtt, *Compassionate Buddha*, p. 85
111. Browne, op. cit., p. 198
112. Suzuki, op. cit., p. 334
113. Ch'en, op. cit., p. 72
114. Suzuki, op. cit., p. 369
115. Sinha, op. cit., p. 100
116. Houghton, op. cit., p. 805

117. Coomaraswamy, op. cit., p. 118
118. Bapat, op. cit., p. xi
119. Morgan, op. cit., p. 382
120. Houghton, op. cit., p. 805
121. Carus, op. cit., p. 42
122. Suzuki, op. cit., p. 390
123. Chatterjee and Datta, op. cit., p. 124
124. Sinha, op. cit., p. 100
125. Browne, op. cit., p. 200
126. Carus, op. cit., p. 81
127. Suzuki, op. cit., p. 347 and S. Radhakrishnan, *History of Philosophy, Eastern and Western*, p. 168
128. Burtt, op. cit., p. 49
129. Carus, op. cit., p. 205
130. Burtt, *Man Seeks the Divine,* p. 222
131. Carus, p. 79 and Browne, p. 190
132. Murty, op. cit., p. 267
133. Burtt, *Compassionate Buddha,* p. 227
134. Browne, op. cit., p. 328
135. Burtt, *Man Seeks the Divine,* p. 222
136. Browne, op. cit., pp. 164-65
137. N. K. Bose, *Selections from Gandhi,* Ahmedabad, 1950, p. 13
138. Thera, op. cit., p. 120
139. Burtt, *Compassionate Buddha,* p. 49
140. Carus, op. cit., pp. 256-57
141. Carus, op. cit., p. 138
142. Suzuki, op. cit., p. 93
143. Ashitsu, The Fundamental Teachings of Buddhism, *The Monist,* Jan., 1894, p. 175
144. Nakamura, op. cit., pp. 146-47

BIBLIOGRAPHY

1. Bapat, P. V., *2500 Years of Buddhism,* Delhi, 1964
2. Bhattacharya, Haridas, ed., *The Cultural Heritage of India,* Vol. I, Calcutta, 1953
3. Burtt, Edwin A., *Man Seeks the Divine,* New York, 1957, Ch. IX
4. Brutt, Edwin A., *The Teachings of the Compassionate Buddha,* New York, 1955
5. Carus, Paul, *Buddha and The Gospel of Buddhism,* Chicago, 1915
6. Ch'en, Kenneth K. S., *Buddhism, The Light of Asia,* New York, 1968
7. Conze, Edward, *Buddhism, Its Essence and Development,* New York, 1951
8. Coomaraswamy, Ananda K., *Buddha and The Gospel of Buddhism,* New York, 1964
9. Cowell, E. B., F. Max Müller, and J. Takakusu, trs., F. Max Müller, ed., Buddhist Mahayana Texts, Vol. XLIX, *Sacred Books of the East,* Oxford, 1894

10. David, T. W. Rhys, tr., F. Max Müller, ed., Buddhist Suttas, Vol. XI, *Sacred Books of the East,* Oxford, 1881
11. Dutt, N., *Buddhist Sects in India,* Calcutta, 1970
12. Fausset, Hugh T., *The Flame and The Light,* London and New York, 1958
13. Humphreys, Christmas, *Buddhism,* London, 1955
14. Kaplan, Abraham, *The New World of Philosophy,* pp. 237-66
15. Kapleau, Philip, *The Three Pillars of Zen,* New York, 1967
16. Kennett, Juju, *Selling Water by the River,* New York, 1972
17. King, Winston, *In the Hope of Nibbana,* La Salle, 1964
18. Koller, John M., *Oriental Philosophies,* Part II
19. Morgan, Kenneth, *The Path of the Buddha,* New York, 1956
20. Murti, T. R. V., *The Central Philosophy of Buddhism,* 2nd ed., London, 1960
21. Rahula, Walpola, *What the Buddha Taught,* New York, 1962
22. Saddhatissa, H., *Buddhist Ethics, Essence of Buddhism,* London, 1970
23. Sangharakshita, Bhikshu, *The Three Jewels,* London, 1967
24. Sinha, Jadunath, *Outlines of Indian Philosophy,* Calcutta, 1965, Chs. V, VI
25. Smart, Ninian, *The Religious Experience of Mankind,* New York, 1969, pp. 77-112
26. Suzuki, D. T., *Essays in Zen Buddhism,* London, 1953
27. Suzuki, D. T., *Outlines of Mahayana Buddhism,* New York, 1963
28. Thera, Piyadassi, *The Buddha,* Ancient Path, London, 1964
29. Warren, Henry C., *Buddhism in Translations,* New York, 1963
30. Watts, *The Way of Zen,* New York, 1966

Chapter 8: Indian Epistemology and Logic

References

1. In Vedānta the word viṣaya stands for the object and the word viṣayin for the subject of knowledge. But in Nyāya the word viṣayin stands for knowledge and the knower, i.e. the Ātman is different from the viṣayin. Advaitins regard Brahman as of the nature of knowledge (Jñāna). This is perhaps under the influence of Buddhism which undermined the concept of Ātman. Advaita reinstated the Ātman, but accepted it as Jñānarūpa or having the nature of knowledge.

Bibliography

1. Barlingay, S. S., *A Modern Introduction to Indian Logic,* Delhi, 1965
2. Bhatta, Annam, *Tarka Dīpikā*
3. Bhatta, Annam, *Tarka Saṃgraha*
4. Bhattacharya, Kalidas, *Philosophy, Logic and Language,* Bombay, 1965
5. Burt, Edwin A., *In Search of Philosophic Understanding,* New York, 1965, Chs. 8, 9
6. Datta, D. M., *The Six Ways of Knowing,* Calcutta, 1960
7. Dharmakirti, *Nyāya Bindu*
8. Hiriyanna, M., *Outlines of Indian Philosophy,* London 1932
9. Jere, Atmaram Shastri, ed., *Bhaṣā Pariccheda and Muktāvali* by Visvanatha, *Dinakarī* by Pancānana

10. Koller, John M., *Oriental Philosophies,* New York, 1970, Ch. 6
11. Krishna, Isvara, *Sāṃkhya Kārikā*
12. Patañjali, *Yoga Sūtras*
13. Śaṅkarācarya, *Sāriraka Bhāṣya*
14. Sharma, D., *The Differentiation Theory of Meaning in Indian Logic,* The Hague, 1969
15. Sharma, D., *The Negative Dialectics of India,* East Lansing, 1970
16. Sinari, Ramakant A., *The Structure of Indian Thought,* Springfield, 1970
17. Sinha, Jadunath, *Outlines of Indian Philosophy,* Calcutta, 1962
18. Vidyabhushan, Satischandra, *A History of Indian Logic,* Delhi, 1971

Chapter 9: METAPHYSICS

REFERENCES

1. P. T. Raju, *Introduction to Comparative Philosophy,* Lincoln, 1962, p. 257
2. Swami Nikhilananda, *The Upanishads,* New York, 1962, pp. 33 ff.
3. D. M. Datta, *The Chief Currents of Contemporary Philosophy,* Calcutta, 2nd edition, 1961, p. 21
4. S. Radhakrishnan and Charles A. Moore, *A Sourcebook in Indian Philosophy,* Princeton, 1957, pp. 589-97
5. See Taittirīya Upaniṣad, II
6. Chāndogya Upaniṣad, VI
7. Dale Reippe, *The Naturalistic Tradition in Indian Thought,* Seattle, 1961, pp. 67-72
8. S. C. Chatterjee and D. M. Datta, *An Introduction to Indian Philosophy,* Calcutta, 1960, p. 57
9. Karl Potter, *Presuppositions of India's Philosophies,* Englewood Cliffs, 1963, p. 146
10. N. Dutt, *Buddhist Sects in India,* Calcutta, 1970, p. 95
11. K. Damodaran, *Indian Thought, A Critical Survey,* London, 1967, p. 112 ff.
12. M. Hiriyanna, *Outlines of Indian Philosophy,* London, 1932, p. 238 ff.
13. Hiriyanna, op. cit., p. 235
14. Ninian Smart, *Doctrine and Argument in Indian Philosophy,* London, 1964, p. 77
15. Hiriyanna, op. cit., p. 383
16. Charles A. Moore, *The Indian Mind,* Honolulu, 1967, p. 140 ff.
17. S. Radhakrishnan, *Indian Philosophy,* London, 1948, p. 166
18. Hiriyanna, op. cit., p. 383
19. Radhakrishnan and Moore, op. cit., p. 508

BIBLIOGRAPHY

1. Annambhatta, *Tarkasaṃgraha* (Notes by Athalyes Bodas)
2. Barth, A., *The Religions of India*
3. Carpenter, J. E., *Theism in Medieval India*
4. Chatterjee, S. C. and D. M. Datta, *Introduction to Indian Philosophy,* Calcutta, 1960, 6th ed.
5. Dasgupta, S., *History of Indian Philosophy,* Vols. I to IV
6. Deussen, Paul, *Outlines of Indian Philosophy*

7. Garbe, Richard, *The Philosophy of Ancient India*
8. Ghate, V. S., *Vedānta*
9. Griffith, R. T. H., tr., *The Hymns of the Ṛig Veda*
10. Hiriyanna, M., *Outlines of Indian Philosophy*, London, 1951
11. Hume, R. E., tr., *The Thirteen Principal Upaniṣads*, Oxford, 1921
12. Jaini, J., *An Epitome of Jainism*
13. Joshi, G. N., *The Evolution of the Concepts of Ātman and Mokṣa in the Different Systems of Indian Philosophy*, Ahmedabad, 1965
14. Keith, A. B., *The Sāṃkhya System*
15. Koller, John M., *Oriental Philosophies*, New York, 1970, Ch. 5
16. Lyon, Quinter M., *The Great Religions*, New York, 1957, Ch. XV
17. Müller, F. Max, *Six Systems of Indian Philosophy*
18. Nakamura, Hajime, *Ways of Thinking of Eastern People*, Honolulu, 1964, Part I
19. Nikhilananda (Swami), *The Gospel of Sri Ramakrishna*, Madras, 1944
20. Radhakrishnan, S., *Indian Philosophy*, Vols. I & II, New York, 1927
21. Raja, C. Kunhan, *Some Fundamental Problems in Indian Philosophy*, Delhi, 1960
22. Raju, P. T., *Idealistic Thought in India*, Cambridge, 1953
23. Raju, P. T. and Alburey Castell, *East-West Studies on the Problem of the Self*, The Hague, 1968
24. Ranade, R. D., *A Constructive Survey of the Upanishads*
25. Ranade, R. D., *Mysticism in Maharashtra*
26. Sinha, Jadunath, *Outlines of Indian Philosophy*, Calcutta, 1962
27. Sircar Mahendranath, *Comparative Studies in Vedāntism*
28. Smart, Ninian, *The Religious Experience of Mankind*, New York, 1969
29. Smith, Huston, *The Religions of Man*, New York, 1958, Ch. 2
30. Stcherbatsky, Th., *The Central Conception of Buddhism*
31. Stcherbatsky, Th., *The Soul Theory of the Buddhists*
32. Suzuki, D. T., *Outlines of Mahayana Buddhism*, New York, 1963
33. Thibaut, tr., *Samkara on Vedānta Sūtras*
34. Tomlin, E. W. F., *The Oriental Philosophers*, New York, 1963, Ch. 6
35. Vidyabhushan, S., tr., *The Nyāya Sūtras of Gotama*

Chapter 10: Social Philosophy

References

1. Darśana stands for "religious knowledge," "a doctrine or theory prescribed in a system" and "a system of philosophy." It also means "knowing, understanding, perceiving and foreseeing" (Apte, V. S.: 1963). Darśana, thus, is aimed at jñāna (knowledge). According to the Gītā, knowledge of soul (13/2, 7-11) and realization of unity in diversity (18/20) constitute the essence of the highest jñāna. Hence, by derivation, Darśana implies realization of the unity of universe as the manifestation of Brahman.
2. Manu 12/91
3. The Gītā: 3/22, 25; 4/6, 13; 5/14, 15
4. Mānava-dharma-śāstra iv, 239; also see Prabhu, P. H., *Hindu Social Organization*, pp. 30-34

5. Apte, V. S., *Sanskrit-English Dictionary*
6. Bhatt, G. S., Brahmo Samaj and Arya Samaj and the Church-Sect Typology: *Review of Religious Research*, Vol. 10, No. 1: 1968
7. Gokhale, B. G., *Indian thought through the Ages*, p. 25
8. Mahābhārata: Karṇaparva: 69/58
9. Prabhu, P. H., *Hindu Social Organization*, pp. 79-80
10. Mānava-dharma-śāstra: vi 92, also see Gokhale, B. G., *Indian Thought through the Ages*, p. 29
11. To bring out its real import, dharma is popularly as well as scripturally contrasted with what is not dharma (adharma). Following Bhāgvata Purāṇa, Prabhu mentions five types of adharma, viz. vidharma (dharma contrary to one's own dharma), para-dharma (dharma laid down for others), upa-dharma (dharma consisting of doctrines opposed to established morals or of hypocrisy), chhala-dharma (which is dharma in name only, not in truth) and dharmabhāṣa (which is the result of the dictation of one's sweet will and not according to one's own aśrama)—see Prabhu, P. H., *Hindu Soc. Org.* pp. 27-28.
12. Zimmer, Heinrich, *Philosophies of India*, p. 35
13. Mahabharata, XII, Ch. 8; also see K. V. Rangaswamy Aiyangar, *Aspects of Indian Economic Thought*, pp. 23-24
14. Arthashastra, tr. by R. Shamasastri, p. 12
15. Prabhu, P. H., *Hindu Social Organization*, p. 80
16. Gokhale, B. G., *Indian Thought Through the Ages*, p. 82
17. The Wam Marg, the Left Path, was intended to attain supernatural power through orgiastic and magical practices. As for example, "wine, flesh, fish, mudra, (cakes) copulation procure salvation in every age" (Kali Tantra). 'When admitted to orgies, all varṇas become dvija; but leaving them they become different (Kularnava Tantra). "If a man falls over drinking but drinks again on rising up, he is freed from the cycle of rebirths" (Mahanirvana Tantra).' Excepting mother's vagina, let every man enjoy all vaginas. Vedas, Śāstras and Purāṇas are like ordinary prostitutes (Gyanasankalini Tantra). "Cohabitation with a woman in menses is as meritorious as bathing in the sacred tank of Pushkar (in Ajmer), with a Chaṇḍāl woman (fallen and low caste woman) as a pilgrimage to Kāśi (Varanasi), with a Chamar woman, i.e. a woman from the caste (chamar) of skinners and tanners, as bathing in the Gaṅgā at Prayag (Allahabad), with a laundress (woman from the caste of washerman) as a pilgrimage to Mathura, the birthplace of Kriṣṇa, with a prostitute as a pilgrimage to Ayudhya, the birth-place of Rama" (Rudrayamala Tantra). These examples have been picked up from Dayānanda's Satyarth Prakash, translated by Durga Prasad (pp. 286-93) to which reference may be made for other such details and for the reaction of the Right Path towards them. Such thoughts and practices have always remained confined to secret cults and have never been approved of as part of dharma. Being only of academic and historical importance now, they do represent a kind of reaction to the Vedic tradition which followed the downfall of Buddhism.

18. The eight forms of marriage are: The Brāhma (gift of a daughter to a man of good character and learned in the Vedas invited by the father); The Daiva (the gift of the daughter to a priest); The Ārṣa (giving of daughter in marriage to the bridegroom, after receiving a cow and a bull, or two pairs of these from the bridegroom); The Prajāpatya (gift of the daughter with the address of the mantram 'may both of you perform together your dharma'); The Gāndharva (marriage by mutual love and consent); The Āsura (marriage involving payment of brideprice as mostly practised by tribes and castes); The Rākṣasa (the forcible abduction of a maiden from her lower house); The Paishācha (marriage by stealth, seduction of a girl who is sleeping, intoxicated or disordered in intellect (Prabhu: ibid., pp. 151-52). The law today recognizes only the Brāhma, the Gāndharva and the Āsura.
19. Garuda Purāṇa, 108
20. For details see Gokhale, B. G., *Indian Thought Through the Ages*, Ch. 4
21. Prabhu, P. H., *Hindu Social Organization*, p. 83
22. Māhabhārata, Śāntiparva: 242, 15; also see Prabhu, P. H., *Hindu Social Organization*, Chs. 6 (Family) and 8 (Varna)
23. For detailed study see Pandey, Raj Bali, *Hindu Samskaras*
24. Dayānanda, *Satyarth Prakash*, tr. by Durga Prasad, pp. 72-73
25. The tradition of the varṇa system enjoins upon a man to take his mate from the varṇa he belongs to or from the varṇas lower than his. As a corollary of this, a female has to choose her spouse either from her varṇa or from varṇas higher than her varṇa. These ways of choosing a mate are socially idealized as anuloma marriage. Marriage of a woman with a male from a varṇa lower than her, is pratiloma marriage which is not illegal but undesirable and sinful as it leads to miscegenation of varṇa. These are based on the ideal of savarṇa marriage, i.e. marriage in the same varṇa. However, they allow a wide range of choice to the Brahmin male and Śūdra female and a very restricted range of choice to the Brahmin female and Śūdra male.
26. The sacred thread of the Brāhmin is to be made up of cotton, that of the Kṣatriya of flax and that of the Vaiśya of wool. This traditional injunction is no more in practice. However, in the countryside in the linguistic region of Oudh, the main distinction relates to length of the sacred thread of various castes, the sacred thread of the Brahmin being the longest, that is, twenty-four rounds folded around four fingers set together.
27. The Gītā: 14/3-19
28. Rigveda, X, 90, 12; also see Prabhu, P. H. ibid., Chapter 8
29. Mahābhārata, Śāntiparva 188, 1-17
30. In the dialogue between the King Yudhishthira and Nahusha, the Python (Maha. Vanparva 180. 33-39), the former tells the latter, "It is therefore that those who have grasped the essentials of dharma have known that character (shila) is the principal desirable thing." "On this theory," writes Prabhu, "further, every person at birth, is no better than shudra; his character-traits as expressed in his behaviour later show him to belong to the Brahmin (or

any other) varna." Quoting Śatapatha Brāhmaṇa (XI, 5, 4, etc.) Prabhu emphasizes that after upanayana one becomes a dvija, a twice born, and till upanayana every man is just like śūdra (Prabhu, P. H., ibid., pp. 111, 306-7). Holding the same view, Dayānanda draws support from Manu (X 65): "If a person born of a shudra or low caste family possesses the virtues, habits and tendencies of the Brāhmins, Kśatriyas and Vaiśyas, he should be classed with them according to his merits. In like manner, if a person born of a Brāhmin, Kṣatriya or Vaiśya's family, possesses the merits, habits and nature like those of śūdra, he should sink to the level of the śūdras (Satyartha Prakash, p. 86). For detailed study see P. H. Prabhu, *Hindu Social Organization,* Ch. 8 and for caste and varṇa Irawati Karve's *Hindu Society—An Interpretation,* Chs. 1-4.

31. Gokhale, B. G., *Indian Thought Through the Ages,* p. 100
32. Tulsidasa, *Rāmacharitamānasa,* tr. by Atkins, A. G.: Vol. III, The Beautiful Chaupai 51: p. 1024
33. Shwetashwataropnishada: 4/5: See also the Gītā: 14/6-8 see Patañjala, Yoga-Sutras IV 7 and Vyāsa & Vāchaspati on it (Prabhu, ibid., 39)
34. Karve, Irawati, *Hindu Society—An Interpretation,* pp. 56-59
35. In the Mahābhārata (Vanparva, Adhyāya 207) there occurs a dialogue between Dharma-Vyadha, The Dutiful Hunter, and the Brāhmin on the ways of dharma. In spite of being from the highest caste, the latter (the Brāhmin) went to the former of the butcher caste (vyādha) to receive instructions in dharma for the Hunter knew it better than the Brahmin. In that dialogue, the Hunter tells the Brāhmin: "Any number of things can be said as regards the dharma and adharma of our actions. But he who adheres to his dharma acquires a great fame. To stick to one's karmas is certainly in keeping with the dharma. And, Karma carried out in this matter, i.e., in accordance with one's dharma does not stick to or pollute the individual even though the karma happens to be that of killing animals. To abandon one's own duties here in this world is sinful." And, therefore, whatever befalls one because of one's present birth, must be adhered to as the most essential part of dharma and the path of social mobility through rebirths. Also see Prabhu: ibid., pp. 24-25.
36. Srinivas, M. N., *Social Change in Modern India,* pp. 6, 7
37. Anguttara Nikaya, III, pp. 149, 151; also see Gokhale, B. G., ibid., p. 160
38. Gokhale, B. G., ibid., p. 163; Mahābhārata, XIII, 96, 35; Mānavadharma-śāstra, VII, 111-12
39. *Young India,* Jan. 5, 1942; also Oct. 15, 1931
40. Shamasastry, *Arthashastra,* p. 8
41. Mukerji, Radha Kamal, *A History of Indian Civilization,* pp. 18-21
42. Vyas, K. C., *Social Renaissance in India,* pp. 16, 19
43. Sarkar, Benoy Kumar, *The Positive Background of Hindu Sociology,* pp. 618-35
44. Vyas, K. C., ibid., p. 69; also Ch. 2; and also Shastri, Shiva Nath, *History of Brahmo Samaj,* Vol. II, Ch. 4
45. This resumé of Dayānanda's thought is based on Satyartha Prakash.

46. Vachaspati, Indra Vidya, *History of Arya Samaj* (in Hindi), Part I, Ch. 1
47. See The Ārya Samaj, Lajpat Rai
48. The resumé of Vivekananda's thoughts mainly based on Swami Ranganathananda's *The Meeting of East and West in Swami Vivekananda*
49. For details, Natrajan, S., *A Century of Social Reform in India*
50. Vyas, K. C., ibid., p. 150 and Wolpert, Stanley A., *Tilak and Gokhale*, p. 67
51. Gandhi, M. K., *My Philosophy of Life* and *All Religions Are True*, ed. by Anand T. Hingorani
52. See introduction to the *Third Five Year Plan*
53. Majumdar, D. N., *Races and Cultures of India*, Chs. 9, 10
54. The Hindu Marriage Act of 1955
55. Bhatt, G. S., Trends and Measures of Status Mobility Among the Chamars of Dehradun, *The Eastern Anthropologist*, Vol. XIV, No. 3
56. Madan, T. N., The Joint Family—A Terminological Clarification, in *Family and Marriage*, ed. by John Mogey
57. Kapadia, K. M., *Marriage & Family in India*, Ch. 10
58. Zinkin, Taya, *India Changes*, Chs. 4, 5, 6
59. Majumdar, D. N., *Races and Cultures of India*, Chs. 9, 10
60. For details on Caste: Srinivas, M. N., *Caste in Modern India, Social Change in Modern India*; Andre Beteille, *Castes: Old and New*; Taya, Zinkin, *Caste Today*
61. Karve, Irawati, *Hindu Society—An Interpretation*, p. 88; specially see Ch. 3 on Indian Philosophy and Caste
62. "Sanskritization is the process by which a 'low' Hindu caste, or tribal or other group, changes its customs, ritual, ideology and way of life in the direction of a high, and frequently, 'twice born' caste. Generally such changes are followed by a claim to a higher position in the caste-hierarchy than that traditionally conceded to the claimant caste by the local community" (Srinivas, M. N., 1966, p. 6; Oxford, 1952, p. 30). It operates through any of the three models, viz. the Brāhmin, the Kṣatriya and the Vaiśya depending entirely on the nature of the dominant cast of the region under reference. "Again, the agents of Sanskritization were (and are) not always Brāhmins." Sanskritization is not "Brahmanization" as certain vedic rites are confined to the Brāhmins and the two other twice born castes. It is also not Hinduization for a group may Sanskritize itself without designating itself as Hindu. It is "an extremely complex and heterogeneous concept" and as a conceptual term it is an "awkward" term (*The Far Eastern Quarterly*, Vol. XV, No. 4, 1956). Along with it has been noted the process of de-Sanskritization.

In Benoy Kumar Sarkar's study of *The Positive Background of Hindu Sociology* (Book I, Allahabad, 1937) one comes across such expressions as "the Sanskritization of Tamil Culture Proceeded step by step" (p. 372), or, Shivaji's first and foremost ambition in this regard (the cultural nationalism) consisted in 'Sanskritizing Persian words and phrases of daily existence in public, civic, administrative or political life' (pp. 507, 8) or 'we shall now point to one or two other Sanskritizings or Hinduizings of the Persian texts' (p. 538). Here, thus, Sanskritization stands for the process of ideational acculturation through the sacred literature in Sanskrit language and use of Sanskrit words and also scripturally prescribed rituals. It implies Hinduization and Brahmanization though it may not be so.

As Sarkar puts it, "The process by which the non-Indians, non-Aryans, non-Brahmans, the Vrātyas, the Śūdras, the wild tribes and what not have got themselves Indianized, Aryanized or Brahmanized constitute the most solid realities of race history and cultural development in every nook and corner of Indian and in every epoch of India's growth . . . . The very category "expansion of Hindu Culture" implies nothing but this democratization or rather impact of the masses upon the main stock of Hindu institutions and ideals" (p. 473). Lacking historical perspective, Prof. Srinivas's formulation conceptualizes only one way process, from the higher, the dominant to the lower, whereas it has been a two-way process of acculturation between the Vedic and non-Vedic traditions.

63. Sarkar, Benoy Kumar, *The Positive Background of Hindu Sociology*, p. 473
64. Myrdal, Gunnar, *The Challenge of World Poverty*, Ch. 7

BIBLIOGRAPHY

1. Aiyangar, Rangaswami K. V., *Aspects of Indian Economic Thought*, Varanasi (Banaras) 1934
2. Beteille, Andre, *Castes—Old and New*, Bombay, 1969
3. Chambliss, Rollin, *Social Thought from Hummurabi to Comte*, New York, 1954, Ch. 5
4. Damodaran, K., *Man and Society in Indian Philosophy*, New Delhi, 1970
5. Desai, A. R., *Social Background of Indian Nationalism*, Bombay, 1948
6. Gandhi, M. K., *My Philosophy of Life*, and *All Religions are True*, ed. by Anand T. Hingorani, Bombay, 1961, 1962
7. Gokhale, B. G., *Indian Thought Through the Ages*, Bombay, 1961
8. Hutton, J. H., *Caste in India*, Oxford, 1946
9. Kapadia, K. M., *Marriage and Family in India*, Oxford, 1959
10. Karve, Irawati, *Hindu Society—An Interpretation*, Poona, 1961
11. Lajpat Rai, *The Arya Samaj*, Longmans Green, London, 1915
12. Lamb, Beatrice P., *India, A World in Transition*, New York, 1968
13. Madan, T. N., The Joint Family—A Terminological Clarification, in *Family and Marriage*, ed. by John Mogey, Leiden, 1963
14. Majumdar, D. N., *Races and Cultures of India*, Bombay, 1965
15. Malhotra, S. L., *Social and Political Orientations of Neo-Vedantism*, Delhi, 1970
16. Mukerji, Radha Kamal, *A History of Indian Civilization*, Part I, Bombay, 1958
17. Myrdal, Gunnar, *The Challenge of World Poverty*, London, 1970
18. Natrajan, S., *A Century of Social Reform in India*, Bombay, 1959
19. Noss, John B., *Man's Religions*, New York, 1956, Ch. 7
20. Pandey, Raj Bali, *Hindu Samskaras*, Banaras, 1949

21. Prabhu, P. H., *Hindu Social Organization,* Bombay, 1963
22. Radhakrishnan, S., *Eastern Religions and Western Thought,* New York, 1959, Part IX
23. Sarkar, Benoy Kumar, The Positive Background of Hindu Sociology (Book I, *Introduction to Hindu Positivism*), Allahabad, 1937
24. Sastri, Sivanath, *History of Brāhmo Samaj,* Calcutta, 1919
25. Spratt, P., *Hindu Culture and Personality,* Bombay, 1966
26. Srinivas, M. N., *Caste in Modern India and Other Essays,* Bombay, 1962; *Social Change in Modern India,* Berkeley and Los Angeles, 1966
27. Swami Ranganathananda, *The Meeting of East and West in Swami Vivekananda,* Calcutta, 1968
28. Vachaspati, Indra Vidya, *History of Arya Samaj* (in Hindi) Part I: Sarvadeshik Arya Pratinidhi Sabha, Delhi, 1957
29. Vidyarthi, L. P., ed., *Aspects of Religion in Indian Society,* Meerut City, 1961
30. Vyas, K. C., *Social Renaissance in India,* Bombay, 1957
31. Vyas, Ram Narayan, *The Universalistic Thought of India,* Delhi, 1970
32. Wolpert, Stanley A., *Tilak and Gokhale—Revolution and Reform in the Making of Modern India,* Berkeley and Los Angeles, 1962
33. Zimmer, Heinrich, *Philosophies of India,* New York, 1959
34. Zinkin, Taya, *India Changes,* New York, 1958
35. Zinkin, Taya, *Caste Today,* London, 1963

Chapter 11: Indian Ethics

References

1. A. T. Embree, ed., *The Hindu Tradition,* New York, 1966, p. 278 ff
2. O. L. Chavarria—Aguilar, ed., *Traditional India,* Englewood Cliffs, 1964, p. 70
3. See W. De Bary, *Sources of the Indian Tradition,* New York, 1958, p. 13 and S. Dasgupta, *Indian Idealism,* Cambridge, 1962, p. 50
4. I. C. Sharma, *Ethical Philosophies of India,* Lincoln, 1965, p. 273 ff (revised edition, Harper Torchbooks, 1970)
5. William Garber, *The Mind of India,* New York, 1967, pp. 218 ff.
6. S. Dasgupta, *History of Indian Philosophy,* 1963, Vol. I, pp. vii ff
7. The Bhagavadgītā, II, 51-52
8. C. Sharma, *Indian Philosophy, A Critical Survey,* London, 1962, pp. 21-22
9. The Bhagavadgītā, II, 56
10. Ibid., II, 57
11. M. K. Gandhi, *My Religion,* Bombay, 1955, p. 57
12. R. A. Sinari, *The Structure of Indian Thought,* Springfield, 1970, pp. 189-90
13. S. Radhakrishnan, *Eastern Religions and Western Thought,* New York, 1959 pp. 33-34
14. The Bhagavadgītā, III, 13
15. Swami Prabhavananda and F. Manchester, *The Spiritual Heritage of India,* New York, 1963, p. 97
16. C. Sharma, op. cit., p. 24

BIBLIOGRAPHY

1. Aiyer, P. S., *Evolution of Hindu Moral Ideals,* Calcutta, 1945
2. Chan, Wing-tsit, et al., *The Great Asian Religions,* Toronto, 1969, Chapter 4
3. Hopkins, E. W., *Ethics of India,* New Haven, 1924
4. Khantipalo, Phra, *Tolerance: A Study from Buddhist Sources,* London, 1964
5. King, Winston, *In the Hope of Nibbana, An Essay on Theravada Buddhist Ethics,* La Salle, 1964
6. Lacy, Creighton, *The Conscience of India,* New York, 1965
7. Mahadevan, T. K., *Truth and Non-Violence,* Delhi, 1970
8. Mukerjee, R., *The Dynamics of Morals,* London, 1950
9. Nakamura, Hajime, *Ways of Thinking of Eastern People,* Honolulu, 1964, Ch. 13
10. Radhakrishnan, S., *Eastern Religions and Western Thought,* New York, 1959, Part III
11. Raju, P. T., *The Philosophical Traditions of India,* London, 1971
12. Ranganathananda, Swami, *Eternal Values for a Changing Society,* Calcutta, 1958
13. Ray, B. G., *Gandhian Ethics,* Navajivan, 1950
14. Reddy, V. M., *Values & Value Theories*
15. Scott, Roland, *Social Ethics in Modern Hinduism,* Calcutta, 1953
16. Sharma, I. C., *Ethical Philosophies of India,* New York, 1970

Chapter 12: CONCEPTS OF MAN

REFERENCES

1. S. N. Dasgupta, *A History of Sanskrit Literature, Classical Period,* Vol. I, Calcutta, 1947, p. 16
2. S. Vishnu Suktankar and S. K. Belvalkar, *The Mahabharata,* Poona, 1956
3. Raghuvamsa Nirnaya, *Mahakalidasa,* Bombay, 1944, p. 28
4. S. Radhakrishnan, *The Bhagvad Gītā,* London, 1960, p. 201
5. Sri Aurobindo, *Essays on the Gītā,* Pondicherry, 1949
6. Swami Akhilānanda, *Hindu Psychology,* London, 1960, p. 54
7. Swami Abhedānanda, *How To Be a Yogi,* Calcutta, 1943, pp. 99-111
8. Nemicandra, *Dravyasamgraha* (*Sacred Books of the Jains*)
9. Mallisena, *Syad-vada-manjari,* Chowkamba, Banaras, 1968, pp. 149-51
10. Buddhist Suttas, *S. B. E.,* Vol. XI; see also A. K. Coomaraswamy, *Buddha and the Gospel of Buddhism,* p. 116 ff
11. Sāṃkhya-Pravacana-sūtra with the commentary of Aniruddha and the Bhasya of Vijñānabhiksu
12. Sāṃkhya Kārikā, Iswara Krishna, Theosophical Society Publication, Bombay, 1924
13. Surendranath Dasgupta, *A History of Indian Philosophy,* Vol. 1, Cambridge, 1951
14. Sarvadarśana Saṃgraha, Mādhavāchārya, Rtl. E. B. Cowell and A. E. Gough, London, 1914, p. 80
15. Hariharananda Aranya, *Patañjala Yoga-darsana*
16. D. M. Datta, *Six Ways of Knowing,* London, 1932, vide Introductory
17. Nyāyamañjari, pp. 160-70

18. Madhavacarya—Sarvadarśana saṃgraha, trns. by Cowell and Gough, Ch. XI, 1961
19. Jaimini-Mimāṃsā sūtra (with Sabara's Bhāṣya)
20. Ganganath Jha, *Prabhakara Mimamsa,* pp. 6-28, 1911
21. Madhavācārya, Nyāyamalavistara
22. Sastradipika and Slokavarttika Sūtra (2)
23. Ganganath Jha, *Mimamsa sutra of Jaimini* (Eng. trans. Allahabad)
24. V. S. Ghate, *The Vedanta Bhardarkar,* Oriental Research Institute, Poona, 1926
25. V. L. Sastri, *One Hundred and Ten Upanisads,* Bombay, 1948
26. Minor Upaniṣads, Advaita Ashram, 1938
27. Madhava, Upaniṣad-bhāsya
28. Paul Deussen, *The System of Vedānta,* Chicago, 1912
29. Max Müller, Srī Bhāsya (with commentary and translation, *Sacred Books of The East Series,* 1966)
30. G. Thibaut, The Vedānta-sūtras with commentaries, *Sacred Books of The East* Series
31. Paul Deussen, *The Philosophy of the Upanishads,* 1908
32. Romain Rolland, *Mahatma Gandhi,* Delhi, 1969
33. S. Radhakrishnan, *Mahatma Gandhi 100 Years,* Gandhi Peace Foundation, Delhi, 1968, p. 308
34. Edward J. Thompson, *Rabindranath Tagore, His Life and Work,* Oxford, 1926
35. Sigfried Estborn, *The Religion of Tagore,* Christian Literature Society For India, Madras, 1949
36. Fellowship of the Spirit, Harvard University Press, Cambridge, 1961
37. Paul Schilpp, ed., My Confessions vide *the Philosophy of S. Radhakrishnan,* New York, 1952
38. *Kalki, The Future of Civilization,* New York, 1934, p. 30
39. S. Radhakrishnan, *The Hindu View of Life,* London, 1960
40. Sri Aurobindo, *The Human Cycle,* New York, 1950, p. 261
41. Sri Aurobindo, *The Ideal of Human Unity,* New York, 1950, p. 157
42. Sri Aurobindo, *Superman,* Calcutta, 1944, p. 1
43. Sri Aurobindo, *The Life Divine,* New York, 1965, p. 907
44. Sri Aurobindo, *Conscious Evolution and The Destiny of Man,* Pondicherry, 1965
45. S. Radhakrishnan, *Eastern Religions and Western Thought,* New York, 1959, p. 354
46. Georg Bühler, Laws of Manu, *Sacred Books of the East,* New York, 1969, p. 25
47. C. Moore, *The Indian Mind,* Honolulu, 1967, p. 323
48. S. Radhakrishnan, op. cit., p. 54
49. N. K. Bose, *Selections from Gandhi,* Ahmedabad, 1950, p. 26
50. Moore, op. cit., p. 300
51. Moore, op. cit., p. 270
52. S. G. Champion and D. Short, *Readings from World Religions,* Greenwich, 1959, p. 148 and W. T. De Bary, *Sources of the Indian Tradition,* New York, 1958 p. 61
53. Paul Carus, *The Gospel of Buddha,* Chicago, 1915, pp. 74-75

BIBLIOGRAPHY

1. de Chardin, Pierre Teilhard, *The Future of Man*, London, 1964
2. Dasgupta, Surendranath, *Indian Idealism*, Cambridge, 1962
3. Eliade, Mircea, *Yoga, Immortality and Freedom*, New York, 1958
4. Hiriyanna, M. *Outlines of Indian Philosophy*, London, 1932
5. Hutchison, John A., *Paths of Faith*, New York, 1969, Ch. 6
6. Krishnamurti, J., *Talks With American Students*, Berkeley, 1973
7. Levy, John, *The Nature of Man According to the Vedanta*, London, 1956
8. Nakamura, H., *Ways of Thinking of Eastern People*, Ch. 9
9. Narain, Dhirendra, *Hindu Character*, Bombay, 1957
10. Nikam, N. A., *Philosophy, History and The Image of Man*, Bombay, 1973
11. Organ, Troy, *The Hindu Quest for the Perfection of Mab*, Ohio, 1970
12. Radhakrishnan, S., *The Hindu View of Life*, Macmillan, 1962
13. Raju, P. T., *Indian Concepts of Man*
14. Reddy, V. Madhusudan, *Mankind on the March*, Hyderabad, 1972
15. Saksena, Shri Krishna, *Essays on Indian Philosophy*, Honolulu, 1970
16. Sinari, Ramakant A., *The Structure of Indian Thought*, **Springfield, 1970,** Ch. 2
17. Tagore, *The Religion of Man*

Chapter 13: ŚAṄKARA

REFERENCES

1. Śaṅkara's commentary on the Brahma-sūtra, I, iii, 33
2. *brahma satyaṁ jaganmithyā jīvo brahmaiva maparah*
3. See T. M. P. Mahadevan, *Gauḍapāda: A Study in Early Advaita*, University of Madras, 3rd ed., 1960, p. 247
4. Māndūkya-kārikā, III, 17
5. Ibid., III, 18
6. Śaṅkara's commentary of the Māṇḍūkya-kārikā, III, 17
7. X, 90, 1-3; Macdonnell, Vedic Reader, pp. 195-97
8. I, 164, 46; Griffith, Hymns of the Ṛig-veda, Vol. I., p. 292
9. Bṛihadāraṇyaka upaniṣad, III, iv, 2
10. Ibid., II, iv, 5
11. Ibid., II, iii, 6
12. Ibid., II, IV, 14
13. Ibid., IV, iii, 7
14. Taittirīya-upaniṣad, II, 1
15. Bṛihadāraṇyaka-upaniṣad, III, ix, 28.7
16. Śaṅkara's commentary of the Bhagavad-gītā, XIII, 12
17. Śvetāsvatara-upaniṣad, VI, 19
18. Taittirīya-upaniṣad, III, 1
19. Chāndogya-upaniṣad, III, xiv, 2
20. Śaṅkara's commentary on the Brahma-sūtra, I, i, 2
21. Śaṅkara's commentary on the Īśā-upaniṣad, 4
22. Śaṅkara's commentary on the Brahma-sūtra, I, i, 11

23. Śaṅkara's commentary on the Māṇḍūkya-kārikā, III, 19
24. Śaṅkara's commentary on the Brahma-sūtra, I, iv, 3
25. See Śaṅkara's adhyāsa-bhāṣya
26. Śaṅkara's commentary on the Brahma-sūtra, I, iv, 3
27. Śaṅkara's commentary on the Bṛihadāraṇyaka-upaniṣad, III, iii, 1
28. Taittirīya-upaniṣad, III, 1
29. Śaṅkara's Kena-upaniṣad-vākya-bhaṣya, III
30. Śaṅkara's commentary on the Brahma-sūtra, II, iii, 41
31. Śaṅkara's commentary on the Māṇḍūkya-kārikā, III, 15
32. Śaṅkara's commentary on the Taittirīya-upaniṣad, II, 1
33. III, ii, 3
34. Atma-bodha, 4
35. Śaṅkara's commentary on the Īśā-upanisād, 2
36. Atma-bodha, 3
37. See Sankara's introduction to the Kena-upaniṣad-vākya-bhāṣya
38. Śaṅkara's introduction to Kena-upaniṣad-pada-bhāṣya
39. Śaṅkara's commentary on the Brahma-sūtra, I, i, 1
40. III, 2
41. Śaṅkara's commentary on the Brahma-sūtra, I, i, 4
42. Śaṅkara's Atma-bodha, 44
43. Śaṅkara's commentary on the Māṇḍūkya-kārikā, IV, 98
44. Śaṅkara's commentary on the Brahma-sūtra, I, i, 4

Bibliography

1. Burtt, Edwin A., *Man Seeks the Divine,* New York, 1957, Chapter 10
2. Deutsch, Eliot, *Advaita Vedānta, A Philosophical Reconstruction,* Honolulu, 1969
3. Deutsch, Eliot and J. A. B. von Buitenen, *A Source Book of Advaita Vedānta,* Honolulu, 1971
4. Geunon, Rene, *Man and His Becoming,* New York, 1958
5. Hiriyanna, M., *The Essentials of Indian Philosophy,* London, 1948, Chapter 7
6. Isherwood, Christopher, ed., *Vedanta for Modern Man,* New York, 1951
7. Mahadevan, T. M. P., *The Philosophy of Advaita*
8. Murty, Satchidananda, *Revelation and Reason in Advaita Vedānta,* New York, 1959
9. Prabhavananda, Swami and Christopher Isherwood, trs., *Shankara's Crest-Jewel of Discrimination*
10. Prabhavananda and Christopher Isherwood, *The Spiritual Heritage of India,* New York, 1963, Chapter 16
11. Satprakashananda, Swami, *The Methods of Knowledge According to Advaita Vedānta*
12. Tattwananda, Swami, *The Quintessence of Vedānta,* Kalady, 1960
13. Thibaut, George, tr., F. Max Müller, ed., Vedānta Sūtras, Vol. XXXIV, XXXVIII, *Sacred Books of the East,* Oxford, 1904

Chapter 14: Śaiva Siddhānta, Viśiṣṭādvaita, Dvaita

Bibliography

1. Devasenapathi, V. A., *Human Bondage and Divine Grace*

2. Devasenapathi, V. A., *Śaiva-Siddhānta*
3. Dhavamony, Mariasusai, *Love of God According to Śaiva Siddhānta*, Oxford, 1971
4. Hiriyanna, M., *The Essentials of Indian Philosophy*, London, 1948, Ch. VIII
5. Hopkins, Thomas J., *The Hindu Religious Tradition*, Belmont, 1971
6. Madhva, *Commentaries on the Brahma-sūtra, Gītā and Upanishads*
7. Madhva, *Vishnu Tattva Nirnaya*
8. Prabhavananda, Swami and Frederick Manchester, *The Spiritual Heritage of India*, New York, 1963, Chs. 19, 21
9. Radhakrishnan, S., Chairman, Editorial Board, *History of Philosophy, Eastern and Western*, London, 1952, Vol. I, Ch. XIV
10. Radhakrishnan, S. and Charles Moore, *A Sourcebook in Indian Philosophy*, Princeton, 1957, Ch. 15
11. Raju, P. T., *Idealistic Thought in India*, Cambridge, 1953
12. Rāmānuja, Commentaries on the Brahma Sūtra and the Gītā
13. Rāmānuja, Vedārtha-Saṃgraha
14. Reyna, Ruth, *Introduction to Indian Philosophy*, Bombay, 1970, Ch. 22
15. Sharma, B. N. K., *Madhva's Teachings in His Own Words*
16. Sinha, Jadunath, *Outlines of Indian Philosophy*, Calcutta, 1963, Ch. 16
17. Thibaut, George, tr., G. Max Müller, ed., Vedānta Sūtras with Ramanuja's Commentary, Vol. XLVIII, *Sacred Books of the East*, Oxford, 1904

Part V: The Modern Period

References

1. D. S. Sarma, *Hinduism Through the Ages*, p. 90
2. Sarma, op. cit., p. 75
3. D. M. Datta, *The Chief Currents of Contemporary Philosophy*, p. 134. For Bhattacharya's writings see *Studies in Philosophy, Krishnachandra Bhattacharya* by Gopinath Bhattacharya, Progressive Publishers, Calcutta.
4. P. T. Raju, *The Philosophical Traditions of India*, p. 237

Chapter 15: Aurobindo

Bibliography

1. Sri Aurobindo, *Essays on the Gītā*, New York, 1950
2. Sri Aurobindo, *The Human Cycle*, New York, 1950
3. Sri Aurobindo, *The Ideal of Human Unity*, New York, 1950
4. Sri Aurobindo, *The Life Divine*, Pondicherry, 1960
5. Sri Aurobindo, *The Mother*, Pondicherry, 1949
6. Sri Aurobindo, *A Practical Guide to the Integral Yoga*, Pondicherry, 1965
7. Sri Aurobindo, *The Synthesis of Yoga*, Pondicherry, 1971
8. Sri Aurobindo, *Thoughts and Aphorisms*, Pondicherry, 1971
9. Sri Aurobindo, *Thoughts and Glimpses*, Pondicherry, 1964
10. Bruteau, Beatrice, *Worthy to the World, The Hindu Philosophy of Sri Aurobindo*, Cranbury, 1971
11. Chaudhuri, Haridas, *Integral Yoga*, London, 1970
12. Chaudhuri, Haridas, *The Philosophy of Integralism*, Pondicherry, 1967

13. Colaco, Paul, *The Absolute in the Philosophy of Aurobindo Ghose*, Rome, 1954
14. Diwakar, R. R., *Mahayogi Sri Aurobindo*, Bombay, 1962
15. Maitra, S. K., *An Introduction to the Philosophy oj Sri Aurobindo*, Banaras, 1945
16. Naravane, V. S., *Modern Indian Thought, A Philosophical Survey*, Bombay and New York, 1964, Ch. 7
17. Pandit, M. P., *The Teaching of Sri Aurobindo*, Madras, 1959
18. Radhakrishnan, S. and Charles Moore, *A Sourcebook in Indian Philosophy*, Princeton, 1957, Ch. XVI
19. Reddy, V. Madhusudan, *Sri Aurobindo's Philosophy of Evolution*, Hyderabad, 1966
20. Roy, A., *Sri Aurobindo and The New Age*, London, 1940
21. Srivastava, Rama Shanker, *Contemporary Indian Philosophy*, Delhi, 1965, Part III
22. Vyas, Ram Narayan, *The Universalistic Thought of India*, Bombay, 1970, Part II, Ch. 21, p. 105-111

Chapter 16: Rabindranath Tagore

References

1. *Gītāñjali*, poem 73, Macmillan, 1938
2. See article captioned "Sahitya Tattva" by Rabindranath Tagore. (*Prabasi*, 1341, Vaishakh)
3. Poem—'Ananataprem'
4. No. lxxvii
5. No. 56
6. *Sadhana*, p. 48
7. Ibid., p. 52
8. *A Tagore Reader*, Amiya Chakravarty, ed., Macmillan, 1961, p. 208
9. *Sadhana*, pp. 64-65
10. See *Dharma*, p. 107
11. *Lover's Gift* and *Crossing*, pp. 66-67
12. See *Janmadine*
13. No. 35
14. *Tagore Reader*, p. 268
15. *Nationalism*, p. 110
16. *Tagore Reader*, p. 268
17. Ibid., p. 199
18. *Towards Universal Man*, p. 146
19. Ibid., pp. 155-56
20. Ibid., p. 330
21. Ibid., p. 51
22. Ibid., p. 323
23. *Sadhana*, p. 18
24. *Gītañjali*, no. 30
25. *Sonar Tari*, poem entitled 'Vaishnava Kavita'
26. For a fuller account of Tagore see my book, *The Philosophy of Rabindranath Tagore*, Progressive Publishers, Calcutta, 1970

BIBLIOGRAPHY

1. Chakravarty, A., *A Tagore Reader,* New York, 1961
2. Naravane, V. S., *Modern Indian Thought, A Philosophical Survey,* Bombay and New York, 1964, Ch. 5
3. Raju, P. T., *The Philosophical Traditions of India,* London, 1971, Ch. 14
4. Ray, Benoy G., *The Philosophy of Rabindranath Tagore,* Calcutta, 1970
5. Sarma, D. S., *Hinduism Through the Ages,* Bombay, 1967
6. Sarma, D. S., *The Renaissance of Hinduism in the Nineteenth and Twentieth Centuries,* Benaras, 1944, Ch. IX
7. Sen, Sachim, *The Political Thought of Tagore,* Calcutta, 1947
8. Srivastava, Rama Shanker, *Contemporary Indian Philosophy,* Delhi, 1965, Part II
9. Tagore, Rabindranath, *Nationalism,* London, 1917
10. Tagore, Rabindranath, *The Religion of Man,* New York, 1931
11. Tagore, Rabindranath, *Sādhanā, The Realisation of Life,* New York, 1915
12. Tagore, Rabindranath, *A Tagore Testament,* New York, 1954
13. Tagore, Rabindranath, *Towards Universal Man,* New York, 1961
14. Thompson, Edward, *Rabindranath Tagore,* Oxford, 2nd ed., 1948
15. Verma, Rajendra, *Rabindranath Tagore, Prophet Against Totalitarianism,* New York, 1964

Chapter 17: RAMAKRISHNA

REFERENCES

1. C. Isherwood, *Ramakrishna and His Disciples,* Calcutta, p. 64
2. It is very difficult to ascertain when Gadādhar became known as Ramakrishna. If given that name by his parents, why was he not called it in childhood? Another view is that Totā Puri gave him the name. A third is that Rani Rashmani's son-in-law did when he came to Daksineswar.
3. Orthodox tāntrikas advise eating fish and meat, drinking wine, making passion-kindling gesticulations and copulating.
4. See Swami Nirvedananda's article on Ramakrishna in *The Cultural Heritage of India,* Vol. IV, p. 672
5. See *The Sayings of Ramakrishna,* Compiled by Swami Abhedānanda (Ramakrishna Vedanta Math, Calcutta) for the different sayings quoted here.
6. F. Max Müller, *Ramakrishna His Life and Sayings,* London, 1898, p. 134
7. Max Müller, op. cit., p. 171
8. See A. C. Das, *A Modern Incarnation of God,* p. 251
9. See *Completer Works of Swami Vivekananda,* Vol. IV, p. 187

BIBLIOGRAPHY

1. Abhedānanda, Swami, *The Sayings of Ramakrishna,* Calcutta, 1946
2. Bhattacharyya, Haridas, ed., *The Cultural Heritage of India,* Calcutta, 1956, Vol. IV
3. Budhananda, Swami, *The Complete Works of Swami Vivekananda,* Calcutta, 1959, 8 volumes
4. Chatterjee, S., *Classical Indian Philosophies; Their Synthesis in the Philosophy*

of Ramakrishna, Calcutta, 1963
5. Chatterji, P. *Studies in Comparative Religion,* Calcutta, 1972
6. Das, A. C., *A Modern Incarnation of God,* Calcutta, 1958
7. Diwakar, R. R., *Paramahamsa Ramakrishna*
8. Farquhar, John N., *Modern Religious Movements in India, Mystic,* Conn., 1968
9. Isherwood, Christopher, *Ramakrishna and His Disciples, Calcutta,* 1965
10. King, Winton, *Introduction to Religion, A Phenomenological Approach,* New York, 1968, Ch. 14
11. *Gospel of Sri Ramakrishna According to M*, Madras, 1924
12. Naravane, V. S., *Modern Indian Thought, A Philosophical Survey,* Bombay and New York, 1964, Ch. 3
13. Nirvedananda, Swami, *Sri Ramakrishna and Spiritual Renaissance,* Calcutta, 1940
14. Ray, B. G., *Religious Movements in Modern Bengal,* Visva-Bharati, 1965
15. Rolland, Romain, *Thr Life of Ramakrishna,* Calcutta, 1930.
16. Saradananda, Swami, *Sri Ramakrishna, The Great Master,* Madras, 1956
17. Sarma, D. S., *The Renaissance of Hinduism in the Nineteenth and Twentieth Centuries,* Banaras, 1944, Chs. VI, VII
18. Srivastava, Rama Shanker, *Contemporary Indian Philosophy,* Delhi, 1965, Part I
19. Spiegelberg, Frederic, *Living Religions of the World,* Englewood Cliffs, 1956, Ch. 6
20. Vivekananda, Swami, *Complete Works of Swami Vivekananda,* Lecture entitled "My Master," Vol. IV, Calcutta, 1963

Chapter 18: Gandhi—A Modernist Heresy

Bibliography

1. Bose, Nirmal K., *Selections from Gandhi,* Ahmedabad, 1946
2. Bose, Nirmal K., *Studies in Gandhism,* Calcutta, 1962
3. Datta, D. M., *Philosophy of Mahatma Gandhi*
4. Diwakar, R. R., *Glimpses of Gandhi*
5. Diwakar, R. R., *Satyagraha, The Pathway to Peace*
6. Fischer, Louis, ed., *The Essential Gandhi,* New Jersey, 1961
7. Fischer, Louis, *Gandhi: His Life and Message for the World,* New York, 1954
8. Gandhi, M. K., *All Religions Are True,* Bombay, 1962
9. Gandhi, M. K., *Hind Swaraj*
10. Gandhi, M. K., *My Religion,* Ahmedabad, 1955
11. Gandhi, M. K., *Sarvodaya,* Ahmedabad, 1957
12. Gandhi, M. K., *The Story of My Experiments with Truth,* Washington, 1960
13. Kher, V. B., *In Search of the Supreme*
14. Mahadevan, T. K., *Gandhi, My Refrain,* Delhi, 1973
15. Mahadevan, T. K., *Nonviolence After Gandhi,* Delhi, 1968
16. Naravane, V. S., *Modern Indian Thought, A Philosophical Survey,* Bombay and New York, 1964, Ch. 6
17. Ramabhai, Suresh, *Vinoba and His Mission,* Sevagram, 1954
18. Ramachandran, G. and T. K. Mahadevan, eds., *Gandhi, His Relevance for Our Times,* New Delhi, 1967

19. Ramachandran, G. and T. K. Mahadwan, eds., *Quest for Gandhi,* New Delhi, 1970
20. Ray, B. G., *Gandhian Ethics,* Navajivan, 1950
21. Reddy, V. N. K., *Sarvodaya Ideology and Acharya Vinoba Bhave,* Hyderabad, 1963
22. Srivastava, Rama Shanker, *Contemporary Indian Philosophy,* Delhi, 1965, Part IV
23. Verma, Surendra, *Metaphysical Foundations of Mahatma Gandhi's Thought,* New Delhi, 1970

Chapter 19: Epilogue

References

1. S. Radhakrishnan, *Eastern Religions and Western Thought,* New York, 1959, p. 39
2. A. Chakravarty, *A Tagore Reader,* New York, 1961, p. 209
3. Charles Moore, *The Indian Mind,* Honolulu, 1967, p. 273
4. Chakravarty, op. cit., p. 278
5. R. Tagore, *Towards Universal Man,* New York, 1961, p. 65
6. R. Tagore, *Isa Upanishad*
7. Ibid.
8. S. Radhakrishnan, op. cit., p. 52
9. S. Radhakrishnan, op. cit., p. 43
10. Katha Upanishad, II, 2, 12
11. M. K. Gandhi, *My Religion,* Ahmedabad, 1955, p. 127
12. R. Tagore, *Isa Upanishad,* p. 41
13. N. K. Bose, *Selections from Gandhi,* Ahmedabad, Calcutta, 1950, p. 25
14. Wm. De Bary, *Sources of the Indian Tradition,* New York, 1958, p. 245
15. S. Radhakrishnan, op. cit., p. 55
16. Gandhi, op. cit., p. 124
17. S. Radhakrishnan, op. cit., p. 47
18. Swami Vivekananda, *Works,* Vol. II, p. 385
19. Keshub Chunder Sen, *Lectures in India,* London, 1901, Vol. II, p. 121
20. Moore, op. cit., p. 178
21. Moore, op. cit., p. 179
22. Gandhi, op. cit., p. 2
23. Sen, op. cit., p. 10
24. Gandhi, op. cit., p. 12
25. Sen, op. cit., p. 16
26. D. M. Datta, *Contemporary Philosophy,* Calcutta, 1961, p. 578
27. Sen, op. cit., p. 112
28. F. Max Müller, *Ramakrishna, His Life and Sayings,* London and Bombay, 1898, p. 99
29. Gandhi, op. cit., p. 10
30. Max Müller, op. cit., p. 158
31. John Yale, *What Religion is in the Words of Swami Vivekananda,* London, 1962, p. 10
32. Max Müller, op. cit., p. 157
33. M. K. Gandhi, *All Religions Are True,* Bombay, 1962, p. 4

34. Max Müller, op. cit., p. 152
35. Gandhi, op. cit., p. 13
36. D. S. Sarma, *Hinduism Through the Ages,* Bombay, 1967, p. 73
37. D. S. Sarma, *The Renaissance of Hinduism,* Benares, 1944, p. 296
38. P. T. Raju, *Indian Concepts of Man,* p. 38
39. Sarma, op. cit., p. 276
40. S. Radhakrishnan, op. cit., p. 353
41. S. Radhakrishnan, op. cit., p. 42
42. Chakravarty, op. cit., p. 209
43. Sarma, op. cit., p. 270
44. Tagore, *Universal Man,* p. 331

BIBLIOGRAPHY

1. Arapura, J. S., *Radhakrishnan and Integral Experience,* Calcutta and New York, 1966
2. Bouquet, A. C., *Comparative Religion,* Middlesex, 1941, Ch. 12
3. Burt, Edwin A., *In Search of Philosophic Understanding,* New York, 1965, Chapters 10, 11
4. Burtt, Edwin A., *Man Seeks the Divine,* New York, 1957, Ch. 14
5. Murty, K. S. and K. Ramakrishna Rao, *Current Trends in Indian Philosophy,* Waltair, 1972
6. Naravane, V. S., *Modern Indian Thought, A Philosophical Survey,* Bombay and New York, 1964, Ch. 1
7. Nikhilananda, Swami, *Hinduism, Its Meaning for the Liberation of the Spirit,* London, 1958
8. Radhakrishnan, S., *Eastern Religions and Western Thought,* New York, 1959
9. Radhakrishnan, S., and J. H. Muirhead, *Contemporary Indian Philosophy,* London, 1936 & 1952
10. Raju, P. T., *The Philosophical Traditions of India,* London, 1971, Ch. 14
11. Rao, M. V. Krishna, ed., *Glimpses on Religion, Philosophy and Mysticism,* Bangalore, 1971
12. Ray, B. G., *Contemporary Indian Philosophers,* Kitabistan, 1947
13. Riepe, Dale, *The Philosophy of India and Its Impact on American Thought,* Springfield, 1970
14. Sarma, D. S., *Hinduism Through the Ages,* Bombay, 1967
15. Sarma, D.S., *The Renaissance of Hinduism in the Nineteenth and Twentieth Centuries,* Benaras, 1944, Ch. 13
16. Sinari, Ramakant A., *The Structure of Indian Thought,* Springfield, 1970, Ch. 12
17. Smart, Ninian, *The Religious Experience of Mankind,* New York, 1969, Ch. 11
18. Srivastava, R. S., *Contemporary Indian Philosophy,* Delhi, 1965

GLOSSARY

As an aid to western students especially a glossary of more commonly used terms is provided. A suggested pronunciation (in parentheses) has been included also although the reader should be cautioned that unanimous agreement as to pronunciation is not always achieved. One difficulty is that even within the United States there are variations in dialect.

ACĀRYA (*ah char yah*) a teacher, preceptor, title given to learned Brahmins or outstanding teachers.

ĀDṚṢṬA (*awe dris ta*) unseen power, invisible, unseen.

ADVAITA (*awe doi ta*) non-duality, monism, indivisibility, Vedānta philosophy of the oneness of reality, advocated by Śaṅkara in contrast to the Dvaita philosophy of Madhva and the qualified monism, Viśiṣṭādvaita of Rāmānuja.

AGNI (*ugh nee*) fire, God of fire, other early Gods included Ganeśa (elephant-headed god), Hanumān (the monkey god) and Yama, Indra, Varuṇa and Kubera, the four guardians of the universe.

AHAṂKĀRA (*a hung car*) the self, ego, principle of individuation, self-consciousness, flaunting of one's self.

AHIṂSĀ (*a him sah*) non-violence, non-injury, non-killing.

AMITĀBHA (*a me ta vh*) The Buddha of the Pure Land or Western Paradise, the merciful, gracious saviour.

ĀNANDA (*a nan dah*) bliss, supreme joy, one of the three attributes of the Absolute, the others being cit (knowledge, consciousness) and sat (being, existence).

ANEKĀNTAVĀDA (*awne kanta vada*) Jain doctrine of many standpoints and the manifoldness of reality, the plurality of reality and the limitedness of one's judgments.

AṆU, last but the smallest material particle.

AṚHAT (*orre hut*) The perfected disciple or saint, one who has entered Nirvāṇa.

ARTHA (*orre tha*) wealth, material well-being, one of the four ends of man the other being kāma (love, pleasure, enjoyment), dharma (ethical living, righteousness) and mokṣa (spiritual perfection, freedom, deliverance, salvation).

ĀŚRAMA (*ah sra maw*) the four stages of life—brahmacārin (student), gārhasthya (householder), vānaprastha (forest dweller) and Sannyāsin (homeless wanderer).

ĀTMAN (*ath mon*) self, spirit, soul, ātman is the individual self or spirit and Ātman the Supreme Self or Spirit. In contrast to the Buddhist anātman doctrine of ultimate selflessness or denial that there is no absolute, continuing self.

AUM (*ohm*) the sacred syllable indicating the Absolute (Om also).

AVATĀRA (*ava taar*) an incarnation of the Deity.

AVIDYĀ (*awe v dwa*) ignorance, nescience, lack of knowledge.

BHAKTI (*vhok ti*) an attitude of love, faith and devotion to God. Bhakti yoga one of the means of union with God, the others being karma yoga, the way of unselfish works, jñāna yoga the way of knowledge and, rāja yoga the way of concentration and mind control.

BHIKṢU (BHIKKU-Pali) (*vic shoe*) Religious mendicant, Buddhist monk.

BODHI (*bo dhi*) knowledge of God, enlightenment, divine knowledge.

BODHISATTVA (*bo dhi sha tta*) A perfect one who refrains from entering Nirvāṇa in order to aid others to attain it, one who has Bodhi, knowledge personified.

BRAHMĀ (*brahm ha*) The creator, one of the Hindu Trimūrti or Trinity, the other being Viṣṇu (Vishnu) the preserver and Śiva (Shiva) the destroyer (of the impure so that the pure may replace it), the three principles of coming into being, existing, and going out of existence.

BRAHMAN (*brom hun*) The infinite, the Absolute, Ultimate Reality, Supreme Spirit. One who has knowledge of God as one, a highly knowledgeable person.

BRĀHMAṆA, a highly knowledgeable person (originally), member of the priestly caste, the other castes being Kṣatriya (warriors, protectors), Vaiśya (merchant, trader) and Śūdra (server, peasant).

BUDDHI (*bu dhi*) intellect intelligence, the faculty of direct perception.

CĀRVĀKA (*char vak*) the philosophy of materialism or the materialist.

DARŚANA (*dar shun*) to view the holy presence of God, a way of thought or interquotation, to see.

DEVA (*dee va*) divine, a god.

DHARMA (DHAMMA-Pali) (*dhr ma*) religion, way of life, virtue, moral order, righteousness, social and moral order, duty, code of conduct, metaphysically the universal universal laws of nature by which nature operates.

DHYĀNA (*dha na*) meditation, the seventh stage in Yogic practice.

DUHKHA (*du kha*) suffering, pain, misery, first of the Buddhist four noble truths.

DVIJA (*dwi ja*) twice born, one's natural birth and the second birth into the spiritual life when invested with the sacred thread.

GAUTAMA (GOTAMA-Pali) (*gau ta ma*) Buddha's family name.

GHĀT (*ghaat*) bathing place on a river bank with steps leading down.

GUṆA (*gu na*) attribute, characteristic, property, constituent. The three guṇas of prakṛiti are sattva (virtue, brightness, illuminating), rajas (passion, activating) and tamas (ignorance, darkness, sluggishness, restraining).

GURU (*guru*) spiritual preceptor or guide.

HĪNAYĀNA (*hina yan*) Lesser vehicle or way, associated with later Theravada Buddhism in South-East Asia as contrasted with Mahāyāna, the Great Vehicle or broader way of Northern Buddhist schools.

ĪŚVARA (*ish wara*) God in personal form, Brahman with attributes (Saguṇa in contrast to Nirguṇa Brahman).

JĪVA (*gee vha*) individual soul.

JÑANA (*gan*) knowledge, knowledge of the Divine.

KARMA (*car ma*) action, law of cause and effect (in Buddhism dependent origination), the good or evil results or effects of past actions, law of ethical consequence, religious act or ritual.

KARUṆĀ (*coru na*) compassion for all beings.

KOṢA (*ko sha*) sheath, the five sheaths enveloping the soul or self—the bodily, vital, mental, intellectual and sheath of bliss.

KṚṢṆA (*chris na*) an incarnation of Viṣṇu.

LĪLĀ (*lee la*) Brahman's joyful creative activity.

MAHĀ (*ma ha*) great.

MAITRĪ (METTĀ-Pali) (*moi three*) friendship.

MANAS (*ma nash*) mind.

MANTRA (*mon tra*) a Vedic sacrificial hymn, verse, incantation.

MĀRA (*ma ra*) the tempter (Buddhism), the evil one.

MĀRGA (*mar go*) path, way, road.

MĀYĀ (*ma yah*) the view that all phenomenal existence is an illusion, relativity of thought, the unexplainable power of Brahman.

METTĀ (*metta*) good will.

MOKṢA (*moksha*) spiritual perfection, liberation, freedom from rebirth.

NIRVĀṆA (NIBBAṆA-Pali) (*nir vana*) extinction, blowing out, state of final enlightenment, transcendental state, the ultimate goal sought by the Buddhist.

PARAMĀTMAN (*param ath mon*) Supreme Self or Spirit, godly person.

PRAKṚITI (*pra kri ti*) mother nature, in Sāṃkhya primeval matter prior to differentiation, the second principle.

PRĀṆA (*pran*) breath, life force, breath of life, prāṇāyāma, the fourth stage in Yogic practice.

PŪJĀ (*poo ja*) worship, ritual of worship, worship service, offerings to God.

PURĀṆAS (*poo ra na*) old, ancient religious texts.

PURUṢA (*puh roo shah*) in Sāṃkhya the cosmic spirit, the first principle postulated, spiritual, subjective, immaterial, indestructible.

RĀMA (*raam*) an incarnation of Viṣṇu.

ṚISHI (*ri she*) seer.

ṚITA (*reeta*) an early concept, the natural order, the cosmic order, the order or orderliness of things, synonymously moral order, the right, the good.

SĀDHANĀ (*shah dha na*) spiritual discipline.

SĀDHU (*shah dhu*) an ascetic, one who does sādhanā.

ŚAKTI (*shak ti*) strength, moral strength, female part of the Ultimate Principle, wife of Śiva.

SAMĀDHI (*shaw ma dhi*) the eight and last stage of intense concentration and unawareness of externals in Patañjali's yoga philosophy.

SAṂSĀRA (*song chara*) cycle of rebirth, the round of worldly life.

SAṄGHA (*song gha*) Buddhist assembly, order of monks.

SARVODAYA (*char bo doi*) enlightenment of all, Gandhi's ideal of the well-being of all.

SATYA (*satya*) Truth.

SMṚITI (*smri ti*) Religious knowledge written and handed down by human beings, traditional knowledge in contrast to Śṛuti—revealed knowledge or religious knowledge transmitted verbally such as the Vedas.

ŚŪNYA (*shoon nya*) the void, emptiness.

SUTRA (*shoe tra*) a sacred thread worn by members of the three upper castes, figuratively that which runs through and holds together, a collection of writings by the founder of a sect or philosophy.

TANTRA (*tan tra*) esoteric literature especially of the Śiva-Śakti schools, a treatise on the worship of Śakti.

TAPAS (*ta posh*) penance, austerity.

VARṆA (*varna*) caste, colour.

YŌGA (*yoe ga*) Union with God, a system of physical, mental and spiritual discipline leading to such union associated with Patañjali.

INDEX

Indian thought : an introduction / edited by Donald H. Bishop. —
New York : Wiley, [1975]

xv, 427 p : 22 cm.

"A Halsted Press book."
Includes bibliographies and index.
ISBN 0-470-07580-5

Erratum slip tipped in.

1. Philosophy, Indic—Addresses, essays, lectures. I. Bishop, Donald H.

B131.I5 1975 181'.4 73-13206
MARC

Library of Congress 75